MW00479849

The Rise and Fall
of the Brezhnev Doctrine
in Soviet Foreign Policy

The New
Cold War
History

John Lewis
Gaddis,
editor

The Rise and Fall
of the Brezhnev Doctrine
in Soviet Foreign Policy

Matthew J. Ouimet

The University
of North Carolina
Press
Chapel Hill and London

© 2003 The University of North Carolina Press

ALL RIGHTS RESERVED

Manufactured in the United States of America

Designed by Cameron Poulter

Set in Stone Serif by Keystone Typesetting, Inc.

The paper in this book meets the guidelines for permanence
and durability of the Committee on Production Guidelines
for Book Longevity of the Council on Library Resources.

Library of Congress Cataloging-in-Publication Data

Ouimet, Matthew J.
The rise and fall of the Brezhnev Doctrine
in Soviet foreign policy / Matthew J. Ouimet.
p. cm. — (New Cold War history)
Includes bibliographical references and index.
ISBN 0-8078-2740-1 (cloth: alk. paper)
ISBN 0-8078-5411-5 (pbk.: alk. paper)
1. Soviet Union—Foreign relations—Europe, Eastern.
2. Europe, Eastern—Foreign relations—Soviet Union.
3. Soviet Union—Politics and government—1953–1985.
4. Soviet Union—Military policy. 5. Soviet Union—
Foreign relations—1945–1991. I. Title. II. Series.
DJK45.S65 O89 2003
327.47—dc21
2002008796

cloth 06 05 04 03 02 5 4 3 2 1
paper 06 05 04 03 02 5 4 3 2 1

For my parents,
Alan and
Mary Ouimet,
who taught me
to love history
and to argue creatively

And for
Herbert J. Ellison,
my mentor and friend

Contents

Acknowledgments

I AM INDEBTED to a great many institutions and individuals for providing their insights and assistance with this book, though, of course, all of the views expressed herein are my own. The American Council of Teachers of Russian furnished a United States Information Agency grant that enabled me to conduct research in Moscow during the 1994–95 academic year, and I am deeply obliged to its very helpful staff. Thanks also to the University of Washington Graduate School and Department of History, The Henry M. Jackson School of International Studies, and Phi Alpha Theta Historical Honors Society for supplying the additional funding needed to support my work in the Russian State Archives.

While in Moscow I received repeated assistance from the staff and directors of the Institute of the World Economy and International Relations (IMEMO) and the Institute of International Economic and Political Studies (formerly the Institute of the Economics of the World Socialist System), as well as the Center for the Preservation of Contemporary Documentation. I would especially like to recognize IMEMO director Nodari Simonia, Natalia Stepanovna, Igor Zevelev, Vladimir Khoros, Svetlana Glinkina, Nikolai Bukharin, I. I. Orlik, A. A. Iskenderov, and Sergei Mironov for their insightful suggestions on the direction of my research. I am also grateful to the many former Soviet officials who agreed to be interviewed for this study, especially Army General A. I. Gribkov, Aleksandr Yakovlev, Georgii Shakhnazarov, Nikolai Kulikov, Sergei Grigoriev, Valerii Musatov, and I. N. Kuz'min. Their personal observations and experiences served to breathe life into many of the issues and concerns that lay buried in the dark recesses of Moscow's communist bureaucracy.

During the 1999–2000 academic year I had the remarkable opportunity of working as a research scholar at the Woodrow Wilson Center's Kennan Institute for Advanced Russian Studies. I owe a great deal to the incredible staff of the Wilson Center, the Kennan Institute, and the Center's Cold War International History Project, and I thank their directors, Lee Hamilton, Blair Ruble, and Christian Ostermann respectively, for the hospitality and support that I received during my stay. While at the Kennan Institute I had the opportunity to present my findings to an extraordinarily informed and experienced audience of scholars, federal intelligence analysts, and former congressional staffers. Many of these individuals had direct experience in the shaping of an American response to the Brezhnev Doctrine, and I am very grateful to them for sharing their insights with me. Additionally, I had the great opportunity to work with a fine young scholar named Jon Kakasenko, who, as my intern, did a truly impressive job translating and transcribing the many interviews that I conducted in Moscow. Jon's future looks bright, and I am honored to have played a small role in his professional training.

This work has benefited extensively from the careful consideration and useful recommendations of many brilliant scholars. Fostering the project in a variety of ways from its infancy were Herbert J. Ellison, James Felak, and Christopher Jones, who provided encouragement and thoughtful advice that has proven invaluable to its completion. It was an unexpected pleasure to discover that Chris Jones had been awarded a fellowship at the Wilson Center during my tenure there. His input during the later stages of this project was invaluable to me. Of equal value were the careful suggestions of John Lewis Gaddis and Ambassador Robert L. Hutchings, whose patient attention to detail never flagged despite the many drafts of this manuscript that they each received. Thanks additionally to Robert Tarleton for providing impetus for this project, and to Oscar Bandelin and David Curp for their support at its close.

Portions of this work appeared as part of an article entitled "Reconsidering the Question of Soviet Intervention in Poland, 1980–1981: A Crisis of Divergent National Interests," published in July 2000 in the *Slavonic and East European Review*. I would like to thank the editor of the journal for permission to include the relevant material from the article in this book.

Finally, I would like to recognize the boundless patience and enthusiastic support of my wife, Julie, which persisted even when this project took her to strange and intimidating lands both inside and outside the Capital Beltway for years on end. Words cannot express the love and humble respect I owe her, but I will gladly spend a lifetime repaying the debt.

Abbreviations

AFL-CIO	American Federation of Labor and Congress of Industrial Organizations
BBC	British Broadcasting Corporation
CC	Central Committee
CIA	Central Intelligence Agency
CMEA	Council for Mutual Economic Assistance
CPC	Communist Party of China
CPSU	Communist Party of the Soviet Union
CSCE	Conference for Security and Cooperation in Europe
CSCP	Czechoslovak Communist Party
CSSR	Czechoslovak Socialist Republic
CTK	Ceskoslovenska Tiskova Kancelar (Czechoslovak News Agency)
DiP	Doswiadzcenie i Przyszlosc (Experience and Future)
DS	Durzhavna Sigurnost (Bulgarian State Security)
EC	European Community
EEC	European Economic Community
FRG	Federal Republic of Germany (West Germany)
GDR	German Democratic Republic (East Germany)
IEMSS	Institut Ekonomiki Mirovoi Sotsialisticheshoi Sistemy (Institute of the Economics of the World Socialist System [Bogomolov Institute])
ILO	International Labor Organization
KGB	Komitet Gosudarstvennoj Bezopasnosti (Committee for State Security)
KOR	Komitet Obrony Robotnikow (Workers' Defense Committee)
KPN	Konfederacja Polski Niepodleglej (Confederation for an Independent Poland)
KSS	Komitet Samoobrony Spolecznej (Committee for Social Self-Defense)
MFA	Ministry of Foreign Affairs
MRBM	Medium-range ballistic missile
MVD	Ministerstvo Vnutrennykh Del (Ministry of Internal Affairs)
NATO	North Atlantic Treaty Organization
NEM	New Economic Mechanism
NKVD	Narodnyi Komissariat Vnutrennykh Del (People's Commissariat of Internal Affairs)
NSC	National Security Council
NZS	Niezalezne Zrzeszenie Studentow (Independent Students' Union)
OPEC	Organization of Petroleum Exporting Countries
PAP	Polska Agencja Prasova (Polish Press Agency)

PCC	Political Consultative Committee
PCI	Partido Communista Italiano (Communist Party of Italy)
PDPA	People's Democratic Party of Afghanistan
POW	Prisoner of war
PPR	Polish People's Republic
PRL	Polska Rzeczpospolita Ludowa (Polish People's Republic)
PZPR	Polska Rzeczpospolita Partia Robotnicza (Polish United Workers Party)
SALT	Strategic Arms Limitation Talks
SED	Sozialistische Einheitspartei Deutschlands (Socialist Unity Party of Germany)
TASS	Telegraficheskoe Agenstvo Sovetskogo Soiuza (Telegraphic Agency of the Soviet Union)
UN	United Nations
USSR	Union of Soviet Socialist Republics
WTO	Warsaw Treaty Organization (Warsaw Pact)
ZOMOs	Zmotoryzovane Odwody Milicji Obywatelskiej (Mechanized Units of the Citizens Militia)

The Rise and Fall
of the Brezhnev Doctrine
in Soviet Foreign Policy

Introduction

CHRISTMAS DAY 1989. The audience in the concert hall of East Berlin's
Schauspielhaus sat in excited anticipation as Maestro Leonard Bernstein
raised his baton to begin the fourth movement of Beethoven's Ninth
Symphony. It was a moment filled with remarkable historical import and
hope for the future. On stage, musicians from both East and West Germany, as well as France, the Soviet Union, and the United States, combined their talent in a single gesture that bore witness to the extraordinary transformation that was then sweeping through Eastern Europe.
Caught up in the spirit of the moment, Maestro Bernstein had altered one
word of the famous Choral Symphony to commemorate the unprecedented nature of the evening's celebration. The substitution of this single
word—*freiheit* in place of the traditional *freude*—transformed the poetry of
Schiller's "Ode to Joy," on which Beethoven had based his magnum opus,
into the "Ode to Freedom." The promise of what had come to pass seemed
at that moment to defy any possibility of cynicism or irony. The yoke
of communist authoritarianism in Europe was finally giving way before
a wave of popular demonstrations clamoring for legitimately elected governments. Planned economies were already starting to introduce elements of the free market in their commercial relations both domestically
and internationally. Meanwhile, in the city that the world once expected
would give birth to a global conflagration, Cold War hostility had suddenly given way before a giddy sense of international altruism. The phenomenon that would come to be known as the "Revolutions of 1989" was
in the process of reshaping the postwar order in Europe as the Cold War
rushed toward its stunning conclusion.

Hardly a month earlier, the Berlin Wall that had separated East and
West Germany since 1961, the very icon of Cold War antagonism, had
literally collapsed. With picks and sledgehammers, bulldozers and jack-
hammers, families separated for decades began to tear down this embodi-
ment of the Iron Curtain which had divided Europe since the end of
World War II. Newspapers across the world broadcast the news in letters
inches high. Communist control was collapsing in Eastern Europe. Before
the end of the year, every country in the Soviet bloc would overturn the
Party's legal monopoly on power in favor of free elections and constitutional democracy. In most countries this process was so peaceful and

evolutionary that, by December, many were already referring to it as the "velvet revolution."[1] The power of civil society had triumphed against the armed might of authoritarian governments while Moscow, the erstwhile guarantor of communist monopoly rule, stood by and watched.

Where were the Soviet divisions that had intervened time and again between 1953 and 1979, propping up communist regimes from Berlin to Kabul? What had happened to the countless pledges of "fraternal assistance" that Moscow had once offered as part of its commitment to "socialist internationalism" in bloc relations? Had the Soviets chosen to intervene with military force, the Revolutions of 1989 might well have gone down to defeat. After all, earlier reform attempts had collapsed in 1956, 1968, and 1981 thanks to the use, or menacing presence, of Soviet troops. Why not in 1989? Could it be that the collapse of communism in Eastern Europe was due as much to permissive shifts in Soviet foreign policy as to the region's civic activism? Could the Soviet leadership share the responsibility, one might even say the credit, for this astonishing political earthquake with the hundreds of thousands who turned out to defy the region's heavily armed communist apparatus? In short, what had become of the infamous Brezhnev Doctrine and its strict limitation of national sovereignty within the Soviet bloc?

The question of Soviet military restraint in 1989 has been explored over the past decade from a variety of approaches. Virtually all have linked it directly to the public alteration of Soviet East European policy that took place during the Gorbachev era.[2] This initial focus was once certainly understandable. Until the late 1980s, Moscow had given no clear indication whatsoever that it had begun to reexamine commitments in Eastern Europe, to say nothing of abandoning allied communist regimes to their respective political fates. Inasmuch as Cold War–era scholarship was forced to rely heavily on published sources, narrow attribution of Moscow's historic policy shift to Mikhail Gorbachev and his advisers was unquestionably compelling. Indeed, even after the introduction of new archival evidence to the historical record, Gorbachev's reforms still remain an essential, if no longer instigatory, chapter in the story of Moscow's gradual retreat from assertive control in Eastern Europe.

This is not to suggest that scholars have ignored the long-term impact of such external forces as the increasingly unstable nature of East European communist regimes and the U.S. military buildup under Presidents Carter and Reagan.[3] Some have also addressed the socialist economic crises that prompted Moscow to divest itself of East European commitments in order to participate in the international market.[4] Moscow, they correctly point out, simply could not afford to subsidize Eastern Europe any longer as it had in years past.[5] Yet while such studies may recognize the initial appearance of these factors under Brezhnev, they describe them all as having reached the point of influencing Soviet policy, once again, largely under Gorbachev.

While each of these angles provides important insights into the Soviet shift, nearly all suffer from the same temporal limitation confining it to the mid- and late 1980s. Even examinations that spotlight the Brezhnev Doctrine treat this marriage of ideology and military intervention as virtually unaltered from its origins in 1968 until the late Gorbachev era. One book written prior to the collapse of the Soviet bloc suggests that a Soviet state still committed to Marxist-Leninist doctrine would never abandon the notion of "limited sovereignty" in Eastern Europe.[6] Hence it does not even entertain the notion that the Brezhnev regime might have forsaken its own earlier policies. A later approach, written after the Soviet collapse, allows that socioeconomic decline throughout the bloc may have inspired the first fundamental reevaluation of Eastern Europe's role in Soviet military planning since the Khrushchev era. But it too posits that doctrinal changes began only after Brezhnev's death in 1982, with the gradual abandonment of the Brezhnev Doctrine beginning in 1987 during Gorbachev's reform program.[7]

Scholarship in the former Soviet Union has also tended to confine discussion of East European policy shifts to the Gorbachev era. Moreover, it has been Gorbachev's new respect for "common human values" in Europe rather than evolution of socialist ideological perceptions that has featured in most existing studies to date.[8] Few comprehensive examinations of the communist collapse in Eastern Europe have emerged since the fall of the Soviet Union itself, though discussion of Eastern Europe has occasionally surfaced in political commentaries, memoirs, and other personal reflections.[9] While a number of these provide important insights, not one has attempted to offer a comprehensive explanation for the start of the shift in Soviet East European policy that reached its climax in 1989.

In this book I posit that the now famous reforms of Soviet bloc policy in the mid-1980s were not the instigation but the climax of a fundamental transformation in Soviet bloc policy that traces its origins to the late Brezhnev era. Drawing on a broad spectrum of new archival revelations and interviews with former Soviet policymakers, I detail how a radical shift in Moscow's perception of national interests redefined Soviet commitments in Eastern Europe between 1968 and 1981. As concern for Soviet domestic stability eclipsed Moscow's international ideological commitments during the Polish crises of the late 1970s and early 1980s, a dramatic, if gradual, evolution of perceptions rendered military intervention essentially inert as a policy option in Eastern Europe. It was this earlier process, along with the Polish events that brought it to a climax, that set the stage politically and ideologically for Gorbachev's later "new thinking" in bloc policy.

Particular attention is given here to the symbiotic relationship between ideological innovations and Moscow's redefinition of Soviet national interests. Even during the period of Stalinist control in the early 1950s, Moscow's official treaties with the People's Democracies of Eastern Europe offered no formal basis for interfering in the affairs of those nations. Soviet supremacy therefore relied on East European recognition of the Kremlin's ideological primacy in communist relations. As a result, ideological shifts in Moscow often manifested as palpable turns of bloc policy. While the role of ideology in foreign policy has long been a subject of considerable debate, its powerful impact on Soviet perceptions of national interest is undeniable. The former Soviet ambassador to the United Nations, Aleksandr Belonogov, has argued that "the hyperideologization of foreign policy in the past often strongly prevented us [the Union of Soviet Socialist Republics, or USSR] from discerning where our interests lay in the international arena."[10] One might well take issue with Belonogov's implicit suggestion of objective national interests. However, as this book ventures to demonstrate, his testimony to the relative power of communist ideological development in Soviet foreign policy is incontrovertible.

Beginning in the late 1960s, the Kremlin constructed an elaborate ideological framework around the conviction that East European stability was central to the security and well-being of the Soviet Union itself. In 1968, the use of Warsaw Pact forces to ensure the future of Soviet-style communism in Czechoslovakia provided all the evidence that was required to illustrate this point. Recently released working notes of the Kremlin's deliberations before the invasion depict a Soviet leadership focused almost exclusively on the need to guarantee the future of a traditional communist system in Czechoslovakia. Placing a premium on ideological concerns, it refused to differentiate between the interests of the Soviet Union and those of its Warsaw Pact allies. It regarded Soviet "national" interests as extending beyond the borders of their own republics to embrace the East European states as well. Moscow accordingly treated Czechoslovakia as a constituent part of the Soviet nation, the political integrity of which was integral to the national interests of the USSR. Hence a threat to its sociopolitical system elicited the same response as an attack on the Soviet Union itself.

This ideological premium, however, was not impervious to the pragmatic exigencies of national survival; thus by 1981, Soviet perceptions had changed dramatically. As a wave of strikes swept over Poland, the communist authorities in Warsaw appeared to be on the verge of political collapse. A pro-democratic "counterrevolution" seemed poised to overturn Poland's communist system along with the postwar status quo in

Europe. And yet extensive documentary and testimonial evidence now confirms that at the height of the Polish crisis the Soviets abandoned as inconceivable the notion of an invasion to rescue communist rule in Poland. Western sanctions and a collapse of Moscow's international prestige promised to upset the internal stability of the Soviet Union if Warsaw Pact forces moved in to crush the Solidarity trade union movement. At a time when economic stagnation and mounting military expenditures already compromised Soviet growth and development, these kind of repercussions were judged to be at variance with the evolving national interests of the Soviet Union. Should an opposition government come to power in Warsaw, the Kremlin secretly concluded, Moscow would simply have to come to terms with it. The appeals to "socialist internationalism" and "fraternal assistance" which had permeated bloc policy since 1968 had simply become too costly to entertain in practice. Thus as ideological commitments gave way to the requirements of realpolitik in the crucible of Polish civil unrest, the Brezhnev Doctrine expired as a viable part of Moscow's foreign policy arsenal.

Ultimately, the imposition of martial law by Polish forces prevented exposure of this new Soviet position. It became conventional wisdom, even among the Polish leadership and members of the Soviet Party apparatus, that allied forces would have rolled into Poland if Warsaw had failed to crush the national opposition on its own. Nevertheless, memories of what might have been remained with the Soviet leadership as a constant reminder of the need to reform the fundamental assumptions of bloc relations. No longer could Moscow insist on political uniformity within the bloc if it was unwilling to guarantee the viability of allied socialist governments in times of national crisis. The Polish events of 1980–81 had demonstrated that the interests of socialist nations could clash with each other, creating a situation in which national custom divided, rather than united, the bloc. Therefore, Moscow reluctantly began to permit a limited return to Khrushchev's policy of allowing the countries of the bloc to pursue their own "roads to socialism," respective of national traditions and customs. This new permissiveness would hopefully enable local communist regimes to generate some measure of support and legitimacy to replace their reliance on Soviet military might.

Excepting the opposition of a few stubborn hard-liners, this was largely the condition of Soviet attitudes toward bloc relations on the eve of Gorbachev's rise to power in the mid-1980s. The road that he would travel with his program of reforms and "new thinking" had already been laid out for him years earlier in the wake of the Polish Solidarity crisis. No workable alternative existed that might realistically have been expected to ensure communist viability into the next century.

Chapter 1 lays the groundwork for this book with an examination of the decision to send Warsaw Pact forces into Czechoslovakia in 1968. I discuss how the Soviets came to expand their understanding of what constituted a "counterrevolution" from the Hungarian model of violence in the streets to the peaceful, even popular, reform of socialist practice away from established Soviet norms.

Chapter 2 follows with a discussion of Moscow's "normalization" strategy for bringing Czechoslovakia back into the communist fold after the invasion. While apparently successful in the short run, the 1968 intervention had long-term repercussions that would come back to haunt the Soviets. Within the socialist camp, many reform advocates lost hope in the prospects for "socialism with a human face" and began advocating a more fundamental political transformation. Meanwhile, in the global arena, Sino-Soviet tensions exploded into open conflict. Both these threats—the one to communist orthodoxy, the other to Soviet security—underscored the need to tighten allied cooperation throughout the bloc.

Chapter 3 addresses how the Soviets responded to this need with a push to integrate the bloc around a common set of political and economic policies known collectively by the ideological masthead of "socialist internationalism." For the better part of a decade these principles provided the framework for an institutional overhaul of socialist relations in Eastern Europe. At the center of this consolidation campaign was the fundamental assertion of the Brezhnev Doctrine—that bloc nations had both a right and a responsibility to support and defend one another against all foes, foreign and domestic. By the late 1970s, however, the doctrine's assumption that the interests of all socialist nations were fully compatible began to encounter some undeniable exceptions. In the interest of reviving a mired Soviet economy, Moscow sharply raised the price charged to its allies for badly needed energy exports. Later, faced with the collapse of Afghanistan's communist regime, the Kremlin initially refused to provide military intervention on its behalf, despite Kabul's anxious requests for Soviet troops. Only when this ideological imperative overlapped with a perceived threat of Western incursion on the border of the Soviet Union itself did Moscow reverse its position and send troops into Afghanistan. Already, then, the relationship between ideology and national interests was beginning to change as the imperatives of Soviet domestic security took priority over the obligations of socialist internationalism. Moreover, the pace of this realignment would only accelerate as the effort to offer "international assistance" to Kabul degenerated into a military quagmire rife with negative consequences for Moscow's international prestige and plans for economic development.

In Chapter 4 I examine how the Kremlin's carefully crafted system of institutional cooperation started to crumble in the late 1970s as Soviet leaders struggled to cope with flagging economic performance and deepening tensions in socialist Poland. I give particular attention to the Kremlin's fear of Polish Catholic nationalism following the election of Poland's Karol Cardinal Wojtyla to the papacy as Pope John Paul II. Socialist internationalism notwithstanding, Soviet leaders were far more concerned at that time with preventing Polish Catholics from destabilizing the Western Soviet republics than with confronting religious nationalism in Poland. Purely domestic issues within the USSR at this point not only constrained but also began to eclipse Moscow's commitment to stability in the affairs of its allies.

Chapters 5–7 describe how the Polish Solidarity crisis of 1980–81 ultimately forced the Soviet colossus to recognize that fundamental contradictions existed between its new perception of Soviet national interests and the defense of communist rule in Eastern Europe. Though the Solidarity revolution clearly threatened to overturn communist rule in Poland, military intervention was no longer considered an affordable response to the crisis. The Soviet Union simply could not withstand the blow Western sanctions would deal to its national economy and international prestige. In practice, therefore, it was no longer realistic to regard socialist internationalism and its guarantees of "fraternal assistance" as the foundation of political uniformity in bloc relations. The Poles had seen to that. Should some future Solidarity-style reform movement choose to call the Soviet bluff, communist monopoly rule and its attendant system would collapse in a heap, its bankruptcy exposed and undefended. Consequently, it was at this point that the momentum began to increase toward a more permissive Soviet presence in Eastern Europe. The concluding chapter of this book offers a number of reflections on how that momentum ultimately carried Moscow to the advent of Gorbachev's reform program.

1 ★ Evolutionary Counterrevolution

The only thing as important for a nation as its revolution is its last major war. . . . What was believed to have caused the last war will be considered likely to cause the next one.
—Robert Jervis, *Perception and Misperception in International Politics*

IT IS CHARACTERISTIC OF THE IRONY which pervades the entire course of Soviet history that the road to Mikhail Gorbachev's permissive bloc policies began with an effort to eliminate political diversity within the socialist alliance.[1] During the period between January and August 1968, the new Brezhnev leadership sought to define the boundaries of independent policy within the socialist alliance on the basis of ideological orthodoxy. Unlike the remarkable dismantling of communist monopoly rule that characterized the Hungarian Revolution of 1956, the Prague Spring was largely an effort by loyal communists to reform the practice of "real socialism" in Czechoslovakia. As such, it presented the Brezhnev leadership with one of the more intractable legacies of the Khrushchev era and its policy of "separate roads to socialism." To what degree could a member-state of the socialist commonwealth renovate its system and institutions without raising the specter of counterrevolution?

The Hungarian Revolution

From the vantage point of the new Brezhnev regime coming to power in 1964, Nikita Khrushchev's failure to define the limits of "de-Stalinization" in Eastern Europe had resulted in serious instability over the previous decade that could not be allowed to continue. Nowhere were the consequences of this failure more evident than in Hungary. Beginning with the New Course instituted by Khrushchev and Georgii Malenkov throughout the Soviet bloc after the death of Stalin, each step in the direction of correcting past abuses created political tremors in Budapest. Central to the New Course, for instance, was the principle of collective leadership. Unlike the Stalinist-era practice of a single despotic leader in each socialist country, under the New Course the first secretary of the Communist Party was to be a person different from the man running the government. In this way Nikita Khrushchev assumed the post of Soviet first secretary in 1953, while Malenkov became head of the Council of Ministers, or prime minister. Accordingly, Moscow compelled Hungary's Stalinist leader, Mátyás

Rákosi, to surrender the post of prime minister in July 1953 to Imre Nagy, a longtime communist who had spent the years from 1929 to 1944 in the Soviet Union.

Upon assuming his new post, Nagy moved quickly to introduce sweeping reforms to cope with the consequences of Rákosi's heavy industrialization drive. Light industry and food production were established as investment priorities. Peasants were given permission to dissolve collective farms if they desired. Religious tolerance was expanded. Police powers were reduced, and Stalinist internment camps closed. In all sectors of Hungarian life, discussions addressed the further democratization of Hungarian political life.

The Nagy reform program terrified the members of Hungary's party apparatus, most of whom worked alongside Rákosi to oppose any meaningful change. Ultimately, another Soviet development decided this political feud. In January 1955, Malenkov was criticized at a meeting of the Communist Party's Central Committee for favoring light industry over heavy industry and for his agricultural policies. A month later Malenkov submitted his resignation, admitting publicly that "he had not been trained adequately for a role as a government leader."[2] Khrushchev's political ally, Nikolai Bulganin, then became the new Soviet premier. In April, Rákosi similarly overthrew Imre Nagy. The latter lost his position as premier, his seat in parliament, his position on the party Central Committee and Politburo, his membership in the Academy of Sciences, and his university lectureship all in one fell swoop as Mátyás Rákosi abandoned his reform program and resumed full control over the nation.

Rákosi's removal of Imre Nagy in 1955 elicited strong protests from the people of Hungary, particularly the nation's intelligentsia, many of whom openly attacked Rákosi for his excesses during the Stalinist era. Meanwhile, international developments added to their concerns. Following the conclusion of the Austrian State Treaty in May 1955, the Soviet troops who had occupied Hungary since World War II were to have left. However, on 14 May, one day before the signing of the Austrian treaty, Khrushchev concluded a treaty of friendship, cooperation, and mutual assistance with the East European states, including Hungary, that led to the creation of the Warsaw Treaty Organization (commonly known as the Warsaw Pact). As a result, Soviets troops had a legal basis for remaining in Hungary indefinitely.

Only two weeks later, Khrushchev was in Belgrade with Bulganin working to repair the rift that had existed between the Soviet Union and Yugoslavia since 1948. During the visit, Bulganin and Yugoslav leader Josip Broz Tito signed an agreement outlining the basis for reviving mutual respect between their countries. Known later as the Belgrade Declaration, the agreement pledged that separate paths to socialism were permissible within the Soviet bloc. This development only added more fuel to the fire in Hungary, where Nagy's supporters clamored for a turn from the Soviet model embraced by Mátyás Rákosi. Meanwhile, many of these same individuals strongly opposed the new Warsaw Treaty, demanding both the withdrawal of Soviet forces from Hungary and Hungary's withdrawal from the Warsaw Pact.[3] In response, beginning in July 1956, Moscow instructed members of the Soviet military stationed in Hungary to prepare a top secret plan titled "The Special Army Corps's Participation in the Restoration of Order on Hungarian Territory." Code-named VOLNA (WAVE), it was intended to provide protection for the communist leadership in Hungary should popular unrest continue to grow.[4] At the same time, Moscow worked to pacify the Hungarian political scene in July by convincing a reluctant Rákosi to retire for reasons of "hypertension" and move to the Soviet Union.[5] However, the man selected as his successor, Erno Gero, was too closely identified with Rákosi to satisfy those in favor of a return to reform. Although Gero did restore party membership to Imre Nagy in October 1956, the former prime minister remained largely without any official influence.

It was the Polish "October" and Wladyslaw Gomulka's apparent assertion of a "national communist" position in the face of Soviet opposition that provided the spark to ignite the Hungarian explosion.[6] To many in Hungary, it seemed that Moscow might be abdicating its control over the socialist camp. Aware that this belief could have powerful repercussions in Hungary, the Soviet ambassador in Budapest, Yuri Andropov, met between 6 and 19 October with Soviet military leaders to encourage them to step up preparations for Operation VOLNA.[7] Additionally, by 19 October the 108 Parachute Guard Regiment of the 7th Soviet Air Mobile Division was in a state of total battle readiness. By the following day it was boarding planes in Kaunas and Vilnius bound for Hungary.[8] Soviet reinforcements were therefore already arriving in Hungary by the time protests began in Debrecen and Budapest on 23 October. Those in the capital city were especially vocal, involving about fifty thousand people, many of them students from Budapest Polytechnical University. They gathered at the monument to Poland's nineteenth-century general Jozef Bem, hero of the 1848 Hungarian Revolution, and proclaimed their solidarity with the Polish stand against Moscow. By evening, the number of people at the statue had increased to two hundred thousand, some of whom then moved on to topple the large statue of Stalin in the center of the city. Another group of protesters marched to the main radio building to broadcast a series of demands, including a return of Imre Nagy to power, the evacuation of Soviet troops from Hungary, and multiparty elections to the Hungarian National Assembly. It was there, at the radio building, that the first shots of the revolution were fired, most likely by state security guards who were on duty at the time.[9]

Soviet ambassador Andropov wasted no time contacting Moscow with the news that the situation in Budapest was "extraordinarily dangerous," requiring the immediate introduction of Soviet military assistance. At this point, however, the Soviet leadership had not received any such requests from the Hungarians; thus Khrushchev phoned Gero immediately. The Soviet leader told his Hungarian counterpart that he would be willing to send additional troops to quell the popular uprising "if the government of the Hungarian People's Republic would set it [a formal invasion request] down in writing." When Gero pointed out that it would be impossible to call the government together, Khrushchev suggested that the president of the Council of Ministers, Prime Minister Andras Hegedus (then all of thirty-three years old), might draw up the formal request. With this accomplished, Defense Minister Georgii Zhukov received the order to occupy Budapest.[10]

Gero, meanwhile, managed to call a meeting of the Hungarian party leadership, and a number of personnel changes were made in an effort to calm the demonstrators, most important of which was the restoration of Imre Nagy to his former party and state positions. On the following day, the Soviets replaced the unpopular Gero with Janos Kadar, a man who had spent World War II not in the USSR but fighting in the Hungarian underground. Their hope was that the new Nagy-Kadar team would be able to work closely to bring about a negotiated settlement to the national crisis.

As the new prime minister, Nagy moved immediately to restore calm. Indeed, Khrushchev later spoke approvingly of the fact that "Nagy had demanded that the population restore order, and he had signed an order to establish martial law with the authority to take immediate action against anyone who resisted. Nagy had said that the government of the Hungarian People's Republic had invited Soviet troops to Budapest, and that the good movement that the students had started had been taken advantage of by bandits who had stirred up trouble and shootings in the crowds, and as prime minister he demanded that arms be laid down by 1300 hours."[11]

At this early point in the crisis, Khrushchev appears to have had full confidence in Nagy, noting that "within the Hungarian leadership, both in the party and the government, there was a complete consensus of opinion. . . . Imre Nagy is acting decisively and bravely, stressing that on all points he is in agreement with Gero." Indeed, Nagy had gone as far as to issue orders to the Hungarian armed forces on 23–24 October not to resist Soviet troops.[12] Later Soviet testimony suggests that this order was very effective. "The Hungarian army was strong," Defense Minister Zhukov reportedly told a meeting of Soviet armed forces in 1957. "It consisted of 120,000 men, approximately 700 tanks, 5,000 cannons, and a few air force divisions and regiments. The Hungarians are not bad fighters, as we know from our experiences in the two world wars. This army ceased to exist in precisely five minutes [in the 1956 events]." Lieutenant General Yevgeny Ivanovich Malashenko, in charge of the operational section of the Soviet Special Corps Headquarters in Hungary, offers the more realistic appraisal that, while many units of the Hungarian army did defect to support the revolutionaries, most stayed at their posts and obeyed orders during the crisis. Ultimately, however, they played a decidedly minor supporting role to the Soviet forces in the pitched street battles of October and November. Indeed, for most of the October events, they simply remained neutral.[13]

Largely in the absence of assistance from the Hungarian army, then, Soviet forces fought a desperate battle against the revolutionary forces in Budapest for the days between 24 and 28 October. Hungarian communist historians would later portray their opponents as criminals; in fact, most were young, unskilled workers, along with some students, soldiers, and army officers.[14] This presented a significant problem to those who claimed that the uprising was a counterrevolutionary bid by fascist forces to reestablish control in Hungary against the will of the working people. As one ranking member of the Hungarian Party insisted at an October 26 Central Committee meeting, the opposition was "a broad-based, mass democratic movement, seeking to repair socialism and put a stop to the distorted construction of socialism."[15] Although the Central Committee rejected this position, some members, like Janos Kadar, had to admit that "the party leadership had certainly come into conflict with broad strata of the population."[16] It did not take long for this realization to call into question the entire nature of the crisis. Meeting on 27–28 October, the party's Political Committee (similar to the Soviet Politburo) voted to accept the "broad-based democratic movement" interpretation of events, a decision supported by visiting Soviet representatives Anastas Mikoyan and Mikhail Suslov.[17] Reporting back to Moscow, Mikoyan and Suslov recommended adoption of this new line in a bid to "win over the workers' masses." They were even willing to allow "a certain number of petty bourgeois democrat" ministers to be introduced into the Hungarian state leadership as a demonstration of greater democracy. There were, however, limits to what they would countenance. "From our part," Mikoyan noted, "we warned them [the Hungarians] that no further concessions can be made, otherwise it will lead to the fall of the system." Mikoyan was especially adamant about the stationing of troops in Hungary, warning that "withdrawal of the Soviet army will lead inevitably to American troops marching in."[18]

Imre Nagy took his government's concession to the airwaves on 28 October, declaring in part, "The government condemns those views that say that the present mass people's movement is a counterrevolution." That night he returned to the airwaves to discuss how "the events of the last few weeks have developed with tragic speed."[19] However, he then called for the formation of workers councils, for greater democracy, for the dissolution of state security forces, for state-approved pay raises, for a cease-fire, and for a Soviet withdrawal. For the moment, the Hungarian people were satisfied. On 29 October, Soviet forces in Budapest were ordered to cease fire. The following day they received instructions to withdraw from Budapest immediately.

Nagy now faced a jubilant public, convinced that they had successfully held off the great Soviet colossus. With the Hungarian Communist Party in shambles, Nagy found himself carried along by the current of public demands. Not long before, Zoltan Vas, a close friend of Mátyás Rákosi and a leading Hungarian Party member, had said, "Nagy is not an anti-Soviet person, but he wants to build socialism in his own way, the Hungarian way."[20] By the time of the Soviet withdrawal, however, Nagy was no longer convinced of the compatibility of Soviet and Hungarian national interests. Rather, he had begun to express the opinion that satellite status would forever obstruct the building of socialism in Hungary. National independence, he felt, was a precondition for socialism, but it was inconsistent with participation in a bipolar international standoff. He concluded that the blocs should be dissolved. At the same time, he decided that the presence of noncommunist politicians within the government was not sufficient democratization in Hungary. Rather, the postwar political parties ought to be reconstituted and permitted to compete in free and fair elections for the National Assembly.

This was clearly further than the Soviets were willing to go. Indeed, it was further than Janos Kadar was willing to go as well.[21] By 31 October, forces in the Soviet Union were already moving toward the border with Hungary. That same day, Nagy revealed the composition of his newly formed government, which included members of the National Smallholders Party, Social Democratic Party, and National Peasant Party (called the Petofi Party). He also announced that soon he would be starting negotiations on Hungary's withdrawal from the Warsaw Pact.[22]

As Soviet troops began crossing the Hungarian border on 1 November, Nagy decided to dispense with the proposed negotiations. He simply declared Hungary to be a neutral country and appealed to the United Nations for protection from the Soviet Union. That day he addressed a crowd assembled in the center of Budapest, insisting that he had not requested any further Soviet assistance. "At the same time as we renounce the Warsaw Pact," he said, "we also request that Soviet troops be withdrawn."[23] The Soviet press, meanwhile, began running articles suggesting that "Hungarian soldiers and officers who served in Horthy's and Hitler's armies are heading to Hungary from the West."[24]

Moscow's Operation WHIRLWIND began on the morning of 4 November as Soviet troops marched again into Budapest and faced heavily armed resistance. As they entered the city, the new Revolutionary Worker-Peasant Government, led by Janos Kadar, appealed officially to the Soviet Union for help in suppressing the national uprising and restoring order.[25] Repeated requests for Western assistance elicited little more than a U.S.-sponsored resolution in the United Nations to condemn the invasion. Many have credited this anemic response to the invasion's occurrence during the Suez Canal Crisis of 1956, at a point when the United States was incapable of acting in concert with its French and British allies. But the declassification of formerly secret documents in the United States now reveals that in July 1956 the U.S. National Security Council had adopted a policy paper in which "the United States government disavowed any political and military intervention in the Soviet satellites."[26]

Left to their own devices, with a government in turmoil and an army in disarray, the Hungarians had little chance against the full power of the Soviet army. According to a plan worked out on 2 November between Khrushchev and Tito, the Yugoslav government offered Nagy and twelve of his colleagues sanctuary in its Budapest embassy on 4 November. At 4:30 P.M. that afternoon, Soviet ambassador N. P. Firiubin in Belgrade sent a telegram to Moscow that read in part that the Yugoslav vice premier had "contacted Imre Nagy as it had been agreed with Khrushchev. . . . It is still not clear whether or not Imre Nagy made the declaration [about Hungary's withdrawal from the Warsaw Pact] in the name of the government in Budapest. If he made this declaration, then they, the Yugoslavs, will try to have him announce publicly that he made this declaration under the pressure of the reaction. They also intended to negotiate with Nagy, to get him to make an announcement that he supports the government headed by Kadar in Szolnok [a location sixty-five miles outside Budapest where Kadar and his government were holed up until 7 November]."[27] This, notes a later observer, "suggests that the Soviet leaders thought Nagy was basically malleable and could be persuaded to support them."[28] Their efforts were unsuccessful, and the Yugoslavs soon turned Nagy and his colleagues over to Soviet forces, who sent him off to imprisonment in Romania.

On 21 December 1957, over a year later, the Hungarian communists under Kadar finally voted to bring Nagy to trial for his "counterrevolutionary" conduct. In February 1958, however, the Soviets notified Kadar that the date scheduled for the Nagy trial was inconvenient, citing the prospect of an East-West summit between Khrushchev and President Dwight D. Eisenhower. Kadar therefore offered his colleagues two alternatives: either have the trial take place as scheduled, followed by a light sentence, or postpone the trial and level the more severe sentence that had been planned. At Kadar's suggestion, the Hungarian Central Committee voted for the latter, and on 16 June 1958, Imre Nagy was executed.[29]

Kadar's reprisals against the less illustrious Hungarian revolutionaries were often similarly brutal. According to data released from communist archives after 1991, 35,000 people were summoned between 1956 and 1959 to account for their activities during the revolution. Of these, 26,000 were tried, and 22,000 sentenced. Between 1957 and 1960, approximately 13,000 were interned, and from 1956 to 1961, 280 to 300 people were executed for their part in the events of 1956.[30]

In the end, Khrushchev's New Course and its corollary in the Belgrade Declaration had opened a Pandora's box in Hungary that required at least 60,000 Soviet troops to shut. Of these, Soviet sources report 669 officers and soldiers killed, 1,450 wounded, and 51 missing. The same sources claim that as many as 4,000 Hungarians became casualties of the intervention.[31] Looking back over this experience from 1964 and considering the effort that the new Kadar government had to exercise in restoring control over Hungary, the Brezhnev leadership was wary of introducing any further reforms in Eastern Europe.

Another Hungary?

Notwithstanding the harsh crackdown against the Hungarian Revolution, oppositionists continued to confront communist authorities in the Soviet Union and Eastern Europe right through the 1960s. The reformist spirit of de-Stalinization continued to haunt the socialist camp after 1964, unwilling to accept Khrushchev's dismissal as the end of an era. Following the 1965 arrest and conviction in the USSR of authors Andrei Siniavskiy and Yuri Daniel on charges of "anti-Sovietism," Moscow faced a growing battle with dissidents in the Soviet Union itself. Members of the All-Russia Social Christian Union, a group founded in 1964 by four graduates of Leningrad University, were arrested and tried for terrorism in 1967–68. The KGB based its case against the group on its declaration: "The liberation of all peoples from the communist yoke can only be achieved by armed struggle."[32] Meanwhile, in June 1967, Moscow was shocked to see Alexander Solzhenitsyn present an attack on official censorship at the Fourth Writers' Conference in Prague. Aggravating the case was the fact that Solzhenitsyn's address was aimed at the Soviet Union of Writers.[33] By 1968 the dissident problem in the Soviet Union had reached a stage where

Leonid Brezhnev began to speak of "killing off at an early stage these bacilli who could cause us serious harm," while other Politburo members suggested exiling personae non gratae.[34] In Poland student unrest in May 1968 ignited widespread protests against that nation's communist government. Meanwhile, that same month Soviet defense minister Andrei Grechko announced to the Politburo in Moscow that Romania was seriously considering full withdrawal from the Warsaw Pact. He warned that if the Romanians left, the pact would not be able to hold together.[35]

Unquestionably, the greatest challenge to Moscow's authority in the 1960s was the communist government of the People's Republic of China. Tensions between the USSR and its former ally had advanced since the late 1950s to the point that, in 1966, contacts between the Communist Party of the Soviet Union (CPSU) and Communist Party of China (CPC) were continued only at very low levels. Small-scale skirmishes began to erupt along the Sino-Soviet and Sino-Mongolian borders, raising concerns that the Soviet Union might act on Khrushchev's September 1964 threat to use "up-to-date weapons of annihilation" if necessary to defend its frontiers.[36] Moscow faced China's ideological challenge with similar resolve, calling at the Twenty-third CPSU Party Congress in 1966 for "socialist unity" in the face of Maoist divisiveness. By 1968, Mikhail Suslov, Moscow's chief ideologist, was seeking to isolate the Chinese at a meeting of the international communist movement scheduled to convene in November. At a preparatory conference in February 1968, Suslov declared that he would "do everything necessary to create the most favorable conditions for this conference."[37] This included playing down the threat of Czechoslovak revisionism in an effort to avoid alienating potential anti-Chinese allies.[38]

Cast against this backdrop of open challenge to Soviet authority, Moscow did not immediately perceive the relatively late arrival of de-Stalinization in Czechoslovakia as a grave threat. The process began in 1962, when Khrushchev pressured Czechoslovak leader Antonín Novotný to reassess the purges he had overseen between 1949 and 1954, largely against Slovak Communist Party activists.[39] This political embarrassment coincided with a sharp decline in the nation's once widely admired standard of living, providing a welcome opportunity for the Slovak Party to assert itself. Novotný watched in anger as the Slovaks appointed Alexander Dubcek to the position of first secretary in April 1963, thus replacing one of Novotný's key political allies. "By the end of 1966," Joseph Rothschild writes, "the Slovak section of the Communist party had removed from its Presidium and Secretariat all the Prague-oriented, centralizing, terror-implicated satraps whom Gottwald [Novotný's Stalinist predecessor] and Novotny had imposed on it over the previous two decades."[40] Legal and economic reforms followed these political shifts, as the nation struggled to free itself of its Stalinist past and its concomitant distortions. Notions of guilt by "probability, analogy, or class background" were condemned, while central planners discussed modifications of the nation's command economy.[41] Novotný worked hard to impede these forces of change, just as Mátyás Rákosi had once done in Hungary. His efforts climaxed in December 1967, when the embattled Stalinist invited Soviet leader Leonid Brezhnev to Prague in a bid to launch an all-out political coup against the reformers. Brezhnev, however, failed to support him, and in late December the Czechoslovak Central Committee asked Novotný to resign his position as head of the Czechoslovak Communist Party (CSCP). Meeting on 3–5 January 1968, the Central Committee then formally separated the positions of first secretary and president of the republic, appointing Alexander Dubcek to the former and leaving Novotný as the latter. In Bratislava, the Slovak Central Committee elected Vasil Bilak as Dubcek's successor to head its wing of the party.

Former CPSU Central Committee staffer Valerii Musatov recalls how members of the Central Committee responded to Dubcek's election in early 1968: "He's a provincial," they said, "but his attitude toward the Soviet Union is friendly."[42] Despite this initial welcome, it was not long before developments in Czechoslovakia began to drive the country toward a political confrontation with the Kremlin. Under Dubcek's watch, limited experimentation with market economics and independent enterprise quickly led to social and political reforms. Czechs and Slovaks were permitted to travel abroad more freely, while at home social organizations came into existence outside the purview of Party control. In February, Dubcek suggested that Prague might unilaterally establish greater links with the nations of Western Europe, including West Germany, a move that East German Politburo member Kurt Hager warned would subvert and divide the socialist alliance.[43] Public discussion of a parliament free from Party control ensued, and official censorship ended in Czechoslovakia. Dubcek's new government curtailed the powers of the secret police and gradually removed Moscow's designated representatives from the Party and from trade unions.

Soviet patience with these initial reforms finally turned to alarm in March when the outbreak of student protests in Poland raised fears that Czechoslovak initiatives could jeopardize communist rule throughout the bloc. The resignation of Antonín Novotný as Czechoslovakia's president on 21 March only aggravated Moscow's anxiety, as Dubcek failed to consult with the Kremlin on the matter of Novotný's successor. At stake was not only a conservative voice in Prague but traditional Soviet influence as well. Moscow's response was predictably grave. For the first time since Dubcek came to power, Soviet leaders raised the prospect of a Hungarian-style counterrevolution evolving in Czechoslovakia. Speaking at a meeting of the Politburo on 21 March, KGB chairman Yuri Andropov warned that "the methods and forms by which the work is progressing in Czechoslovakia remind one very much of Hungary. In this outward appearance of chaos . . . there is a certain order. It all began like this in Hungary also, but then came the first and second echelons, and then, finally, the social democrats."[44] At this point, however, there was no consensus on the Politburo to support the KGB chairman. Many, including General Secretary Brezhnev, resisted hasty judgment, demanding clarification from Prague. So, on 21 March, with the Politburo still convened, Brezhnev picked up the phone and called Dubcek.

No doubt mindful of the fate that had befallen Imre Nagy in 1956, Dubcek responded to Brezhnev's call with assurances that the situation in Czechoslovakia was safely under control. He worked hard to play down any connection between his policies and those of his Hungarian predecessor. The 1956 invasion had demonstrated that there were definite limits to the extent Moscow would tolerate independence within the socialist commonwealth. Most important, Czechoslovakia could not attempt to leave either the Council for Mutual Economic Assistance (CMEA) or the Warsaw Pact the way the Hungarians had in 1956. At the same time, the extreme nature of the Hungarian case provided the Czechoslovak leader with little guidance for implementing a more measured reform of socialism. Dubcek simply trusted that he could "persuade [the Soviets] in a comradely fashion" to accept the reform program as consistent with both socialist principles and Czechoslovak national traditions.[45] In this spirit, he promised Brezhnev on 21 March that "we will be able to manage the events which are occurring here."[46]

For the time being, Brezhnev was willing to accept Dubcek's assurances, consistent with the Soviet leader's reputation as a vacillating consensus maker. But other members of the Soviet leadership were less easily reconciled and pressed for more resolute dealings with Prague. Among the most apprehensive was Petr Shelest, first secretary of the Ukrainian Communist Party. Ukraine shared a common border with Czechoslovakia, and Shelest feared that the bacillus of reform might spread eastward from Prague into his republic. Most troubling was Dubcek's restoration of national rights to the Ruthenian (Ukrainian) minority in Slovakia and the subsequent revival of the Eastern Rite Catholic Church, a denomination that had been suppressed in the USSR since the late 1940s. Such measures threatened to inflame smoldering nationalism among Ruthenians in Western Ukraine, prompting Shelest to call for an immediate invasion of Czechoslovakia. "What we are talking about is the fate of socialism in one of the socialist countries," he warned the Politburo on 21 March, "as well as the fate of socialism in the socialist camp." Yuri Andropov agreed, and he proposed undertaking military preparations just in case they became necessary.[47]

At a summit in Dresden two days later, the communist leaders of Bulgaria, Poland, and Hungary also called on Moscow to respond more decisively toward the Prague Spring. In the words of then East German leader Walter Ulbricht, "If Czechoslovakia continues to follow the January line, all of us here will run a serious risk which may well lead to our downfall."[48] Confronted with the prospect that communist control in Eastern Europe was indeed on the wane, the Soviets quickly changed their tone in dealings with the Czechoslovaks. They lectured Dubcek's delegation about counterrevolution, warning that it "does not always begin with murders, but often with demagogy, pseudosocialist slogans and appeals to freedom, harmful to the party, the state and social apparat, with the weakening and demoralization of the instruments of power."[49]

Was this the reality that was facing communism in Eastern Europe? Had the reform process begun to run out of control in Prague? The April publication of Dubcek's very liberal "Program of Action" seemed to confirm for Soviet observers that it had. While much of the program merely restated principles enunciated earlier by Nikita Khrushchev, it contained a number of assertions that were bound to alarm Moscow. Most troubling were the stipulations aimed at limiting Party control over the Interior Ministry, a move that would shatter the network of agents Moscow had employed for years in Czechoslovakia. No more comforting were statements that undermined the leading role of the Communist Party in Czechoslovak society through calls for greater political pluralism.[50]

Moscow was unwilling even to consider approval of Czechoslovakia's new Party program. When discussed in the Soviet media, its contents were heavily censored. Meanwhile, it generated a defiant resolve among those few high-ranking Party members who had seen it in full. At the April plenum of the CPSU Central Committee, for instance, the Soviets unambiguously declared, "We will not let go of socialist Czechoslovakia."[51] Members claimed a right to ideological self-defense with their assertion that "bourgeois ideological influence had to be combated, whatever its source."[52] This theme arose again only weeks later when, on 4 May, Brezhnev and others warned the visiting Czechoslovak leadership that the fallout of the Prague Spring would no longer be considered a purely internal affair. The potential consequences it presented to the entire socialist camp were too significant. Speaking to the Politburo on 6 May, Brezhnev condemned the Action Program as "opening possibilities for the restoration of capitalism in Czechoslovakia." Foreign Minister Andrei Gromyko echoed this concern, predicting an eventual counterrevolution and "the complete collapse of the Warsaw Pact."[53]

At Brezhnev's suggestion, the Politburo decided to respond to this prospect with a series of Warsaw Pact training maneuvers in Czechoslovakia. Scheduled to begin in June, these war games were intended as a warning against pursuing any further implementation of the April program. "After this," Brezhnev punned, "everyone will understand that you cannot play games with us."[54] According to the briefing given to socialist allies in May, the maneuvers would also aim to "support forces [in Czechoslovakia] that would react positively" to the increased pressure and who would then "consolidate and discover forces that will struggle against the counter-revolution."[55] However, only a few days before the exercises were about to commence, these "forces" had yet to be identified. Prompted by their ideological presuppositions, the Soviets postulated the existence of a "healthy nucleus" within the Czechoslovak leadership, although they were unsure of exactly who belonged to it. Therefore, toward the end of May, the Politburo dispatched Aleksei Kosygin to undertake a fact-finding mission in Czechoslovakia.

While in Prague, the Soviet premier received a number of important concessions from Dubcek. Czechoslovakia would remain in the Warsaw Treaty Organization (WTO, or Warsaw Pact) and Council for Mutual Economic Assistance. The Czechoslovak Communist Party would retain its monopoly over state power, while forbidding the creation of new political parties. Moreover, Dubcek agreed to permit the Warsaw Pact exercises in Czechoslovakia beginning in June, following assurances that the maneuvers were intended as "necessary assistance," rather than outside interference.[56]

The fact-finding aspect of the visit turned out far less agreeably for Soviet expectations. On 27 May, Kosygin reported his observations to the Politburo. The news was not good. "Right now there are no other forces in the country apart from the existing Central Committee Presidium [Dubcek and his associates] who could take the situation in hand," he concluded. It was possible to define the Czechoslovak leadership as made up of different political groupings. But Kosygin saw no significant differences of opinion among them on important questions. It also appeared that the only authoritative figures in the Czechoslovak Party were Dubcek; his close ally, Prime Minister Oldrich Cernik; and President Ludvík Svoboda. Kosygin therefore proposed a shift in Soviet attitude vis-à-vis reformist policies and intentions. In his opinion, the Prague leadership was not at fault for the sociopolitical crisis in Czechoslovakia. Dubcek was not an enemy of the Soviet Union, he said, nor was his much-maligned deputy, National Assembly chairman Josef Smrkovsky. Rather, the situation seemed to have developed in accordance with the logic of "class opposition." Finally, Kosygin concluded, rumors of a "healthy nucleus" within the Czechoslovak party were highly exaggerated. Moscow would simply have to hope that the existing leadership in Prague could be counted on to act in concert with Soviet wishes.[57]

This fundamental reassessment of the situation might well have prompted the Politburo to abandon its attempts to divide and conquer the Czechoslovak leadership. But chance intervened. Just as Kosygin finished his presentation, Brezhnev was summoned to the phone. The call was from Ukrainian Party leader Petr Shelest, who was phoning to inform the Politburo about a conversation he had just concluded with the Czechoslovak communist Vasil Bilak.

As first secretary of the Communist Party in Slovakia, Bilak saw the Prague Spring primarily as a vehicle for asserting Slovak autonomy.[58] He therefore focused on the increased federalization promised in the Action Program, while limiting democratic reform in Slovakia.[59] Under Bilak's leadership, the Slovak Party tried to contain the more liberal aspects of the Prague Spring. He had once gone as far as suggesting off the record that the Soviets might support separation of Slovakia from Czech lands if forced to choose between democracy and federalization.[60] In conjunction with senior East European officials, notably Walter Ulbricht of East Germany and Wladyslaw Gomulka of Poland, Bilak hoped to convince the Soviets to remove Dubcek and end the Prague Spring while retaining Slovakia's newly acquired rights under federalization.[61] His discussion with Shelest had been designed to elicit this response, and it created instant panic in Moscow.

"If order is not restored in the country within a month," Bilak had told Shelest, "we will all fly [from power]. Our apostle [Dubcek] will fly as well . . . and we, Slovaks and Russians, will obviously have to liberate Czechoslovakia again." The Slovak leader requested that the Soviets act quickly and decisively, promising that a "second center" in the Czechoslovak Party would support them. Clearly this promise contrasted with the report Kosygin had just presented. However, Brezhnev readily dismissed his colleague's impressions, concluding that Bilak undoubtedly had a more realistic grasp of the existing situation. Discussion of Kosygin's mission to Prague ended abruptly, and the Politburo took up the possibility of collaborating with Bilak's "second center" within the CSCP.[62]

The Impact of Soviet Military Pressure

Having established contact with a member of the "healthy forces" in Czechoslovakia, the Soviets maintained the hope that military pressures would strengthen this "wing" of the CSCP. Therefore, when the joint Warsaw Pact Sumava exercises culminated on 30 June, participating troops were ordered to remain in Czechoslovakia. Local response was indignant, and anti-Soviet passions flared. From Prague, Soviet ambassador Stepan

Chervonenko warned, "The troops must be withdrawn, because in this situation the people don't support the presence of our troops. At the moment relations toward our army are very good. But if we leave our troops here now, everyone will turn against us."[63]

Reactions in Moscow to Chervonenko's recommendation were mixed. Mikhail Zimianin, Aleksandr Shelepin, and Suslov shared the ambassador's concern that military intimidation would destroy any possibility of a political resolution to the Czechoslovak crisis. However, the majority of their colleagues continued to favor the application of pressure along all fronts, including the use of armed intimidation. Nicholas Podgornyi, Arvid Pel'she, P. E. Shelest, Vasiliy Mzhavanadze, and Yuri Andropov all insisted on leaving the troops in Czechoslovakia. Andrei Gromyko and Andrei Grechko went so far as to encourage swift and decisive action. "It is now clear," Gromyko said, that "we cannot avoid military intervention." Perhaps seeking to shake the impression that he had moderately misrepresented the political scene in Prague, the now repentant Kosygin agreed with Gromyko.[64] After consultations with Janos Kadar on 3 July, Brezhnev informed the Politburo that the Hungarian leader also stood in favor of military intervention. It was obvious that the leadership of the Soviet bloc, both in Moscow and in Eastern Europe, was losing patience with the political channels that Ambassador Chervonenko advised.

With the Politburo deadlocked on Czechoslovakia, responsibility for finding a way forward fell by tradition to the general secretary, Leonid Brezhnev. At that point in early July, Brezhnev still held out hope that an invasion could be avoided. "We must now carefully size up whether we are mistaken in our estimation of the situation in Czechoslovakia," he asserted. "All of our measures depend on this."[65] As for the Soviet troops remaining in Czechoslovakia, by 11 July Dubcek was able to convince Brezhnev to begin their withdrawal.[66] Reform advocates in Prague were encouraged in the face of Moscow's apparent indecisiveness as the impact of the earlier exercises came to naught.

Cultivating the "Second Center" in Czechoslovakia

The Soviet inclination to sideline Dubcek in favor of Bilak and his confederates gained considerable momentum in early July when the Czechoslovak leader refused to attend a blocwide summit convening in Warsaw. Seeking to avoid yet another application of multilateral pressure on his government, Dubcek demurred and requested bilateral contacts instead.[67] His refusal seriously upset Brezhnev, who warned Prague that it indicated a new, and implicitly undesirable, state of relations between the CSCP and CPSU. Kosygin, the erstwhile champion of cooperation with Dubcek, now noted ominously that Czechoslovakia was improving its relations with Romania and Yugoslavia, the two states in the region most independent of Soviet influence.[68] Moreover, the support Czechoslovak reformers were receiving from Western European communist parties, such as those in Italy and France, did nothing to allay Soviet concerns. The Prague Spring was steadily undermining Moscow's authority over the world communist movement, and Alexander Dubcek was doing little to avert a major showdown with his socialist partners.

Consequently, by early July, Dubcek had been all but factored out of Soviet plans for the "normalization" of Czechoslovakia, that is, its restoration to Soviet-approved political and socioeconomic norms. Contacts with the so-called healthy nucleus of the CSCP began to intensify along both interparty and military lines. Meanwhile, KGB authorities assured the Politburo that popular sentiment in the Soviet Union was behind a military intervention if needed to establish order in Czechoslovakia. At the Warsaw summit of 14–15 July, Communist leaders from the German Democratic Republic (GDR), Hungary, Poland, Bulgaria, and the Soviet Union issued a joint critique of the situation in Prague despite the absence of a Czechoslovak delegation. Brezhnev's speech at the summit ignored standard accusations of imperialist subjugation in Czechoslovakia and focused instead on the threat posed to democratic centralism and the leading role of the Party.[69] He understood that the Prague Spring was not, as official propaganda increasingly suggested, the result of a covert Western plot aimed at fragmenting the socialist alliance. Rather, Brezhnev was concerned with the prospect that Czechoslovakia's own internal reform might endanger the communist political monopoly in Eastern Europe.

From this perspective, the events transpiring in Czechoslovakia could not be regarded as the internal affairs of a single socialist nation. "This is no longer your affair alone," the five attending allies told the Dubcek government in a communiqué that came to be known as the "Warsaw Letter." "We shall never agree that imperialism should break through the socialist systems by peaceful or violent means, from within or from without, and change the balance of power in Europe to its advantage." Joint action was necessary, the letter concluded, in the interest of collective self-defense. "That is precisely why we maintain that firm resistance to anti-communist forces and a decisive battle for the preservation of the socialist system in Czechoslovakia are not only your duty but ours as well."[70] Never before used in a bloc communiqué, this formulation clearly implied the threat of intervention by Warsaw Pact forces.[71] To Dubcek's objection that the letter was an infringement of Czechoslovak state sovereignty, Brezhnev diplomatically described it not as an ultimatum but as an expression of well-intentioned concern.[72]

Days later the Central Committee of the CPSU in its July plenum approved the conclusions of the Warsaw meeting. The plenum adopted a resolution reasserting the need to ensure "the consolidation of the socialist system on the basis of the principles of proletarian internationalism" in "support of the cause of socialism in Czechoslovakia."[73] This use of the words "proletarian internationalism" underscored the Soviet view that the fate of communism in Prague was the legitimate concern of the entire bloc. It signaled that the faction in Moscow behind intervention was solidifying its influence. Impatient with Dubcek's empty assurances, Brezhnev himself announced to the Politburo on 19 July that the only remaining question was, "Have we exhausted the arsenal of political coercion, have we done everything short of extreme [i.e., military] measures?"[74]

The Soviets had nonmilitary pressures available to them that they might have used to curb the Czechoslovak reform program. Without a doubt, their most important levers of peaceful influence were all economic. Czechoslovakia was heavily dependent on deliveries of subsidized oil and gas from the Soviet Union, and so trade sanctions would have had a strong impact on its economy. But all available information indicates that this lever was never seriously utilized during the Prague Spring crisis. True, Western media reports in April 1968 revealed that Czechoslovak grain supplies had run extremely low, suggesting some form of embargo by the socialist allies.[75] Nevertheless, there is little further evidence that Moscow ever tried to play the economic card with Prague. To do so would have chanced the prospect of Dubcek turning more decisively toward the West for assistance. Moreover, the Czechoslovaks could have responded with countersanctions of their own, cutting off deliveries of uranium and other products.[76] Hence, in terms of "measures short of war," the Soviets were forced to rely on the type of bellicose rhetoric that had characterized their public pronouncements since June.

Mid-July saw this rhetoric stepped up to an increasingly menacing tone. Though the Soviet leadership recognized that the most serious problem in Czechoslovakia stemmed from the communist reform program, it was not yet prepared to address this concern in a public forum. Expressions of ideological concern were better framed in the context of the bipolar international standoff. Therefore, on 19 July an article in *Pravda* claimed to quote a joint Central Intelligence Agency (CIA)/Pentagon plan detailing "ideological sabotage" as prelude to the "liberation of East Germany and Czechoslovakia." It stipulated that "the conduct of direct aggression is to begin when, in the opinion of the plans' authors, ideological sabotage has created the requisite situation."[77] Three days later, on 22 July, *Pravda* again raised the stakes, asking: "Can it be that one should wait until the counterrevolutionary forces become master of the situation in Czechoslovakia before giving battle to them?"[78]

Questions about doing battle with foreign intelligence services and counterrevolutionaries in Czechoslovakia, however rhetorical they might have been, reflect the seriousness with which the Soviets had begun preparing for the prospect of military intervention by late July 1968. Yet the belligerent accusations appearing in the Soviet media that month and later in August were not regarded in Moscow as simply the necessary hyperbole used to justify an imminent invasion. Intelligence reports prepared for the Politburo seemed to confirm the reality of Western subversion in Czechoslovakia. In part this was due to the personal convictions of Ambassador Chervonenko, who forwarded an inordinate amount of sensationalist material to Moscow. A Soviet translator who worked in the embassy later recalled that the material selected for translation from the local press was heavily biased in its discussion of antisocialist activities.[79] Alexander Bovin, a member of the Central Committee's Department for Liaison with Communist and Workers Parties during the crisis, also blames Chervonenko, along with Minister-Counselor Ivan Udaltsov and his boss in the Liaison Department, Sergei Kolesnikov, for creating what amounted to a systematic disinformation campaign. These three officials, he recalls, sent a steady stream of "distorted and very subjective information" to the Politburo designed to give the impression of an imminent counterrevolutionary coup in Prague.[80]

Another facet of this internal disinformation campaign came from KGB officials who presented intelligence reports to the Politburo that intentionally suggested Western subversion was afoot in Czechoslovakia. Starting in the early spring of 1968, the KGB dispatched "illegal" agents to Czechoslovakia, individuals posing as Western journalists, businessmen, or tourists, who were to collect intelligence and carry out active measures against the nation's counterrevolutionary forces. According to former KGB archivist Vasili Mitrokhin, this operation, code-named PROGRESS, was the first time that "illegal" agents were used in large numbers within the Soviet bloc. Mitrokhin describes the mission of the PROGRESS operation as twofold: "to penetrate the allegedly counter-revolutionary groups springing up during the Prague Spring in order to report on their subversive intentions; and to implement a series of active measures designed to discredit them."[81] The active measures undertaken as part of PROGRESS were, according to Mitrokhin, "intended to justify a Soviet invasion by fabricating evidence of a counter-revolutionary conspiracy by Czechoslovak 'rightists' and Western intelligence services." By mid-July 1968, the illegals had successfully planted a cache of arms in Czechoslovakia near the border with West Germany which was "revealed" with great fanfare in the Soviet press as evidence of a counterrevolutionary plot to overthrow the government.[82]

The bogus nature of such intelligence did not trouble the top leadership of the Soviet KGB. Former KGB resident Oleg Gordievsky recounts that the organization was simply incapable of viewing opposition as anything but a plot or conspiracy. It therefore postulated that the troubles in Prague *must* have been the result of Zionist agents working for the West. "Though well aware that most of the evidence of Western conspiracy put on public display was fabricated," Gordievsky writes, "the KGB had no doubt about the reality of the plot." This certainty persisted even when Oleg Kalugin, then a KGB political intelligence officer in Washington, D.C., provided "absolutely reliable documents" that proved American intelligence had nothing to do with the events in Czechoslovakia.[83] A year after the crisis, Kalugin discovered "that the KGB leadership had ordered that my dispatches be shown to no one and that they be destroyed."[84] According to Kalugin, "Attempts at an even-handed report simply did not fit in with the KGB's concept of the way events were shaping up in Czechoslovakia, and therefore never got beyond the KGB."[85] Inasmuch as the Soviet leaders had few other resources to augment their understanding of what was developing in Prague, their perceptions were colored almost entirely by the pessimistic analysis of their intelligence briefings.[86]

As a result, by late July a majority of the Politburo had come to believe that military force was virtually inevitable in Czechoslovakia, and Soviet policies began to shift accordingly. On 22 July, Soviet ambassador Chervonenko delivered to Dubcek a demand that Soviet troops be permanently stationed in Czechoslovakia.[87] Prague refused to permit this but signaled that Czechoslovak forces would not engage the Red Army if it took up positions regardless.[88]

The Kremlin's reversal on the matter of troop withdrawals was characteristic of its increasingly cynical attempts after the Warsaw summit to elicit concessions from Prague through bilateral contacts. Foreign Minister Gromyko continued down this path at the July 19 Politburo meeting, suggesting that "the April and July plena of the Central Committee underscored that we would not let go of Czechoslovakia. . . . I consider a bilateral meeting necessary in this situation. At this meeting we should lay it all on the line for them. Obviously, they will not come over to our suggestions. But then we will deliberately approach the adoption of a decision on extreme measures."[89] In other words, a definitive presentation of Soviet demands, face to face, would clarify the Czechoslovak position once and for all. Gromyko felt sure that the meeting he proposed would clear the way for a decisive resolution of the Czechoslovak crisis by force of arms. As for the international fallout of such measures, Gromyko asserted that it would be negligible. The Johnson administration in Washington, he assured, wanted nothing to do with Czechoslovakia, bogged down as it was with the war in Vietnam.[90] The Soviets had their hands free in their sphere of influence to act as they felt necessary. It simply remained to unite the Politburo behind the intervention by assuring fence-sitters such as Brezhnev that political channels had been exhausted.

In the meantime, the Soviet leadership had already begun to draft a number of statements that would be delivered in the name of the Czechoslovak Politburo and the new Revolutionary Government at the start of the invasion. On the whole, these proclaimed that the Soviet army was uniting with the armies of Poland, Hungary, and Bulgaria to fulfill their "international debt" to the Revolutionary Government. The identity of this new government remained undefined, on the assumption that the presumed "healthy nucleus" of the CSCP would fill its ranks at the outset of the intervention. In the meantime, Czechoslovak authorities were not permitted any input into the declarations that Moscow was carefully crafting on their behalf. Relations with Prague were about to change dramatically as Moscow moved to control the Revolutionary Government of Czechoslovakia by unequivocal diktat.

Exhausting Political Channels

With Dubcek's government already condemned in the prepared intervention statements, the two governments met one last time from 29 July until 3 August to ensure that all political channels had been exhausted. The bilateral meeting took place in Czechoslovakia on its border with the Soviet Union, in the town of Cierna nad Tisou. Brezhnev arrived with an ultimatum to the Czechoslovaks based on the earlier Warsaw Letter. Soviet demands included forbidding all antisocialist organizations, parties, and clubs; assertion of control over the mass media; resurrecting the guiding role of the Communist Party in society; and the removal of certain reformist leaders from their positions. Above all, Moscow desired postponement of the Fourteenth Congress of the CSCP, scheduled for 9 September, which was certain to purge all remaining conservatives from the Party leadership.[91]

It was a list that seemed certain to ensure Czechoslovak refusal, consistent with Gromyko's prediction. Nevertheless, Vasil Bilak notes in his memoirs that he and other conservatives soon realized Dubcek was on the verge of reaching a compromise agreement with Moscow.[92] To circumvent this, an antireformist ally, Antonin Kapek, delivered a note to Brezhnev requesting "fraternal assistance to our Party and our whole nation in dealing a rebuff . . . [to] anti-socialist and anti-Soviet forces." These forces, he argued, had taken over the CSCP and amounted to a "serious danger to the very fate of socialism" in Czechoslovakia. Kapek was the sole signatory of this letter and only a candidate member of the CSCP Presidium. Consequently, he probably carried little weight with the Soviets. Indeed, it is unclear from newly released sources whether Brezhnev ever saw the letter.[93] In any case, the letter did not have its intended impact on the Soviets. Negotiations continued, and a mutually acceptable agreement was concluded.

The two sides met with their Warsaw Pact allies to ratify the compromise agreement at a blocwide summit in Bratislava on 3 August. Moscow agreed to withdraw its remaining troops from Czechoslovakia, and it moved to tone down the antireformist polemics in the Soviet media.[94] In exchange, Dubcek pledged to restore the authority of the Party and guarantee the policies of "proletarian internationalism" in state policies. This particularly amounted to a promise of keeping Czechoslovakia in the Warsaw Pact alliance. But it also involved a broader concession to the Kremlin's limited definition of state sovereignty within the socialist bloc.

This was most clearly enunciated in the Cierna nad Tisou negotiations in an exchange between Premier Kosygin and Alexander Dubcek. "We regard the Warsaw Treaty as a treaty that binds our parties and our peoples together in the face of imperialism," Kosygin told Dubcek. "And now maneuvers are beginning. What are we to think: where is your border and where is our border, and is there a difference between your and our borders? I think that you, Comrade Dubcek and Comrade Cernik, cannot deny that we together have only one border—the one that abuts the West and separates us from the capitalist countries." Clearly seeking to curry Soviet favor at this difficult juncture, Dubcek replied that this had been the case "even up to the Second World War." Kosygin, in turn, made it clear that this arrangement would continue long into the future. "This is a border we will never surrender to anyone," he said. "We say this quite directly and this was envisaged in our state treaties. . . . That border is our common border, and if we must defend it together against the enemy, then how could a dispute arise on this question with the High Command of the Warsaw Pact Armed Forces, which ordered troops to be in a certain region for two to three weeks?"[95]

The Soviet position was clear. State sovereignty could not be allowed to get in the way of common regional interests. The only borders that mattered were those which faced the West. Among the communist nations, borders could not be considered a barrier to the passage of allied forces, even in peacetime. Ultimately, the principle of mutual defense against Western imperialism was sufficient to circumscribe any assertions of state sovereignty that a government or its people might seek to raise against allied troops on their territory.

While the Bratislava agreement stipulated a number of important personnel changes in Prague, it did leave Dubcek and most of his associates in power. Those whom Moscow permitted to remain, however, would face increasing limitations on Czechoslovak sovereignty. Consequently, few on either side of the negotiations saw any real prospects for a lasting agreement coming out of Bratislava.[96] However, Moscow left no doubt that this had been the last time diplomatic means would be used to resolve the Czechoslovak issue. "If you deceive us once more," Brezhnev warned Dubcek at the conclusion of the Cierna nad Tisou negotiations, "we shall consider it a crime and a betrayal and act accordingly. Never again would we sit with you at the same table."[97]

One group that counted on the fragility of the Bratislava compromise was Bilak's conservative cabal. Recognizing that Kapek's note had been unsuccessful in motivating the Soviets to act against Dubcek, Bilak and his confederates drafted another letter to Brezhnev. Ignoring the ongoing negotiations with Moscow, it requested an immediate Soviet intervention of Czechoslovakia. "Conscious of the full responsibility for our decision," it read, "we appeal to you with the following statement." What ensued was a litany of accusations against the "post-January democratic process," designed to convince the Soviets that "the very existence of socialism in [Czechoslovakia] is under threat." Finally came the official entreaty for intervention: "In such trying circumstances we are appealing to you, Soviet Communists . . . with a request for you to lend support and assistance *with all the means at your disposal.* Only with your assistance can the Czechoslovak Socialist Republic be extricated from the imminent danger of counterrevolution." Recognizing that publicity about such a document would put them in jeopardy, the five signatories to this soon-to-be infamous document concluded with the request, "In connection with the complex and dangerous course of the situation in our country, we request that you treat our statement with the utmost secrecy, and for that reason we are writing to you, personally, in Russian." It was signed by Alois Indra, Drahomir Kolder, Antonin Kapek, Oldrich Svetska, and Vasil Bilak.[98]

The letter was delivered to the Soviet delegation during a break in the summit talks. Rather than give it to Brezhnev himself, Bilak arranged through the KGB station chief in Bratislava to meet Ukrainian leader Shelest in the men's lavatory for a handoff. Shelest delivered the letter immediately to Brezhnev, who "expressed deep gratitude" but offered no further response.[99] For the time being it appeared that the Soviets might have a workable diplomatic agreement with Prague. However, Moscow now had the request it needed should intervention prove necessary.

The Decision to Intervene

Within a week of the Soviet-Czechoslovak compromise, Brezhnev was on the phone with Dubcek complaining that the terms of the agreement were not being met. He was especially upset that the personnel changes stipulated in Bratislava had not yet been made. Over the next few days, Dubcek sought to convince the Soviet leader that a removal of cadres could only occur at the next Central Committee plenum in late August or early September. He promised that he fully intended to implement the terms of the agreement, but on a slightly revised schedule. Brezhnev answered that he was tired of promises and discussion. The time had come, he said, for decisive action. If the government in Prague could not take such steps itself, then the Soviets would be forced to take matters into their own hands.[100]

What Dubcek did not know was that a few days earlier, on 10 August, Bilak had complained bitterly to Brezhnev that Dubcek was not intent on implementing the Bratislava agreement.[101] Both men recognized that only two more meetings of the Presidium were scheduled—for 13 and 20 August—before the convening of the Slovak Communist Party Congress on 26 August. This meant that if the conservatives were going to launch a palace coup with Soviet support, it would have to be at one of these meetings, as Bilak would certainly be replaced at the Slovak Congress. This set a deadline both for Czechoslovak compliance with the Bratislava compromise and for Soviet intervention in support of conservative "healthy forces."

Unaware of the precarious position into which his fellow Slovak had placed him, Dubcek responded to Brezhnev's impatience on 13 August with a dangerous tack, suggesting that the Soviet Politburo ought simply to take whatever measures it deemed necessary to resolve the situation in Czechoslovakia. Brezhnev warned Dubcek that he did not recognize the gravity of what he proposed. Was the Czechoslovak leader calculating that the Soviets would be reluctant to upset the upcoming November conference of the international socialist community? After all, Dubcek knew how important this conference was to the Soviet effort at isolating Beijing. Might this have convinced him that he still had some room to maneuver in his dealings with Moscow?[102]

What seems more likely is that Dubcek had begun to suffer from depression or stress that caused him to adopt a fatalistic outlook on the future of his reform program. This is evident in his numerous statements to Brezhnev suggesting that he expected to be removed from power at the next Central Committee plenum. "I would go anywhere to work," he told Brezhnev wearily. "I don't need this responsibility. Let whoever you want take it, let whoever you want become first secretary of the CSCP Central Committee. I can't work any longer without support, under constant attack. . . . My strength has run out; it is not a coincidence that I told you that the new plenum will elect a new secretary."[103]

Brezhnev tried to calm Dubcek by returning to the problem at hand in a businesslike manner. Turning from the issue of past noncompliance, he asked whether the Czechoslovak Presidium would support the Soviet conditions at its next plenum. At this point the distressed and exhausted Dubcek appears simply to have given up his attempt to put off the inevitable, telling Brezhnev point blank that, although he himself remained faithful to the compromise, the Presidium would not be able to carry it out. For Brezhnev, this admission confirmed his worst expectations. Not only had Dubcek lost control of the ruling Presidium, but the Presidium appeared to have lost control of the general situation in Czechoslovakia.[104] Political options had now been thoroughly explored and exhausted. The road was wide open for a military resolution of the Czechoslovak "counterrevolution."

Among the first alerted were the "healthy forces" in Prague and Bratislava. Soviet ambassador Chervonenko met secretly with CSCP conservatives Alois Indra and Oldrich Pavlovsky on 14–15 August and confided that Soviet troops would "move into action on the night of 20 August" to support creation of a "provisional revolutionary government of workers and peasants." Indra replied with a guarantee that the majority of the CSCP Presidium and Central Committee, the Czechoslovak National Assembly, and the government would support the putsch when the Soviets arrived. Chervonenko passed Indra's promise along to the Soviet Politburo.[105]

News of the impending intervention also found support among most of the Warsaw Pact allies.[106] Ulbricht and Gomulka greeted the Soviet decision with particular satisfaction, noting that it was high time the alliance took decisive action in Czechoslovakia. Indeed, Ulbricht had reported to Moscow after a meeting with Dubcek on 13 August that Prague had secret ties with Bonn and Romania and that it planned to leave the Warsaw Pact.[107] Fresh from a last-minute meeting with Dubcek himself, Janos Kadar declared Hungary's readiness to participate in all actions granting "assistance to the Czechoslovakian people."[108] When the leaders of Poland, Hungary, East Germany, and Bulgaria met in Moscow on 18 August to discuss final preparations for the invasion, each reportedly "expressed complete and unanimous agreement with the assessment and conclusions of the Politburo of the CPSU Central Committee."[109]

Onetime Dubcek ally Zdenek Mlynar has suggested that the Soviets received a green light at this crucial point in mid-August from, of all places, the Johnson White House. He writes that on 18 August Brezhnev received assurances from President Johnson that the United States would respect the integrity of the Soviet sphere of influence in Czechoslovakia and Romania.[110] There is little in the published diplomatic papers of the Johnson administration to confirm this remarkable claim. It is true that U.S. policy from the start of the Prague Spring had been to remain assiduously uninvolved in Czechoslovak affairs.

The U.S. ambassador to the Soviet Union at the time, Llewellyn "Tommy" Thompson neatly summed up this policy in a telegram to the Department of State on 22 July 1968. "Although there are many pros and cons," Thompson wrote, "I am convinced that our present posture on Czech affair is the correct one particularly in absence any request from Czechs for a change. They should be in the best position to judge effects of any actions or statements on our part. Any appeal to the Soviets would necessarily reveal weakness of our position by what we would not and could not say. Moreover, I believe that on balance such appeal would strengthen the hands of the hardliners rather than those who oppose intervention." Thompson noted that regardless of how the Soviets proceeded, they stood to lose. "Soviets have left themselves little ground to retreat," he suggested, "and have already paid a big price in the Communist as well as the free world by their crude handling of this affair. If Czechs face them down, Soviet prestige will suffer and other members of the camp will be encouraged to greater independence. If they use force the free world will be deeply shocked, NATO strengthened, hope of reducing military expenditure by agreement with US jeopardized, etc. Moreover internal dissatisfaction with Soviet leadership would increase."[111]

It is important to note, however, that this "hands-off" policy was not intended to be interpreted by the Soviets as permissiveness. Indeed, on the same day as Ambassador Thompson stressed these points to Secretary Dean Rusk, the latter met with Anatoly Dobrynin, the Soviet ambassador to the United States, for discussions on the developments in Czechoslovakia. Rusk was concerned about allegations of U.S. involvement that had recently appeared in the Soviet press. An official State Department "memorandum of conversation" for that meeting indicates that Rusk took the opportunity of noting, "This was the first time that anybody had spoken officially to Ambassador Dobrynin about the Czech situation." Consistent with Ambassador Thompson's telegram, Rusk did not offer any warnings of possible U.S. action to deter the Soviets from intervening in the Prague Spring. Nor did he offer any recognition of the Soviet sphere of interest in Eastern Europe. Instead, he simply objected to the allegations that had appeared in the Soviet press of any "NATO Western plot against Czechoslovakia involving the Pentagon and CIA." Rusk stated emphatically that these were entirely untrue, adding that "no one knew better than members of the Soviet Embassy the restraint the U.S. had exercised in regard to Czech developments."[112]

Of course, the secretary allowed, "the feelings of the American people were perfectly understandable in matters of this kind." They went back to Thomas Jefferson, the Declaration of Independence, and the conviction that peoples have the right "to order their own affairs themselves." Rusk concluded that if the accusations being mounted against the United

States were intended as a "pretext to lay a basis for some future action against Czechoslovakia," the U.S. government "would deeply regret it and it could not possibly have anything but a very negative effect on our relations, all the more so if the U.S. was to be presented as a scapegoat." The president of the United States, he underscored, "took these allegations very seriously."[113]

Dobrynin reportedly denied that the allegations had been intended as a pretext or excuse for anything. Beyond that, however, he simply replied that he would report the conversation to his government. The State Department memorandum concludes with the comment that "Dobrynin appeared to be considerably worried, possibly due to the U.S. démarche but most likely by the general state of affairs in regard to Czechoslovakia. He was distinctly not his usual genial self."[114]

This appears to have been not only the first but also the last time that a member of the U.S. government had any official communication with the Soviets regarding the Prague Spring prior to the August invasion. As noted, Secretary Rusk's comments hardly constitute the "green light" that Mlynar claims President Johnson gave to Moscow in advance of the invasion. Yet the message that Ambassador Dobrynin took back to the Soviet Politburo certainly implies otherwise. The version of this conversation found in the Presidential Archive in Moscow includes a sentence that is not in the memorandum housed at the U.S. Department of State. The Russian version suggests that Rusk informed Dobrynin in part that "the USA has been against interference in the affairs of Czechoslovakia from the very start. This is a matter for the Czechs first and foremost. *Apart from that, it is a matter for the Czechs and the other nations of the Warsaw Pact.*" Russian historian R. G. Pikhoia concludes from this statement that "for the political leadership of the USSR it had become clear—realization of 'extreme measures' would not elicit active countermeasures from the USA."[115] This perception was undoubtedly the source of Gromyko's aforementioned assertion in July that the United States could be counted on to remain uninvolved in Czechoslovakia. Rightly or wrongly, the Kremlin clearly had reason to proceed with its plans confident that the threat of a forceful response from NATO was unlikely.

Thus, by mid-August, the intervention was ready to go. The military details had been largely worked out during the Warsaw Pact exercises in May and required little additional attention from Soviet leaders. Political guidelines were also ready, as reflected in the "Declaration of the Presidium of the CSCP Central Committee and Government of the Czechoslovak Socialist Republic." Worked out in late July, the declaration asserted that the intervention was taking place at the initiative of the Czechoslovak Presidium. It outlined the future of Czechoslovakia's domestic and foreign policies and listed the limited privileges that would be permitted to the citizens of Czechoslovakia following the invasion. Moreover, it placed friendship with the Soviet Union and other socialist nations at the top of Czechoslovakia's foreign agenda. On the eve of the invasion the Politburo instructed Ambassador Chervonenko to deliver the text of the declaration to Bilak and his coconspirator Alois Indra. Chervonenko's instructions read simply, "This document is material that can serve our friends as an aid in working out their appeal to the people."[116] The Soviet ambassador was to deliver a similar text to Czechoslovak president Svoboda in Prague at 11:20 P.M. on 20 August, an hour before the start of the intervention. "If the president reacts positively to the request of the fraternal nations," Moscow instructed Chervonenko, "then you can tactfully relay to him . . . the accompanying text of his appeal to the army and the people."[117]

Chervonenko carried out his assignment as written, and President Svoboda immediately phoned Brezhnev, refusing to approve the invasion. To avoid extensive bloodshed, however, he promised that the Czechoslovak army would not resist. At 12:30 A.M. on 21 August 1968, Soviet-led Warsaw Pact forces invaded and began to occupy the sovereign state of Czechoslovakia. True to his word, Svoboda ordered the armed forces not to fight back.[118]

The Politburo resolution that initiated the intervention summed up Moscow's final consensus on the Czechoslovak counterrevolution. It read in part:

> Having comprehensively analyzed the conditions and situation in Czechoslovakia during the last few days, and having similarly considered a request from members of the Presidium of the CSCP Central Committee and government of the CSSR [Czechoslovak Socialist Republic] to the USSR, Poland, Bulgaria, Hungary, and the GDR requesting military assistance in the battle against counterrevolutionary forces, the Politburo of the CPSU Central Committee unanimously considers that the recent developments in Czechoslovakia have taken a very dangerous turn. Rightist elements operating with clear and covert support from imperialist reactionaries are preparing a counterrevolutionary overthrow. . . . Considering that the USSR and other fraternal parties have already exhausted all political means of influence on the government of the CSCP in trying to encourage it to rebuff rightist, antisocialist forces, the Politburo of the CPSU Central Committee feels that the moment has come for the shift to active measures in defense of socialism in the CSSR and unanimously resolves: to render assistance and support to the communist party and people of Czechoslovakia through military force.[119]

Conclusion

Assessments of Moscow's decision to invade Czechoslovakia have traditionally focused on the dimension of state security that supposedly defined the scope of Soviet commitment throughout Eastern Europe. "As with Hungary in 1956, Moscow responded with overwhelming force to a perceived threat to its strategic military position in Central Europe," reads one typical account.[120] Relying heavily on a rational-actor model of analysis, these assessments have tended to view ideology as little more than a mask concealing Moscow's true intention: maintaining its buffer zone in Eastern Europe against Western invasion. In so doing, they upheld Hans Morgenthau's maxim that "the true nature of [foreign] policy is concealed by ideological justifications and rationalizations."[121]

However, the new sources of information released following the collapse of communism in 1989–91 reveal the powerful degree to which Soviet ideological perceptions influenced the decision to invade. While security interests certainly factored into the overall equation, the central concern motivating the Brezhnev leadership in 1968 was the growing conviction that communist rule was on the brink of collapse in Czechoslovakia.

From the point at which hard-liners such as Andropov and Shelest began comparing the Prague Spring to the Hungarian Revolution, Soviet discussions focused intently on preventing a return to social democracy in Czechoslovakia. Military measures were considered, but not in the context of defending against a hostile West. Indeed, any serious talk of Western infiltration is distinctly absent from these early Soviet debates. Rather, the use of force was to be arrayed against Czechoslovakia's domestic political opposition. Its attempts to reconsider the Party's vanguard role in society, the use of state security organs, and the prospect of multiparty politics outraged even Kremlin moderates such as Brezhnev.

On the basis of these ideological concerns, the Soviet understanding of what constituted "counterrevolutionary" activities broadened considerably. From an outlook based on the Hungarian experience, Moscow evolved a more complex perception of political jeopardy that did not involve armed insurgency or riots in the streets. Instead, peaceful reformism and ideological evolution within the Party itself were what seemed poised to undermine socialist norms in Czechoslovakia. Ultimately, of course, these political developments were linked to broader security issues, such as the integrity of the Warsaw Pact. This enabled the KGB to foster the impression that the West was using Dubcek to weaken and destabilize the socialist alliance. Nevertheless, the accounts of Politburo discussions held through the winter, spring, and summer of 1968 show little real concern over a Western threat to Soviet bloc security interests. At stake was not the safety of the region but its political uniformity.

By July, the Soviet leaders had fully transformed their understanding of what constituted an open counterrevolution against socialist power. As Karen Dawisha astutely observes, "Until the end of July, there was a tendency for Soviet statements to compare the events in Czechoslovakia with those in Hungary in 1956. Since there was no armed insurrection and no bloodshed in Czechoslovakia, it was argued, there was no counterrevolution. But by August, the influence of the Hungarian experience had diminished, and with that diminution a mental barrier to invasion was removed."[122] Although this shift began as early as March, it took some time for it to develop into a general consensus. The last straw that solidified a united front appears to have come as late as Dubcek's conversation with Brezhnev on 13 August. His admission that the Prague government had no intention of instituting the political controls outlined in Bratislava confirmed Soviet fears that a counterrevolution was indeed under way. It satisfied even the most moderate Politburo opponents of military intervention, ending the indecisiveness that had characterized earlier responses.

At the same time, it is essential to recognize the international conditions that made military intervention a feasible option for the Soviet Union in 1968. By the late 1960s, the trend toward East-West détente found Washington and the Western alliance reluctant to champion the principle of East European sovereignty against assertions of Kremlin influence. Moreover, the United States was far too busy coping with the hostilities in Vietnam to consider any kind of forceful response to Soviet aggression in the summer of 1968. Consequently, Moscow was able to act with relative impunity against those it considered "counterrevolutionaries" in Eastern Europe.

What is perhaps most remarkable about the Soviet risk analysis was the Kremlin's willingness to jeopardize bloc unity in the face of the widening Sino-Soviet split. Tensions with the People's Republic of China had been rising for years, and Beijing was openly trying to supplant Moscow as head of the international communist movement. Thus, both militarily and ideologically, China posed a very significant threat to Soviet interests. Yet in the face of this threat, the Brezhnev regime still chose to intervene with armed force in Czechoslovakia. This says a great deal about the degree to which it equated political stability in Eastern Europe with the vital national interests of the Soviet Union. From Moscow's vantage point in 1968, the evolutionary counterrevolution under way in Prague posed as great a danger to the political integrity of the Soviet Union as it did to the communist monopoly in Czechoslovakia. It was this conviction that ultimately lay behind the decision to send hundreds of thousands of Warsaw Pact troops into Czechoslovakia on 21 August 1968.

2 ★ "Normalization" and Orthodoxy

> When those states which have been acquired are accustomed to live at liberty under their own laws, there are three ways of holding them. The first is to despoil them; the second is to go and live there in person; the third is to allow them to live under their own laws, taking tribute of them and creating within the country a government of a few who will keep it friendly to you.
> —Niccolò Machiavelli, *The Prince*

THE EVOLUTION OF THE MODERN NATION-STATE has inspired many memorable reflections on the fundamental relationship between military force and political power. Amid the fruits of this bountiful intellectual harvest stands a pithy aphorism, attributed alternatively to Napoléon Bonaparte and William Ralph Inge (1860–1954): a man may build himself a throne of bayonets, but he cannot sit on it. The 1968–69 "normalization" of Czechoslovakia is a fascinating case in point.

Once the Soviet-led armies of the Warsaw Pact had occupied Czechoslovakia, they faced the daunting prospect of reestablishing socialist norms as the basis of the nation's political and social life. "Normalization," then, amounted to an attempt to restore conservative, pro-Soviet rule in Czechoslovakia. In addressing this task, Moscow quickly discovered that many of its previous perceptions had been poorly informed and mistaken. Chief among these was the belief that conservative "healthy forces" represented a powerful voice in the Czechoslovak Party and government. The scene that faced the arriving Soviet troops shattered this assumption. The Czechoslovak quislings, it turned out, represented a small minority of the CSCP who had acted independently to torpedo the Prague Spring. The vast majority of Czechs and Slovaks responded to the invasion, as to Dubcek's subsequent arrest, with indignation and open protest. Under these conditions, the political normalization of Czechoslovakia became a protracted affair quite unlike the coup envisioned in Moscow.

Though faced with an unexpected political debacle from the outset of the intervention, Soviet leaders failed to question the validity of the information being fed to them through the carefully programmed channels of the KGB and Foreign Ministry. Encountering nearly monolithic condemnation from the people of Czechoslovakia, they nevertheless failed to reconsider their conclusions about the counterrevolutionary objectives of the Prague Spring. Not surprisingly, therefore, Soviet occupation policy relied heavily on extensive interference and covert action rather than political engagement of the Czechoslovak people at large.

The resulting campaign of enforced orthodoxy became the model of Brezhnev's East European policy for more than a decade. Reflecting on the "lessons" of 1968–69, the Brezhnev leadership resolved to run a tighter ship in Eastern Europe against the possibility of further crises. Dubbed the "Brezhnev Doctrine of Limited Sovereignty" by Western observers, the new policy line would rely on the implicit threat of military intervention to prevent any deviation in the region from Soviet-approved norms. In this way, the Kremlin sought to perpetuate communist monopoly rule in Eastern Europe, free from the instability that reformism and diversity had unleashed in the past.

A Rude Awakening

Despite the overwhelming military superiority of the six hundred thousand Warsaw Pact troops taking up positions throughout Czechoslovakia, the Soviet intervention plan began to unravel politically right from the start. Relying on assurances from Bilak, Indra, and the KGB, the Soviet leadership was counting on a promised CSCP conservative majority to voice their support for the intervention. Conservative hopes collapsed, however, when two of those expected to join the coup, Frantisek Barbirek and Jan Piller, proved uncooperative. This fatally compromised the quisling majority on the Presidium, leaving them unable to hold up their end of the grand conspiracy. Instead they were compelled to sit by and watch as their Warsaw Pact allies encountered political condemnation from every level of Czechoslovak society.

The early political setback also meant that the Presidium received its first notification of the operation from Czechoslovakia's minister of defense, Martin Dzur, rather than from its own conservative faction. Placed under arrest in his own office by two Soviet officers, Dzur was permitted one phone call to inform Dubcek of the invasion. The call left the Presidium in a state of shock. No doubt reflecting back over his last conversations with Brezhnev, Dubcek took the news deeply personally. "So they did it after all," he cried, "and to me!" Offering his resignation to the Presidium on the spot, the defeated first secretary lamented, "If they have something against me, why don't they deal with me directly? I don't care if they string me up by the ribs, I would, in any event, answer for everything."[1] His reformist colleagues, however, would not hear of it. Supported by President Svoboda, the Presidium convinced Dubcek to withdraw his resignation. In the absence of military resistance, they felt, political solidarity was essential to an effective national response. This would be the key to preserving some semblance of state sovereignty when the smoke of the invasion began to clear. As Zdenek Mlynar later recalled, "Talk now began about no one resigning and how all the legally-constituted organs had to remain intact; no new organs must be set up, nor could there be any personnel changes under pressure from the intervention."[2] Thus the nation's highest political body would remain at the forefront of the popular resistance. Because Moscow sought to justify the intervention with assertions that the ruling government had requested allied assistance, its active opposition to the invasion dashed any chance of a swift normalization.

With the collaborators still a part of the Presidium, the cause of solidarity in the face of adversity was itself compromised. In these first hours of the intervention, both opponents and defenders of the Soviet action sat together, baffled about how to respond to the arriving occupation forces. In the tension of these awkward hours, the quislings struggled to cope with their complicity in what was befalling the nation. At one point Bilak, apparently terrified for his life, cried out in despair, "Alright lynch me! Why don't you kill me?" Unaware then of his pivotal role in preparing the invasion, Bilak's colleagues largely ignored his outburst.[3]

If fellow conspirators shared Bilak's profound sense of responsibility for the crisis, they did not express themselves as openly. In fact, they soon began to exploit an unexpected opportunity to shift the blame for the invasion onto Dubcek, and they pressed their advantage assertively. The distraught Czechoslovak leader provided them with an opening when he chose to share for the first time the contents of a letter he had received from Brezhnev three days earlier. The letter presented a litany of attacks on the Prague leadership for violating the Bratislava agreement, the consequences of which had only now become fully apparent. The conspirators seized on this letter and Dubcek's earlier reluctance to reveal its contents as proof of *his* ultimate responsibility for the invasion. Dubcek had received what they argued was a clear warning from Moscow and had recklessly ignored it. For the time being, then, these accusations sufficiently muddied the waters of discussion, obfuscating the matter of quisling complicity.

The prevailing confusion over the issue of guilt notwithstanding, reformers and conservatives revealed their true colors in the debate over how to *respond to* the intervention. As the Presidium worked frantically to draft an appeal to the Czechoslovak people, conservatives adamantly refused to condemn the invasion as a violation of international law. The issue was internal to the socialist community, they asserted, and thus should not be discussed outside their "common household." From the conservative viewpoint, of course, the invasion did not violate Czechoslovak national sovereignty. While no one mustered the courage to say so openly, the collaborators viewed the operation as an extension of "fraternal international assistance" to the people of Czechoslovakia. Moreover, they were keenly aware that the occupation had begun in conjunction with their own fervent requests. Once again, though, Bilak's failure to deliver a majority of the Presidium compromised the pro-Soviet position. Despite conservative objections, the balance of the Presidium adamantly asserted the necessity of mobilizing the international community against the invasion.[4]

By 1:30 A.M. the Presidium had adjourned its meeting, and the reformers settled in to await the arrival of Soviet forces.[5] Bilak and the other collaborators left the building immediately and sought refuge at the Soviet embassy.[6] Soviet forces arrived around 4:00 A.M. and placed the remaining leaders under guard. Five hours later Soviet troops arrested Dubcek and a handful of leading reformers, "in the name of the revolutionary tribunal led by comrade Alois Indra."[7] The men were taken into Soviet custody and soon found themselves aboard a plane bound for Moscow. The balance of the Czechoslovak leadership was released and allowed to respond to the crisis as each individual saw fit.

On the following day, 22 August, Prague was stirring with efforts to cope with the political vacuum in the capital. Meeting at the Hotel Prague, the CSCP Central Committee (CC) had been in session since the afternoon of the previous day. Though its original discussions had called for a statement in support of Dubcek, by 22 August the arrival of Bilak, Indra, and other collaborators under Soviet protection sharply altered the tone of the meeting.[8] With Bilak now acting as chairman, it issued a statement calling on the people of Czechoslovakia to "respect the harsh reality in which we have found ourselves and which cannot be changed at once." Rather than demanding the release of the nation's duly appointed leaders, it read simply, "Delegated members of the Presidium of the CSCP CC are entering into contact with the command of the forces of the other five Warsaw Pact countries with the aim of assuring accelerated normalization."[9]

At the same time, however, the Central Committee declaration also supported the Presidium's earlier statement, condemning the invasion as "contrary to the fundamental principles of international law."[10] Although they had undermined the effort to support Dubcek and his allies, the quislings were clearly unwilling, at this point, to come out in full support of the invasion. Czechoslovakia was under occupation, but its political fate had yet to be resolved. Bilak and his fellow collaborators therefore remained reluctant to reveal their actual positions, out of concern for the repercussions that might follow an unfavorable political outcome.

Meanwhile, in the Prague suburb of Vysocany, Czechoslovak Party reformers secretly convened the Extraordinary Fourteenth CSCP Congress, which had been scheduled for September. In contrast to the proceedings of the Central Committee meeting occurring across town, the Vysocany

Congress sought to preserve the reform process in the face of a conservative putsch. It accordingly elected a new, more liberal Presidium, with Dubcek at its head. Conservatives such as Bilak and Piller, who were not in attendance, were not reappointed. If allowed to stand, therefore, the results of the congress promised to remove all conservative influence from the Party leadership in Prague.

The Vysocany Congress was not alone in demonstrating how seriously Bilak and his political allies had misrepresented Czechoslovak public opinion to Moscow. In streets and public squares across the nation, the grassroots response to the invasion also bristled with loud indignation. Viktor Suvorov, a Soviet officer who participated in the occupation, relates how the people of Prague surrounded Soviet tanks and pelted the exasperated invaders with abuse. "We're here at the request of your government," shouts one Soviet political officer in his account. "Then name even one of the members of the government who invited you to interfere in our affairs," the crowd responds. "Comrades!!!" cries the officer, appealing to socialist unity. "We are not your comrades!" comes the reply from Czechs, who now begin to hit the political officer across the face. As the officer goes for his pistol, other soldiers pull him back from the crowd. "Fascist devils!" he screams at them. "You're the fascists!" holler back the Czechs.[11] In a related instance, Mlynar relates how the Soviet troops guarding Dubcek and his allies "closed the windows so that the crowd, which had gathered outside beyond the cordon of paratroopers, could not be heard singing the national anthem and shouting slogans and chanting Dubcek's name."[12]

Within days, resistance flyers expressed popular opposition toward the invaders. "Long live Dubcek," one began. "Long live Mr. President Svoboda. Long Live our legal Government and National Assembly. Don't provoke—Ignore—Be clever—Invisible—Only cool reason will work wonders—There are many quiet and effective means—In this is our strength."[13] The flyers also voiced outrage at those who had collaborated with the Soviets. On the morning of 22 August one appeared that read, "There is only one response to traitors, the contempt of the nation and the refusal to have anything to do with them. Down with the traitors! Long live the free Republic!"[14]

Thus marshaled from both above and below, public opinion in Czechoslovakia coalesced solidly into open, albeit peaceful, opposition to the Soviet-led intervention. While resistance was most ubiquitous in the Czech lands, it quickly spread eastward following rumors that Slovakia might be annexed by the Soviet Union.[15] As a result, within the first few days of the intervention, Moscow found itself in control of the entire country but opposed by the overwhelming majority of Czechoslovakia's Party and society.

In light of these conditions, the most immediate problem facing the Soviets and their political allies in Czechoslovakia was the formation of a new government that could legitimize the planned normalization. Earlier difficulties notwithstanding, Soviet hopes continued to lie with the Czechoslovak collaborators and their supporters. While under Soviet protection at the August 22 Central Committee meeting, however, the quislings remained in constant fear of their compatriots. Indeed, at the conclusion of the meeting, Bilak and Indra chose to ride in a Soviet armored vehicle from the Hotel Prague back to the Soviet embassy, rather than accompany their colleagues by car. While crossing the Vltava River, their armored transport found itself deadlocked in traffic owing to an accident between a tram and some Soviet military vehicles. The commander of their armored car suggested to the two men that they transfer to another car, but they refused. They did not want to be seen in public getting out of a Soviet military vehicle. As a result, Mlynar recalls, "they sat inside the steel-plated monster for almost an hour under the hot August sun. They arrived at the embassy in a pitiful condition and in a miserable frame of mind."[16]

Back at the Soviet embassy, Soviet first deputy prime minister K. T. Mazurov and Ambassador Chervonenko tried in vain to encourage the formation of a Revolutionary Government.[17] To their frustration, Kosygin's conclusions of late May proved correct. No effective alternative to Dubcek's leadership existed in the CSCP. An abortive attempt was made to try and bring President Svoboda into cooperation with a new government, but the president withheld his support. Responding to Jan Piller, the mouthpiece of the rump Presidium in negotiations with the Soviets, Svoboda declared, "If I were to do anything of the sort, the nation would have to drive me out of this Castle like a mangy dog."[18] His refusal to cooperate was decisive. Without Svoboda, the conservatives simply did not have the courage to face their countrymen. Negotiations toward creation of a new, pro-Soviet government would have to be adjourned to Moscow, where Svoboda would insist on the participation of Dubcek and the other incarcerated reformers. For a time, then, occupied Czechoslovakia was left rudderless, in a state of political chaos.

Coping with the Unexpected: The Early Soviet Response

Amid this disappointment and confusion, Soviet military personnel did surprisingly little to ensure a restoration of political order. At the outset of the invasion, the principal military objective had been achieving control over the full territory of Czechoslovakia. Consequently, the initial orders to Soviet-led ground forces appear to have concerned only rules of engagement, particularly with possible North Atlantic Treaty Organization

(NATO) intervention forces. Speaking on 13 August, Defense Minister Andrei Grechko told members of the Defense Ministry that Moscow "cannot exclude the possibility that NATO's forces will invade the CSSR from the West." He concluded that "if that happens, we will have to act in accordance with the situation."[19]

Viktor Suvorov conveys a similar impression in his description of the night of 19 August, when the invasion forces first received their orders. Their instructions focused exclusively on identifying friend from foe. In the words of Suvorov's commanding officer, "The white stripe is the distinguishing mark of our forces and those of our allies. All military hardware of Soviet or allied construction without a white stripe must be neutralized, preferably without force. Tanks without stripes and other military hardware should be immediately destroyed without warning and without a command from above in a confrontational situation. If you should encounter any NATO forces, you are to stop immediately and hold your fire until otherwise commanded." Suvorov's officer concludes his instructions by observing, "Our objective is to take control of as much territory as possible. Then let the diplomats decide where the border will run between Eastern and Western Czechoslovakia. It is a matter of honor that Eastern Socialist Czechoslovakia should be larger than the western part."[20]

Soviet forces were thus clearly focused on the prospect of encountering military resistance from either the Czechoslovak army or NATO. Their orders therefore concerned questions of combat and tactical objectives rather than political interference in Czechoslovak affairs. Yet once occupation forces had taken up their positions in the country, one might have expected them to become more extensively involved in the political goals of the intervention. This had certainly been the pattern of Soviet conduct in Eastern Europe in the early postwar period.[21] It is interesting, therefore, to consider the list of orders issued by the Allied Command on 22 August. It presents a surprisingly laissez-faire position on the part of the military: (1) Do not disarm Czechoslovak army units; (2) Withdraw from areas where Czechoslovak troops are stationed; (3) Withdraw from small localities; (4) In large towns, station military units in parks and open areas; (5) Refrain from blocking buildings of state and Party organs of the Czechoslovak Socialist Republic; (6) Banks should function normally; and (7) All allied troops will be supplied out of their own resources.[22]

Available evidence indicates that the military appears to have adhered strictly to these instructions, despite the paroxysm of public indignation jeopardizing Moscow's political objectives. The scholar Fred Eidlin, a first-hand witness to these events, recounts that "although buildings housing

Party and state agencies were surrounded by military forces, and in some cases entered by them, official bodies continued to meet, deliberate, and communicate with the world outside."[23]

Why didn't the Soviets close down the existing government and install their chosen successors? If one recognizes that Moscow relied on misleading reports confirming conservative strength in the CSCP, Soviet objectives come into focus. The ad hoc behavior of Soviet forces at the start of the invasion was largely the consequence of a Soviet leadership scrambling to cope with the unexpected. Having fulfilled their expressly military mission, the occupiers were unprepared to undertake an aggressive role in the subsequent normalization, expecting Czechoslovak conservatives to do so themselves. The political setbacks of the initial occupation therefore necessitated a fundamental reassessment of the situation on the ground in Czechoslovakia if Soviet resources were to be effective in the long run.

Saving Face at the Moscow Talks

As Czechoslovakia met the invasion with angry demonstrations, Moscow scrambled to stabilize the political crisis. Svoboda's refusal to cooperate and the results of the Vysocany Congress made it clear that a compromise would have to be struck with the deposed reformists. Indeed, President Svoboda is said to have gone as far as threatening suicide if Dubcek and the other arrested leaders were prohibited from participating in talks about the future of Czechoslovakia.[24] While dramatically heroic, such threats were probably unnecessary. As Mlynar later reasoned, "Moscow had no one else to negotiate with in the end but the Dubcek leadership. Its agents had failed to carry off an internal putsch, and it was out of the question for Moscow to deal with the leadership elected by the Fourteenth [Vysocany] Congress."[25] Haunted by this troubling realization, on 23 August Brezhnev and company met with the Prague leadership—both conservatives and reformers—at the Kremlin in Moscow. In addition to the representatives from Prague and their Soviet "hosts," the Moscow talks of 23–26 August also included the other East European leaders involved in the intervention. Some were strongly against considering a political solution in which Dubcek might retain control of the government in Prague. Bilak's original plan, relayed to Brezhnev in the final days leading up to the invasion, had envisioned creation of a Revolutionary Government with Drahomir Kolder as first secretary. This government was then supposed to have rounded up about forty thousand reform supporters for a perfunctory trial by "special tribunal." The highest-ranking officials among them were to have faced the death penalty.[26] Based on the observation that Dubcek was arrested in the name of Alois Indra, Soviet operational directives appear to have altered some of the details of this plan. And obviously even the revised plan had fallen through in the early hours of the invasion.

However, during the Moscow talks, East European leaders Ulbricht, Gomulka, and Todor Zhivkov, opposing "capitulation" to the reformists, offered an alternate plan. They proposed the establishment of a "worker-peasant government without Dubcek" that would be installed under Alois Indra. Once installed, Zhivkov argued, this government could then proceed with the "liquidation of the reactionary bands in Prague and Bratislava." Meanwhile, Soviet embassy officials in Prague also endorsed the creation of a "national unity" government behind Indra. But Brezhnev rejected these ideas as "unrealistic" and "easier written than done" under existing circumstances. When Gomulka continued to advocate the idea to Kosygin, the latter replied, "Do not convince me, but the sixteen million Czechoslovaks!"[27]

A return to the status quo antebellum was out of the question; that would have dealt a crushing blow to Soviet international prestige and leadership within the socialist camp. Thus it remained to coerce Dubcek to toe the Soviet line. While in Moscow, Dubcek faced threats of torture and violent repression of civilian demonstrations if he did not sign an agreement that seriously circumscribed his reform program. Indeed, the discussions even broached the possibility of a war in Eastern Europe. As Brezhnev warned, "If the rightists introduce such hysteria from underground stations, do they really think that the Soviet, Hungarian, German, and Bulgarian forces will simply leave? This cannot happen. At the same time, this impression could lead to war. We have to overcome this danger, but on principles acceptable for you, for us, and for the socialist countries."[28] Premier Kosygin painted a similarly stark choice for Dubcek, stating very directly on 23 August, "There are two alternatives, war or an agreement."[29]

Although the prospect of war with the socialist alliance was simply too dangerous to hazard, the reformers tried to steel themselves bravely before such threats. Speaking later about their initial resistance to Moscow's demands, Josef Smrkovsky explained, "We took into consideration the fact that at a certain point there is nothing left to do but reject any kind of solution involving accommodation—that it is sometimes better, in the interest of the honor and character of a people, to expose one's breast to the bayonets."[30]

Eventually this kind of brinkmanship brought the talks to the point of collapse. Moscow was in no mood to negotiate. The stern tone Brezhnev adopted in addressing Dubcek reflected this in no uncertain terms.

> We in the Kremlin came to the conclusion that we could not depend on you any longer. You do what you feel like in domestic politics,

even things that displease us, and you are not open to positive suggestions. But your country lies on territory where the Soviet soldier trod in the Second World War. We bought that territory at the cost of enormous sacrifices and we shall never leave it. The borders of that area are our borders as well. Because you do not listen to us, we feel threatened. In the name of the dead in World War Two who laid down their lives for your freedom as well, we are therefore fully justified in sending our soldiers into your country, so that we may feel truly secure within our common borders. It is immaterial whether anyone is actually threatening us or not: it is a matter of principle, independent of external circumstances. And that is how it will be, from the Second World War until eternity.[31]

Despite the finality of such statements, Dubcek assumed a hard negotiating position with Brezhnev, misjudging his own bargaining position. Eventually, on 26 August, the Soviets simply got up and walked out on the discussion. This was the Kremlin's trump card, and it worked well. After the Soviet departure from the negotiating chamber, Dubcek almost collapsed from stress and had to be sedated. When he calmed down he yielded to the appeals of his colleagues, who now called for reason rather than bloodshed. Under pressure from the rest of the Czechoslovak delegation, Dubcek agreed to meet the Soviet terms.[32]

The details of the Moscow Protocol were very reminiscent of the earlier deals embodied in the Warsaw Letter and the Bratislava agreement. Dubcek agreed to sack a number of leading government reform figures, to reimpose controls on the mass media, and to strengthen political and military cooperation with the other socialist bloc nations. He also promised to coordinate European policy with Moscow and its allies. Finally, the Czechoslovak leadership would refuse to recognize the results of the Extraordinary Fourteenth CSCP Congress.[33] In return, the Soviets allowed Dubcek and most of his cabinet to return to their posts, and Soviet troops were removed from urban centers in Czechoslovakia. The document did not settle the future status of Soviet troops in the country, but Moscow agreed to raise the issue at a later discussion.

Reassessment and the Search for Long-Term Stability

Following the conclusion of the Moscow Protocol, the Soviet leadership turned from the matter of saving face to working out a more agreeable long-term approach for Czechoslovakia. Dubcek had already convinced the Soviet leaders that he was not a good long-term gamble. But cultivation of a viable, trustworthy nucleus of conservatives within the Czechoslovak Party would require time. Meanwhile, Dubcek's reform-oriented government would retain control in Prague, albeit under close Soviet supervision. To sustain the facade that the CSCP had requested and supported the Warsaw Pact intervention, new appointments would take place only later, at a normal Czechoslovak Party plenum. Patience was an essential part of the effort to justify the planned normalization campaign.

The turn in Moscow toward a more politically feasible long-term solution for Czechoslovakia necessitated consideration of both fundamental objectives and previous mistakes. Understandably, this reassessment began with an elementary question: Had the operation really been necessary? Obviously, Soviet official statements asserted that it had been. But did such confidence color the views expressed behind the closed doors of the Kremlin and Central Committee offices? Archival evidence suggests that it did.

According to a report prepared for the Politburo in the first weeks of the occupation, despite the unanticipated political setbacks, the Soviet leadership did not regret its decision to intervene militarily in Czechoslovakia. The decision to send in troops is held in the report to have been a "wise, courageous, and timely" move necessary for circumventing a restoration of capitalism in Czechoslovakia.[34] In the postwar era, the assessment argues, modern anticommunist tactics were focused on undermining communist states through "peaceful explosions from within." Consequently, Soviet armed forces merely fulfill their "sacred international duty" when repressing "counterrevolutionaries" in the fraternal socialist countries. The report refers to the growing list of incidents since World War II when this had proven necessary—East Germany (1953), Hungary (1956), and Czechoslovakia (1968). Inasmuch as international capitalism was thought to be continuing its efforts to encourage similar problems in other socialist states, the lessons learned in the invasion of Czechoslovakia are portrayed as important precedents for the future of the Soviet bloc.[35]

Thus from the perspective offered in the Politburo assessment, the invasion of Czechoslovakia was necessary first and foremost to stem the growing influence of foreign, antisocialist elements in Czechoslovakia. Although this conviction had led to a political debacle at the outset of the intervention, Soviet leaders proved either unwilling or unable to question it. The picture was perfectly consistent with their ideological worldview and so contributed to the "groupthink" phenomenon in Politburo considerations.

In the face of such axiomatic convictions, evidence and proof were decidedly secondary concerns. As the report admits, Soviet intelligence had failed to martial sufficient confirmation of foreign agents operating in support of the rightist "counterrevolutionaries." From Moscow's perspective, however, this complication did not challenge established analyses. It was important chiefly because it compromised the Soviet propaganda campaign. Effective propaganda required more compromising material that threw light on Western intelligence activities in Czechoslovakia. For this reason, not for corroboration of established conclusions, the assessment demanded more attention to verification.[36]

The matter of misinformed perceptions aside, it is not hard to fathom the Soviet concern for effective propaganda in the weeks following the invasion. Poor propaganda, from Moscow's point of view, had been the fundamental cause behind the embarrassing public relations breakdown at the outset of the intervention, both in Czechoslovakia and around the world. Polish leader Wladyslaw Gomulka voiced concern about this as early as 24 August, when he lamented, "The actual correlation of forces in Europe has already changed. Czechoslovakia is actually outside the Warsaw Treaty Organization and the Czechoslovak army as well. We have only the territory of Czechoslovakia, but we have neither a majority of the nation, nor the party, nor the army."[37]

Moscow's analysis confirmed this impression and blamed it on inadequate propaganda. The Soviets felt that they had lost the battle for public opinion in Czechoslovakia within the first week of the intervention because the invasion had effectively taken place in a propaganda blackout. On the basis of unreferenced opinion polls, the November assessment purports that, prior to the intervention, 50 to 60 percent of the Czechoslovakian people supported the theoretical entry of Soviet troops. However, by the end of the first week, according to Soviet figures, 75 to 90 percent of Czechoslovakians condemned what they saw as a Soviet occupation of their country. The report credits this to the more effective efforts of the anti-Soviet opposition in Czechoslovakia.[38]

Clearly, the relative information blackout that attended the start of the intervention did nothing to mitigate the widespread sense of shock felt by the Czechoslovak people. As early as 4:30 A.M. on 21 August, Czechoslovak radio in Prague had broadcast the Soviet-authored "proclamation of the Presidium" justifying the intervention.[39] Additionally, by 5:40 A.M. Radio Vltava, broadcasting in Czech and Slovak from East Germany, had begun to read a similar bulletin from the Telegraphic Agency of the Soviet Union (TASS).[40] However, the proclamation did not reach the Czechoslovak News Agency (CTK) until 8:00 A.M. Moreover, confusion had ensued when CTK workers refused to transmit it. In the end, the statement went out over the home service of Radio Moscow in early afternoon, more than twelve hours after the start of the invasion.[41]

The Soviet media campaign was replete with similar miscalculations. Thousands of propaganda leaflets printed in Czech which should have been distributed at the start of the invasion appeared only after five or six days. The same problem occurred with specially printed Czech issues of *Pravda* and other Soviet periodicals. It was not until 30 August that

Zpravy, the newspaper of the occupation forces, began to appear.[42] Moscow also failed to seize immediate control of the Czechoslovakian media. This left the intervention open to criticism from an unsympathetic press corps, whose opposition was damaging.[43]

Considering the traditional Soviet reliance on agitation and propaganda to mobilize popular sentiment, the blackout at the start of the invasion was certainly unusual. As with much of the early intervention, its shortcomings resulted largely from Moscow's political miscalculations. On the strength of the intelligence provided by both the KGB and the Czechoslovak conspirators, Moscow had anticipated strong support from within the CSCP. Moreover, as noted above, unidentified public opinion polls provided to the Politburo showed 50 to 60 percent of Czechoslovak society in favor of a hypothetical intervention. While this hardly indicated a promise of "wide support," it goes a long way toward explaining the overconfidence reflected in Moscow's anemic propaganda offensive.

Poor propaganda was also held to have been responsible for the international condemnation that followed the intervention. According to the November assessment, Soviet representatives should have prevented discussion of the intervention in the United Nations (UN). Moscow might have arranged earlier with the Czechoslovak foreign minister to issue guidelines for the nation's representatives at the UN and in all embassies abroad. These would have prepared Czechoslovak diplomats in advance to justify the Soviet-led action to the international community. (The possibility that they might not have been so inclined is not addressed in the briefing.) This supposedly would have frustrated the efforts of "bourgeois state activists" to exploit the situation in Czechoslovakia for their own ends.[44]

With respect to the military performance of the Warsaw Pact troops, the Soviet assessment was rather more positive. The one general criticism leveled against the military for future reference was that tanks and heavy artillery should not have been kept out of the central streets and squares in major cities. The absence of such armored deterrents meant that the rhythm of life continued as normal in urban Czechoslovakia despite the occupation. This lent itself to widespread passive resistance throughout the country. Anti-Soviet demonstrations broke out on a number of occasions, free from a visible threat of overwhelming force. Although a small amount of military hardware made its way to major downtown areas, it was spaced to a degree that left it vulnerable to potential sabotage. The clear lesson for the Soviets was that it was wiser to create a constant visual reminder of overwhelming force in an important urban center under occupation, even in the absence of active military resistance.[45]

With its fundamental perceptions excepted from reconsideration, the

Kremlin still required an acceptable explanation for the operation's political fiasco. Ironically, it found a scapegoat in the KGB. Yet its grievance with the intelligence agency did not stem from the misinformation it had received in the months prior to the invasion. Instead, the Politburo focused its criticism on the shortcomings of the "special services," KGB teams charged with rooting out the antisocialist opposition in Czechoslovakia. In particular, it faulted the special services for failing to plant agents inside the Czechoslovak reform movement in the months before the August invasion. This facet of operation PROGRESS had apparently borne little fruit. As a result, when the movement created a parallel underground structure in March 1968, it rendered unsuccessful all later Soviet efforts to penetrate it. This was a serious mistake, the assessment concluded: "An early underground organization on the scale of an entire government at the highest party and state levels is an unprecedented occurrence. It is a serious danger. Its overcoming is possible only as a result of a deep internal penetration by our special services."[46] Failure to infiltrate meant that Soviet agents could not effectively misinform and demoralize, introduce schisms, inspire mutual mistrust, or encourage organizational paralysis within the reform movement.[47]

Nevertheless, the KGB remained at the center of the Kremlin's revised normalization strategy. Immediately following the invasion, it began to coordinate the activities of "illegal" agents from the Soviet Union and other bloc countries in a late effort to "penetrate the Czechoslovak 'counter-revolutionary underground,' émigré groups and hostile intelligence services."[48] Moreover, for the balance of the intervention it directed a comprehensive disinformation campaign to manipulate the political situation facing the Dubcek government. This scheme stipulated the development of a "broad plan of special disinformation measures" that would either encourage mistrust between the rightist leaders or compromise them in the eyes of the masses.[49] The first week of the intervention had shown the power of public opinion behind Dubcek. Through its new program of covert action, Moscow would compromise Dubcek's authority with the masses to the point where he could be safely removed for good. At that point Moscow's handpicked allies in the CSCP would replace the reformist government and ensure the return to political orthodoxy.

In addition to its compromising element, this ambitious plan also required intensive work with Czechoslovak conservatives to prepare them for decisive action. The early days of the intervention had demonstrated the problem of conservative paralysis in the face of popular outrage. Moscow acknowledged this lesson and vowed to engage in more preparatory efforts the second time around. In the language of the Politburo's assessment, active support of pro-Soviet elements was "possible only through individualized work with each person . . . and through use of the full arsenal of well-known means."[50] Although these means were not discussed in great detail, they included both legal and illegal activities on the part of Soviet agents. "It is necessary to use the presence of our troops in Czechoslovakia to strengthen our illegal positions," the report recommended. "It is not enough to implement specialized work merely from the legal position of an ambassadorial position. We ought to create ten to twelve powerful, illegal positions in key points of the country, and from these positions we should carry out extensive work stimulating the activities of healthy elements, exposing to decay, compromise, and isolation the activities of the counterrevolutionaries."[51] In this way, the KGB would utilize whatever means possible to assure the eventual installation of a conservative, pro-Soviet regime in Czechoslovakia.

Moscow's assertion of political and administrative control went well beyond even the expanded mission of the KGB and its PROGRESS operatives. It also involved direct actions on the part of the Soviet leadership to ensure observance of acceptable political norms in occupied Czechoslovakia. "We're talking here about the most decisive interference in the affairs of Czechoslovakia," the assessment confessed, "about the application of pressure along all lines right up to the presentation of ultimatums." Recognition of the essentially illegal nature of the invasion itself conveniently legitimized any further acts, regardless of how they might contradict international law. In a moment of complete frankness the report cautioned against acting indecisively in order to avoid the appearance of direct interference in the affairs of a sovereign socialist nation. Such efforts, it stated, are "not only naïve, as the dispatch of troops is the most extreme act of interference in a state's affairs, but also fallacious, as the rightists are using this noninterference and our indecisiveness to strengthen their positions and to demoralize healthy [i.e., pro-Soviet] forces."[52]

The Soviets were especially anxious to gain effective control over the Czechoslovakian Ministry of Internal Affairs. Without full oversight of this key institution, they felt, "stabilization of the crisis in Czechoslovakia has been impossible." This was not a new discovery. Brezhnev's discussions with Dubcek before the invasion had consistently demanded greater discipline in the ministry, including replacement of its head, Josef Pavel. Pavel had remained, however, and became a considerable obstacle to the Soviet normalization process. Regarding the intervention as a hostile invasion, he recalled two state security officials suspected of collaboration and sought criminal proceedings against all ministry employees who had "committed punishable acts in connection with the forcible measures" of the occupation.[53]

"Independent of political regulation," the Politburo reassessment said of the Internal Ministry, "it was necessary from the first days [of the intervention] to interfere in a most decisive and radical manner in the activities of this very important organ and to control all of its positions."[54] Failure to do so had left the reformers in a powerful position. From Moscow's point of view, the Ministry of Internal Affairs under Pavel remained the most important rightist lever of control in Czechoslovakia. "At present," the briefing noted, "the [ministry] organs are not only incapable of resolving these problems, but they are actively opposing the Soviet state security organs." Soviet control of the ministry, the report speculated, would enable Moscow to strengthen the fundamentals of Soviet-style socialism and root out foreign instigators of "counterrevolution." As such, it was essential to overhaul its staff with cadres who would collaborate with the Kremlin.[55]

Another bulwark of the revised normalization program was Soviet control of the mass media in Czechoslovakia. Concern for the power of the free media had long troubled Moscow, beginning with the easing of censorship in early 1968. The hostile press coverage that met the invading Warsaw Pact forces accentuated and justified those earlier apprehensions. Moscow could not hope to assert its revised program of disinformation without full media cooperation. Thus, in addition to replacing the personnel at the Ministry of Internal Affairs, the November reassessment called for appointment of "sympathetic" elements to head the Czechoslovak media.[56]

With the ministry and the media in conservative hands, the normalization could proceed apace with its revised stratagem. Soviet agents were now to encourage the polarization of opinions within Czechoslovakia's governmental and Party organs in a bid to isolate and remove rightist proponents. The Soviets would also seek to inflame and exploit reformist disillusionment with Dubcek's postinvasion policies. From Moscow's perspective, reformist criticism, in conjunction with the increasingly complex political situation, conspired to damage Dubcek's authority. "Therefore," the November assessment plotted, "it is necessary to support this critical direction in every way possible. In the given situation, extremist elements are our allies. We must depose Dubcek with the hands of the rightists and then finish him off, along with his political authority." To ensure the success of this scenario, pro-Soviet elements in the Czechoslovakian leadership were to portray themselves as disgruntled rightists, loyal to the cause of reform but critical of Dubcek and his policies. "This political masquerade is absolutely essential if the new [pro-Soviet] cadres are to establish themselves," the assessment declared. All measures at Moscow's disposal, ranging from ideological persuasion to compromising individuals and economic pressure, were to be utilized to this end.[57]

While details still remain scarce, it is clear from the memoirs of KGB archivist Vasili Mitrokhin that Moscow conducted its normalization campaign very much along the lines laid out in the November assessment.[58] To the extent that the situation warranted, Moscow viewed even the most direct forms of interference—to the point of ultimatums—fully justified. Moreover, it did not require open counterrevolution or even peaceful reforms of socialism to condone this. The postinvasion normalization plans show that all it took was a situation of political instability and the presence of an untrusted leader.

Consequently, as it processed the lessons of Czechoslovakia, Moscow began to move toward a bloc policy of enforced orthodoxy and increasingly centralized control. In the process, the Soviets failed to grasp the most fundamental lesson of their experience: that the Prague Spring was a logical domestic response to the excesses of Soviet-style socialism. Would the invasion have taken place if this lesson had been recognized from the outset? Perhaps, as the reforms of the Prague Spring would still have evoked fears of counterrevolution in the bloc. In the long run, however, Moscow might well have turned its attention after 1968 to reforming socialism in a controlled fashion. Instead, it worked to consolidate its East European neighbors behind a status quo party line that made few allowances for divergent state interests or national character. While some would argue that socialism was unreformable under any circumstances, it is not difficult to see how the course Brezhnev chose to take undermined any hope for a lasting normalization.

Reaping the Harvest of Patience

Though Moscow had refused to deal with the central issue of the crisis, attention to tactical details eventually paid big dividends. Much of this success was owed to the self-control and discipline of the Czechs themselves. Already by the second day of the invasion, factory work had resumed to a limited extent in response to appeals broadcast on the radio. Two days later, on 24 August, a West German correspondent observed that life appeared to be returning to normal in Prague. Streetcars were operating, and shops were open for business.[59]

In time the political objectives of the normalization also began to fall into place as pro-Soviet elements asserted increasingly antireformist positions. Slovakia's first secretary, Gustav Husak, proved the most promising. Husak had been spotted at the Moscow discussions in August as a possible ally. Shortly thereafter, at the Slovak Party Congress, he had rejected the convocation of the Extraordinary Fourteenth CSCP Congress, though it had appointed him in absentia to the Party's new Presidium.[60] Husak did not come out publicly in support of the invasion and was not connected to Bilak's quisling cabal. Instead, his public appearances reflected a pragmatic attitude toward the Moscow Protocol. Speaking seven months after the invasion, in March 1969, he reasoned that "I do not intend to describe the Moscow settlement as a historic victory. . . . We should not indulge in illusions: what else was there to do?"[61] Indeed, Husak initially appeared to stand by the reformist government with his declaration, "I fully back Dubcek's conception; I took part in its formulation. I am going to give him my full support; either I shall stand by him or I shall go."[62]

Like Bilak and other Slovak leaders, however, Husak actually viewed the liberal aspirations of the Prague Spring with mistrust and resistance. After the invasion, while Dubcek and others attempted to keep the Action Program alive in the Czech lands, Husak worked to curtail its achievements in Slovakia. Moreover, as spring prepared to break anew over occupied Czechoslovakia, the Slovak leader stood ready to overturn the hopes of the previous year. Only weeks after he had pledged to stand by Dubcek or resign, a crisis broke out in Prague that afforded a ready opportunity. The Czechoslovak victory over the Soviet Union at the world ice hockey championship in Stockholm touched off demonstrations in Prague at the end of March. In the confusion, the office of the Soviet airlines, Aeroflot, was set on fire. Conservatives immediately attributed the fire to right-wing "counterrevolutionaries" and attacked Dubcek for his failure to maintain order. Striking while the iron was hot, they and their Soviet patrons clamored to take on Dubcek for a second time, eight months after the August invasion.

The confrontation went exactly as Moscow had planned months earlier. With Dubcek weakened by the concessions of the Moscow Protocol, the well-positioned conservatives asserted themselves aggressively. On 11 April, as Dubcek struggled to defend himself against conservative critics, Husak made a speech in Nitra in which he directly attacked Dubcek's reform program. His words rang with ideologically charged polemics. "Anti-social and opportunist forces strove to crush and destroy the political power of the working people in this state," he said of the Dubcek era, "to undermine the leading role of the Party, the power of the state apparatus, to wreck the unity of the working people."[63] The defamation campaign proved extremely effective under Husak's leadership. Less than a week after his speech, at the April 17 CSCP Central Committee plenum, Husak replaced Dubcek as first secretary of the statewide Party.

Husak's appointment to the position of first secretary effectively ended reformist attempts to revive the Prague Spring and its progressive Action Program. With Dubcek out of power, Husak moved to consolidate control of the Party and state bureaucracies. The resulting purge saw more than five hundred thousand members expelled from the Party, including, ultimately, Dubcek himself.[64] Through it all, Dubcek continued to assert his loyalty to both Moscow and socialism, as in an interview given to *Look* magazine in July 1969, while he was working as Czechoslovakia's ambassador to Turkey.

Responding to the Western reporter's suggestion that Dubcek was a democrat, the former first secretary offered assurances of his abiding loyalty to both socialism in general and Moscow in particular. "Yes, but if it were necessary for me to fight the enemies of Socialism," Dubcek asserted, "I would fight. They pretended that I was practicing anti-Sovietism. On the contrary, I have never thought that my policy would be developed outside our alliances and friendship with our Socialist friends. These are not merely words. I have always been tied to the Socialist parties and to the Soviet Union. I have always been and I always will be against manifestations of anti-Sovietism. . . . As far as the anti-Socialist forces are concerned, I wanted, first of all, to consolidate the leading role of the party. I was against all opposition to the party, against the restoration of the Social Democratic party."[65] Unfortunately for Dubcek, by August 1968 the forces of reform driving the Prague Spring had broken free of his control, shattering for good his credibility with Moscow. Husak's decisive purge of reform advocates from the Party and government ensured that the new leader would face no such challenges in the era of bloc consolidation.

The peaceful and orderly transfer of power to conservative hands was perfectly in line with Moscow's wishes. Soviet leaders gave their blessing to Husak's new domestic program, relieved that their pressures for political "normalization" could finally proceed unimpeded. In October 1969, the CSCP and CPSU signed a joint statement which declared that strengthening Marxist-Leninist ideology and defending socialist democracy were their most important common goals. Notably, the statement stipulated that "this must be carried out in a bitter and continuous struggle against anti-socialist views and concepts within the communist movement." Its deliberate language amounted to an ideological broadside aimed at both Prague Spring reformers and Maoist radicals. The term "antisocialist" here included, first, bourgeois nationalism, followed by left-wing opportunism and revisionism.[66] The message was clear. In the socialist commonwealth there could be only one acceptable route, namely, the narrow path charted for all in Moscow. The era of reform, begun nearly fifteen years earlier by Khrushchev's de-Stalinization program, had come to an end in Eastern Europe. The notion of "separate paths to socialism" was no longer acceptable. A new era of enforced orthodoxy and Soviet centralization of power had begun.

The Fallout of the Invasion

The near-term realization of Moscow's goals in Czechoslovakia led most observers on both sides of the Iron Curtain to regard the intervention as a decisive Soviet victory. Even in the high-profile arena of East-West confrontation, the negative repercussions of the operation were both muted and short-lived. Relations with the West experienced some short-term setbacks, particularly for the approval of the recently concluded Nuclear Non-Proliferation Treaty.[67] Movement on the Strategic Arms Limitation Talks (SALT) was also delayed, as President Johnson refused to travel to Leningrad in September 1968 and his successor, President Nixon, hesitated to reestablish contacts in 1969.[68] Ultimately, however, the pressing need to involve Moscow in negotiations with North Vietnam eclipsed American indignation, and Washington soon proved willing to mend fences in the interest of détente.

The impact of the invasion was far less auspicious within the less publicized socialist community. The U.S. ambassador to the Soviet Union, Llewellyn "Tommy" Thompson, had foreseen this in a number of the telegrams that he sent to Washington in advance of the August invasion. On 2 August 1968, for instance, he had written that "if the Soviets, by using whatever means are necessary, are able to restore an orthodox regime in Czechoslovakia, they could at least for a time hope to consolidate their hold over a smaller portion of the bloc. The eventual price they would have to pay for this would, however, doubtless be great, including their relations with non-ruling Communist parties."[69] Thompson's prediction was remarkably accurate. As Soviet historian Roy Medvedev observes in *On Socialist Democracy*, the intervention sparked "an extremely serious crisis in the international communist movement."[70] In the Soviet Union, according to Andrei Sakharov, "the hopes inspired by the Prague Spring collapsed. And 'real socialism' displayed its true colors, its stagnation, its inability to tolerate pluralistic or democratic tendencies, not just in the Soviet Union but even in neighboring countries. . . . For millions of former supporters, it destroyed their faith in the Soviet system and its potential for reform."[71] This was particularly true of the Soviet intelligentsia to whom the invasion was a crushing blow. For the six who led a brief protest against the invasion in Red Square on 25 August, it signaled a return to neo-Stalinist politics. "For all its hesitations and half-measures," they felt, "the Khrushchev era would soon seem like a paradise lost."[72] This sentiment was widely held. Seeking to sum up the impact of August 1968, the Soviet novelist Vasily Aksyonov described it as "a nervous breakdown for the whole generation."[73]

At the level of interstate relations, the invasion fallout was again most significantly experienced within the socialist community. It created instant tension with the East European nations that had not taken part in the operation. Relations worsened with Yugoslavia and Romania, which worried that their own assertions of independence might face a Soviet military response. Both thereafter worked to develop special military units whose mission was to respond extensively to an invasion force.[74] Albania, for its part, used the invasion as an excuse to leave the Warsaw Pact.[75] As for the nations remaining in the Soviet-led alliance, the invasion confirmed that autonomous political reforms would no longer be tolerated. While some experimentation continued in the economic sector, particularly in Hungary, the invasion and subsequent normalization of Czechoslovakia put an end to the political implications of Khrushchev's de-Stalinization process. It would be incorrect to characterize the new era as "neo-Stalinist," as Brezhnev's leadership never returned to the widespread terror and iron control of the 1930s. By 1969, however, it had become clear everywhere in the Soviet bloc that Moscow sought to crush Khrushchev's legacy of "separate roads to socialism."

In the broader international socialist movement, the invasion seriously damaged Moscow's ability to mount a united front against the Chinese. The conference that Mikhail Suslov had long planned so as to isolate Beijing did finally convene in June 1969. But the Soviets found it exceedingly difficult to exert their leadership over the parties in attendance, many of whom still vigorously denounced the violation of Czechoslovakia's national sovereignty.[76] The West European "Eurocommunists" were the most severe critics: "The Soviet invasion of Czechoslovakia in 1968 was the last straw," Spanish communist leader Santiago Carillo later wrote. After the invasion, "any idea of internationalism ended for us."[77] Facing this type of dissent, the Soviet leadership could hardly hope to contain the Chinese ideological offensive as planned.

Ironically, this combination of the intervention followed by a distinctly anti-Chinese international conference only served to complicate the tensions facing Moscow in the south. Sino-Soviet tensions escalated rapidly, prompting China to alter its domestic and foreign policies to counter what it perceived as a new threat from Moscow. In Beijing, Chinese defense minister Lin Biao, Mao's likely successor, is said to have warned the Chinese Communist Party Politburo of an impending Soviet attack. In preparation, he issued Directive no. 1 in October 1968, putting the entire country on war footing.[78] The result was an outbreak of hostilities along the Sino-Soviet border on 2 March 1969, in which Chinese forces allegedly ambushed a Soviet border patrol unit on Zhen Bao/Damansky Island, killing an officer and his thirty men.

From seventeen divisions in 1965, Soviet forces in the region reached twenty-seven divisions by 1969. Moscow also began to station strategic weaponry in the border zone, including SS-4 medium-range ballistic missiles (MRBMs), short-range SCUD and FROG (Free Rocket over Ground) missiles, and an antiballistic missile system.[79] In discussions addressing the perceived Chinese threat, Soviet defense minister Andrei Grechko is said to have recommended use of a "nuclear blockbuster" against Chinese industrial targets. Others reportedly called for surgical strikes against Chinese nuclear facilities.[80] For a number of months it was unclear what might happen. As the world looked on during the summer of 1969, Moscow faced the prospect of open war with a socialist country only a year after its invasion of Czechoslovakia. By placing greater stock in their ideological interests vis-à-vis Eastern Europe, the Soviet leadership had invited very real challenges to its own domestic security.

Aleksei Kosygin and Chou En-lai finally met on 11 September 1969 to negotiate an end to the hostilities. Their four-hour meeting achieved this goal successfully. According to the Soviet account of these discussions, the two sides agreed to "observance of the existing border, the inadmissibility of armed confrontations, [and] the withdrawal of troops of both sides from direct contact in controversial sectors."[81] Significantly, however, Moscow was forced to accede to continued Chinese attacks on its leadership of the international communist movement. A secret Soviet assessment of the negotiations sent to the leadership of the East German Socialist Unity Party (SED) underscores that Chou "justified the current forms of 'polemics' which are being used by the Beijing leaders as having nothing in common with theoretical discussions, and referred to the statement of Mao Zedong to the effect that 'polemics will continue for 10 thousand more years.'" Anxious to dispel the winds of war on the southern frontier, Kosygin was forced to accept this declaration, allowing that "polemics on controversial issues are permissible." But he added that "over the whole history of the struggle with communism, imperialism has never received a greater gain than that which it has as a result of the deepening, which is not our fault, of the PRC's differences with the Soviet Union and other Socialist countries."[82]

Coming on the heels of the largely disappointing conference of socialist parties in June, the Sino-Soviet agreement of September 1969 further eroded the influence of the Soviet model in the communist community. Nevertheless, Moscow's implicit threat of military intervention became the cornerstone of socialist bloc unity throughout the coming decade. It would not be until the end of the 1970s that another crisis would test this new doctrine of force and Moscow's resolve in applying it. In the meantime, throughout what Russians would come to call the "era of stagnation," Brezhnev and his fellow Soviet leaders would continue to rely on increasingly damaging ideological inflexibility in dealings with their socialist neighbors.

Conclusion

The invasion and normalization of Czechoslovakia in 1968–69 constituted a watershed in the history of Soviet bloc policy. In the course of this two-year period, Moscow shifted sharply away from its post-1953 permissiveness and redefined regional parameters that would continue for more than a decade. In the words of Robert Hutchings, Soviet policy after 1968 reflected an "adjustment of doctrine . . . born of necessity to be sure—

in the direction of socialist solidarity and away from Khrushchev's acceptance of 'separate roads to socialism.' "[83] The new archival evidence from former Soviet and East European collections corroborates this general impression in language far stronger than most existing historical accounts ever dared to suggest. The picture that emerges from behind the veil of official secrecy is one of profound Soviet interference in Czechoslovak affairs at every level of society. Belying all statements to the contrary, Moscow made violation of Czechoslovak state sovereignty the cornerstone of its normalization program.

Few statements embody this worldview better than Brezhnev's private justification for the invasion leveled on Dubcek in late August 1968. This exchange brought into sharp focus the truth of how Soviet perceptions of Czechoslovakia, its leadership, and its historical relationship with the Soviet Union defined Moscow's response to the Prague Spring. It is hardly an exchange between the leaders of two sovereign states. Rather, Brezhnev addresses Dubcek in the manner of a feudal lord dressing down a disloyal vassal. Czechoslovakia is not recognized as an independent country but as a constituent part of the Soviet Union, bought and paid for by the Red Army's liberation effort in World War II.

It is this assertion that most evidently illustrates the essential role of Eastern Europe in Brezhnev's perception of Soviet national interests. There is no indication from Brezhnev's words, from Politburo discussions, or from Soviet actions that Moscow regarded Eastern European political stability as anything less than an integral part of its own national interests. This is why, despite any clear threat to Soviet territorial interests, Brezhnev lectured Dubcek about endangering "common" security interests. Defined as broadly as they were, Soviet national interests would identify any political threat to socialism in Eastern Europe as a challenge to its domestic security. A loss of Soviet political control in any one of the bloc nations, particularly those on its periphery, would therefore represent a clear and present danger in the eyes of the Brezhnev leadership. It was on the basis of this perception of Soviet national interest that the Warsaw Pact "justifiably" invaded the sovereign territory of an allied nation. From Moscow's perspective, the intervention had been a crusade for self-preservation, worthy of the political and substantial economic costs it entailed. Indeed, before lapsing into its extensive critique, the Politburo assessment began with a strong statement approving of the invasion as "wise, courageous, and timely" and a manifestation of the Red Army's "sacred international duty."

This commitment to a profoundly ideological perception of national interests locked Soviet policy into a vicious circle of its own making. Convinced that the Prague Spring had been the work of foreign agents, Moscow undertook its own covert operation to subvert and destroy it. Though in control of the entire country within the first days of the invasion, it discovered the difficulty of translating military force into political legitimacy. And so the Soviet leadership reframed the aims of the intervention from military objectives to political manipulation. Reliance on tanks and troops gave way to the use of "special forces" and the strategic application of ultimatums. All necessary means, legal or illegal, were employed to compromise the authority of the reformist government while strengthening its conservative opponents. Through it all, ideological perceptions identified friend and foe, justified the flaunting of national and international law, and proscribed any serious reconsideration of the causes behind the Prague Spring.

As a result, orthodoxy and bloc cohesiveness became the watchwords of Soviet policy in Eastern Europe. The experience of Czechoslovakia ensured that persistent ideological convictions would strictly define socialist relations for the balance of the Brezhnev era. Having failed to process the lessons of managed political reform in Czechoslovakia, in future crises Moscow would be forced to rely on the central conclusions of 1968—namely, how to mount an effective intervention.[84]

As the experience of 1968 had shown, however, the intrinsic weakness of the Brezhnev Doctrine was reliance on force and stealth to solve political problems. Czechoslovak reformism had sought a way of managing political, social, and economic change in a modern socialist nation. This had been the central issue at the heart of Soviet bloc development since the death of Stalin in 1953, and in 1968 it remained to be effectively addressed. Hungary's experience in 1956 had shown that a full-scale withdrawal from the socialist commonwealth was not an option. Alexander Dubcek and his political allies had attempted to transform Czechoslovakia within socialist norms and in accordance with liberal national traditions. The Soviet invasion signaled that this approach to reform was equally unwelcome in the bloc. Yet the normalization of Czechoslovakia relied heavily on the nation's self-discipline and political moderation. A future crisis in a more stubbornly independent state, such as Poland, could not expect to meet this kind of cooperation. Therefore, as the bottom line to socialist legitimacy in the bloc, the Brezhnev Doctrine had a very distinct Achilles' heel.

As a result, the legitimacy problem festered behind the facade of socialist life well into the next two decades. In 1975, Mlynar observed that "six years after, the leading representatives of the politics of 'consolidation' are still trying to convince the Czechoslovak people that here 'in reality' there was Hungary of 1956, even though no one saw it and therefore they have to 'fashion' in the 'heads of people' that which reality didn't show."[85] To many loyal communists from Moscow to Madrid, this process was more than disillusioning. Contributing to the disaffection across an entire generation of communists worldwide, it was a propaganda disaster that undermined efforts to unite the international socialist movement firmly behind Soviet leadership. By introducing an implicit, but widely recognized, doctrine of limited sovereignty, it disrupted interstate relations with many neighboring states in both Europe and Asia. Most important, it left the Soviet Union committed to a policy that anathematized any effort to reform the practice of socialism along truly popular lines. Intent on ensuring a single model of socialist practice in the bloc, Moscow now staked its European sphere of influence on a single trump card—that of military intervention.

3

Socialist Internationalism and National Interest

Soviet troops have gone into Czechoslovakia—
friendship knows no boundaries.

Why did they send our troops into Afghanistan?
They were going alphabetically.
—Soviet anecdotes

The State therefore must make a choice: either to give up its continuous
effort and doom its borders to continuous unrest . . . or else to advance
farther and farther into the heart of the savage lands . . . where the
greatest difficulty lies in being able to stop.
—Chancellor Aleksandr Gorchakov, 1864

BY REDEFINING IN 1968 the notion of what constituted a "counterrevolution," the Brezhnev leadership sought to institute a fundamentally new era in socialist bloc relations. Under this altered regime, the Soviet leadership identified a threat to traditional socialist norms anywhere in the bloc as a menace to its prestige and stability. Moscow effectively guaranteed communist rule in Eastern Europe against all enemies, both foreign and domestic, by explicitly subordinating the national interests of its allies to the welfare of the entire socialist community.

This outlook informed the Kremlin's effort to deepen socialist integration on the grounds that common interests demanded common policies. Economic integration, political consolidation, a return to ideological orthodoxy, and inter-Party cooperation became the new watchwords of Soviet bloc relations. Failure to hold fast to this general line anywhere would theoretically constitute a danger to socialism everywhere, particularly as the bloc faced a rapidly changing international environment. Consequently, the threat of military intervention hung perpetually over Eastern Europe like the sword of Damocles throughout the 1970s and early 1980s. The Soviets and their allies referred to this consolidation under duress as "socialist internationalism." In the West, it was regarded as a predictable consequence of the new Brezhnev Doctrine.

One can discern two distinct phases within the Brezhnev consolidation era. The first, from 1971 until mid-1976, witnessed a renewed stability and optimism in the bloc, as Eastern Europe entered a period of new prosperity and higher living standards. By contrast, the period between 1976 and the early 1980s saw the entire region decline rapidly into serious economic and political instability. Government efforts to maintain social order as living standards began to fall failed to prevent open disaffection toward communist rule. International political developments provided additional impetus to this decline. Eurocommunism began to offer an alternative to the Soviet model of communist rule so stringently enforced since 1968. Meanwhile, the Helsinki Final Act and its stipulation of human rights provisions gave a growing dissident population a handy weapon to wield against communist authority.

By the end of the 1970s, Moscow faced an important decision. If it continued to define stability in Eastern Europe as an integral part of Soviet national interests, it would soon find itself drawn into a maelstrom of economic and political crises. On the other hand, the alternative could well be a toppling of communist rule in some key states, if not throughout the entire bloc. Such a shift in what Moscow called the "correlation of forces" between East and West would come as a blow to the international communist movement, not to mention Soviet foreign policy.

By the late 1970s, the promises of socialist internationalism were increasingly inconsistent with the perceived interests of the Soviet Union itself. The 1979 invasion of Afghanistan saw the Kremlin choose to honor the former, convinced that Soviet security was, for now, inextricably bound to the fate of Afghan communism. Ultimately, the consequences of this action proved to be far more destabilizing than Moscow had anticipated. On the eve of the 1980s and of a new crisis in Poland, the Kremlin leadership was already reassessing the importance of domestic stability to Soviet national interests. In time, this new perspective would have far-reaching implications for the future of communism in Eastern Europe.

The Brezhnev Doctrine

On 11 September 1968, less than a month after the invasion of Czechoslovakia, an article by political theoretician Sergei Kovalev appeared in *Pravda* arguing that the intervention had been a justifiable act of collective self-defense. "Foreign imperialists," in league with "internal émigrés," had allegedly turned the Prague Spring into a "peaceful counterrevolution . . . no less insidious" than a violent rebellion. Kovalev therefore concluded that the defense of socialist norms required "vigilance" on the part of all communists.[1] Two weeks later, on 26 September, Kovalev published another article in *Pravda* in which he argued that "the weakening of any link in the world socialist system has a direct effect on all socialist countries." As a result, all were said to have an "internationalist duty" to defend socialism, just as those states involved in Czechoslovakia had defended the "fundamental interests of the socialist commonwealth."[2] Where did this remarkable assertion leave the integrity of territorial sovereignty within the socialist camp? Did the new doctrine amount, as many Western observers contended, to a limitation of sovereignty in the bloc? Kovalev offered no indications, doubtless because the truth would have led to considerable dissension in socialist ranks. Indeed, Romania's vitriolic criticism of the invasion was founded precisely on this point.

Yet, for this same reason, the Soviets could not simply ignore the issue of national sovereignty. At the Fifth Congress of the Polish United Workers Party (PZPR) on 12 November 1968, Leonid Brezhnev asserted that it was not at all at variance with socialist internationalism. "Socialist states," he argued, "stand for strict respect for the sovereignty of all countries. We resolutely oppose interference in the affairs of any states and the violation of their sovereignty." At the same time, he added, socialist states have a right "to protect the blossoming of their country, the good and well-being of the broad mass of working people on the path to creating a society free from all oppression and exploitation." Hence, sovereignty was implicitly subordinate to the broader interests of socialist internationalism. The right to defend the "gains" of socialism, while not entirely incongruous with respect to national borders, occasionally had to take precedence. In Brezhnev's words, "When external and internal forces hostile to socialism try to turn the development of a given socialist country in the direction of the restoration of the capitalist system, when a threat arises to the cause of socialism in that country . . . this is no longer merely a problem for that country's people, but a common problem, the concern of all socialist countries."[3] Although publicly denying the existence of any new doctrine, statements like these left the matter of East European sovereignty very much unresolved.[4]

The concept of socialist internationalism had begun to take shape in the earliest days of the Bolshevik movement as *proletarian* internationalism. This earlier variant had its origins in the famous rallying cry of the *Communist Manifesto*, "Workers of all nations, unite!" According to Marx and Engels, working-class people must recognize that the division of the world into different nations only facilitates their exploitation. The worker has no legitimate state loyalties. Rather, he should remain dedicated to the liberation of his class from bourgeois exploitation throughout the world.

The emergence of new socialist states after World War II prompted Soviet ideologists to proclaim the birth of *socialist* internationalism. Defined as brotherly cooperation among all nations of the socialist camp, it was the logical evolution of proletarian internationalism into the realm of interstate relations. In time, any clear distinction between them began to erode as ideologists used the terms "socialist" and "proletarian" interchangeably. For much of the postwar era, however, proletarian/socialist internationalism remained undistinguished as but one of many arrows in Moscow's ideological quiver. It featured briefly in Khrushchev's justification for the 1956 Soviet invasion of Hungary, but by the early 1960s it again commanded relatively little attention in either Soviet or East European policy statements. Only after 1968 did proletarian/socialist internationalism become the ideological hinge pin of Soviet East European policy. Nevertheless, Moscow could legitimately argue then that the principle was far from new. "The CPSU has . . . always set forth the principles of proletarian internationalism," wrote one ideologue in 1976, "guided by them in its domestic and foreign policy, and has actively used them as a weapon in the struggle against imperialism and reaction."[5]

Was this merely cynical opportunism on Moscow's part, an ideological boondoggle applied to justify Soviet aggression and imperial control? Certainly many Western scholars and politicians have seen it as such. Indeed, some contemporary Russian scholars argue for this interpretation as well.[6] From their perspective, 1968 did not represent a significant turning point in Soviet policy toward Eastern Europe. Rather, they contend, Moscow's long-term use of military control and intimidation in the region simply acquired a more extensive ideological explanation under Brezhnev.[7]

The shift toward a more strict interpretation of socialist internationalism had begun to appear within the context of socialist relations as early as 1964 with Khrushchev's call for a greater coordination of blocwide foreign policy, but Khrushchev was removed from power before he could realize this objective. When his successor, Leonid Brezhnev, attempted the same type of integration in 1965, the leaders of both Czechoslovakia and Romania demanded a greater say in the formulation of common foreign policies. This proved more than Brezhnev had bargained for, so he relented for the time being.[8]

Brezhnev's retreat created a brief vacuum in the direction of bloc relations which contributed to the increasingly divergent initiatives taking place in Prague. Meanwhile, after December 1966, the West German political coalition of Chancellor Kurg Georg Kiesinger and Foreign Minister Willy Brandt began to seek improved relations with the governments of Eastern Europe. In the absence of more efficient Soviet coordination, this early *Ostpolitik* split the socialist camp. While Romania and Bulgaria were willing to entertain better ties with the Federal Republic of Germany (FRG), Poland and East Germany were not.[9] Ultimately, Bulgaria backed down, but Romania established diplomatic relations with Bonn in early 1967.

The rapprochement between Romania and West Germany elicited strong condemnation from the rest of the bloc. Nevertheless, Moscow still failed to exert decisive control, and the Prague Spring continued to draw Czechoslovakia further down the road of reform. By mid-1968, Soviet policy had become very unclear in Eastern Europe. Until August, no one knew what, if anything, Moscow was prepared to do to stop the spread of Czechoslovak liberalization. Once the invasion had clarified this point, Soviet leaders returned to the matter of blocwide integration and enforced cohesion within the socialist alliance.

The Brezhnev Doctrine and its reinterpretation of socialist internationalism consequently represented a reimposition of Soviet authority on the basis of earlier experience. It was, in short, an evolution of doctrine to meet the perceived demands of contemporary realities. East European national sovereignty had been effectively limited since 1945. The Soviet interventions in East Germany (1953), Hungary (1956), and Czechoslovakia (1968) merely reconfirmed this fundamental reality. In the first two instances, Moscow had responded to open, violent rebellions against communist rule. Czechoslovakia, on the other hand, had introduced a new definition of "counterrevolution" in bloc relations. For the first time Moscow had invaded a sovereign socialist country whose government and society had been working peacefully for the reform of Stalinist institutions.

The argument that these reforms had constituted an "insidious" rebellion against traditional socialist norms carried broad implications for the future of socialist bloc relations. Soviet interventionism now became a lever to ensure observance of common policies in all spheres of political and economic life. Meanwhile, socialist internationalism provided a theoretical basis for this evolution of Soviet policy which was consistent with both past and present sensibilities. Although it seemed to ripen in step with the necessities of the Kremlin's foreign policy, the theory did not constitute a purely cynical justification of Soviet realpolitik. As Hélène Carrère D'Encausse wisely points out, "The theoretical development of inter-socialist relations in the years following the invasion of Czechoslovakia was much more than an *a posteriori* program of justification for a coup. Begun in fact under the compulsion to explain and justify this reaction, this developed ideology was later designed to define the political program of the USSR in Eastern Europe and to provide it with a clear legitimacy and a clear direction."[10] The Soviet leadership, like any other government, operated within the policy options defined by its ideological worldview. At the same time, this worldview continued to evolve to meet the challenges of modern life. It was this marriage of theory and action which drove the transformation of Soviet East European policy after 1968.

Detente, Legitimacy, and the Drive for Bloc Cohesion

In large part the issue that motivated Moscow's reorientation was the emergence of centrifugal forces in the bloc, introduced by Khrushchev's permissive "separate roads to socialism." But developments in the international arena also informed and reinforced the trend toward integration because of their potential challenge to bloc unity and cooperation. Largely as a result of the deepening conflict with China, the Soviets now sought normalized relations with the West. This raised the specter of ideological infection in the socialist camp. After all, the Soviet leadership had convinced itself in the course of 1968 that "Western ideological centers" were behind the developments of the Prague Spring. This conviction persisted into the 1970s, détente notwithstanding, prompting doctrinal statements such as this: "In the situation that has arisen, only solidarity around the USSR and tight unity can save the young socialist states from imperialist intervention and the restoration of capitalism."[11] In addition to ideological concerns, the expansion of commercial relations with the West, eventually involving up to one-third of CMEA trade, threatened to disrupt the socialist economic alliance. Hence, to the Soviet leadership, blocwide consolidation seemed necessary to protect the integrity of East European socialism.

Détente did prove an effective cause around which to rally the bloc. In December 1969 a summit of bloc leaders convened in Moscow to adopt a common strategy for approaching the West. A policy of "controlled bilateralism" emerged at this meeting as the guiding principle behind Soviet bloc diplomacy. According to this policy, individual East European initiatives were to be consistent with the pace of the entire bloc. Regular consultations with Moscow would ensure that no one state was out of step with the rest. As the basis of renewed regional cooperation, it underwrote changes within both the Warsaw Pact military alliance and the Council for Mutual Economic Assistance.

In conjunction with these issues of foreign policy, the matter of regime viability also fostered Moscow's new consolidation drive. Legitimacy had largely eluded communist governments in Eastern Europe since their inception after World War II. Exacerbating this problem was the fact that popular rejection of both Soviet hegemony and communist ideology had led to increased repression and more extensive social controls in these countries. By the late 1960s and early 1970s, Moscow saw that the viability problem posed yet another clear and present danger to Soviet influence in Eastern Europe. Taken as part of the overall picture involving Czechoslovakia, the escalation of Sino-Soviet conflict, and the beginning of East-West détente, it threatened to undermine the very foundations of the Soviet bloc. Therefore, from Moscow's perspective, consolidation stood to resolve the challenges to socialism originating both within and outside the Soviet bloc.

Internationalism therefore assumed a new importance in Soviet bloc policy, proclaimed as essential to the main objectives of the world socialist movement. Everything from the creation of a new socialist society to international détente, peace, and social progress was now seen as contingent on the process of bloc integration.[12] In the estimation of Soviet ideologist I. Dudinskii, this process demanded above all "working out a general line pertaining to an agreed-upon circle of domestic and foreign policy issues, realizing coordinated action, and working out cooperative plans and programs." Such an effort, he concluded, would require "support among the masses for a spirit of collectivism, internationalism, a realization of the need for brotherly friendship and mutual support of all peoples of the socialist nations, and a cooperative defense of the conquests of socialism."[13]

It was this last assertion pertaining to "cooperative defense" which remained problematic. If one of the fundamental principles of socialist internationalism was respect for national sovereignty, what were the limitations on cooperative defense? Most Soviet accounts argued that any attempt to import counterrevolution into one of the socialist states constituted legitimate grounds for either bilateral or multilateral military assistance. If the "achievements of socialism" faced any kind of threat, military or political, the Soviet Union and its allies had an obligation to respond decisively.[14]

This was the ideological basis underlying Moscow's consolidation efforts after 1968. Much of it amounted to little more than an airing out of mothballed boilerplate formulas such as "indestructible brotherhood," "collective action," and "struggle for national liberation and social progress." What was new, however, was the degree to which the new policy couched its recognition of national sovereignty and independence within strict statements of ideological orthodoxy. As Brezhnev remarked in a 1976 speech, the principles of internationalism in the socialist camp included "revolutionary solidarity, unified action, full independence and sovereignty, freedom in the selection of paths and forms for the creation of a new societal structure, comradely mutual assistance, and a belief in the ideas of Marxism-Leninism."[15] This was a new type of policy that blended neo-orthodox political control with the appearance of multinational decision making. When addressing issues of little real import, Moscow even appeared to be occasionally "outvoted" by its junior East European partners. Meanwhile, on all vital questions, Soviet apparatchiks and Party ideologists oversaw the strict reassertion of the Soviet political model across the board.[16]

Moscow chose to coordinate the integration process along existing institutional lines rather than create a new organization based on the Comintern of the 1920s and 1930s. While some, especially the East German communists, favored a new Comintern, most regarded it as an outmoded tool of Stalinist repression in Eastern Europe. And so, in June 1969, the leaders of the Soviet bloc nations met in Moscow to discuss the more palatable alternative of reforming the WTO and CMEA. On 18 June, the Soviet Communist Party daily, *Pravda*, announced their decision to rely more heavily on "natural" ideological coordination, including "bilateral consultations, regional meetings, and international conferences" to coordinate bloc policies.[17] Structured in the traditional pyramidal model of democratic centralism, these regular consultations would occur at every level and in all spheres of national life. Periodic summit meetings would form the apex of the pyramid, while military and diplomatic, economic, and other bureaucratic interaction made up its base.

On the face of it, the new coordination seemed to decentralize regional decision making away from Moscow. Each of the allied states took turns chairing the multilateral meetings, which lent an appearance of democracy and egalitarianism to the proceedings. On the one hand, this built up East European morale, as it "represented a new and somewhat paradoxical Soviet confidence in a multilateral approach to problems of alliance management and, derivatively, in the ability of their more loyal allies, chiefly the Bulgarians, Czechoslovaks, and East Germans, to help ensure that the desired consensus would prevail in multilateral negotiations."[18] On the other hand, in practice it remained clear that the Soviets continued to play the role of primus inter pares, engineering the results of all major discussions through "directed consensus."

Overcoming East European Resistance

Occasionally this practice required the application of considerable Soviet pressure on its allies. One such instance saw Moscow engineer the removal of Walter Ulbricht as head of the East German Socialist Unity Party in 1971. Ulbricht had begun to upset Moscow with insinuations that the Soviet leadership could learn from the experience of East German communism.[19] Ulbricht would have to be replaced, the Soviets decided, with a leader who kept his nose out of ideological questions. His removal turned out to be a hard-won but significant victory for Soviet consolidation in Eastern Europe. His successor, Erich Honecker, immediately moved toward closer ties with the Soviet Union. Speaking at the Eighth Party Congress of the SED, Honecker declared that consultations with Moscow had "intensified systematically," which he predicted would lead to unprecedented unanimity on questions of ideology and foreign policy.[20]

Another memorable case of Soviet pressure involved an open threat of military action against Romania in the early 1970s. Relations between Moscow and Bucharest had been strained since Nicolae Ceausescu came to power in 1965 with his characteristic brand of nationalistic communism. Following the invasion of Czechoslovakia, he declared publicly that "attempts to justify mistakes and the emergence of new theses which are contrary to Marxist-Leninist principles such as the thesis of 'limited sovereignty' only complicate matters and hinder the process of remaking . . . unity."[21] To punctuate this position, in 1972 the Romanian Grand National Assembly passed a measure stipulating that "only elected Party and state bodies, and not unspecified groups therein, are entitled to ask for political, economic, or military assistance from other countries."[22]

In the years that followed the events of 1968, the Romanian maverick also formed a tacit alliance with Yugoslavia to resist the expansion of Soviet control in the Balkans. From Moscow's perspective, Ceausescu's timing could not have been worse. With the Sino-Soviet rift exploding into open conflict along the Ussuri River in 1969, China attempted to engineer its own rapprochement with the Balkan states, especially Yugoslavia and Albania, to undermine Soviet influence in the socialist world. When Ceausescu's speeches began to teem with references to a "Balkan zone" in 1971, the Hungarian press warned of a pro-Chinese, anti-Soviet "Tirana-Belgrade-Bucharest axis."[23] Fears in the Kremlin transformed from a concern for bloc unity to alarm about the potential security threat on the southwestern Soviet frontier. Moscow responded with a show of force as two divisions of Soviet airborne troops took up positions in Bulgaria not far from the Romanian border. In time, a combination of intense political, military, and economic pressure convinced Ceausescu to accept the trappings of multilateral integration in both the CMEA and the WTO. Moreover, as in the case of Ulbricht's resignation, these Romanian concessions advanced considerably the cause of Soviet-led coordination in bloc relations.

Moscow used coercion to impose economic uniformity as well, most notably in its relations with Hungary. Hungarian leader Janos Kadar had begun experimenting with economic modernization in the mid-1960s, eventually settling into a policy called the New Economic Mechanism (NEM) by 1968. Among other things, the NEM program involved some decentralization of economic authority, as well as limited competitiveness in both domestic and foreign market relations. Kadar argued that NEM was not an exercise in national communism but a Marxist-Leninist policy for building socialism which took into account Hungary's peculiar framework.[24] At first in 1968, Moscow seemed to accept this explanation, provided that Kadar's reforms did not stray into politics.

However, most of the Soviet leaders harbored deep suspicions about the liberal character of the reforms themselves. These suspicions erupted into protests in late 1969 against the "confusion and potential ideological contraband" that the Soviets feared NEM was unleashing in Hungary.[25] The Kremlin began to attack alleged "nationalist manifestations" and "Zionist intrigues" in Hungary which Kadar seemed unable to control. Rumors began to circulate that Mikhail Suslov was working hard to have Kadar removed from his position as first secretary. Indeed, in May 1972, under heavy pressure from Moscow, Kadar offered his resignation to the Hungarian Party, to take effect in early 1973. But at a secret session of the Hungarian Central Committee, Kadar received a unanimous vote of approval that seemed to validate his economic policies.[26] Hence, Moscow and Budapest seemed to have reached a stalemate on the issue.

The draw was short-lived. At its November 14–15 Central Committee plenum, the Hungarian Party essentially abandoned NEM in favor of a return to traditional Soviet-style economic policies. Leading reform advocates were sacked in favor of more conservative apparatchiks, though Kadar stayed on as first secretary. For the time being, the demands of bloc integration took precedence over Hungary's peculiar economic interests.[27]

Thus it was that the Soviets successfully employed all the levers at their command in securing adherence to a new uniformity in blocwide socialist development. Whether the issue was political (as in the GDR), military (as in Romania), or economic (as in Hungary), the assertion of Soviet pressure and leadership relentlessly overcame all regional intransigence. As a result, within a few years Moscow was able to impose a number of fundamental reforms across the entire alliance. Among these, the most important were the 1969 Budapest Program of the WTO and the 1971 Comprehensive Program within the CMEA.

Reform within the Warsaw Treaty Organization

From a military perspective, consolidation of Soviet leadership within the socialist camp addressed Moscow's fervent desire to avoid any further military action against its allies. True, Soviet propaganda continually implied a willingness to use force. But after the difficult normalization of Czechoslovakia, Moscow did all that it could within the bounds of unity to avoid having to act on this promise. As Robert Hutchings observes, "For the nearer term, the Soviet drive for socialist integration had the more limited aim of preventing a reoccurrence of the events of 1968 by creating within the Soviet bloc an interdependence so thorough and a system of consultation and coordination so pervasive that recourse to direct military coercion would be rendered unnecessary."[28]

The transformation of the WTO got under way with the conclusion in March 1969 of the Budapest Reform Program. Signed by bloc leaders only months after the invasion of Czechoslovakia, the Budapest Program created three new bodies designed to facilitate increased integration. The Committee of Defense Ministers, Committee for the Coordination of Military Technology, and Military Council seemed to strike a balance between increased Soviet control and a greater East European voice in decision making. For instance, while the Committee for the Coordination of Military Technology facilitated Soviet supervision of East European defense establishments, it also provided greater opportunities for technology exchange within the bloc. This both solidified Soviet oversight and addressed East European concerns about burden sharing in military development. Additionally, the Committee of Defense Ministers for the first time subordinated the Soviet commander in chief of the WTO Joint Command to the East European defense ministers.[29] In practice, however, Moscow surrendered very little to the collaborative process. Despite the official checks and balances set up to give each member-nation an equal say, Soviet decisions nearly always prevailed over any opposition. As in political discussions, military issues were also resolved through the process of "directed consensus." The fact that Soviets held nearly every top bureaucratic post within the alliance certainly facilitated this arrangement.[30]

Under its new configuration, the Warsaw Pact was especially useful for advancing a general foreign policy line for the entire socialist alliance. As Brezhnev pointed out at the Twenty-fourth CPSU Congress of 1971, in addition to traditional bilateral contacts, bloc foreign policy would now evolve largely through the discussions of the WTO Political Consultative Committee.[31] Though it seemed to surrender its leadership role to the collaborative process, as elsewhere the Soviet Union usually determined the outcome.

It was in the realm of purely military affairs that the reforms were at their most controversial. Included in the Budapest Program was a measure called the New Statute on the Joint Armed Forces. While mentioned in the general discussion surrounding the program, the New Statute was never published in full, therefore its details remained obscure. What is known is that the statute provided for the supranational integration of Warsaw Pact forces under undisclosed conditions. During certain joint exercises or in time of war, East European forces would fall under direct Soviet control, with orders bypassing their own high commands. Giving the official designation of the title "Joint Command" to what amounted to the Soviet General Staff did not obscure the genuine significance of this measure.[32] Ambiguous statements about the permanence or extent of Joint Command control caused serious disagreements among the socialist states. Nicolae Ceausescu, for one, objected that "the idea of yielding a part of the right of command and leadership of the army, however small, by the party and government is inconceivable."[33] The official Soviet line was that the troops assigned to the Joint Command "are not withdrawn from the jurisdiction of the command of the countries in question."[34] Yet it is not clear how Moscow reconciled this position with the very real subordination of East European command and control defined in the New Statute. As the Poles did not adopt this measure until 1979–80, it would seem that it remained a hotly debated issue throughout the 1970s.[35]

Despite the presence of some controversy, the Budapest Reforms were a decisive first step in the Soviet consolidation of political and military affairs in Eastern Europe. As a show of this deepening integration, in 1970 the Warsaw Pact staged Brotherhood-in-Arms, the first ever pactwide military exercises in bloc history. Intended as a demonstration of socialist internationalism, the maneuvers also sought to emphasize a collective commitment to the inviolability of the German Democratic Republic and the Ulbricht regime at the outset of the détente process. They accordingly reaffirmed socialist solidarity and the consolidation process as both timely and relevant.[36]

The unprecedented maneuvers also signaled the persistence of serious tensions within the socialist alliance, especially between Moscow and Bucharest. Although the East German press had announced prior to their October commencement that the Romanians would participate in the exercises, Bucharest sent only a few officers to act as observers.[37] Ceausescu was insistent that Romania retain control over its military forces, in part owing to his desire not to get drawn into another Soviet-led intervention. But above all, the Romanian leader sought to ensure Romania's relative independence and territorial integrity. This priority underwrote the aforementioned 1972 Law on National Defense, as well as Ceausescu's rejection of the New Statute on the Joint Armed Forces. Indeed, throughout most of the 1970s Ceausescu's contumacious independence repeatedly frustrated efforts to cement a common foreign policy within the WTO. June 1974, for instance, found him publicly complaining that Moscow was attempting to secure "extraterritorial transit rights" through Romania. That same year, as well as four years later in 1978, Ceausescu rejected further Soviet proposals in the Political Consultative Committee (PCC) to tighten the WTO joint command.[38]

Romania's resistance notwithstanding, during the 1970s the Warsaw Pact assumed an official role as the watchdog of political stability and Soviet influence in Eastern Europe. By securing institutional recognition of its dominant position in the alliance, the Budapest Reform Program solidified Moscow's control over the region both politically and militarily. Through its effective supremacy on the PCC, the Soviets began to realize their long-held objective of coordinating common foreign policy initiatives toward the West, all the while using the Warsaw Pact to underwrite stability in the bloc. As Robert Hutchings reflected at the time, "The continued presence of some thirty Soviet divisions in Eastern Europe . . . provides a constant reminder—one not altogether unwelcome among the leaders of the East European regimes—that the military might of the Soviet Union is the ultimate guardian of the political status quo in the region."[39] Meanwhile, the introduction of multilateral collaboration into this effort, while largely perfunctory, did have a positive impact on allied morale. In this way the Budapest Program assumed a central importance in the Soviet integration of socialist Europe.

Alongside the Warsaw Treaty Organization, the second of the two institutional pillars supporting the socialist alliance was the Council for Mutual Economic Assistance. Also referred to as Comecon, the CMEA came into existence in 1947 as Moscow's response to the American Marshall Plan for the economic reconstruction of postwar Europe. For more than ten years, the new economic alliance existed in name alone. Its member-nations remained in a state of virtual autarchy until Khrushchev proposed greater bloc integration in the late 1950s following the twin stimuli of the Hungarian Revolution and formation of the European Economic Community (EEC).

The CMEA received its first charter in 1960, which focused, as its title suggests, on the "basic principles of the international socialist division of labor." A serious disagreement immediately developed between the bloc's industrial and agrarian tiers. Northern industrial states such as the GDR, Czechoslovakia, and the Soviet Union proposed a fixed division of labor within the CMEA, whereas the southern Romania and Hungary, supported by agricultural Poland, objected to the prospect of remaining underdeveloped in perpetuity.[40]

This dispute deepened still further in 1962 when Khrushchev called for the creation of a supranational planning and decision-making body for the CMEA.[41] Due largely to Romanian resistance, this and all other efforts to introduce joint economic planning across the bloc in the early 1960s met with little success. According to Hungarian economist Tibor Kiss, deputy department chief of the Hungarian Institute of Planned Economy, the whole initiative "forgot that the perfection of multilateral coordination . . . did not depend simply on improving methods but was primarily a question of self-interest. The joint-planning concept disregarded actual production conditions in the socialist countries and the objective necessity of maintaining their economic independence."[42] Clearly the lesson of Khrushchev's failure was that any attempt to integrate the socialist economies of Eastern Europe would have to take into account the southern priorities of industrial development and economic sovereignty.

Soviet economic planners revisited the idea of international plan coordination in 1969, five years after Khrushchev's ouster. Consistent with the overarching goals of bloc solidarity, economic integration now also promised to buffer the anticipated disruption caused by opening the socialist bloc to increased Western commerce. Following the Twenty-fifth CMEA Session in Bucharest that July, the details of an impending integration finally appeared in the press. A year later, at the Twenty-sixth CMEA Session of July 1972, the alliance announced the impending coordination of its 1976–80 national five-year plans.[43]

After months of consideration, the Twenty-seventh CMEA Council Session in June 1973 formally elected to use the Coordinated Five-Year Plan of Multilateral Integration Measures as the basis for implementing socialist economic integration. The plan remained short on details, however, appearing more as a show of unity than a practical step toward deeper integration. Meetings in the Crimea a month later revealed that plan coordination would be limited to enterprises engaging in international trade within the CMEA. Nevertheless, official reports declared this to be the start of more-extensive economic consolidation in years to come. The GDR and the USSR introduced elements of this new integration as early as 1974. The other nations of the alliance followed in their 1976–80 five-year plans.[44] By 1977, member-governments were already preparing to expand the integration of national economic plans into the 1981–85 period.

Like the Bucharest Reform Program, the integration of CMEA member economies included a number of high-profile concessions to East European governments. Mindful of Khrushchev's earlier failures, Soviet leaders proclaimed that the new initiative, titled Comprehensive Program for the Further Extension and Improvement of Cooperation and the Development of Socialist Integration by the Comecon Member Countries, would harmonize the disparate levels of economic development that existed in the CMEA. The southern tier nations would remain inviolate in matters of national sovereignty, they promised, while still cooperating in tighter production and trade. Additionally, a new "interested party" principle offered member-nations the choice of opting out of any joint investment project. Prior to the implementation of the Comprehensive Program, all nations of the bloc had been required to participate in CMEA joint projects once adopted. Under the "interested party" principle, nonparticipating nations would not be required to render support, though they would subsequently lose their veto over implementation decisions of that project. This arrangement enabled Moscow to circumvent the obstruction of nettlesome East European vetoes, while seeming to permit greater freedom of action in bloc relations.

The CMEA approved nine new joint investment projects after 1972 under the new agreement. Of these, however, eight involved investment in the Soviet economy, most notably the Orenburg natural gas pipeline. The ninth was located in Cuba. Not one provided collective investment in the economies of Eastern Europe. Rather, like the Orenburg project, most entailed the harnessing and delivery of Soviet energy resources to the region. As this imbalance began to elicit allied objections in the late 1970s, the Soviets chose to de-emphasize the projects altogether rather than adopt more egalitarian investment criteria. As a result, by the early 1980s, many earlier initiatives remained uncompleted for lack of sufficient investment capital.[45]

Another source of tension that the new reforms failed to overcome was the question of market mechanisms in socialist bloc trade. Despite the fact that many East Europeans, particularly the Hungarians, desired a more market-oriented integration, Moscow insisted on the preservation of centralized prices in both domestic and interstate trade.[46] Competitive advantage and relative scarcity were antithetical to socialist internationalism, the Kremlin felt, and so had no business defining the bases of CMEA commercial relations. Cooperation, not competition, was the key to bloc integration. The notion that a "viable" industry could be driven out of business because it was not competitive on the international market remained an anathema in the socialist world. After all, the policy of guaranteeing full employment ensured that Eastern Europe and the Soviet Union were replete with such uncompetitive enterprises. The division of labor under socialism ought to secure and maintain the individual economic complexes of its members. In place of international competition, socialist integration would oversee their organization into an interstate economic complex.[47] Seeing little chance for an agreement, the Hungarians and others were forced to table divisive issues such as nonquota ties, price formation in foreign trade, and the convertibility of trade. This virtually guaranteed that socialist economies would remain obsolescent and uncompetitive on the world market.

Perhaps the most formidable obstacle standing in the way of the program's implementation was, again, Romania. When Romanian participation appeared in doubt, however, Moscow simply threatened to cut off its deliveries of iron ore, vital to Romania's enormous refining industry. The threat worked. Ceausescu ultimately agreed to conclude both a Soviet-Romanian trade protocol on coordination of economic plans as well as a new treaty of friendship, cooperation, and mutual assistance with the Soviet Union.[48] Following the conclusion of these agreements in July 1970, the economic component of the Soviet consolidation effort was approved for implementation over the course of the following fifteen to twenty years.

Nevertheless, East European governments continued to regard the notion of increasing economic integration with suspicion. Despite changes made to address earlier concerns, the bloc's less developed nations continued to worry about being locked forever into disadvantageous trade positions. Romania was not the only nation concerned about infringements on its political and economic sovereignty. Nearly all multilateral agreements and communiqués touching on the Comprehensive Program included statements stressing the importance of safeguarding national sovereignty within the bloc. Consequently, the nature of long-term economic integration within the CMEA remained largely undefined thanks to this perpetually troublesome issue.

Yet even if the socialist allies had managed to reach an accord on economic reform, the Comprehensive Program remained an unlikely objective. To begin with, the program relied to a great extent on ties between the socialist nations which simply did not exist: in the early 1970s the member-states of the CMEA had yet to develop significant contacts between their national economies. Additionally, the program's reliance on plan coordination, rather than market principles, reinforced a dependence on bilateral, barter-style trade. Multilateral debt clearing was thus very difficult, if not impossible. The program also hampered technological innovation because of its reliance on administrative decisions in the sphere of technical cooperation and exchange. Finally, the burden of contributing to joint investment projects in the USSR, deemed necessary to ensure a continuous supply of cheap energy resources, slowed the growth of some of the poorer socialist economies. With time, this seriously undermined the East European commitment to the CMEA. By contrast, the Twenty-fifth Congress of the CPSU in 1976 praised the advances made in a number of sectors including cooperative exploration of natural resources, joint construction of massive industrial complexes, increased interenterprise cooperation among bloc nations, and growing scientific and technical exchange.[49] This divergence of views offered yet another indication that the interests of the bloc nations in practice were nowhere near as common as their propaganda suggested.

Soviet Bloc Consumerism

One of the most significant economic developments of the Brezhnev era was the growth of consumerism, known popularly as "goulash communism" in many nations of the socialist commonwealth. This trend began in the wake of Polish riots that broke out in 1970 when the government in Warsaw raised the price of staple food products just before the Christmas holidays. The riots led to serious political instability in Poland and the use of deadly force against antigovernment demonstrators. Polish leader Wladyslaw Gomulka, in power since 1956, was forced to resign under Soviet pressure and was replaced by Edward Gierek.

The lesson of the Polish experience—that governments could rise and fall on the strength of consumer demand—did not go unnoticed. Respect for consumerism became the watchword of communist legitimacy in Eastern Europe. Bulgaria's experience was exemplary of what ultimately occurred throughout the bloc. In December 1972 the Bulgarian government resolved to raise the standard of living of its average citizen, primarily by increasing wage levels. Within a few years this policy created a considerable inflationary overhang, as the Bulgarians had little on which to spend their savings. Sofia consequently sought to expand opportunities for its citizens to travel, participate in winter sports, and engage in tourism. Bulgaria also increased its imports of consumer goods, planned to constitute 15 percent of all imports by 1975 and 20–25 percent during the 1976–80 five-year plan.[50] This, the government felt, would make up for Bulgaria's failure to produce sufficient quantities of these goods itself. The result was an unprecedented expansion of consumerism in Bulgaria, fueled by a sharp increase in light industrial imports. This pattern of events was repeated throughout the bloc in the course of the early and mid-1970s.

Ironically, despite the new appreciation of consumer demand, the production of light industrial goods actually declined in Hungary, Bulgaria, and the USSR during this period. Moreover, even in those countries where consumer goods production did expand, the start of this growth can often be traced back to the 1966–70 five-year plan, casting into doubt the credit widely given to post-1968 economic integration measures.[51] Indeed, the growth rate of heavy industrial goods actually outstripped that of consumer goods production everywhere except Hungary during the period 1961–74.[52]

Consequently, the defining element of goulash communism was not the growth of light industrial production but the import of Western consumer goods into socialist markets. The problem this presented, of course, was that import-driven consumerism carried a heavy financial cost. While the added expense posed few difficulties for the Soviet Union, the same could not be said for the comparatively resource-poor nations of Eastern Europe. Lacking the natural endowments of the USSR and specializing in agriculture or low-quality industrial output, the East Europeans could not sustain a steady influx of consumer imports on the strength of their exports alone. Instead, they began to assume mounting debts. While receiving loans from foreign governments, both Soviet and Western, East European communists also availed themselves of the commercial wealth flowing out of the Middle East during the oil crisis. The theory was that foreign investment, both private and governmental, would enable a modernization of their industrial base and an expansion of exports. This, in turn, would facilitate repayment of debts while continuing to fund necessary consumer imports. For a time the policy seemed to be remarkably successful. A combination of Soviet trade subsidies and Western credits enabled the region's communist governments to garner an unprecedented degree of political stability.

As communist governments came to rely on consumer satisfaction to provide political stability, Western concerns and sensibilities acquired a new currency in the region. The days of relative political and economic autonomy were gone forever. Meanwhile, the failure to make light industrial production an abiding priority seriously jeopardized the quest for communist legitimacy. "Despite the concern expressed by the leaders of

Eastern Europe to increase the supply of consumer products, priority continues to be given to heavy industry and producer goods," one contemporary account warned. "Rising expectations will be difficult to satisfy under these conditions."[53]

Although Eastern Europe's collective hard currency debt rose by 480 percent during the period 1973–78, Czechoslovakia was the only state in the bloc whose industrial stock benefited from the foreign loan program. Moreover, even Czechoslovakia failed to translate this modernization into increased export earnings. In the meantime, agricultural exports, one of the region's traditional contributions to the world market, declined as governments sought to keep shops full and consumers well fed. Investment funds either went to pay for consumer imports or simply dissipated in the hands of inefficient or corrupt bureaucratic managers. Consequently, the long-run impact of goulash communism was an economic catastrophe in Eastern Europe that invited indebtedness, ensured wide-scale industrial obsolescence, and constrained exports.

Moscow, meanwhile, gave no indication that it recognized the increasing reorientation of Eastern Europe away from the CMEA toward Western markets, focusing instead on the oil crisis and the degree to which it had apparently crippled capitalist economies. Soviet scholars bragged that the CMEA was able to cover the needs of its constituents, "thanks to a coordinated policy in the development of the energy and raw materials branches of industry."[54] In reality, it was Moscow's willingness to provide oil and gas to the bloc at deeply discounted prices that insulated the region from the international crisis. Hardly the stuff of mutual economic benefit, bloc stability would last only as long as the Soviets agreed to forgo lost profits. For the time being, though, it ensured a dependence on Moscow that complemented the overall direction of Soviet economic consolidation in Eastern Europe.

Bilateral Treaties Formalizing Socialist Internationalism

The central political development of the 1970s that formed the backdrop for the Budapest Reform Program and the Comprehensive Program was the formalization of socialist internationalism in a web of new bilateral treaties. While multilateral agreements within the WTO and CMEA took on a greater visibility after 1968, bilateral treaties, particularly those concluded with Moscow, remained the backbone of socialist unity. Beginning with the Soviet-Czechoslovak treaty of 1970, these bilateral conventions legally recognized the claims of socialist internationalism and, by association, its doctrine of limited sovereignty.

The first of these, signed between the Soviet Union and Czechoslovakia in May 1970, underscored the "internationalist duty of the socialist countries" to defend the "socialist gains" and strengthen the "unity and solidarity of all countries of the socialist commonwealth." Prague and Moscow pledged to work toward an "international socialist division of labor," "socialist economic organization," and the "all-round cooperation" of state and public organizations. A commitment to the cause of integration employed terms rarely seen outside the context of Soviet nationalities questions. It spoke of the "drawing together [*sblizhenie*] between the peoples of the two states." In the Soviet ideological glossary the term "sblizhenie" was linked indissolubly with the notion of *sliianie*, or "merger."[55] In the early years of Soviet Russia, the progress from sblizhenie to slianie became the ideological foundation for the unification of the various Soviet republics into a single state. Its new use in formulating a long-term outlook for the future of Soviet–East European relations was fully consistent with Moscow's continuing process of integration and consolidation. Efforts to establish a trend toward supranational integration were already afoot in the WTO and CMEA, as previously noted. The assertion of sblizhenie in a formal diplomatic agreement was the political component of this effort. Its importance was reflected in Brezhnev's 1976 statement at the Twenty-fifth Congress of the CPSU: "This process of gradual sblizhenie of the countries of socialism is quite certainly being developed these days as in conformity with natural law."[56]

However, Moscow faced an uphill battle for broader recognition of this process among its remaining allies. As usual, the Romanians proved the most resistant. Consequently, the Soviet-Romanian treaty of July 1970 differed considerably from the earlier Soviet-Czechoslovak agreement. In military relations, for instance, mutual defense obligations were limited to external threats, a formal recognition of Romania's right to opt out of any internal police actions such as the 1968 invasion of Czechoslovakia. References to the defense of socialist gains were conspicuously absent. Nor was there any mention of any sort of sblizhenie between the USSR and Romania. Although the treaty did voice support for "socialist internationalism" in general, it was careful to reassert each nation's "sovereignty and national independence, equality, and non-interference in . . . internal affairs." Romania's bilateral treaties with the other nations of the bloc reflected similar reservations on integration.[57] Those concluded between the other allies and Moscow occupied a variety of points along the political continuum between the Soviet-Czechoslovak and Soviet-Romanian agreements.

By 1977, with Eastern Europe increasingly beholden to the Soviet economy, bilateral relations between Moscow and its client-states took on a far greater degree of uniformity. With the wholesale rewriting of the Soviet constitution, a series of new bilateral agreements were concluded, all of which formally recognized the principles of socialist internationalism in bloc integration. All contained passages bearing considerable resemblance to the earlier formulations of the Soviet-Czechoslovak treaty of 1970. In place of largely unspecified references to an "international socialist division of labor" which had appeared in earlier agreements, the new treaties clearly committed their signatories to the objectives of the 1971 Comprehensive Program. These included deepening economic integration, as well as the once hotly debated policy of coordinating national economic plans. All contained references to the process of sblizhenie said to be drawing the bloc into ever closer relations. All affirmed the internationalist duty to protect the "historic gains of socialism."[58] The conclusion of the 1977 bilateral treaties accordingly marked the pinnacle of Moscow's efforts to impose orthodox uniformity in the bloc. Soviet and East European national interests were now formally linked under the umbrella of socialist internationalism. Behind the facade of increasing pluralization and democratization, the Soviet Union had achieved a degree of control unprecedented in the post-Stalin era.

The Tide Begins to Turn

From Moscow's vantage point, the first half of the 1970s was a time of relative stability and economic success. The Twenty-fourth Congress of the CPSU set the tone for the decade in 1971 with its official encouragement of stability, integration, and cooperation in bloc relations. Mass media faced new state controls after the onset of East-West détente and subsequent expansion of dissident activity. Concern for economic stagnation rose in general, while consumerism became a universal answer to the question of popular legitimacy. Within the ranks of the common people, well-stocked stores fostered hope that Eastern Europe would soon enjoy a considerable improvement in its overall standard of living. Meanwhile, in foreign policy, Moscow secured its borders with China during the 1970s, while coordinating international protests against America's presence in Vietnam.

Nevertheless, despite these apparent successes, the Soviets continued to face resistance from within the international socialist movement at awkward moments. The story of its efforts to coordinate a voting bloc at the Conference for Security and Cooperation in Europe (CSCE) in Helsinki is a useful case in point. Begun in November 1972, the "Helsinki process" brought together all the European states (except Albania and the Vatican) with Canada and the United States for talks intended to finalize the political boundaries of postwar Europe. For three years the talks continued, becoming the touchstone of East-West détente. They involved a great deal of give-and-take, negotiation, and compromise on both sides of the Iron Curtain, with issues divided thematically into three groups, or "baskets," for discussion.[59] The first basket, "Security in Europe," provided for confidence-building measures in security and disarmament and determined ten principles on which all international relations ought to be based.[60] Basket 2 addressed cooperation in economics, science, and technology, including promotion of tourism and migrant labor. Basket 3 established standards on humanitarian rights, including the free movement of information and ideas, as well as educational exchanges. The Final Act, signed during a summit convened 30 July–1 August 1975, pledged to continue the CSCE process in the future.[61]

Preparatory talks between Moscow and its political allies on the eve of the Helsinki conference revealed an immediate divergence of opinion on ideological issues. Independent parties, including the Yugoslavs, Romanians, and some West Europeans, were determined to resist what they saw as a return to the Soviet control of the 1930s when Moscow had ruled over the Communist International with an iron hand. A common political line, they argued, "must be based upon genuine consensus; it must emphasize the principles of autonomy, equality, and noninterference in interparty relations (with the important corollary that no special status should be accorded to the CPSU); it must contain no criticism of any party, present or absent (e.g., the Chinese); it must deal with political action, not with ideology; and in any case it was not to be binding upon any party."[62]

The challenge to Moscow's leadership was direct and uncompromising. Western observers began to speak of the possibility that a rift was developing in the international communist movement. Soviet commentators admitted to this possibility themselves in the face of undeniable defiance.[63] The dispute complicated plans to hold a pan-European conference of communist parties prior to the signing of the Helsinki Accords. Moreover, when the communist conference finally did convene in Berlin on 29–30 June 1976, Moscow's prospects for leadership on the continent were on the verge of a crippling setback.

Leading the attack on Soviet primacy were the West European "Eurocommunists," led by the Spanish, Italian, and French communist parties. In contrast to Soviet bloc traditions, the Eurocommunists asserted the importance of respecting both human rights and the independence of each national party. In the run-up to the June conference, the head of the Spanish delegation asserted in an interview, "As far as we are concerned, this process of preparation is helping to reemphasize, in a new form, a very important principle: the independence of the Communist parties."[64] Later, at the conference itself, Enrico Berlinguer, leader of the Communist Party of Italy (PCI), explained that Western European communists desired a nonideological state of democratic organization, political pluralism, autonomous trade unionism, religious freedom, and freedom of expression.[65] The Eurocommunist position amounted to a rejection of Soviet-bloc socialism in favor of West European social democracy, complete with its so-called bourgeois liberties. Consistent with this position, the Euro-communists were even willing to work "within the framework of the international alliances" of Western Europe, including NATO and the European Community (EC), organizations traditionally seen as hostile to the cause of world communism.[66]

The Eurocommunist opposition had a profoundly negative impact on socialist unity. By the close of the Berlin Conference, the Soviets had lost a great deal of prestige within the international movement. Indeed, the final communiqué of the conference made no mention of socialist inter-nationalism. The Eurocommunists simply would not agree to it. As a member of the French delegation commented, "Conferences like this one do not appear to us to correspond any longer to the needs of our time. Since any elaboration of a strategy common to all our parties is hence-forth absolutely ruled out, it seems opportune to seek new forms of col-lective encounters, more lively, flexible and effective." Of course, Moscow attempted to paint a good face on the limited agreements that did come out of the conference. "It was a noteworthy milestone in the development of international solidarity, an event of enormous significance in the his-tory of the international communist movement," declared one Soviet observer.[67] Ironically, he was correct. The meeting had been a landmark in the history of socialist unity. But its significance lay in its crippling blow to the cause of internationalism in the socialist camp, not in its successes. It illustrated that the very principle on which Moscow had built its con-solidation initiative—proletarian/socialist internationalism—remained unconvincing to many parties within the communist movement itself. As such, the meeting implicitly defined the limits of Moscow's leadership both practically and ideologically.

Another unanticipated consequence of the Berlin fiasco lay in its strengthening of ties between the Eurocommunists and the emerging ranks of East European dissidents. As noted above, because ideological differences had delayed the conference by a year, it had failed to coordi-nate a common line on the question of human rights for use in the negotiation of the 1975 Helsinki Final Act. Western efforts to pin down the Soviets on the issue of human rights had been the central challenge that Moscow had to face during the long Helsinki process. The Kremlin's main objectives had been to secure Western recognition for the political status quo in Europe for the first time since World War II and to expand East-West economic cooperation. As for the "third basket" of human rights agreements, former Soviet ambassador Anatoly Dobrynin admits, Moscow simply sought to diminish the significance of these negotiations, "for it still believed humanitarian issues to be domestic matters."[68]

Consequently, Dobrynin continues, "when the treaty was ready and the third basket emerged in its entirety before the members of the Politburo, they were stunned. . . . Many had grave doubts about assuming international commitments that could open the way to foreign interference in our political life."[69] Foreign Minister Andrei Gromyko defended the wording that his team had negotiated with the West, noting that "the main goal for the Soviet Union for many years had been the general recognition of the postwar boundaries and the existing political map of Europe, which would amount to a major political and propaganda victory for Moscow." He also underscored the extensive economic benefits that basket 2 promised the Soviet bloc. Ultimately, he concluded, the Soviet government alone would define what constituted interference in its domestic affairs. "We are masters in our own house," he reportedly told the rest of the Politburo.[70]

He could not have been more wrong. Soon after the Helsinki Final Act was signed, the third basket became what Dobrynin astutely calls the "manifesto of the dissident and liberal movement, a development totally beyond the imagination of the Soviet leadership."[71] Activists in the Soviet Union and Eastern Europe responded to the Final Act by organizing groups intended to hold the bloc's communist parties to their promises on human rights. Inasmuch as the dissidents shared considerable common ground with the Eurocommunists, the two groups supported each other well into the 1980s. As Lucio Lombardo Radice of the PCI Central Committee observed in December 1976, "It is inevitable that the socialist opposition to socialist governments in the East . . . should link itself at least ideologically with Eurocommunism. It is equally inevitable that the Italian, French, or Spanish 'model' should become a political problem for the ruling communist parties of Eastern Europe."[72]

After the 1976 Berlin Conference, Eurocommunists not only provided ideological support to dissidents but occasionally even defended them against state persecution. The French Party, for example, successfully secured the release of the Soviet dissident Leonid Plyushch, while the PCI supported Polish dissident Jacek Kuron's call to investigate the Polish United Workers Party on behalf of striking Polish workers.[73] The true significance of this development would become clear in the course of the following decade when reformist communist factions and dissident movements such as Solidarity in Poland would be instrumental in turning the region away from the Soviet model altogether.

Another factor that compromised the stability of the Soviet bloc in the late 1970s was Moscow's decision to raise the price of oil in transactions with Eastern Europe. Since 1958 the Soviet Union had been providing oil to most of its East European allies at prices that changed every five years to reflect the average price of oil on the world market during the preceding five-year period.[74] By 1974, this formula found the Soviets providing oil to the bloc at an 80 percent discount from world market prices. When the price of oil shot up on Western markets during the Organization of Petroleum Exporting Countries (OPEC) crisis, the opportunity costs of these subsidies also increased exponentially. This left Moscow with a dilemma. The interests of its own stalled economy demanded that Moscow seek to recoup some of the losses it was suffering in Eastern Europe. More expensive oil would presumably prompt the East Europeans to economize on oil use, while discouraging excessive dependence on Soviet subsidies. But the Soviets also wanted to cushion the impact of the world oil crisis on the socialist economic community.[75] A choice had to be made between preservation of Soviet national interests and subsidization of East European communism, two elements long considered free of any contradictions.

Despite its persistent assertion of socialist internationalism, Moscow chose to protect its own interests, introducing a special price increase in 1975, after which the price of oil would change *every year* based on the average of the previous five years. The result was a doubling of the price for Soviet oil on the CMEA market by 1976.[76] Ten-year, low-interest loans were made available to help the socialist allies cope with the new pricing formula.[77] Nevertheless, higher prices for Soviet oil came as a shock to the East European client-states. While reaching nowhere near the price of oil on the world market, this inflationary surprise drastically altered East European terms of trade with the Soviet Union. Moreover, as the decade wore on and elevated world prices began to work their way into the Soviet pricing formula, the East Europeans watched these terms decline further.

Within only a few years, the oil shock seriously exacerbated the deepening economic crisis in Eastern Europe. By 1978, Western lenders had begun to worry about their investments in the Soviet bloc, and thus borrowing conditions became tighter. Repayment periods shortened and interest rates rose, leaving Hungary, Poland, and the GDR on the verge of a crippling liquidity crisis.[78] East European governments were forced to slash imports and introduce austerity measures. In an effort to cushion consequent shocks in domestic markets, exports declined as well. The result was a steadily descending economic spiral in every nation of the Soviet bloc that threatened to sabotage regional stability.[79]

Afghanistan

The tug-of-war between socialist internationalism and Soviet national interests surfaced again at the end of the 1970s in the Soviet decision to invade Afghanistan. Its new energy policies notwithstanding, the Soviet leadership had spent the 1970s proclaiming an unshakable commitment to the political stability of its socialist allies. The national interests of the USSR, according to socialist internationalism, were indistinguishable from those of its allies. A threat to communist rule in any one nation constituted a threat to the entire community. For many years after the invasion of Czechoslovakia, this type of rhetoric had cost the Soviets very little. Local communists had managed well on their own by manipulating the carrot and stick of consumerism and police action. It was not until Afghanistan joined the socialist camp at the end of the 1970s that the Brezhnev Doctrine finally faced its next proving ground.

The communist government of Nur Mohammad Taraki took power in Afghanistan with a bloody coup on 27 April 1978.[80] The takeover came as a complete surprise to the Soviet leadership, which learned first about it from a Reuters news agency bulletin. The coup plotters had chosen not to inform the Soviets in advance, fearing that Moscow might have tried to discourage the move in light of the weak revolutionary situation in Afghanistan. Former first deputy foreign minister Georgii Kornienko writes that this is precisely what Moscow would have sought to do, "inasmuch as from the Marxist point of view there was no revolutionary situation in the country and relations between the Soviet Union and Afghanistan under King Zahir-shah, and later under Daoud, . . . were on the whole friendly."[81] That impression was later borne out shortly after the coup when the Afghan communist party, the People's Democratic Party of Afghanistan (PDPA), split along factional lines, with Taraki and his deputy prime minister, Hafizullah Amin, freezing their onetime ally, Babrak Karmal, and his followers out of power.

Once the takeover had taken place, Kornienko continues, Party ideologues in Moscow, particularly Mikhail Suslov and Boris Ponomarev, immediately came to regard Afghanistan as one of the socialist countries, similar in its developmental pattern to socialist Mongolia.[82] A few months after the coup, on 5 December 1978, Moscow signed a twenty-year treaty of friendship and cooperation with Taraki and began providing extensive assistance and advisory personnel to Afghanistan. By early 1979, Taraki's harsh domestic policies had engendered open resistance from Islamic freedom fighters, the mujahideen, and a civil war erupted.

Moscow's initial reaction to the start of hostilities in Afghanistan was to increase deliveries of weapons and other material in support of the government forces there. Consistent with the principles of socialist internationalism, its first concern was for the preservation of communist rule that Taraki warned was in grave danger from mujahideen "counterrevolutionaries." On 17 March, as the fate of Afghan communism seemed to hinge on the outcome of an ongoing battle in Herat, Taraki requested Soviet military intervention.[83] Foreign Minister Andrei Gromyko encouraged his colleagues on the Politburo to consider the proposal seriously. He urged "under no conditions can we lose Afghanistan. We have already lived in peace and good neighborliness for sixty years. So if we lose Afghanistan now, it will drift away from the Soviet Union, and that will deal a serious blow to our [foreign] policy."[84] For Gromyko, the fate of communist rule in Afghanistan was closely tied to Soviet national interests. Perceived as part of the global ideological struggle with the West, the collapse of communism in Afghanistan would amount to a major setback for the Soviet Union.

Inasmuch as military establishments are accustomed to contingency planning, the Soviet Ministry of Defense had already considered a number of invasion scenarios for Afghanistan and was ready to act as soon as the Kremlin gave the word. The one remaining question facing Soviet leaders was whom their forces would be fighting when they got to Afghanistan. That is, would the common people side with the opposition against the Red Army?[85] Importantly, world opinion does not appear to have given the Soviets pause at this stage of the discussion. Kosygin certainly recognized there would be states that would oppose the efforts of Taraki's government to reassert its authority in Afghanistan. Among them would likely be Iran, Pakistan, China, and the United States. Nevertheless, there was little concern for how these or other nations might respond to a Soviet intervention. "We must work out a political decision keeping in mind that we will be labeled the aggressor," Yuri Andropov counseled, "but this notwithstanding, under no circumstances can we lose Afghanistan."[86] Of course, Taraki would have to issue a public request for assistance in order for Moscow to justify the invasion. "Without an appeal from the government of Afghanistan," Andrei Kirilenko underscored, "we cannot send in troops." When Kosygin next spoke with Taraki, he would have to make this abundantly clear. Moreover, Taraki would have to alter his military tactics to stop the indiscriminate shelling of rebel-held positions. This was fast turning the nation's religious activists into enemies of the government and would consequently frustrate the Soviet military effort.

With these cautions in mind, Kosygin summed up the Politburo's conclusions. "We are all of one mind," he said, that "we cannot let Afghanistan go. Hence, we must work out first of all a political document and use all possible political means to help the Afghan government to fortify itself, to offer assistance, which we already noted, and, as an extreme measure, to consider a resolution of military action."[87] As Vladimir Bukovskiy observes, this decision was taken ten months prior to NATO's decision to place tactical nuclear weapons in Europe and without any discussion of acquiring warm-water ports in the Arabian Sea.[88] It proceeded entirely from the ideological and political considerations of defending communist rule in Afghanistan. The socialist community was to be preserved no matter how the international community regarded Soviet aggressiveness. Moscow would not allow Afghanistan to drift out of its sphere of influence.

Within twenty-four hours, however, the Soviet position shifted dramatically. The day after the Politburo reached its initial decision, Kosygin spoke again with Taraki about the prospect of Soviet military intervention.[89] Taraki repeated his request for Soviet assistance but shied away from a high-profile invasion. Rather, he suggested that Soviet soldiers of Central Asian extraction slip into Afghanistan wearing Afghan uniforms. After all, he pointed out, Iran and Pakistan had been sending Islamic volunteers into Afghanistan in this way to join the mujahideen. Kosygin complained that Taraki was oversimplifying the question. Of particular concern to Moscow was the matter of whom the people of Afghanistan would support. The Iranian revolution, which had taken place only months earlier, had seen the people pull together against the United States and all others who proclaimed themselves defenders of Iran. Surely the same response was possible, if not likely, from the people of Afghanistan in the face of a Soviet invasion.

Taraki's response radically altered the Kremlin's willingness to consider sending in troops. If Soviet armed forces did not support government defenders in Herat, he argued, communism rule would soon collapse in Afghanistan because of its lack of any significant popular support.[90] While the government continued to have faith in its own armed forces, it had become increasingly isolated. From Moscow's perspective, this changed everything. As KGB chief Andropov noted to his colleagues on 18 March, "We have to consider very, very seriously the question of in whose name we will send troops into Afghanistan." It was not clear that Afghanistan was developing along socialist lines, he pointed out. Religion continued to wield enormous influence in Afghan society. Nearly the entire rural population remained illiterate, and the national economy was backward even by Soviet standards. If the only way that the Afghan revolution was to succeed was at the end of a Soviet bayonet, then it was not worth saving. It simply did not merit the military risk.[91]

Gromyko agreed completely with Andropov. Reversing his earlier position, the foreign minister returned to the question of against whom Soviet forces would be fighting. Certainly it would be against the entire Afghan people, he said. If Taraki's government could not attract any popular support, then Afghanistan was not yet ripe for communist revolution. Moreover, he continued, Moscow would be putting a lot on the line if it launched an invasion. The Kremlin's earlier nonchalance regarding international opinion had been a mistake. Everything the Kremlin had been working to achieve in terms of reducing international tensions, reducing armaments, and maintaining détente with Western political leaders would be undermined. China would also have ammunition to use against the Soviet Union in branding it an aggressor nation. Consistent with UN statutes, the Afghan people would be legally justified in requesting assistance from other nations on the grounds of collective defense against aggression. Finally, the war in Afghanistan was an internecine conflict into which the Soviet Union had not been officially invited. "In a word," Gromyko concluded, "what we have here is an affair in which the government of the country, as a result of serious mistakes it has made, has found itself not on top of things and not enjoying the necessary support of the people."[92]

Andropov advised that the Politburo reconsider its decision concerning the dispatch of troops into Afghanistan. "I think we should tell Taraki directly," he said, "that we support all of their actions, that we will supply the [material] assistance which we agreed upon yesterday, and that under no circumstances can we send troops into Afghanistan."[93] The other members of the Politburo were in full agreement. Once again, in Brezhnev's absence, Kosygin summed up the conclusions of the discussion. "In a word," he said, "we are not changing anything concerning aid to Afghanistan with the exception of the dispatch of troops."[94] The Soviet leadership remained willing to provide whatever material support Taraki might need to consolidate his power. But that was the length to which socialist internationalism extended in this case. Protection of Moscow's military assets and international prestige took precedence over the preservation of communist rule in Afghanistan, at least for now. During a secret visit by Taraki to Moscow on 20 March, the Soviet leadership adhered strictly to this line, arguing that dispatch of the Red Army to Afghanistan would only further complicate the situation there. In the end, Brezhnev offered what seemed to be the final word on the issue. "We have looked at this question from all sides," he told Taraki. "We have carefully considered it, and I will say directly: this should not be done."[95]

In the months that followed, the Kremlin leadership remained committed to avoiding a war in Afghanistan, notwithstanding repeated requests from the Afghan leaders to reconsider.[96] Although several hundred Soviet troops were dispatched to safeguard the helicopters and other material provided to the Afghan communists, a full-scale intervention remained out of the question.[97] Consideration of the issue always returned to the negative consequences an invasion would bring down on the Soviet Union and its foreign policies. At the top of Moscow's new list of concerns stood the fate of the disarmament process, the SALT II treaty, and détente with the West. An invasion, the Soviets now recognized, would devastate East-West relations, thereby upsetting many Soviet accomplishments of the past decade.[98] Détente had prompted an evolution in the way Moscow perceived its interests at home and abroad. No longer would it intervene strictly on the basis of principle as it had in Czechoslovakia, especially to save a communist coup in the Third World.

Ultimately, however, Moscow was prompted to reevaluate its interests in Afghanistan. In September 1979, fighting broke out within the Afghan communist party itself. Taraki was killed in a battle with forces loyal to Deputy Prime Minister Amin, who promptly assumed control in Kabul. Moscow was not at all pleased with Amin's rise to power. His policies were far more repressive than Taraki's, particularly within the Afghan communist party itself. In his bid to consolidate power, Amin proved willing both to shoot dedicated communists and to negotiate with supporters of the "counterrevolution." Worst of all, he made a number of overtures to the United States and its allies on the grounds of maintaining a "more balanced [foreign] policy" toward the West. This point caused serious apprehension in the Kremlin, as it opened the door to increased American influence over Afghanistan. Although Amin continued to agree with Soviet policy recommendations, he also alleged that Soviet agents had made attempts on his life in mid-September. Moreover, he and his close advisers continued to hint at the possibility of Soviet repression occurring in Afghanistan.[99]

In short, Amin earned the reputation of being a loose cannon in the socialist camp. Not only did he dare to flout Moscow's authority but he also threatened to give Western governments a foothold on its southern borders. Analysts in the KGB gradually began to speculate that the Afghan leader was an operative of the CIA.[100] While it is clear that no one was suggesting as much in September 1979, one can see from what suspicions this rhetorical accusation might have stemmed.

International developments outside of Afghanistan also seemed to be changing for the worse in the fall of 1979. The presence of U.S. warships in the Persian Gulf, along with widespread rumors that Washington was planning an invasion of Iran, seriously concerned Soviet military leaders, particularly Defense Minister Dmitrii Ustinov. A U.S. invasion of Iran, Ustinov felt, "would seriously alter the military-strategic situation in the region to the detriment of the interests of the Soviet Union. If the USA allowed itself something like this tens of thousands of kilometers from its territory and in the immediate approaches to the borders of the USSR, then why should we fear to defend our position in neighboring Afghanistan?"[101]

On the basis of these new considerations, October 1979 found the Soviet Politburo reexamining the question of intervention in Afghanistan. Without a doubt, the Soviets felt, the future of the "April revolution" that Taraki had initiated in 1978 was now in jeopardy. Amin's policies promised to become very disadvantageous to traditional socialist development in Afghanistan. Moreover, in an apparent bid to free himself from dependency on Moscow, Amin had extended his hand to Washington and other Western powers. In Kornienko's words, it appeared that "Afghanistan could be 'lost' for the USSR and the Americans could become based there, urged on by their 'loss' of Iran."[102]

In this case, Soviet national interests merged quite naturally with the international "responsibility" to defend communist rule in Afghanistan. No longer was it simply a matter of principle. By 1979, Amin's overtures to the United States redefined the issue as a strategic challenge along the defensive perimeter of the Soviet Union. As the Russian historian R. A. Medvedev observes, "A frightening picture was emerging in the minds of the Soviet leaders of American rockets targeted at the Soviet Union from Afghan territory."[103] Former CIA analyst and State Department political adviser Raymond L. Garthoff offers an additional consideration along these same lines. Garthoff points to the fact that Afghanistan shared a twenty-five hundred kilometer border with Soviet Central Asia, a region with an ethnic profile very like that found in Afghanistan. Moreover, as recently as 1978 there had been a Tajik riot against the Russians living in Dushanbe, a city just to the north of the Afghan border. Garthoff writes that "after the Soviet intervention [into Afghanistan] the KGB chief in Muslim Soviet Azerbaijan, Major General Zia Yusif-zade, publicly linked the situation in Afghanistan (and Iran) with alleged American intelligence efforts to exploit Islam in the Muslim republics of the USSR."[104] Moscow therefore had both national security and domestic stability in mind as it chose to flout international condemnation and chance an encounter with the bulk of the Afghan people in support of an admittedly bogus "revolution."

After trying for weeks to establish control over Kabul, the Soviet leaders finally decided in December 1979 to go ahead with the invasion.[105] The largest Soviet invasion force amassed since World War II stood ready for action in the Central Asian and Turkistan military districts, including fifty thousand reservists summoned to active duty. In Kabul, the Soviets had already assembled a force of five hundred men for storming the presidential palace. Indeed, Amin had inadvertently orchestrated his own removal in early December with a request that Moscow secretly dispatch the troops to Kabul for his protection.[106] As in Czechoslovakia, the objective of the invasion would be to replace the ruling government with "healthy forces" loyal to Moscow. Soviet troops would then assist the Afghan army to crush the rebel mujahideen and reestablish communist control throughout the country.

Official approval for the invasion came on 12 December in a resolution titled simply "Concerning the Situation in 'A.'" From what little is written in this document, one can discern that the proposal to send in troops originated with Andropov, Ustinov, and Gromyko. Kornienko suggests that the timing of the decision was not coincidental. That same day a special meeting of NATO foreign and defense ministers had approved the stationing of U.S. medium-range nuclear missiles in Europe. "In other words," Kornienko writes, "the conclusion that had once carried a lot of weight in the eyes of the Soviet leaders, to the effect that the dispatch of troops would have negative consequences on Soviet relations with the West, seemed undermined by the fact that these relations had become strained even without it—there was nothing much to lose, as they say."[107] The decision received the approval of all voting and nonvoting members of the Politburo and was then allowed to proceed.[108]

On 25 December 1979 a massive airlift began transporting Soviet troops into Kabul, with one plane landing every three minutes at Kabul National Airport.[109] Prior to their arrival, the Soviet ambassador had informed Amin that Moscow was dispatching additional forces to Afghanistan as "fraternal assistance." Amin reportedly "welcomed this decision and ordered the general staff of Afghanistan's armed forces to cooperate in every way possible with Soviet troops."[110] Two days later, Soviet special forces seized control of the presidential palace. Amin was killed in the siege and subsequently replaced by the pro-Soviet Babrak Karmal. Before long, seventy-five thousand Soviet troops had joined government forces in the battle against the mujahideen to support the new regime Moscow had installed.

The initial experience of the Soviet troops in Afghanistan hardly suggested what was to follow in the months and years ahead. "As the troops moved in," Garthoff points out, "there were more Soviet casualties from road accidents than from combat."[111] However, it was not long before the Soviets realized that the war in Afghanistan was going to become an intractable military morass. Political rifts between the different wings of the PDPA continued to hobble an Afghan army already crippled by a widespread desertion problem. Soon after the intervention, Garthoff notes, the once 145,000-strong army had shrunk to about a quarter of that size.[112] One high-ranking member of the KGB later confessed, "We made two major errors of judgment: we overestimated the willingness of the Afghan army to fight, and we underestimated the upsurge of Afghan resistance."[113] In February 1980, Soviet troops stepped out of their supportive role and began mounting offensive operations of their own against the opposition forces.[114] By the spring of that year, Soviet forces required as many as 80,000 troops to hold major cities and towns and to protect the Afghan army from mujahideen attacks.[115] (By 1985 this number would rise to 108,000.)[116] As feared, Soviet forces found themselves at war with the vast majority of the Afghan people in support of an unpopular government. "By 1981," Kornienko writes, "for most if not all of the Soviet leaders capable of thinking realistically it had become clear that there could not be a military resolution of the problem in Afghanistan."[117] Time would demonstrate the truth of this early realization. When the

Soviets left Afghanistan in 1988–89, their forces had suffered casualties of 14,453 killed, 53,753 wounded, and 415,932 left seriously ill.[118] Moscow had found its Vietnam.

The diplomatic fallout of the invasion also exceeded Moscow's worst expectations.[119] Détente with the United States collapsed altogether, along with all hope for the ratification of the SALT II arms control agreement. American president Jimmy Carter proclaimed that the invasion posed the greatest threat to international peace since World War II. He declared an embargo of U.S. grain against the Soviet Union and organized an international boycott of the upcoming 1980 Summer Olympic Games, scheduled to be held in Moscow. The grain embargo created particularly serious economic difficulties for the Soviets, as they were forced to procure the shortfall elsewhere at an estimated $1 billion more than American imports would have cost. Shortages of meat and dairy products resulted from the lack of grain for fodder, prompting worker unrest in the Soviet cities of Gorky and Togliatti.[120] While not as thoroughly ruptured, Moscow's ties with Western Europe also suffered in the wake of the invasion. Moreover, because the Soviet economy had become reliant on imports of Western technology, the collapse of relations with the United States increased the relative importance of Western Europe in Soviet foreign policy.[121] Before long, this reliance would become an important check on Moscow's freedom of action in Eastern Europe, as the Polish Solidarity crisis would illustrate.

The invasion carried similarly damaging possibilities for Eastern Europe. At least three Soviet bloc nations, Poland, Hungary, and Romania, were very uneasy about the new war in Afghanistan. They feared the economic consequences that would follow the full collapse of relations with the West. These were among the most indebted of the East European states, and they were most concerned with the continuing availability of Western credits. When the fallout between Washington and Moscow put Wall Street off-limits to the entire bloc, these East European governments turned to Western Europe for financial assistance.[122] Here too, then, West European influence expanded over Soviet bloc affairs on the eve of the 1980s.

It is clear from the assessments of the top Kremlin leaders themselves that the consequences of Afghanistan seriously compromised the interests of the Soviet Union. Speaking in 1983 with United Nations secretary-general Javier Perez de Cuellar, Yuri Andropov admitted that the invasion of Afghanistan had "seriously damaged Soviet relations first of all with the West, secondly with the socialist nations, thirdly with the Islamic world, fourthly with other nations of the 'Third World,' and finally, fifthly, it was extremely debilitating for the internal situation within the USSR, for its economy and society."[123] Lest one suppose that these were platitudes intended as propaganda in the West, Kornienko notes that, later in June 1983, Andropov met with Afghan leader Babrak Karmal and informed him that he "should not count on an indefinitely long presence of Soviet troops in Afghanistan, that it was necessary to carry out the expansion of the government's social base through political methods."[124] Kornienko believes that, had Andropov lived, Soviet troops would have been removed from Afghanistan years before Mikhail Gorbachev ultimately accomplished this difficult task in 1988–89.[125]

At the start of the 1980s, however, the eventual conclusion of the war in Afghanistan still lay shrouded in the mists of time. What Moscow did know was that with its domestic economy in turmoil and its international prestige on the rocks, the Soviet Union would have to scramble to salvage its authority in the world socialist system. The forum chosen for this effort was the April 1980 Paris Conference of European Communist Parties. Soviet objectives in Paris were the same as they had been in Berlin four years earlier. In the name of socialist unity and cooperation, the Soviets sought to expand their consolidation policy to include all the communist parties in Europe. Essentially, then, the Paris Conference was an attempt to reverse the embarrassment Soviet initiatives had suffered in Berlin. Additionally, amid the ruins of East-West détente, the meeting was an attempt to enlist the assistance of the Western parties in salvaging relations with their respective countries.

Rifts in the Eurocommunist movement gave Moscow good cause to believe that its efforts would meet with more success than they had in 1976. The French Party had defected from the Eurocommunist camp, while the Spanish Party was now splintered and weak. Hence, the threat of Eurocommunist unity, which had so thoroughly torpedoed Soviet intentions in 1976, promised to be an insignificant concern in Paris. Ironically, with the Eurocommunists fractured and weak and the Romanians, Yugoslavs, and some West European parties refusing to attend, the Paris Conference only emphasized the lack of cooperation and integration within the socialist camp. Moscow's efforts to assert internationalism in the communist world were unraveling as of early 1980. The absence of Romania, a full member of the CMEA and WTO, from the Paris Conference was a particularly embarrassing example of this centrifugal process at work. If unity meant lining up behind the Soviet Union, the alleged primus inter pares of the socialist commonwealth, then perhaps unity was not the ideal that many of its allies desired.

Conclusion

As the CMEA oil shock and invasion of Afghanistan illustrate, Moscow itself occasionally distinguished between Soviet interests and those of its socialist allies. Historians have tended to view the invasion of Afghanistan as evidence that the Brezhnev Doctrine was alive and well in Soviet foreign policy at the end of the 1970s. Moscow's choice to prop up communism in Afghanistan despite the many consequences Soviet leaders knew would follow an invasion indicates that this perspective is basically sound. Yet the marriage of Soviet national interests and socialist internationalism in the December 1979 decision to go to war is important to note. No longer were Soviet troops intervening on "principle, independent of external circumstances," as they had in 1968. Instability in the socialist camp was no longer sufficient to merit military action, as Moscow's reluctance in March 1979 demonstrated.

By the early 1980s the Soviet bloc was in political, social, and economic disarray. Nations were increasingly forced to attend to their own internal crises, which resulted in a failure to manifest in practice the idealistic commitments of bloc integration. As Robert Hutchings observes, "The grandiose aims associated with socialist internationalism had been rendered increasingly irrelevant by the pressing domestic and international challenges of the day."[126] The Soviet consolidation drive that had begun in the wake of Czechoslovakia had come to depend on the political and economic stability that existed under détente. With its virtual collapse after 1979, this stability proved to have been founded on sand. The bilateral treaties of 1977 had expressed powerful sentiments of unity and cooperation, touting the Kremlin's new definition of socialist internationalism. Communist governments in Eastern Europe had enjoyed a measure of popular support, nurturing Moscow's desire to avoid another military intervention within the bloc. By the end of the decade, however, as the East European debt crisis worsened, Moscow's own oil policy aggravated the instability facing its allies. Soviet foreign policy further complicated East European access to badly needed Western funds with its intervention in Afghanistan. Notwithstanding the availability of low-cost Soviet loans, communist political stability began to fade in lockstep with the region's declining standard of living.

Brezhnev's policy of consolidation based on the principles of socialist internationalism had not enabled the bloc to escape its reliance on Soviet military intervention to guarantee communist rule. At this point, however, Moscow was able to reflect not only on the experience of Czechoslovakia but also on the war in Afghanistan. The former had established a definition of counterrevolution that regarded any departure from the political, social, or economic norms of bloc unity as cause for an allied intervention. But the latter had shown that socialist internationalism and Soviet national interests were not always compatible. Hence, Moscow would soon be forced to reconsider its commitment to communism in Eastern Europe and the costs it was willing to incur for it.

4

★

Socialist Poland—
Asset or Liability?

Listen: take steps this very hour that Russia
Be fenced by barriers from Lithuania;
That not a single soul pass o'er the border,
That not a hare run o'er to us from Poland,
Nor crow fly here from Cracow.
—Alexander Pushkin, *Boris Godunov*

A DECADE AFTER THE INVASION OF CZECHOSLOVAKIA, the Soviets were still working to "normalize" communist rule in Eastern Europe. As détente took a turn for the worse, Moscow asserted bloc cohesion as increasingly vital in managing the decline of commercial relations with the West. But the cause of bloc cohesion continued to face challenges sharply at variance with Moscow's normalization goals. Nowhere was this more visible than in Poland. Nearly a decade of mismanaged growth policies, ballooning national debt, and rising consumer expectations had brought the Polish nation to the point of a popular revolution by 1979. Its Polish United Workers Party (PZPR), under First Secretary Edward Gierek since 1970, had sought to base its credibility on comparatively liberal economic and social policies aimed at winning popular support. However, widespread corruption and misuse of international investments gradually undermined Gierek's efforts, giving rise instead to a nationwide surge of indignant anticommunism. Poles turned from officialdom in all its manifestations and began to create a semilegal civil society, free from Party censors or state controls.

A number of momentous events served to galvanize this popular rejection of state authority. The 1978 election of the Polish Karol Cardinal Wojtyla to the papacy fired the furnace of national pride in Poland more than any event since the capture of Kiev in 1920. As the new pontiff undertook a policy of extensive engagement in Eastern Europe, Poles responded with a renaissance of Catholic activism that quickly spilled over into surrounding states, including the Soviet Union. Meanwhile, nationalists successfully rallied popular emotion around the memory of Polish martyrs executed by the Soviets in World War II. Unforgotten and unforgiven, this crime of a bygone era still loomed large in the public imagination, explicitly discrediting Soviet power and its allies in the Polish government.

With popular dissent and national consciousness on the rise, consumer disaffection began to nurture grassroots trade unionism. Preoccupied with managing what had become a full-scale economic crisis, Poland's communist leadership appeared almost extraneous to Polish society. A sense of "us" versus "them" unified the masses. It had been clear who "they" were since the establishment of communist rule after World War II. By 1980, civil solidarity had finally prompted people to see themselves as a unified "us" as well. In short, a decade of blocwide "normalization" found Poland on the verge of an economic and sociopolitical crisis.

From Moscow's point of view, the emergence of nationalist activism in Poland was the most disturbing facet of these developments. Its openly anti-Soviet tone clearly repudiated the goal of bloc unity and stood to erode socialist internationalism as the ideological cornerstone of Soviet control in Eastern Europe. More important from Moscow's perspective, Polish nationalism, through its links to Catholic activists, threatened to ignite smoldering opposition in traditionally nationalist areas of western Soviet Union. Archival records from this period indicate that Soviet policymakers were becoming acutely aware of their own domestic vulnerability along these lines. While a rejuvenated national consciousness certainly posed problems for Poland's communist government, it threatened disaster in the multinational USSR.

Moscow therefore acted to protect itself from the potentially ruinous tribulations of its neighbors. Driven by a growing realization of Soviet weaknesses, both at home and abroad, Brezhnev and his associates began seriously to reconsider Soviet commitments in Eastern Europe. Gradually eclipsing their concern for the fate of the "socialist commonwealth" was an abiding realization that they had their own domestic problems to worry about, problems that were likely to prove desperate in the long term. While still in its early stages, this redefinition of Soviet national interests involved a reluctant acceptance of extended instability in Eastern Europe that had no parallel in the history of bloc relations. On the threshold of the Polish Solidarity crisis, the full implications of these changing perceptions remained latent. Public pronouncements and private discussions continued to address the fate of communist rule in Poland and elsewhere in the region as intrinsic to Soviet international commitments. Increasingly, however, East European realities would test these commitments, forcing Moscow to choose between domestic stability and socialist internationalism.

Saddling the Bucking Cow

From the very start of the postwar era, Poland stood out in the Soviet bloc as an aberration. Joseph Stalin himself is reputed to have said that introducing communism in Poland was like "fitting a saddle to a cow."[1] In a

Socialist Poland—Asset or Liability?

regional development scheme characterized by uniformity, socialist Poland gradually emerged as something of a nonconformist. One of the cornerstones of the communist system, collectivized agriculture, was never implemented in Poland on a wide scale. Alongside the fully nationalized heavy industrial sector coexisted a nation of small private farmers in flagrant violation of the Leninist "norms" imposed throughout the rest of the communist world. The spiritual and cultural identity of the Poles was no less unique, as evinced by the powerful role of the Catholic Church in Poland. Thanks to its central place in the Polish national identity, the Church under communist rule was permitted to continue both its liturgical *and* its instructional activities. This was a notable exception to the established Soviet practice of "guaranteeing" the freedom to believe while prohibiting so-called religious propaganda. Such exclusive economic and religious indulgences meant that life in socialist Poland continued to involve a measure of the prewar "bourgeois" ethos traditionally seen as hostile to the development of a communist system.

Additionally frustrating for Moscow was the degree to which this "cow" could act like a raging bull at the most inopportune moments. The first incidence of widespread popular demonstrations against communist rule in Poland occurred on 28 June 1956 when workers at the Stalin engineering works in Poznan took to the streets to protest the nation's worsening economic situation. Bearing placards demanding "bread and freedom," the protesters clashed with Polish security forces in two days of street fighting that left at least fifty-three people dead and hundreds injured. Contributing to the riots had been a sense of popular discontent with the slow pace of de-Stalinization in Poland under First Secretary Edward Ochab. Though put down, the protests created a ripple effect in the bloc, encouraging pro-reform Hungarians, on the verge of their own historic revolution, to believe that Stalinism was being toppled throughout the bloc.[2]

In the months that followed the Poznan riots, the Ochab government collapsed under pressure for reforms. The PZPR subsequently turned for leadership to the more nationalistic Wladyslaw Gomulka, who insisted that the Kremlin remove all Soviet officers and advisers from the Polish military, Party, and government.[3] Facing what appeared to be a subversion of Soviet control in Eastern Europe, Khrushchev flew to Poland in mid-October and burst without warning into an extraordinary plenary session of the Polish Central Committee. "We have decided to intervene brutally in your affairs," he announced, "and we will not allow you to realize your plans." Moments later the Poles received reports of Soviet tanks on "training maneuvers" advancing toward Warsaw. Soviet warships had also entered Poland's territorial waters along the Baltic coast. Refusing to be publicly intimidated, Gomulka demanded that Soviet forces in Poland return to their bases. At Khrushchev's orders the tanks halted but did not withdraw. Negotiations ensued, during which the Soviet leader threatened the Poles with impatient outbursts such as "It doesn't matter what you want; our view is such that we will have to restart the intervention."[4]

Although defiant, Gomulka negotiated desperately to avoid an armed confrontation with the Soviet Union. He offered assurances that Soviet concerns about Poland leaving the bloc were groundless. All Warsaw sought was control over Polish domestic affairs, he explained, in keeping with Khrushchev's own bloc policy.[5] "Poland needs friendship with the Soviet Union more than the Soviet Union needs friendship with Poland," Gomulka pleaded. "Without the Soviet Union we cannot maintain our borders with the West. We are dealing with our internal problems, our relations with the Soviet Union will remain unchanged. We will still be friends and allies."[6]

This was a face-saving solution that Khrushchev was willing to accept in light of what promised to be a very dangerous alternative. Since the start of the crisis, Soviet-born marshal Konstantin Rokossovsky, Poland's minister of defense, had been informing Khrushchev that the Polish army would very likely resist any attempt by the Soviet Union to impose a solution by force.[7] In fact, General Wladyslaw Komar, newly appointed commander of the Internal Security Corps, had deployed troops in defensive positions around Warsaw when Soviet forces showed signs of advancing. Meanwhile, Navy Admiral Jan Wisniewski had ordered Polish ports closed to all Soviet ships.[8] Polish society also turned out in a series of anti-Soviet rallies and discussed the creation of a Worker's Committee for the Defense of Warsaw.[9] Clearly a showdown over Poland would not prove easy for Soviet forces.

Wisely, therefore, Khrushchev chose to accept Gomulka's assurances for the future of Soviet-Polish relations. At the October 24 CPSU Politburo meeting in Moscow, Khrushchev reflected that "finding a reason for an armed conflict now would be very easy, but finding a way to put an end to such a conflict would be very hard."[10] A later communiqué of November 1956 and the subsequent treaty of December 1956 set down more defined restrictions on the stationing of Soviet troops in Poland, stipulating Soviet recognition of and respect for Polish state sovereignty.[11]

The Polish October, as these events came to be known, demonstrated the limits of genuine diversity within the socialist community under Khrushchev. In the end, Khrushchev permitted Gomulka's independent initiatives on such matters as collectivization, provided that Poland remained nominally socialist and a loyal member of regional alliance structures. In Hungary, the Polish October prompted calls for a return to the multiparty politics and military neutrality of the immediate postwar era that quickly crossed over Moscow's ideological tolerance line. Though willing to entertain socioeconomic diversity, Khrushchev would not permit a reversal of communist rule or weakening of the Soviet military presence in Eastern Europe.

From the perspective of the Brezhnev leadership, Khrushchev's gamble on Gomulka turned out to have been well placed. Of course, Moscow made repeated attempts to encourage tighter adherence to blocwide socialist norms. As leading Gorbachev adviser Georgii Shakhnazarov later reflected in his memoirs, "There was literally not a single meeting at the highest level when Brezhnev, fed by his advisers, did not suggest to the Polish leader that it was necessary to liquidate Gomulka's 'mistaken decision' and undertake comprehensive collectivization in order to eliminate what Marxist conformists regarded as a black mark on the reputation of the socialist system."[12] Nevertheless, although the Polish leader never did implement wide-scale collectivization, he proved a far more heavy-handed conservative than his earlier reputation suggested.

Consequently, Poland's later domestic crises of 1968, 1970, and 1976 did not elicit any serious consideration of military intervention from Moscow. In 1968, amid the heady reforms of the Prague Spring, it was Polish intellectuals, rather than workers, who initiated antigovernment demonstrations. When a classic Polish play was closed for having offended the Soviets, members of the Polish intelligentsia demanded that the Party put an end to censorship and restrictive cultural policies. Though a nationalist wing of the PZPR turned out in support of the demonstrators, Minister of Internal Affairs Mieczyslaw Moczar used force and arrests to end the three-day protest. Exploiting the fact that many of those involved were Jewish, the government then embarked on an anti-Zionist campaign against prominent Jews in science, education, and the arts. Many chose to emigrate rather than continue to face persecution and intolerance.[13]

Later unrest in 1970 and 1976 resulted from the nation's mounting economic difficulties and the unwillingness of Polish workers to compromise their basic standard of living. This standard had been guaranteed in part by a freeze on the prices paid for staple food products, which had insulated Polish consumers from inflationary pressures since the early 1960s. These low prices virtually guaranteed an economy of permanent shortages, but when the staple products did appear in the shops, they were very affordable. Ultimately, however, the government had to address the profound imbalances that this economy of perpetual shortage had created. From Gomulka's perspective, December 1970 appeared to be an auspicious time to do this. Early that month his government had signed a treaty with Bonn that normalized Poland's relations with the Federal Republic of Germany. It was an important achievement and was very popular among the Polish people. For the first time since World War II, both East and West Germany effectively recognized the postwar borders of Poland. The question remained, though, of how much support it would generate for Gomulka. American political analyst J. F. Brown writes that "Gomulka and his advisers may well have grossly miscalculated the effect of the normalization treaty by assuming that the popular euphoria would be such as to enable them to get away with both the price increases and their timing."[14] Hence, on 13 December 1970, only weeks before the Christmas holidays, Gomulka increased staple food prices by 36 percent.

Immediately, strikes and riots broke out all over the country. Thousands of shipyard workers protested outside the regional offices of the Communist Party in Gdansk. The Polish Party responded decisively, dispatching 25,000 additional troops to the Baltic Coast—13,000 to Gdansk and 12,000 to Szczecin. Additional forces were sent to Kraków, Poznan, Wroclaw, and Warsaw. In total, the forces employed against the strikers in Poland are reported to have numbered up to 61,000 troops. They were accompanied by as many as 1,700 tanks and other heavy equipment.[15] Under orders from Defense Minister Wojciech Jaruzelski, the Polish troops participated in nearly one hundred repressive operations during the 1970 riots, beginning literally on the first day of the crisis. At this point, the army limited its use of firepower to dropping tear gas on unruly crowds such as that surrounding the Gdansk regional party offices. However, on 15 December, Gomulka and his leadership decided to instruct the army to use live ammunition.

Defense Minister Jaruzelski was responsible for seeing that this decision was carried out. His troops were first to fire a warning shot into the air, followed by another on the pavement in front of the protesters. If this failed to have the desired effect, then they would fire directly into the crowds.[16] As a consequence of Jaruzelski's order, on 16 December Polish soldiers shot and killed scores of striking workers outside the Lenin Shipyard in Gdansk.[17] Soon the violence spread to the cities of Gdynia and Szczecin as well.[18] On 17 December, a day now known as "Black Thursday in Gdynia," soldiers with machine guns opened fire on a crowd of civilians, killing dozens.[19] That same day the government decided to declare a state of emergency along the Baltic coast that would have militarized all harbor activity. Rumors began to spread on 18 December that the army was planning to take over all enterprises. Full-scale martial law appeared to be on the horizon.

Ironically, it was Moscow that undermined Gomulka's plans for a wholesale military crackdown in Poland. Although Gomulka insisted on calling the crisis an emergent counterrevolution, the Kremlin refused to endorse his diagnosis.[20] Only two years after the Prague Spring, Moscow was unwilling to apply this definition indiscriminately to all instances of civil disturbance. Defense Minister Jaruzelski was already doing all that he could to preserve the morale of his troops who were now being asked to fire on their own countrymen. As Andrew Michta observes, "For the Russians, the continuing use of Polish soldiers against civilians was fraught with the imminent danger that another key Northern Tier, non-Soviet Warsaw Pact army would thereby be rendered operationally useless. Coming only two years after the disintegration of the Czechoslovak army in the aftermath of the 1968 invasion, such a state of the Polish army would have seriously weakened the Warsaw Pact position in Central Europe."[21] Add to this the prospect that admission of a counterrevolution in Poland could well have necessitated a massive Soviet military intervention in Poland, again only two years after the invasion of Czechoslovakia.[22] Moscow was hardly going to chance these kinds of repercussions over the question of price stability in Poland when negotiation with the workers was still a viable option.

Lacking Soviet support, Gomulka's government collapsed, and Poland's new communist leader, Edward Gierek, sought to offer concessions that would bring the crisis to an end. On 24 January 1971, Gierek appeared at the gates of the Warski Shipyard in Szczecin, a city in which more than thirty factory strike committees had effectively brought economic life to a standstill. For nine hours Gierek met with strike leaders, many of whom were Party members, and listened to complaints about the official trade unions and their inability to protect worker interests. At the end of the meeting, Gierek promised to redress their grievances, with their assistance; to which the workers shouted enthusiastically, "Pomozemy! [We will help!]" A similar session held the following day at the Lenin Shipyard in Gdansk brought the crisis to an end.[23] In February 1971, Gierek repealed the price increases and promised that future hikes would occur only after consultation with the workers. Attempts to present a cooperative state posture were quite effective in the short run, and many workers felt they could trust their new leader.

However, the years that followed the events of 1970–71 were a time of considerable expectation but little institutional change. Workers who had pledged to help Gierek felt betrayed later that year when the Sixth PZPR Party Congress in December 1971 failed to take any steps toward creating independent Polish trade unions. Many, like the young Lech Walesa, then still an electrician at the Lenin Shipyard, would reflect on this betrayal in their efforts to assert the Solidarity independent trade union movement a decade later. Their disappointment notwithstanding, Gierek's government did initiate a number of significant economic changes in the early 1970s. Economic plan indicators were reduced, implying less centralized control, and new pay incentives were offered to workers for accomplishments on the job. To stimulate production in agriculture, the government took efforts to consolidate private land holdings, to distribute state-owned land to the peasantry, and to increase the availability of small agricultural machinery needed to work those holdings.

The problem was, as Brown points out, "these suggestions, though pointing in the right direction, were timid and unimaginative in terms of the expectations aroused and the demands of the economic situation."[24] The initial steps soon lost any kind of real momentum. Within a year or two, around the same time as Moscow pressured Hungary to abandon its New Economic Mechanism, Gierek also began to turn from support for small peasant farming to favor socialized agriculture. Writing about this coincidence, Brown again notes, "It was later confirmed that the change of both policy and personnel [in Hungary] was due chiefly to Soviet pressure. It is not unreasonable to assume, therefore, that what happened to Hungary also happened in Poland."[25] By 1974, the retreat from reform in Poland had become unmistakable.

Nevertheless, Gierek's efforts to introduce more incentives into the wage system had only worsened an already desperate Polish economy. Timothy Garton Ash observes that "in 1976 basic food prices were still mostly pegged to the 1967 level, while the regime continued to shower money on to the workers."[26] The resultant inflationary imbalance prompted Gierek to hazard another price hike on 25 June 1976. As in 1970, the escalation of prices, by an average of 60 percent, caught most of the country completely by surprise. Poland's legislature, the Sejm, itself did not know about the increases until hours before it was to pass them.[27] Once again worker riots broke out. Workers from the Ursus tractor factory outside Warsaw proceeded to the train tracks and stopped the Paris-Moscow express train. In Radom, a crowd set fire to the local Party headquarters.[28] A popular rumor circulating through Poland at the time suggested that Defense Minister Jaruzelski had refused to call out the army in support of a politically isolated Gierek and that the government was accordingly forced to retreat.[29] Visibly shaken, Prime Minister Piotr Jaroszewicz appeared on television within twenty-four hours to announce that the price hikes would be suspended until a "broad consultation with the working class" could be convened. With the crisis thus defused, the secret police then moved in to arrest those who had participated in the strikes.[30] Polish society had shown once again that it simply would not accept the sacrifices needed to stabilize the national economy on communist terms.

Writing later in 1981, the Polish economist Josef Paestka observed: "The lesson of 1976 had a meaning from which but one conclusion can be drawn—it doesn't pay to take unpopular decisions. Second, the government had neither the understanding nor the readiness to begin real dialogue with society and to win the approval and agreement of the people for the adoption of unpopular measures. This required a change of relations between the government and society that was based on democratization. There was no readiness for this."[31] Whereas the Party viewed the national crisis as an economic issue, Paestka and others recognized that it had evolved into a sociopolitical problem as well. However, Gierek was unprepared to adjust the Party's fundamental relations with society. What followed the events of 1976 therefore took the form of cultural and social half-measures intended to win popular support for the regime. The civil society that took shape as a result of these measures was to prove far more politically vocal than Gierek could ever have anticipated.

Civil Society and the Flowering of Polish Dissent

The emergence of a powerful civil society in Poland, so important in shaping the transformation of Eastern Europe in the 1980s, drew its strength from an unprecedented alliance of Polish workers and intelligentsia that came together after the events of 1976. Previous crises had shown that the government was always able to crush the resistance of a divided society. In 1956, 1970, and 1976 it had been worker protests; in 1968 it was demonstrations by the intelligentsia. Andrej Wajda's monumental film about the events of August 1980, *Man of Iron*, paints this societal division in sharp hues, with leading labor figures refusing to turn out in support of their sons' student protests in 1968. This situation began to change with the creation of the Workers' Defense Committee (Komitet Obrony Robotnikow, or KOR), a group of intellectuals committed to the legal defense of roughly one thousand workers arrested after the 1976 disturbances. In addition to its legal efforts, KOR also organized assistance to the families of those arrested and lobbied the government for their reinstatement at work.[32] The result was a growing sense of solidarity among formerly disparate elements of Polish society in opposition to the Party leadership.

The Workers' Defense Committee also involved increasing numbers of intellectuals in a growing dissident movement. One of its most vocal leaders, a young historian named Adam Michnik, articulated what would become one of its central political visions in a 1976 essay titled "A New Evolutionism." Communist revisionism, he argued, had proven unequal to the task of challenging the status quo under socialism. The 1968 invasion of Czechoslovakia had finished it off as an influential force in bloc politics. Thereafter, demands for fundamental systemic reform were seen as likely to bring in the Soviet Union and thus always resulted in concessions to the state by revisionists and intellectual "neopositivists." Michnik therefore proposed a process of extracting concessions on basic civil liberties. He called this effort "new evolutionism" and directly linked its success to a renewed "faith in the power of the working class, which, with a steady and unyielding stand, has on several occasions forced the government to make spectacular concessions."[33]

Intellectual dissent featured in numerous independent publications enjoying wide circulation after 1976. By the end of the decade, two uncensored literary magazines and at least ten uncensored opinion journals were published in Poland. The nation's largest underground press, Nowa, issued roughly one hundred works between 1976 and 1979, including a Polish translation of George Orwell's classic attack on communism, *Animal Farm*.[34] Meanwhile, at least twenty underground papers regularly reached more than twenty thousand monthly subscribers.[35] These publications offered a channel for dissenting intellectuals to develop a political culture free of communist propaganda and state control.[36]

During these formative years, the new association between workers and intellectuals generated a meaningful discussion of free trade unionism. In September 1977 a number of KOR collaborators organized the unofficial newspaper *Robotnik* (The worker), intent on circulating the idea among Polish workers. Two months later, in November 1977, a former Radom worker named Leopold Gierek (no relation to the Polish first secretary), working with *Robotnik*, formed Poland's first unofficial free-union cell.[37] By 23 February 1978, a coalition of workers and intellectuals founded the Committee of Free Trade Unions in Katowice, arguing that unity would enable resistance to state and Party exploitation of Polish workers.[38] Another Committee of Free Trade Unions for the Baltic Coast came into existence in April. Among its earliest members was Lech Walesa, fired in 1976 from the Lenin Shipyard in Gdansk for speaking publicly about similar initiatives.[39] On May Day 1978, this new committee issued a statement condemning official unions as "a subordinate instrument for the organized exploitation of all social groups." Free trade unions were necessary, it continued, to defend "the economic, legal and human rights of all employees."[40]

With the support of such workers as Walesa, the trade union movement took on an increasingly political tone aimed at transforming the face of socialist Poland. Meeting in Szczecin on 11 October 1979, the Founding Committee of the Free Trade Unions of Pomorze issued the "Charter on Workers' Rights," which read in part, "Only the independent trade unions, which have the backing of the workers whom they represent, have a chance of challenging the authorities; only they can represent a power the authorities will have to take into account and with whom they will have to deal on equal terms."[41] Through statements such as these, KOR set itself on a collision course with Polish state authorities, not to mention Moscow. Almost a year before the outbreak of strikes on the Baltic coast, an organizational leadership was already in place, complete with a progressive agenda for social reform in Poland. Mobilized by publications such as *Robotnik*, the civil alliance between workers and intelligentsia was becoming a powerful alternative to official trade unions and other state-sponsored institutions.

Meanwhile, vocal elements of the PZPR contributed to the scrutiny of Gierek's domestic policies. By the late 1970s, many Polish communists considered themselves members of a "loyal opposition" dedicated to the reform of the Polish Party and state. One such group of a hundred Polish Party intellectuals calling themselves Experience and Future (DiP) convened a discussion circle in November 1978. Though it enjoyed official sanction at its inception, the group lost regime support after its initial proceedings proved too critical of existing policies. It nevertheless released a public assessment of Poland's deepening crisis titled "Report on the State of the Republic" in May 1979.[42] Receiving no official reply, the group released another study, "Which Way Out?," in May 1980.[43] Both DiP reports called for sweeping reforms, including genuine trade unions, limited censorship, and rule by the Sejm rather than the Party.

Challenging the Party's exclusively economic assessment, the DiP defined Poland's national crisis as largely sociopolitical. Simply stated, there was not enough trust between the authorities and the public to generate the popular support needed for effective policies. More astonishing, the DiP asserted that this mistrust originated in the Party's own mismanagement and corruption.[44] "Sooner or later," participants predicted, "there will be an explosion of the kind we have already experienced. It is a matter of secondary importance what specific event will trigger it. . . . The social cost of such explosions is always high. But in this case it could exceed anything we have experienced since the war."[45]

These ideas featured highly in grassroots debates held nationwide as PZPR primary cells prepared for the Eighth Party Congress, scheduled for February 1980. A broad assault began within the Party on elite privileges, on the shortage of consumer goods and supplies, and on the regime's absurd Propaganda of Success. When the congress finally convened, the Party leadership attempted to quiet rather than act on these critiques. In a symbolic nod to reformers, Gierek promised more socialist democracy and fired the unpopular prime minister, Piotr Jaroszewicz.[46] However, these token concessions did nothing to redress the serious issues plaguing Polish society, prompting many to conclude that the government was either unwilling or unable to take the steps necessary to solve Poland's domestic crisis.

Economic Spiral

Certainly the most palpable sign of trouble in Poland during the late 1970s was the nation's deepening economic crisis. In a region plagued with economic decline, the Polish predicament was especially formidable. The riots of 1970 had demonstrated that the pursuit of economic growth at consumer expense had dangerous sociopolitical consequences.[47] Yet the alternative of basing government legitimacy on a rising standard of living soon proved equally perilous. Investment funds borrowed from Western creditors were channeled into industries for which there was little demand on the international market, such as steel, shipbuilding, and petrochemicals. Polish indebtedness swelled as a 69.5 percent increase in gross investment for the 1970–75 five-year plan far outstripped the planned target of 38.5 percent. Meanwhile, an uncontrolled rise in real wages, up 36 percent rather than the planned 17 percent, seriously destabilized the nation's price base, creating powerful inflationary pressures.[48]

Had this expansion rested on a solid base of increasing productivity, it might have realized Gierek's most ardent hopes. But productivity from fixed assets rose only 8.8 percent for the 1970–75 period, notwithstanding the much greater rate of investment.[49] This imbalance did not go unnoticed. By the second half of the decade, the failure to translate investments into increased productivity featured prominently in public discussions. A roundtable discussion in the Party journal *Politika* on 9 April 1977 lamented that "in this particularly favorable period of our development we have failed to create lasting conditions for improvement of the level of efficiency in our economy. We failed to direct the social pressures for higher wages into a process in which higher wages are generated by raising efficiency."[50] While fixed prices preserved the Polish economy from inflation, rising wages guaranteed excess demand and chronic shortages of subsidized goods in the marketplace. Over the 1970–75 period, for example, the growth of monetary income in Poland increased by 90 percent, whereas retail sales rose by only 77.9 percent.[51] The attempt to address these shortages with increased consumer imports saw Poland turn from a net exporter of food to a net importer, with a $4.5 billion deficit in foodstuffs alone for the period 1970–80.[52]

This state of affairs degenerated to the brink of disaster after 1975 when Gierek tried to manage the ballooning national debt by slashing imports. With demand already exceeding the existing supply of consumer goods, the reduction of imports created a serious distribution crisis in the nation's shops and markets. Queuing for food lasted for hours before and after the average working day, the black market flourished, and corruption ran rampant. Public indignation welled up and jeopardized the Party's newly won legitimacy. As one Polish journalist wrote at the time, "People keep asking what's become of all the coal, where these quantities of meat have gone to, and where we ship all those goods if the railroad men and dockers are (as we are told) continually overfulfilling their plans. This list of goods now but never previously in short supply grows longer. Matches are in short supply, drugstores don't carry basic medicines, there is no cotton wool, and buying a newspaper is becoming something of a problem. Nobody tries to explain it rationally, and silence begets anxiety and suspicion."[53] Under such conditions, deterioration of public support for the system was probable, if not inevitable. Writing in 1981, Paestka concluded that "the immediate cause of the emerging sociopolitical conflicts was the danger of a decline in the standard of living among a broad layer of society."[54]

As Gierek worked to balance Poland's economic and social woes, Soviet policies seemed calculated to frustrate his efforts. Notwithstanding the difficulties facing East European societies themselves, Moscow insisted that Poland and its other bloc allies grant expensive economic assistance to countries such as Vietnam, Ethiopia, and Angola. Added to this burden was the sharply rising cost of Soviet oil and gas products within the CMEA, along with Moscow's pressure for participation in Soviet investment projects. The combination was deadly for Poland. Its balance of trade with the Soviet Union had favored Poland at the start of the decade, a factor that had contributed to the growth of national income during the 1970–75 period. By 1979, the balance had shifted toward Moscow, producing a payments crisis in Poland.

The Brezhnev leadership, meanwhile, showed little appreciation for the sociopolitical difficulties facing Gierek's government after it was forced to slash consumer imports. At the Moscow CMEA summit of June 1979, Soviet hosts encouraged even deeper austerity measures to cope with the growing cost of petroleum deliveries.[55] Deeply indebted bloc nations, including Poland, that had undertaken intensive growth programs earlier in the decade suddenly found themselves unable to increase either productivity or inputs. While both Hungary and East Germany had to cope with this problem, Poland's crisis was in a class by itself, owing to the unprecedented scale of Gierek's economic mismanagement.[56] At the end of 1979, Poland's external debt amounted to more than $17 billion, with interest payments of roughly $2 billion due in 1980. Efforts to curtail the assumption of new debt did take hold after 1977; however, despite sharp reductions in imports, the goal of balancing trade with the West by 1980 remained far out of reach.[57] In 1979, seeking to buy time, Gierek's government reportedly considered renewing Poland's membership in the International Monetary Fund where it might receive debt assistance on better terms. But the Kremlin is said to have flatly rejected the notion, once again exhibiting a lack of appreciation for the serious problems confronting Poland's leadership.[58]

By 1980, the debt crisis had advanced to a point where drastic action had to be taken to avoid Poland's declaring national bankruptcy and defaulting on Western loans. In the absence of any extraordinary outside support, the Polish economy was unable to navigate the perilous shoals of criminal mismanagement and consumer demand. The failure of Gierek's import-led growth to lift flagging levels of national productivity resulted in staggering shortfalls for the 1976–80 five-year plan. Gross investment stagnated in 1977 and 1978 and declined 8 percent in 1979. Agricultural production grew at a rate of only 2.8 percent for the period 1976–79, far short of the planned 12–14 percent. Perhaps most important, following a number of years of declining growth rates, Poland's national income actually fell by 2 percent in 1979. This marked the first year of negative growth in the nation's postwar history.[59] The descent continued into 1980, finishing at a net loss of 4 percent for that year.[60]

The deepening economic crisis prompted many of Poland's leading scholars to question the foundations of socialism itself. Could such a highly centralized system ever hope to pull Poland back from the edge of the abyss? "Centralized direction and bureaucratization of socioeconomic relations," wrote Josef Paestka, "paralyzed people's activity and initiative, reducing their role to that of executors rather than coauthors of progress."[61] Paestka also argued that Poland's "crisis of authoritarian methods of management" failed to realize its objectives because it did not consider the realistic capacities of the Polish economy or the logical results of its operation. The reformist tone of his remedy was striking. "To stop this practice," he wrote, "we must either undertake profound political and economic changes or declare political bankruptcy." Indeed, Paestka speculated that the government might have pursued its import-led growth policy despite deepening indebtedness simply in order to ensure a short-term grip on power. If this was the case, he declared somewhat mutedly, the government deserved to be condemned both politically and morally.[62]

Such sharp critique of Poland's past government policy and support for political, as well as economic, reforms were not unusual in and of themselves. Many members of Poland's intellectual elite, Party and non-Party alike, took advantage of the looser censorship in the late 1970s and early 1980s to speak openly about national salvation. What was especially significant about Paestka was the degree to which his writings appear to have influenced a change in Soviet perceptions vis-à-vis Poland's sociopolitical conditions. At the height of the Solidarity standoff in 1981, the official Soviet publishing house Progress issued a Russian-language translation of Paestka's treatise *The Polish Crisis, 1980–1981: What Led to It and What It Teaches*. Progress narrowly distributed the work by special list to leading Soviet policymakers, research institutes, and a select number of closed library collections throughout the USSR. Its subsequent impact on high-ranking members of the Party and state administration was significant.[63]

If Paestka provided the top Soviet leadership with its first serious exposure to the complex nature of the Polish crisis, it was not the fault of Moscow's own East European specialists. Indeed, the leading institute within the Soviet Academy of Sciences charged with reporting to the Central Committee on East European affairs had been warning of an impending political and economic crisis in Poland since the events of 1976. Under the direction of Oleg T. Bogomolov, a former member of the Central Committee staff, the Institute of the Economics of the World Socialist System (IEMSS) pushed in vain for the Kremlin to give Warsaw a green light on necessary reforms.

However, as one frustrated IEMSS scholar later observed, the reports of Bogomolov's institute often got no further than the Polish section of the Central Committee, owing to their apparently radical, pro-reformist, tone.[64] Thus, while top Polish and Soviet specialists agreed on the importance of sweeping reforms in Poland, the Moscow leadership continued to assert an unsympathetic, inflexible, and antireformist position. Gierek consequently had little room in which to maneuver when dealing with the growing costs of Soviet energy imports, investment in the Soviet Union, and international aid to the Third World. Though Poland was on the verge of defaulting on its national debt, Soviet priorities focused on increasing revenues and maintaining an assertive position vis-à-vis the West. Ironically, by 1980, this conflict of interests had begun to fuel popular criticism of the socialist system in Poland.

John Paul II, Ostpolitik, and the Soviet Response

Although the Soviet leadership displayed very little apprehension over Poland's economic difficulties before late 1980, it was very anxious about the growth of Polish nationalism. This was particularly true after the 1978 election of Poland's Karol Cardinal Wojtyla to the papacy. The tight link between Roman Catholicism and the Polish people is readily apparent, even to the casual observer, in the proliferation of tombs, banners, and national monuments that fill Poland's churches and cathedrals. During the partition of Poland from the late eighteenth century until 1918, these constant reminders nurtured the idea of a common Polish national identity. The election of a Polish pope in 1978 fired old nationalist sentiments in a wave of religious activism unprecedented in postwar Poland. While further galvanizing Polish civil society, they threatened to spark nationalist brush fires throughout Eastern Europe, including in the traditionally Catholic areas of the Soviet Union itself. Only a few months after Ayatollah Khomeini came to power in Iran, the Soviet leadership began to worry about facing a rising wave of religious activism on both its western and southern fronts.[65] A Polish pope, Foreign Minister Gromyko warned privately, could well incite his compatriots just as the Ayatollah had the people of Iran.[66] Moscow therefore regarded the pope and all Catholic activism as a challenge to Soviet domestic stability, working hard to prevent its spread into the USSR.

Agents of the Soviet KGB posing as visitors from the West had been watching Cardinal Wojtyla very carefully for years and had even tried unsuccessfully to recruit him as an unsuspecting informant. According to former KGB archivist Vasili Mitrokhin, as early as 1971 the young Polish cardinal appeared to be "the leading ideological influence on the Polish church" and a "potential threat to the Communist regime" in Poland.[67] His election to the papacy in 1978 consequently set off alarms in Moscow regarding how the new pope would address the communist system under which he had spent much of his adult life.

The Soviets did not have to wait long to find out. Prior to his election to the papacy, Cardinal Wojtyla had been planning a highly publicized pilgrimage to commemorate the nine hundredth anniversary of the death of Poland's heavenly patron, Saint Stanislaw.[68] His departure for Rome in 1978 did not alter these plans. In a Christmas message read from the pulpits of his former archdiocese in 1978, the new pope proclaimed that "using modern language we can see in St. Stanislaw an advocate of the most essential human rights on which man's dignity, his morality, and true freedom depend."[69] This statement reiterated themes central to the pope's message since the publication of his first encyclical, *Redemptor Hominis*, which implicitly linked communist excesses with the fascist crimes of the early twentieth century.[70]

Allusions like these underscored convictions in Moscow that the new pope was a danger to communism who should not be permitted to return to his homeland. In early 1979, Leonid Brezhnev shared this concern with Polish first secretary Gierek. Gierek was certainly sympathetic, having already considered refusing to grant permission for the visit. But he was forced to recognize that popular sentiment made a refusal politically impossible. "How can I not receive the Polish pope since the majority of our compatriots are of Catholic faith, and for them the election was a great feast," the Polish leader insisted. "Well, do what you want," Brezhnev reportedly told him, "so long as you and your Party don't regret it later."[71] On the eve of the pope's arrival, the PZPR sought to ensure that regrets would not be necessary by issuing an unusually defensive statement on the secular nature of the Polish People's Republic (PPR). The pope's visit would in no way alter this fact, the government warned, nor would it challenge the Party's leading role in society.[72]

As it turned out, the pope's visit did all of this and more. For nine days in June 1979, John Paul II visited six Polish cities preaching freedom from fear to his countrymen. Defying the ideological assumptions of Marxism-Leninism, the pontiff proclaimed, "Remember this: Christ will never

Socialist Poland—Asset or Liability?

agree to man being viewed only as a means of production, or agree to man viewing himself as such. He will not agree that man should be valued, measured, or evaluated only on this basis. Christ will never agree to that!"[73] Later, during a visit to the former Nazi death camps in Oswiecim (Auschwitz), he repeated his earlier equating of communist "totalitarianism" with the crimes of Nazi Germany. "Is it enough," he asked, "to put man in a different uniform [and] arm him with the apparatus of violence? Is it enough to impose on him an ideology in which human rights are subjected to the demands of the system, completely subjected to them, so as in practice not to exist at all?"[74]

The national response was euphoric. During the Pope's appearance in Warsaw's Victory Square, Poles chanted spontaneously, "We want God, we want God, we want God in the family circle, we want God in books, in schools, we want God in government orders, we want God, we want God."[75] It was an experience of profound cultural and spiritual solidarity that gave the nation a powerful sense of its separation from communist authority. In the words of one Polish political scientist, the visit was a "psychological earthquake, an opportunity for mass political catharsis."[76] Later, Solidarity spokesman Janusz Onyszkiewicz described how the pontiff's public appearances enabled Poles to recognize the strength of their burgeoning civil society. When the pope came, he helped people to see that "the 'we' was clear: 'we' are the society, and the country is ours. 'They' [the communist authorities] are just an artificial crust."[77]

During those historic days of June 1979, a profound sense of national unity and moral regeneration emerged which would have a defining influence on the events of 1980–81. As Timothy Garton Ash has observed, "There is no doubt that the communist 'power' was heading for a crisis anyway. . . . But the form the explosion took in 1980—the quiet dignity of the workers, their peaceful self-restraint, the rhetoric of moral regeneration, the ban on alcohol, the breadth of spontaneous social support—this follows from the mass experience of that fantastic pilgrimage in June 1979. It is hard to conceive of Solidarity without the Polish Pope."[78]

Polish authorities were overwhelmed by the fallout from the pope's visit. Vasili Mitrokhin recalls that members of the Polish Party, "faced with the Pope's 'ideological subversion' of the Communist regime, felt that the ideological battle had been lost."[79] On 9 September, the Soviet KGB delivered to the CPSU Central Committee a summary of a report titled "Concerning the Position of Poland in the Vatican's Strategy and Policy" prepared by the Polish Institute for the Study of Contemporary Problems of Capitalism.[80] According to the attached KGB memorandum, its central conclusion was that Poland's uniquely open religious culture was the ideological Achilles' heel of the entire socialist alliance in the battle with the Vatican. If the Church was not challenged in Poland, the report warned, it would soon begin to transfer its power to support religious activists in other socialist countries.[81]

Within two months, in early November, a pro tem commission within the CPSU Central Committee issued its own assessment titled "Concerning Measures for the Opposition of Vatican Policy in Relation to the Socialist Countries." Like the Polish study, this assessment framed John Paul's activities as a direct assault on the "sociopolitical and ideological norms of the socialist societal structure." Vatican policy, it said, particularly toward the youth of the bloc, constituted "direct interference in the internal affairs of the fraternal nations."[82]

However, what was most troubling from Moscow's perspective was the degree to which Vatican publications and radio broadcasts seemed likely to revive Catholic activism within the Soviet Union itself, particularly in Lithuania, Latvia, Ukraine, and Belorussia.[83] In these Western Republics, parts of which had been annexed by the USSR during World War II, religious identity was tightly linked to nationalist resentment of Soviet repression. It had not been long, for instance, since the dramatic self-immolation of Romas Kalanta, a nineteen-year-old Lithuanian, who died in the center of Kaunas on 14 May 1972 while crying out "Freedom to religion! Freedom to Lithuania! Russians out!" This cry rang through the streets of Lithuania for two days as thousands of protesters were put down by the Soviet army. A month later, four more people repeated Kalanta's act, eliciting a second restoration of order by authorities.[84] This sort of unrest only served to corroborate intelligence that the KGB had been receiving from Vatican operatives since 1968 suggesting that the Catholic Church sought "to shatter the Soviet Union from within with the help of ideological sabotage."[85] Religious activism, therefore, naturally elicited fears of domestic instability in the minds of the Soviet leadership.

To counter this threat, the Central Committee Secretariat sought to exploit divisions within the Church itself by invoking the international peace movement. Agents from the Polish, Czechoslovak, and Hungarian intelligence agencies had penetrated the Vatican and were believed to be in a position to influence both the Pope and the Roman congregation.[86] As one KGB report admitted, "Apart from experienced agents, towards whom John Paul II is personally well disposed and who can obtain an audience with him at any time, our friends have agent assets among the leaders of Catholic students who are in constant contact with Vatican circles and have possibilities in Radio Vatican and the Pope's secretariat."[87] By manipulating these assets, the Soviets hoped to encourage dissension within the Church that might undermine support for John Paul's anticommunist initiatives.[88]

On the domestic front, the Central Committee instructed the Soviet of

Religious Affairs of the Council of Ministers to take whatever means necessary to encourage disunity among Catholics.[89] The effort to discredit the Catholic Church in the USSR accordingly assumed a new priority. Government organs received instructions to redouble their efforts against underground Catholic movements, while underscoring the "freedoms of conscience" that supposedly existed under the Soviet constitution. Leading Soviet scholars began to contrast the writings of Catholic "extremists" with evidence that Soviet communists worked alongside "believers" in the international "struggle for peace." One high-profile article, written by Professor M. Mchelov and published that November in *Pravda*, stressed that communists "support statements by religious leaders in favor of détente, in defense of peace among peoples and against the arms race."[90] It implied that any attention to nettlesome questions of morality and religious practice in the Soviet bloc amounted to a rejection of peaceful coexistence in favor of global confrontation. State propaganda agencies such as TASS, Gostelradio USSR, Goskomizdat USSR, and the All-Union "Knowledge" Society depicted John Paul II as a reactionary bent on increasing tensions between East and West.

Meanwhile, the KGB received instructions to publish materials abroad "by special channels" that underscored the problems that such "dangerous tendencies" could create for the Church in the socialist bloc. This directive came in conjunction with special "eyes-only" instructions not revealed in the already "top secret" Central Committee memorandum. These directed the intelligence agency to work with the Soviet Ministry of Foreign Affairs "to study the question of further steps in acting against the negative aspects of the Vatican's 'Eastern Policy.'" For the time being, however, such "further steps" remained undefined.[91]

In its effort to cultivate a moderate wing within the Church, the Central Committee Secretariat even considered permitting the Vatican to appoint additional bishops in the Catholic dioceses of Latvia and Lithuania. This would have marked a significant departure in Soviet religious policy. For decades Moscow had used its veto over episcopal appointments to ensure that the number of bishops remained very low in the Baltics, thus restricting Catholic activities there.[92] Consequently, Baltic Catholics relied heavily on assistance from the Polish episcopate. The appointment of additional bishops, it was felt, would curtail Polish religious influence in favor of more moderate, Moscow-approved clerics. However, this suggestion appears to have been either unworkable or too radical for conservative Party leaders, as it was removed from the final draft of the Central Committee's report.[93] It is nevertheless a significant indicator that influential circles within the Central Committee were looking for ways to contain Polish instability at the borders of the Soviet Union. Motivated by this preeminent concern, the Secretariat sent copies of its analysis and directives to the Party central committees in Lithuania, Latvia, Ukraine, and Belorussia.[94]

The Secretariat's request for further input on this issue received a response in February 1980 from the Soviet of Religious Affairs. Titled "Concerning the Sociopolitical and Ideological Activities of the Vatican in the Contemporary Era," the new study forwarded to the Central Committee was the work of scholars from the Academies of Science and Social Sciences. Adhering to the spirit of the Central Committee's earlier analysis, the scholars' report began with a distinctly positive assessment of the pontiff's positions on international peace and disarmament. It pointed, for instance, to his support for the SALT II agreement and condemnation of the American-led boycott of the 1980 Moscow Olympic Games, both of which were consistent with Soviet interests.[95] Regarding the threat facing Eastern Europe, the scholars had little of substance to offer short of warning that the Vatican's human rights campaign threatened to drive the Church hierarchy into direct confrontation with communist authorities.[96]

What most concerned the Soviet academicians was the prospect that Catholic initiatives might ignite the flames of religious nationalism in the Western Soviet republics. In Lithuania the Church was allegedly inspiring an underground group called the Committee for the Defense of the Rights of Lithuanian Catholics. Efforts to revive the Uniate Catholic Church in Ukraine, denied legal status since 1951, appeared equally as subversive.[97] Like the Central Committee Secretariat before them, the scholars singled out the Polish clergy for its particularly reactionary brand of Catholicism, which had to be kept out of the Western Republics at all costs. They conceded that this was not easily done, as Polish clerics entered the country in the guise of tourists, only to distribute unapproved religious literature, hold illegal religious services, and encourage confrontation with Communist authorities.

No doubt unaware that it had previously been vetoed, the scholars reasserted the notion of permitting the appointment of more Catholic bishops, as well as increasing both the number of Catholic seminarians and the availability of religious materials in Lithuanian, Latvian, and German. They reasoned that rendering Soviet Catholic dioceses independent of the Polish episcopate was worth some concessions in Soviet law. Once religious activities came "above ground," local authorities could expand their control over the network of now more visible Catholic organizations. The resulting atmosphere would subsequently strengthen the hand of the government against "religious extremism," the Uniate Church, and other undesirables.[98]

As academy scholars offered their estimation of the threat posed by

Catholic nationalism, the Soviet press continued to provide a steady diet of antireligious propaganda. In May, *Soviet Latvia* ran an article by I. Grigulevich titled "Accommodating to Reality: Religion in Today's World," which for the first time directly challenged the papacy of John Paul II. A very popular piece among the propaganda elite, the article was reprinted in four additional papers between May and September 1980.[99] What was most noteworthy about the article was the degree to which it downplayed John Paul's challenge to East European communism. "The statements that the pope made during his visit to Poland," it read, "give reason to believe that he supports the line of John XXIII, who provided a kind of ideological foundation for the Church's need to cooperate with a socialist state."[100] Considering the stir that the pope's 1979 pilgrimage set off in Warsaw and Moscow, this statement must have been offered as a concession to establish terms for Soviet-Catholic coexistence. The author of the article reserved his criticism for the Vatican radio broadcasts reaching Soviet Catholics. "Certain programs are openly inflammatory in nature," he charged, "and are aimed at kindling religious fanaticism." Vatican propaganda threatened to exacerbate the problem of religious nationalism in the Soviet Union. "In condemning socialism and communism," the author wrote, 'Catholic radio broadcasters distort the socialist states' policies on religious and nationalities questions."[101]

This widely disseminated article offers a striking example of how Moscow had come to reexamine its East European commitments in the broader context of Soviet national interests. In contrast with the Polish assessment of late 1979, Soviet analysis by mid-1980 focused almost exclusively on the protection of domestic stability within the Soviet Union. After witnessing the Vatican's ideological offensive in the pontiff's native land, Moscow fully expected the Church to extend its initiatives from Poland into the other nations of the region. This perception informed a defensive response on the part of Soviet policymakers and scholars who sought to isolate the Western republics from the religious explosion engulfing East-Central Europe.

When affairs in Poland moved toward a boiling point in the summer of 1980, this matter would take on a new importance as Moscow's efforts to contain the Polish labor crisis reflected its earlier struggle with religious nationalism. On 16 September 1980, in the wake of the Polish Gdansk Accords, a committee composed of the heads of the departments of propaganda, foreign political propaganda, and international affairs finally submitted the academicians' February report to the Central Committee.[102] The Central Committee in turn adopted the report and called for a meeting in November with representatives of the Soviet media to outline the Kremlin's position vis-à-vis Vatican policy.[103] The link was not coincidental. In the months to come, Soviet policy toward the Polish labor crisis would reflect many of the elements present in this earlier attempt to contain the spread of religious nationalism.

A final word must go toward examining the Soviet antireligious campaign in light of the later attempt to assassinate John Paul II. On 13 May 1981, with the Solidarity crisis at its height in Poland, a Turkish terrorist named Mehmet Ali Agca fired several shots at the pope in St. Peter's Square from a distance of less than twenty feet. The pontiff was wounded in the stomach, right elbow, and left hand and was rushed to Rome's Gemelli Clinic. Though he lost 60 percent of his blood from internal hemorrhaging, the pope survived a five-hour operation and recovered to meet with and grant forgiveness to his would-be assassin, sentenced on 22 July 1981 to life imprisonment. The event prompted immediate speculation that the Soviets had been behind a plot to kill the pope. Italian prosecutors linked Agca to a group of Bulgarian conspirators, and international suspicions tied the Bulgarians to Moscow.[104] As for Agca himself, after originally confessing that he had acted alone, he later spoke both of Bulgarian and militant Islamic involvement when it became clear that his handlers were not planning to break him out of prison.[105]

Compelling evidence regarding the Bulgarian-Soviet connection eventually emerged in July 1981, when Iordan Mantarov, a deputy commercial attaché from the Bulgarian embassy in Paris, defected to the West. Meeting with French intelligence, Mantarov confirmed that Bulgaria had been behind the plot to kill the pope, in close cooperation with the KGB. He claimed to have learned this from Dimiter Savov, a high-ranking officer in Bulgaria's intelligence agency, the Durzhavna Sigurnost (DS).[106] According to Savov, the KGB concluded in 1979 that American national security adviser Zbigniew Brzezinski had engineered the election of fellow Pole Karol Wojtyla to the papacy in order to take advantage of Polish unrest and undermine Soviet-Polish ties. He argued that Moscow had become suspicious of the new pope immediately after his election because of the coincidence of growing instability in Poland. When conditions began to worsen and John Paul began to support the independent trade union movement, KGB officials met with the Bulgarians to find a way to "eliminate" the pontiff. Though hearsay, French intelligence agents believed Mantarov's account, as they were able to confirm the truth of other information Savov had provided.[107]

Italian state prosecutor Antonio Albano came to similar conclusions on the basis of some twenty-five thousand pages of documentation and testimony. In his seventy-eight-page report filed with the court in June 1984, Albano asserted: "The Bulgarian secret services had a specific political interest in killing John Paul II. The imposing rise of Solidarity in Poland in the summer of 1980 and consequent social convulsions constituted a most acute crisis for the socialist states of Eastern Europe. This was perceived as a mortal danger to their political cohesion and military strategy. And since Poland's ideological collapse was mostly due to the fervid religious faith of the population, sustained and helped above all by the first Polish Pope in history, the Polish rebellion might be greatly weakened and fragmented [by his] physical elimination." Albano was somewhat less direct in his suggestion of Soviet involvement. "In some secret place," he hints, "where every secret is wrapped in another secret, some political figure of great power took note of this most grave situation and, mindful of the vital needs of the Eastern bloc, decided it was necessary to kill Pope Wojtyla."[108] His veiled reference to Winston Churchill's famous description of Russia as "a riddle, wrapped in a mystery, inside an enigma" clearly indicated that the state prosecutor believed the plot had begun in Moscow.

However, while copious evidence ties the conspiracy to Sofia, there remains precious little to confirm Soviet complicity. Western suspicions have therefore tended to return again and again to the tight relationship that existed between Bulgaria's Durzhavna Sigurnost and the Soviet KGB. According to Stefan Svirdlev, a DS officer who fled Bulgaria in 1971, each of the Bulgarian agency's seven departments was controlled by a KGB adviser reporting directly to Moscow.[109] Additionally, beginning in the early 1970s, the Soviets began to rely on Bulgarian agents to carry out their "wet affairs"—the Soviet term for clandestine violent operations abroad.[110]

Was the assassination attempt in St. Peter's Square an example of such collaboration? Even within the KGB itself, opinions varied. In 1981, before his own defection to the West, former KGB officer Oleg Gordievsky solicited the impressions of those with whom he worked. About half were convinced that the KGB would never undertake a "wet affair" of such magnitude through the Bulgarians. The other half asserted that it had been KGB Department 8 of Directorate S—special operations—that had coordinated the plot. Tellingly, some of this second group suggested to Gordievsky that they regretted Agca's failure to kill the pope.[111] Vasili Mitrokhin is no more certain on the question. While admitting that the KGB would have been "overjoyed" if the pope had been killed, he saw no evidence in the agency's archives of collusion in the affair.[112]

What the new archival documentation does provide is valuable insight into the essential question of possible Soviet motives. For instance, it confirms Mantarov's claim that Wojtyla's election set off alarm bells in Moscow, particularly when he began to encourage Poland's emergent civil society. Most important, though, the secret reports presented to the Central Committee in 1979 and 1980 suggest that Moscow's leading concern was the growth of Catholic nationalism in the Soviet Union. By comparison, social stability in Eastern Europe assumed only secondary importance. The remarkable implication of the Grigulevich article that Catholic propaganda was a far greater menace within the Soviet Union than in Poland evinced this position in an unusually pubic forum.

Therefore, hypothetically speaking, the Soviets had more than one motive for murdering the pope. In addition to those of political cohesion and military strategy outlined by Mantarov and Albano, there was the far more compelling consideration of domestic stability in the western Soviet republics. By the summer of 1980, it had become evident that religious nationalism was on the march here, something that the Soviet leadership viewed as a real threat to domestic stability. Convinced that the new pope was behind this, the Soviets had a very strong reason for wanting him out of the way.

In light of what later transpired in May 1981, the Secretariat's directive of November 1979 to take whatever measures needed in countering John Paul's anticommunist policies certainly rings with added resonance. Could it be that the assassination was the outcome of the secret instructions issued to the KGB "to study the question of further steps in acting against the negative aspects of the Vatican's 'Eastern Policy' "? Only the appearance of further evidence can say, though Western intelligence specialists who Carl Bernstein and Marco Politi have interviewed on this subject "ridicule the notion that a paper trail to the Kremlin might exist."[113] Should one be found, however, researchers will require much greater access to Soviet archival collections before the truth of this conspiracy is laid to rest.

Katyn

As the ideological antithesis to socialist integration, the specter of nationalism invariably worried Moscow whenever it appeared emergent in the bloc. The Kremlin's response to the growth of religious activism after 1978 was a clear case in point. Another was its attitude toward expressions of Polish nationalism in spring 1980 coinciding with the fortieth anniversary of the Katyn Forest Massacre. If the renaissance of Poland's Catholic identity was serving to galvanize its emergent civil society, it was the recollection of a wartime tragedy that promised to incite that society, and possibly other nations, against Moscow.

Polish history is so full of misfortune and strife that Poles have traditionally regarded themselves as the "Christ among nations," suffering for the redemption of the world. In this sad context, few incidents stand out more distinctively in the Polish mindset than the Katyn Forest Massacre. In the first weeks of World War II, consistent with secret protocols concluded with Nazi Germany, Soviet forces occupied and annexed eastern Poland. Soviet authorities then began widespread arrests of suspected nationalists, resisters, and other "class enemies" believed to constitute a threat to Moscow's control in the region. Between January and July 1940, these people were deported en masse, most to sparsely populated areas of Siberia and Kazakhstan. Estimates of the number of deportees vary. Official figures from the People's Commissariat of Internal Affairs (NKVD) suggest a total between 330,000 and 340,000, while others place the number closer to 1.2 to 1.6 million.[114] The conditions in which they were forced to live during the deportations were subhuman and evocative of the Nazi Holocaust. Families traveling in winter spent weeks in unheated railroad cars, practically without food, and in unsanitary conditions.[115] One *New York Times* reporter described how Poles were left in Siberia, "dumped there to get along as best they can or to perish if they are not strong enough to survive."[116] Few were. "Deaths were a frequent occurrence," writes Keith Sword. "The starvation diet weakened resistance to various illnesses. The dead were sometimes buried beside the railway line, if the guards could be persuaded to open the doors. But often either the train did not stop or the guard would not open the door. In such circumstances, the tiny forms of babies had to be pushed through the window while the carriage was still in motion."[117] At least one account suggests that by October 1942, some 900,000 deportees had died from this ordeal, including 50,000 children.[118]

Although these deportations bore the stamp of finality for most, the Soviet leadership under Stalin chose to deal more resolutely with Poles whose profession rendered them capable of organizing popular resistance to Moscow. These included the best of the Polish intelligentsia, thousands of Polish military officers, politicians, bureaucrats, large landowners, police officers, jailers, industrialists, lawyers, judges, doctors, Catholic priests, and even store and hotel owners.[119] On 5 March 1940, the head of the Soviet NKVD (predecessor to the later KGB), Lavrenty Beria, sent a top secret dispatch to Stalin informing him that nearly twenty-six thousand such individuals awaited their fate in camps located in Belorussia and what was now Western Ukraine. On the basis of class and professional factors, Beria argued that these men were "sworn enemies of Soviet power, full of hate toward the Soviet system." All, he insisted, were guilty of anti-Soviet agitation, and would likely continue if freed from confinement. "Every one of them is only waiting for release," he warned, "so as to have the chance to take an active part in the struggle against Soviet power." From the perspective of Soviet state interests, the prisoners in question represented the seeds of nationalist insurgency. There could be no question that their very existence was a menace to the "normalization" under way in the occupied territories. As such, their fate was sealed.[120]

Beria's recommendation to Stalin was simple and to the point: "Consider them a special case punishable by the death penalty—execution." These executions were to take place in the absence of normal legal procedures or documentation. According to directives approved by the Politburo, the matter was to be carried out "without subpoena of the arrested parties and without formal charges, resolved closure of the case, or formal indictment."[121] The Polish prisoners were simply to disappear without a trace, their pending cases left open should it ever become necessary to disavow the executions.

Stalin and a majority of his colleagues on the Politburo adopted Beria's recommendations without alteration. The execution order bears the signatures of Stalin, Kliment Voroshilov, Viacheslav Molotov, and Anastas Mikoyan, along with notes in the corner indicating the support of both Mikhail Kalinin and Lazar Kaganovich.[122] It was carried out in April and May following transport of the prisoners to a variety of locations in Ukraine. Historians and forensics experts have worked for decades to discover exactly what happened to them there, and how they were killed. The conclusions of these investigations are haunting.

Though not all were murdered in Katyn, the story of those who were has commanded the most attention, because of the later discoveries there. It is believed that 4,443 prisoners sent from the Kozielsk POW camp to Gniezdovo were taken by buses to the Katyn Forest near Smolensk. There, according to accounts pieced together by medical examiners and Polish historians, "two NKVD men grabbed each prisoner by his arms. They quickly determined whether to tie his hands and put a choke knot on his neck or whether just to control him with the grip of their own hands while leading him directly to the nearby grave. Polish officers who were still strong enough to struggle were attacked by additional NKVD men. Some suffered crushed skulls, many had their overcoats tied around their heads, some were gagged by stuffing sawdust into their mouths. A number had their elbows tied tightly together behind their backs. Very many were stabbed with four-cornered Soviet bayonets. . . . Some of the victims were searched and robbed of watches, rings, etc."[123] All were executed with a bullet through the base of the skull fired from German "Walther" 7.65 millimeter pistols.

Another six thousand Poles from a camp in Ostashkovo were simply taken to NKVD headquarters in Kalinin. There, within the building's inner prison, they were taken to the staff lounge, one by one. "Each man was asked his surname, first name, and date of birth," a witness later recalled. "Then he was taken to the room next door, which was soundproofed, and shot in the back of the head." As at Katyn, German pistols were used for the executions in Kalinin, because it was feared unreliable Soviet weapons would "overheat with heavy use."[124] A similar fate met most of the remaining prisoners condemned in Beria's March 5 dispatch.[125] From the Soviet point of view, the operation appeared a complete success. The deputy minister of the interior responsible for carrying out the executions, Vsevolod Nikolayevich Merlukov, received the Order of Lenin on 27 April 1940 for his efforts. Similarly, the 140 NKVD executioners all received financial bonuses, promotions, and decorations for a job well done.[126]

However, Moscow had not heard the last of its Polish victims. By October 1941, only a few months after the German invasion of the USSR, Soviet efforts to reorganize the Polish armed forces under former Polish POW General Wladyslaw Anders prompted a search for their missing officers. Of fourteen Polish generals taken prisoner in 1939, only two could be found; of three hundred high-ranking officers, only six.[127] A subsequent investigation revealed that nearly fifteen thousand POWs from the Kozielsk, Ostashkovo, and Starobelsk POW camps were unaccounted for after their transport west to Smolensk in April 1940.[128] Anders and the head of the Polish government in exile, General Sikorski, sought an explanation from Stalin at a meeting on 3 December 1941. The Polish prisoners, Stalin flatly replied, had fled to Manchuria.[129] Further efforts by the Poles to ascertain the fate of their missing compatriots through official channels were fruitless.

Ironically, it was the retreating German army that discovered mass graves in Katyn Forest in February 1943, thrusting the issue of the missing Polish officers into the international spotlight. Moscow responded with shocked indignation to suggestions that it was responsible, accusing the Germans of killing the Poles themselves in a bid to destabilize the anti-Hitler alliance.[130] But despite the German bullets used in the executions, independent German, Polish, and multinational investigations all agreed that the murders had been committed in the spring of 1940 when the region was still under Soviet control. After the Polish government in exile demanded an investigation by the International Red Cross, Moscow broke relations with it and began organizing the Union of Polish Patriots from which it would later seek to form a pro-Soviet Polish government.[131]

Though recognizing the likelihood of Soviet culpability, the Western Allies sought to downplay the Katyn affair in the interest of prosecuting the war against Hitler. The Germans, after all, stood to enjoy considerable propaganda value from their discovery. In the British Foreign and Colonial Office, Sir Frank Roberts admitted to a colleague, "It is obviously a very awkward matter when we are fighting for a moral cause and when we intend to deal adequately with war criminals, that our Allies should be open to accusations of this kind."[132] In his memoirs Winston Churchill later remarked, "It was decided by the victorious Governments concerned that the issue should be avoided and the crime of Katyn was never probed in detail."[133] In the United States, it was not until 1951 that the American government officially recognized Soviet guilt in the matter.[134] By this time, however, it was too late to have an impact on the history books behind the Iron Curtain. Thanks to the establishment of communist rule in Poland, tight Soviet control over Warsaw ensured that Moscow's version of the truth remained unchallenged. When the United States Congress released its findings of Soviet culpability in 1951, the Polish government published a work of its own, *Prawda o Katyniu* (The Truth about Katyn), that reasserted Moscow's official position.[135]

Despite Warsaw's complicity in this historical ruse, by the late 1950s the new head of the KGB, Aleksandr Shelepin, began to wonder how long the Soviet Union could keep the truth of Katyn a secret. On 3 March 1959, almost exactly nineteen years after Beria's fateful dispatch to Stalin, he sent a top secret, handwritten memo to First Secretary Nikita Khrushchev. It expressed Shelepin's concern that eventually "some kind of unforeseen circumstance" might expose the truth of the NKVD executions if thousands of surviving files pertaining to the matter were not destroyed. Such a revelation, he warned, would have an "entirely undesirable impact on our government."[136] Khrushchev and the Politburo agreed with Shelepin and ordered the destruction of all files pertaining to the executions, with the exception of Beria's original dispatch, the Politburo orders, Shelepin's letter, and the destruction order itself.[137]

Yet the international community, especially in the West, remained unconvinced by decades of Soviet claims, and the controversy lived on into the Brezhnev era. By the 1970s, even behind closed doors, Soviet policymakers continued to regard any attempt to examine the matter critically as an anti-Soviet "campaign." And so, when the British Broadcasting Corporation (BBC) decided to broadcast in April 1971 a documentary film based on Louis FitzGibbon's book *Katyn—a Crime without Parallel*, Moscow decried the program as a falsification of history. It cautioned London's Foreign Office to take "measures against the distribution of such slanderous materials in England intended . . . to damage relations between our countries."[138] The British government, of course, did nothing of the sort, and Soviet indignation went unassuaged. Further objections arose the following year when a collection began in London to build a monument to the victims of Katyn dating the executions to 1940.[139] A Central Committee memo sent around to the Politburo at the time read in part: "Recently, imperialist centers of ideological sabotage, especially the powerful Western radio stations, have often begun to return to the so-called Katyn Affair with the well-known Goebbels interpretation [of Soviet guilt]. . . . In connection with the upcoming thirty-fifth anniversary of the crime committed by German fascists in the Katyn Forest (fall 1976), this provocational anti-Soviet campaign could grow in strength."[140] This was certainly not the language of a group that is knowingly misrepresenting history. Rather, it suggests how pervasive the contrived historical interpretation had become even among the highest echelons of Soviet power.

Having fully embraced the argument of Soviet innocence since the 1940s, the Polish communist government also expressed anxiety over the planned memorial. "Recognizing the danger and harms of such propaganda," read a Soviet Central Committee memo from March 1976, "our Polish friends have approached the Soviet Embassy in the PPR with a proposal for Soviet-Polish consultations with the aim of working out possible joint countermeasures."[141] Clearly Warsaw favored collaboration with Moscow inasmuch as its own reputation was on the line as well, particularly with respect to its own people. Belief in Soviet responsibility for the massacre nonetheless remained widespread in Poland. As another CPSU Central Committee report written in March 1976 lamented, "Catholic preachers in their homilies to the Polish faithful often mention with anti-Soviet implications the 'tens of thousands of innocent victims, the best (elite) of Polish society.' In the PPR, our embassy informs us, there are many people who are inclined to believe such anti-Soviet fabrications."[142] From the Soviet point of view, efforts such as the London memorial campaign were "clearly" intended to incite this kind of anti-Soviet sentiment in Poland. Moreover, Moscow feared the explosive consequences it promised to unleash in Poland given its long nationalistic tradition.

By 1980, with much of the country convinced that widespread food shortages were due to the shipment of Polish goods to the Soviet Union, the spark of Katyn posed a clear threat to Soviet-Polish relations and overall bloc integration. In March, with the fortieth anniversary of the executions approaching, Soviet diplomats in Poland began monitoring preparations by KOR and an allied group, the Confederation for an Independent Poland (KPN), to hold a memorial demonstration. It was to take place in a Szczecin cemetery on 13 April. Some weeks before, a pamphlet had appeared which told the story of the massacre, complete with accusations of Soviet guilt. Included was an unprecedented call from Pope John Paul to his countrymen requesting prayers for the victims of Katyn on the appointed day. Completing the linkage of nationalism and religion, the pamphlet bore the signatures of the Szczecin episcopate alongside those of the KOR leadership.[143] When the day arrived, organizers placed 250 flags bearing the words "Victim of Katyn" on as many mock grave sites set up within the cemetery. However, Polish police quickly rounded these up and destroyed the fake graves, along with the flags. Leaders of a student group who had attended the memorial with leaflets of their own were arrested, and their leaflets were confiscated. Police similarly crushed a second memorial service that convened on 27 April, arresting nine of its organizers.

Shortly thereafter, on 26 May, the Soviet consul in Szczecin, P. Timofeev, sent off a report to Moscow that, no doubt accurately, branded the memorials as profoundly anti-Soviet and antisocialist.[144] The significance of encountering widespread opposition across Polish society did not elude Timofeev. "Notwithstanding the existence of internal differences among the antisocialist groups," he wrote, "this April they coordinated their anti-Soviet actions and worked together." Particularly troubling to him was the participation of the Catholic hierarchy, right up to the pope himself. "As is clear from the leaflets," he remarked, "the church took part in the anti-Soviet action together with other hostile groups, something that has not been observed until recently."[145] Considering their abiding concern with religious nationalism, Timofeev's observations must have confirmed Moscow's deepest suspicions about the Polish Catholic "menace."

Further confirmation attended a May 13 dispatch sent to Moscow from the Soviet consul in Gdansk, L. Vakhrameev. Vakhrameev reported that the dissident Polish Youth Movement, a group associated with KOR, had begun distributing flyers in late April calling people to a demonstration in memory of the Polish constitution of 1791. The meeting convened at the Mariacki Cathedral in Gdansk on 3 May. After celebrating Mass, over fifteen hundred people lined up to lay flowers and banners on the grave of the Polish hero Jan Sobieski. Among the banners were some that read simply "Remember Katyn." Concluding the demonstration was a series of speeches by leading proponents of Polish civil society. "Their presentations," wrote Vakhrameev, "carried a maliciously anti-Soviet, antisocialist character and contained attacks against the existing state structure in the PPR, the leaders of the PZPR, and the government, whom they charged with the collapse of the economy and an unwillingness to provide society with a sufficient standard of living. They pointed to the country's lack of independence and its complete submission to the Soviet Union, to the absence of 'personal freedom,' etc. They charged the USSR with the 'massive extermination of Poles during World War II,' and with the 'occupation' of Afghanistan and 'Eastern Polish lands.' Appeals were made to remember Katyn."[146]

Although the organizers of the Gdansk rally received three months of detention, Polish police admitted this would have little impact on their activities. Indeed, the authorities with whom Vakhrameev spoke all told him "that the subversive efforts of the opposition are becoming ever more active; and they are becoming more legal while taking a clearly anti-Soviet and antisocialist direction." Recognizing that a widespread crackdown would ultimately prove necessary, the authorities focused on rallying Party supporters and stepping up ideological work.[147] By the standards of previous experience, this move appeared rather insightful. After all, the riots of 1976 had seen the government forced to retreat when the army under General Jaruzelski refused to fire on fellow Poles. In the years that followed, the Polish opposition had grown far stronger. Therefore, any future confrontation would demand close coordination within the ranks of the PZPR and the Polish armed forces.

By early August it became clear that the police who had met with Vakhrameev had estimated the opposition correctly. Despite the three-month detention of dissident activists after the May rally in Gdansk, another demonstration convened in Warsaw's Powozki Cemetery on 1 August.[148] However, by now Soviet diplomats in Poland had far more pressing concerns. On that same day, strikes had broken out along the Baltic coast which threatened to disrupt an already fragile economy. The great Polish Solidarity crisis had begun.

Conclusion

Standing at the threshold of the Solidarity crisis, Moscow could not have known that it faced the beginning of what would become the collapse of communism in Eastern Europe. Nevertheless, all the factors that would eventually lead to the downfall of communist regimes in 1989 were already coming together in Poland by August 1980. Informed by the failure of previous efforts to reform communist rule in Czechoslovakia, Polish civil society had begun to nurture an alternative national culture, separate from, and occasionally in opposition to, the state and Party. Galvanized by common religious and patriotic issues, encouraged by a new Polish pope, and motivated by the memory of Soviet barbarity, Poles increasingly voiced their desire for a type of "normalization" sharply at variance with that under way in the region since 1968.

Most important, however, this period saw the first evidence of Moscow's growing perception that Eastern Europe had become a serious liability to Soviet national interests. Racked by mounting debt, low productivity, and mounting consumer demand, the empire in Europe constituted an ever increasing burden on the Soviet economy. Meanwhile, its zealous patriots and religious activists threatened to reignite the flames of nationalism throughout the region, including in the western republics of the Soviet Union. Normalization along Soviet lines, therefore, appeared to have resolved precious little in over a decade. Perhaps sensing the futility of this effort, in the face of the mounting Polish crisis Soviet leaders expressed far more concern for their own domestic stability than they did for the fate of bloc integration. Rather than regarding East European instability as a challenge to Soviet national interests, Moscow focused on containing regional instability at the borders of the USSR. Unlike in 1968, when domestic concerns were peripheral to the imperative of "normalizing" Czechoslovakia, by 1980 the Soviet commitment in Eastern Europe had weakened considerably. Though policy statements continued to trumpet the principles of socialist internationalism, events in the bloc underscored the hazards of being tied tightly to the fortunes of Moscow's East European neighbors.

It is one of the interesting ironies of history that Polish developments encouraged Moscow to reevaluate the challenges East Europe posed to Soviet domestic security. For centuries Poland had been the causeway of choice for invading armies bound for the Russian heartland. After the first Polish-Lithuanian invasion defeated the armies of Tsar Boris Godunov in the seventeenth century, Russia faced Napoléon's legions in the nineteenth and German invaders twice in the twentieth, all through this same route. For this reason, Moscow had traditionally regarded a stable, friendly Poland as essential to Soviet national security. Against this strategic backdrop, Moscow's apparent insouciance toward the growing instability in Eastern Europe at the end of the 1970s is striking. Existing archival materials offer little evidence of the ideological or strategic apprehension mentioned by Iordan Mantarov and Antonio Albano in the context of the plot to kill John Paul II. Indeed, Moscow's documented response toward papal initiatives in Eastern Europe sharply contrasts with the attention given to Catholic activism in the Soviet Union itself.

The matter of Katyn was also perceived almost exclusively through the prism of Soviet interests, which in light of the complexities of Polish-Soviet relations is not surprising. After all, the Poles who suffered deportation and execution in 1940 had lived in the part of Poland that was later incorporated into the Soviet republics of Belorussia and Ukraine. These were the areas, in addition to similarly occupied Lithuania and Latvia, where Moscow was working in the 1970s to compromise the influence of the Polish clergy. Assertions of Soviet guilt could very easily have fed the fires of nationalist opposition in the towns and cities from which Beria's victims had come. Certainly the discovery of papal support behind the April demonstration in Szczecin must have confirmed such suspicions in the minds of the Soviet leaders. By 1979 they were already convinced that the Catholic Church was working to feed anti-Soviet nationalism in the western republics. Vatican encouragement on the Katyn issue, given where the victims were from, could only have affirmed this conviction.

On the eve of the outbreak of strikes on Poland's Baltic coast, Soviet propaganda continued to speak of bloc unity, mutual support, and fraternal assistance. Even classified diplomatic correspondence evinced an interest in the problems plaguing Soviet bloc allies. In practice, however, by the late 1970s, the place Eastern Europe had once occupied in the estimation of Soviet national interests had begun to give way before anxiety about the damage that regional crises could inflict on Soviet domestic stability. As the strikes on the Baltic exploded into the Polish Solidarity crisis of 1980–81, this evolving perception of Soviet national interest would prompt the Kremlin to reevaluate completely its East European commitments.

5 Military Assistance to Poland in 1980?

If they don't understand that we are bringing them mathematically
flawless happiness, it is our duty to force them to be happy.
But before we use our weapons, we will try words.
—Yevgeny Zamyatin, *We*

THE EMERGENCE OF THE SOLIDARITY independent trade union in Poland was unquestionably the most important event in the history of the Soviet bloc since the 1968 invasion of Czechoslovakia. Moscow's decision to crush the Prague Spring had effectively shattered popular support for the reform of communist rule in Eastern Europe. In 1980 the Solidarity crisis began the final transformation of East European civil society away from communism, ending in its final collapse nine years later. Fundamental to this process was the simultaneous movement of Soviet bloc policy away from socialist internationalism. The civil war in Afghanistan and explosion of religious nationalism in Poland had begun to demonstrate that the costs of internationalist commitments were at times sharply at variance with Soviet national interests. Consequently, the transformation of Polish labor unrest into a national opposition movement during the summer and fall of 1980 raised important questions for the Soviet leadership.[1] Was this the start of an antisocialist "counter-revolution" in Poland? If so, what were its prospects for success, both in Poland and elsewhere in the region? Could the Polish Communist Party be trusted to manage the situation itself? If not, what were the likely consequences of a Warsaw Pact intervention? Finally, and most important, was it in the best interests of the Soviet Union to absorb those consequences in support of communist rule in Poland? The newly available evidence suggests that in the early months of the crisis provisions were made to bring as many as eleven additional divisions to battle-ready status to assist the Northern Group of Forces in a conceivable invasion of Poland. Ultimately, however, only a fraction of these were actually mobilized by the end of 1980 as Soviet initiatives focused on encouraging, threatening, and cajoling Poland's communist government into crushing the Solidarity movement itself with a minimum of allied assistance. Meanwhile, the Soviets worked to contain the spread of the movement, lest similar unrest compromise the already fragile domestic stability of the Soviet Union.

As one Polish regime after another continued to make concessions to opposition demands, each sought to reassure Moscow of its commitment to the defense of socialism. Unconvinced, the Kremlin launched what amounted to a "cold war" offensive of high-profile maneuvers along the Polish border with the forces it had readied to assist Warsaw in an imposition of martial law. This policy culminated in the extraordinary December Warsaw Pact summit at which Poland's allies convinced the Polish leadership that they might intervene on their own against Solidarity if active measures were not immediately adopted. In the wake of this feint, an uneasy calm settled over Poland as its citizens continued to fear the worst, while Moscow and its allies hoped for the best. Respecting Warsaw's entreaties, allied military assistance would be held in abeyance—at least until it appeared that the Poles could no longer manage on their own to defend communist rule in their country. But it remained anyone's guess as to what would happen if and when that juncture was reached.

Poland Goes on Strike

George Santayana's oft-quoted aphorism that "those who cannot remember the past are condemned to repeat it" might well have been engraved in stone over the portals of communist power in Warsaw. Had it been, one speculates, Poland might well have gone in a direction very different from the path it ultimately traveled. Instead, the Solidarity crisis of 1980–81 began in exactly the same manner as Poland's preceding two crises. On 1 July 1980, seeking to "rationalize" the sale of heavily subsidized staple goods in Polish markets, the Gierek government introduced surprise price hikes across the nation. The move involved very little fanfare, in the hope that it might pass unnoticed by much of the population.[2] As in years past, however, public indignation spread swiftly through society, prompting Polish workers to respond immediately with a wave of strikes. Gierek's regime argued desperately in the official press that economic conditions made the price increases unavoidable, but to no avail. Its economic arguments went unheeded, and work stoppages continued to spread. The government went as far as offering wage concessions of 10 percent that rendered the price hikes virtually meaningless. Nevertheless, the striking workers refused to go back to work.[3]

Their grievances, it turned out, were not entirely economic in nature. A number were distinctly political. In mid-July, for instance, the ten thousand employees of Lublin's FSC truck factory demanded a reduction of police and army privileges, along with greater freedom of the press. The Lublin railway workers included calls for work-free Saturdays and independent trade unions "that would not take orders from above."[4] Some went as far as blocking the rail lines linking Poland with the Soviet Union, concerned that badly needed foodstuffs were being shipped to Moscow for the 1980 Summer Olympic Games.

The unrest in Lublin carried especially serious ramifications for Soviet-Polish relations. Not only were the strikes anathema to the orthodox Soviet-style socialism of the Brezhnev era, but the rail lines that ran through Poland were essential to Moscow's European military strategy. Edward Gierek warned members of the PZPR Politburo on 18 July that "if this drags on, questions can be expected from the Soviet comrades."[5] The Lublin press reflected on this reality with intimations of "anxiety among our friends" in the socialist alliance.[6] Meanwhile, the Czechoslovak newspaper *Tribuna*, on 16 July, attacked what it viewed as an outbreak of "petty bourgeois ideology," liberalism, and individualism in Poland. As Czechoslovak dailies were often used as a mouthpiece for Soviet warnings, this article suggested Soviet concern over adverse developments in Poland. For the time being, though, the Soviet press limited its coverage to citations from Gierek blaming the country's economic problems on heavy rains and widespread flooding.[7]

Late July found Gierek in the Crimea for his annual vacation and consultations with the Soviet leadership. The visit afforded ample time for Brezhnev and his colleagues to engage the Polish leader on how to manage the explosive situation back home. Their recommendations called for swift action before the strikes blossomed into a wholesale attack on socialism and Poland's ties with Moscow. Socialist internationalism, they argued, ought to inspire a broad assault against anti-Soviet and antisocialist nationalism. The situation called for aggressiveness on the part of Polish authorities, for "appropriate attacks" rather than defensive posturing.[8] From Moscow's perspective, the strikes represented the latest manifestation of the same Polish nationalism that had been threatening to compromise Soviet domestic stability since the late 1970s. Consequently, Moscow's earliest instructions to the Polish government focused on restricting the spread and impact of nationalism, rather than on dealing with labor or economic questions.

While Gierek relaxed on the beaches of the Black Sea discussing Polish nationalism with Brezhnev and company, KOR ideologue Jacek Kuron was making international headlines with his assertion that the strikes were intended to have a political impact. Speaking in early August to the West German journal *Der Spiegel*, Kuron said that Poland would require a period of three years to reform its way out of its debilitating socio-economic crisis. Change had to come slowly, he claimed, to avoid provoking a Soviet intervention. In time, though, he predicted that the nation's political evolution would move Poland in the direction of democracy and regular elections.[9]

On 14 August this prospect suddenly became far more likely when seventeen thousand employees of the Lenin Shipyard in Gdansk put down their tools and joined the nationwide stoppage. This was a moment of great symbolic and historical significance, as it had been the Gdansk shipbuilders who had suffered the most casualties during the antigovernment riots of December 1970. Since then, they had enjoyed considerable prestige in Poland's emergent civil society, and their strike in mid-August 1980 immediately inspired copycat stoppages along much of the nation's Baltic coast. What had been a nettlesome labor dispute suddenly became a national opposition movement virtually overnight.

The earlier claims of Jacek Kuron notwithstanding, worker demands were largely apolitical at the outset of the Lenin Shipyard strike. They called for the right to broadcast Catholic Mass on the radio, reinstatement of a number of dismissed workers (including the soon-to-be-famous Lech Walesa), wage increases, the right to strike, strike pay, and a monument to the victims of the December 1970 government crackdown.[10] Before long, however, trade union activists and KOR representatives rushed to join the shipyard's strike committee, and these original demands grew to include a call for independent unions in Poland. The expanded strike committee argued that, far from being a revolutionary provocation, this demand was merely consistent with Convention 87 of the International Labor Organization (ILO), an agreement signed and ratified by the Polish People's Republic.[11] At the same time, its members recognized the need to temper any further demands, lest they occasion a Soviet invasion of Poland. When, for instance, one member advocated an end to censorship of any kind in Poland, KOR representative Bogdan Borusewicz replied decisively, "You know what happened when they abolished censorship in Czechoslovakia?" The parallel was clear to all present, and the proposal was rejected. A further call for free national elections also met defeat out of concern for what was felt to be Moscow's predictable response.[12]

Soviet press reports eventually seemed to justify such cautiousness. On 15 August, *Pravda* ran an article that condemned "narrow nationalist positions" in general as a violation of proletarian internationalism. "Bourgeois nationalist and revisionist concepts," it declared, amounted to attacks on "socialist practice" and Marxist-Leninist norms.[13] This was precisely the type of language that had appeared in Soviet editorials prior to the invasion of Czechoslovakia. It indicated in no uncertain terms Moscow's apprehension over Polish developments and their "nationalist" challenge to regional stability.

Warsaw, meanwhile, held a very different view of the strikes. On 18 August the PZPR Politburo member responsible for Poland's internal security, Stanislaw Kania, met with Gdansk Party secretary Tadeusz Fiszbach for a briefing on the situation at the Lenin Shipyard.[14] It was Fiszbach who only a few months earlier had spoken to Soviet consul Vakhrameev about the inevitability of direct confrontation with the Polish opposition. Now, however, the Gdansk Party secretary adopted a considerably more moderate stance. The strikes, he told Kania, were legitimate working-class protests that ought to be dealt with politically rather than with force.[15] Fiszbach's recommendation was consistent with warnings from Admiral Ludwik Janczyszyn, the commander in chief of Poland's navy, that Polish sailors would not fire on the workers if the government attempted a crackdown. Kania, therefore, left Gdansk resolved to find a negotiated solution in dealing with the strikers.[16]

Warsaw's subsequent political strategy began with a public admission that the Party had, in years past, committed a number of "errors" in economic policy. Kania offered his sympathy, promised an end to earlier mistakes, and asked the strikers to get back to work. But the Lenin Shipyard refused to capitulate on its twenty-one demands.[17] A few days later, at the Fourth Plenum of the PZPR Central Committee convening on 21–23 August, Prime Minister Edward Babiuch was fired in favor of the relatively unknown Jozef Pinkowski. Nevertheless, this bit of political scapegoating also failed to persuade the Baltic strikers to leave their pickets.

Therefore, under growing pressure from Moscow, the new Pinkowski government began to consider more forceful options in dealing with the crisis. A special task force, code-named Lato-80 (Summer-80), was established under Deputy Interior Minister General Boguslaw Stachura for possible use in crushing the opposition by force of arms. However, while a number of PZPR hard-liners felt that martial law should be implemented immediately, the majority remained reluctant to approve widescale bloodshed. Moreover, Kania and most of his colleagues on the PZPR Politburo felt that it was simply a "fantasy" to consider mounting an operation of such magnitude without extensive preparations.[18] "Sending in the army means the use of weapons," said Defense Minister Jaruzelski in a meeting with the PZPR Politburo on 27 August. "Once in, the troops cannot withdraw. The Citizens' Militia is trained for such operations; it has batons and gasses and does not need to use firearms." But, he continued, "society must be prepared for such measures and must be fully aware of the consequences."[19] Should that time come, General Stachura promised the Politburo on 29 August, the troops of the interior ministry would "exterminate the counterrevolutionary nest in Gdansk."[20] For now, though, Warsaw would continue to search for a political solution to the crisis.

Soviet demands that Warsaw get tough with the opposition certainly played an important role in prompting the consideration of more forceful options. Following an August 19 speech by Gierek warning of threats to socialism in Poland, the Soviet press issued its first statement directly addressing the Polish strikes. Without clearly identifying any particular group or individual, the article spoke of "antisocialist forces" at work in Poland.[21] Again, Moscow's language harkened back to the days preceding the 1968 invasion of Czechoslovakia. As if to underscore this connection, 22 August saw an appeal to "real socialist unity" appear in the Czechoslovak Party daily, *Rude Pravo*, complete with entreaties for loyalty to Moscow on all fronts. The Czechoslovak article condemned all who asserted concepts such as national sovereignty and national/state interests that challenged international socialist unity. "The aim of ideological bourgeois activities," it argued, "is to disrupt the unity of the socialist community, to sever individual countries from real socialism and to return them to the path of capitalist development. Our own experience in this is more than instructive. . . . They start by attacking the leading role of the communist parties, above all the Soviet Union, the strongest and most powerful country of real socialism."[22]

By late August, Moscow had begun to watch the events unfolding in Poland with increasing attention. According to Kania's memoirs, Edward Gierek had been inquiring about the possibility of Soviet military intervention on his behalf since mid-August. Thus far, Moscow had yet to respond to his entreaties directly.[23] In the wake of the 1979 invasion of Afghanistan, such a momentous step would require more careful deliberation. For the time being, Moscow was inclined to have the Poles handle the situation themselves. A secret letter delivered to Gierek on 27 August by Soviet ambassador Boris Aristov demanded decisive action on the part of the PZPR to resolve the crisis.

Meanwhile, the Soviets had begun to form their own pro tem commission charged with keeping the Soviet leadership abreast of developments in Poland. Chaired by ideology chief Mikhail Suslov, the committee included Yuri Andropov (KGB chairman), Andrei Gromyko (minister of foreign affairs), Dmitrii Ustinov (minister of defense), Konstantin Chernenko (head of the Central Committee's General Department), Mikhail Zimianin (Central Committee secretary for ideology and propaganda), L. M. Zamiatin (head of the Central Committee Department of Foreign Propaganda), Ivan Arkhipov (first deputy chairman of the USSR Council of Ministers who dealt largely with external economic relations), and Oleg Rakhmanin (first deputy head of the Central Committee Department for Liaison with Communist and Workers Parties of the Socialist Nations).[24]

This new Suslov Commission, as it came to be known, was inclined from the start to view the Polish crisis as a challenge to the very foundations of communist rule in Eastern Europe. Accordingly, one of its first actions, dated 28 August 1980, was to recommend increasing the battle readiness of Soviet forces in the Baltic, Belorussian, and Transcarpathian Military Districts "in case military assistance is provided to the PPR."

Signed by each of the five Politburo members on the commission (Suslov, Gromyko, Andropov, Ustinov, and Chernenko), this recommendation called for the requisitioning of up to twenty-five thousand military reservists and six thousand vehicles to bring a total of three tank divisions and one mechanized rifle division to full combat readiness along the Polish frontier. Within a day or two, by the end of August, these instructions had been implemented, and the four divisions were in place. The commission memorandum also made provision for the prospect that further requisitions might be required in the future. "If the situation in Poland deteriorates further," the memo read, "we will also have to fill out the constantly ready divisions of the Baltic, Belorussian, and Transcarpathian Military Districts up to wartime level. If the main forces of the Polish Army go over to the side of the counterrevolutionary forces, we must increase the group of our own forces by another five–seven divisions. To these ends, the Ministry of Defense should be permitted to plan the call-up of as many as seventy-five thousand additional military reservists and nine thousand additional vehicles."[25]

Commission members also voiced their determination to defend Polish socialism in the national press. The August edition of the journal *Kommunist* carried an article by Oleg Rakhmanin that explicitly linked the Polish events to the "counterrevolutions" of years past. Wrote Rakhmanin, "The lessons of history connected with the events in Hungary in 1956, Czechoslovakia in 1968, and still more the fresh example of Afghanistan show what great importance is connected to the ability of the workers' vanguard [i.e., the Communist Party] to mobilize the people for defense of the revolution, relying here on the support of its friends and allies in the international arena, on class brothers."[26] The article rang with appeals to the kind of "fraternal assistance" that Eastern Europe had come to know well after decades of repeated Soviet military intervention. It sent a clear signal that Moscow regarded the Brezhnev Doctrine to be alive, well, and pertinent to the developments in Poland.

The threat of outside intervention was lost on no one involved in Poland's emergent opposition. In their ongoing negotiations with the government, the strike committees heard time and again that any new union would have to recognize the "leading role of the Party" in Polish society. Otherwise, state negotiators intimated, Moscow might conclude that the Party had lost control of the situation. And everyone knew what consequences that was likely to bring.[27] In response, the strikers offered assurances that "our demands are intended neither to threaten the foundations of the socialist regime in our country, nor its position in international relations, and we would not support anyone who wanted to exploit the present circumstances to that end; on the contrary, we would oppose them."[28] Aware that the government was preparing plans for martial law in late August, the strike committees were eager to give it whatever assurances were necessary to reach a mutual agreement on their chief demand—the formation of independent trade unions in Poland.

Thanks in no small part to the desire on both sides to avoid violent confrontation, the August strikes concluded peacefully with the signing of agreements in Szczecin (30 August), Gdansk (31 August), and Jastrzebie (3 September). Known collectively as the Gdansk Accords, these agreements contained a number of state concessions, including the formation of independent trade unions, wage increases, an increase in the national meat supply (scheduled to begin in December), and increased access to the media for both the new unions and the Catholic Church.[29] Of these, opposition leader Lech Walesa most valued the new unions as the key to worker interests, both present and future. As he declared an end to the strike at the Lenin Shipyard, Walesa stated plainly, "We got all we could in the present situation. And we will achieve the rest, because we now have the most important thing: our IN-DE-PEN-DENT SELF GOVERNING TRADE UNIONS. That is our guarantee for the future."[30]

The new unions took shape at breakneck speed. On 17 September, delegates from thirty-five new independent unions met at the Hotel Morski in Gdansk. Representing over 3 million workers in thirty-five hundred factories, the delegates founded an umbrella organization to coordinate their activities.[31] They named it Solidarnosc, "Solidarity" in English, and appointed Lech Walesa chairman of its Provisional Coordinating Commission. After years of preparation, Poland's civil society finally had an officially recognized voice.

Damage and Risk Analysis

Moscow was uncompromising in its condemnation of the Gdansk Accords, which it regarded collectively as a very serious defeat in the struggle against antisocialist forces. On 1 September, the day after the Gdansk agreement had been signed, *Pravda* carried an editorial warning that "enemies of Poland" were seeking to overturn the status quo in Eastern Europe. Without going into the details of the accords, it strongly implied that the PZPR would have to be coaxed into reneging on its pledges. Otherwise, the article suggested, Poland would be guilty of violating its obligations to the Warsaw Pact alliance.[32]

Poland's East European neighbors took their cues from Moscow in covering the conclusion of the strikes. East German radio broadcasts on 3 September spoke of a threat to "real socialism" from opposition forces in Poland.[33] The following day, Czechoslovakia's *Rude Pravo* called for a "joint defense of the gains of socialism," warning that "counterrevolution was not asleep" in Eastern Europe. Echoing the Soviet line, it asserted that "enemies of socialism" sought to upset Polish-Soviet ties while infecting the entire communist movement with "democratic-socialist revisionism."[34] This type of rhetoric once again offered Moscow an opportunity to publish harsh criticism of Polish events without taking full responsibility for acting on the views these articles expressed. On 6 September, for instance, *Izvestiia* published a Czechoslovak editorial that directly equated Polish developments to the 1968 Prague Spring. "We have seen for ourselves," it read, "that counterrevolution does not sleep. It has entrenched and camouflaged itself, and is biding its time."[35]

Behind closed doors at the Kremlin, Soviet leaders invoked similar sentiments. Convening on 3 September, the CPSU Politburo addressed the question of what policies its representatives would recommend to the Polish leadership at an upcoming summit meeting. A summary of the proposed talking points, forwarded that same day to Brezhnev, Andropov, Gromyko, and Rakhmanin, condemned the accords as "essentially signifying the legalization of an antisocialist opposition in Poland." The Soviets expressed their conviction that "inasmuch as the opposition intends to continue the struggle to achieve its objectives and the healthy forces of the Party and society cannot acquiesce to regressive movement in Polish society, the compromise that has been achieved will most likely be temporary."[36] From the Kremlin's perspective, then, the problem facing the Soviets was how to get the Polish leadership to prepare a "counterattack to recover lost positions within the working class and among the people." While political flexibility was one possible route, the Politburo also proposed that "in the event of necessity, it would be advisable to use the contemplated administrative means"—that is, the plan for martial law already under consideration in Warsaw.[37] At this point, however, the Soviets did not indicate a preference for "administrative" measures over political negotiations, provided that the PZPR successfully reasserted its authority in Poland. Indeed, Moscow had already begun to demobilize the four divisions that had been brought up to battle readiness on 28–29 August in support of a possible Polish crackdown.[38]

Whatever path Warsaw chose to take, it would certainly require considerable political willpower to defeat Solidarity. Consequently, Moscow strongly favored a purge within the PZPR in order to ensure organizational and ideological coherence in the struggle to come. The proposed purge was to include "necessary changes in the leading organs" at a promptly convened Party congress. Thus cleansed of "unhealthy" elements, the new Central Committee might work to undermine the August and September compromise agreements. In the meantime, public opinion would have to be mobilized against the new independent trade unions while the regime worked fast to infiltrate them with Party loyalists. Failure to do this in 1968 had been seen as one of the principal shortcomings of Soviet policy toward the Prague Spring counterrevolution. Success this time around, Moscow felt, would enable "necessary measures to expose the political colors and designs of the opposition ringleaders."[39]

Control of the Polish media was another fundamental concern, as it had been twelve years earlier in Czechoslovakia. Although the concessions granted in the Gdansk Accords broadened access to the press, it was up to the Polish regime to define precisely what type of language would be considered antisocialist and in contravention of Polish state law. Here, from Moscow's vantage point, was a loophole that could be used to reestablish effective Party control over the press even under the new agreement.[40] The Soviets also suggested that careful oversight of television, radio, and the activities of Western "bourgeois journalists" working in Poland could further limit the ability of the opposition to influence popular opinion. Meanwhile, the Party should use the media to "show" that "the events in Poland had been caused not by the shortcomings of the socialist system, but by mistakes and miscalculations as well as by some objective causes (natural disasters, etc.)."[41]

An additional function of the press from Moscow's perspective was its role in promoting the interests of bloc cohesion. Once under full state control, the Polish press ought to "objectively depict the economic advantages Poland enjoys from broad cooperation with the USSR and other fraternal nations." It was hoped that this would "dispel the widespread slander that one of the causes of the present difficulties in supplying the people of the PPR with consumer goods is supposedly their delivery to the countries of socialism."[42] As indicated earlier, the lion's share of this vitriol on the part of Polish society had been aimed at the Soviet Union, and Moscow clearly recognized the adverse implications of such sentiments for Polish-Soviet relations.

The Kremlin did not have to wait long for a response to this list of concerns. Consistent with Moscow's desire for change within the top Polish leadership, Stanislaw Kania formally replaced Edward Gierek in the position of PZPR first secretary on 6 September. Inasmuch as Kania was reported to have been in control behind the scenes since 16 August, Gierek's removal did not follow entirely from the Soviet recommendations of 3 September. However, Kania must have assured Moscow of its wishes, judging from several agreements signed on 10–11 September extending $155 million in additional food and industrial deliveries to Poland.[43] In addition, the Soviets postponed $260 million in Polish debts while providing a further $260 million in credits at a low ten-year rate of repayment.[44] The fact that the Soviets reached these agreements with Poland's Deputy Premier Miezcyslaw Jagielski was quite significant, as he had been the Polish Party negotiator who had signed the Gdansk Accords on 31 August.

Jagielski's welcome, along with the aid he received, suggested that Warsaw and Moscow had reached an understanding regarding the struggle against Poland's new opposition movement. From Moscow's perspective, this understanding involved a strategy of divide and conquer aimed at separating Polish workers from the troublesome intelligentsia. Coverage by TASS of Poland on 12 September, for instance, drew a distinction between workers striking for socioeconomic reasons and the activities of openly "antisocialist" intellectuals.[45] Three days later, on 15 September, the Soviet consul general in Gdansk, L. Vakhrameev, cabled the Foreign Ministry in Moscow that the genuine worker discontent underlying the summer strikes did not obviate the fact that hostile elements were exploiting worker unrest to undermine the existing political system.[46] The strikes, he argued, were part of a "carefully thought-out and organized action of opposition antisocialist forces," as evinced by the Gdansk strike committee and its twenty-one demands. Indeed, Vakhrameev was convinced that the strikes had been planned years in advance.[47] Opposition forces, he suggested, had taken advantage of worker responses to the July price hikes in an attempt to launch a "silent, creeping counterrevolution." In addition to manipulating worker discontent effectively, the antisocialist elements were also alleged to have engaged in blatant harassment of those who chose to oppose the strikes.[48] The events of August and September show, the consul general admitted, that "on the wave of mass strikes on the [Baltic] Coast and in the country, [the oppositionists] managed to achieve unquestionable success."[49]

In sizing up the actions of the Polish leadership, Vakhrameev estimated that it had failed above all to perceive the radically new situation it faced. Describing how officials first tried to localize the disturbances with selective economic concessions, he observed that "our friends tried to solve the problem with old methods, but in totally different, new, conditions." This "tactic," he continued, was predictably unsuccessful. Poland had degenerated into a situation of "dual power" in which most factory Party cells had become paralyzed.[50] Consequently, the government had little choice but to compromise with the strike committees. It was, Vakhrameev argued, "the only correct way in the deepening crisis to a peaceful resolution of the conflict."[51] The Party, after all, was struggling to retain its legitimacy in Polish society while "an underestimation of the criticism and pain of the workers, the presence of formalism and slowness, of bureaucratism and administration in the style of an economic apparatus, of Party and other social organizations, has led to a sapping of Party authority, to the loss of worker trust and of belief in the Party's ability to solve problems."[52] Indeed, the consul general added, this dissatisfaction with the existing regime had even prompted some Party members to join the strikes. Thus, the disorientation and pessimism of Polish society had also worked its way into the ranks of the PZPR itself.

Vakhrameev adopted a decidedly ideological position in his policy recommendations. He concurred with the "many honest communists" he claimed to know in Poland who contended that the crisis stemmed from poor political indoctrination of Polish society in years past. Members of the PZPR suffered from a profound sense of self-doubt and confusion, he argued, which only exacerbated this lamentable situation. Consequently, Moscow could best contribute to a satisfactory outcome of the crisis by attending to its ideological origins. In the interest of the entire socialist commonwealth, Moscow ought to forward to the Soviet consulate (presumably in Gdansk) as soon as possible literature in Polish and Russian ("or at least in Russian") on the themes "V. I. Lenin on trade unions," "V. I. Lenin on ideological work," and "V. I. Lenin on the role of the Party in society."[53] Beyond this, Vakhrameev suggested that the Soviet external trade organization assist Poland in meeting contractual agreements through deliveries of materials required for shipbuilding and repair.[54]

Unlike similar impressions that were prohibited from reaching the top leadership in 1968, such consideration of legitimate worker unrest, Party mismanagement, and popular disillusionment tempered Moscow's conviction that an antisocialist counterrevolution was under way in Poland. It was, after all, impossible to ignore the popularity of the opposition movement that had reached into every corner of Poland's extensive civil society since the founding of Solidarity on 17 September. Private farmers had begun to call for their own independent unions. Students formed an Independent Students' Union (NZS). Professionals such as historians and journalists also met in their own associations with demands for "new officers, new statutes, less censorship, more truth!"[55]

What the Vakhrameev dispatch also illustrates is that, like the Prague Spring before it, the emergent Solidarity crisis was chiefly interpreted in ideological terms as an internal challenge to communist control in Eastern Europe. While this conclusion certainly had military ramifications, it was not the security of the bloc that appeared under attack but rather the region's political system. Soviet press coverage early in the crisis reinforced this orientation quite assertively. Seeking to exploit Polish fears of German revanchism, one article appearing in *Pravda* on 20 September under the pen name "A. Petrov" alleged provocatively that Solidarity was actually the work of West German activists eager to set up Gdansk (formerly the East Prussian city of Danzig) as the capital of Poland. However, rather than asserting the presence of a security threat, the article focused on the danger to Poland's socialist system. It warned that "as the situation becomes more stable, there is an increase of the activities of circles hostile to socialist Poland and their instigatory and subversive work."[56]

In years past, such an assessment would have elicited active consideration of military intervention. Indeed, contacts from the Polish embassy in Moscow, speaking with American diplomats in mid-September, confided that "the Polish Government is more concerned now about the possibility of Soviet invervention [sic] than it was two weeks ago immediately after the strike settlements." Significantly, though, the Polish source in question "did no [sic] however, believe Moscow had by any means reached a decision on any specific measures."[57] His sense of the situation in the Kremlin was right on target. By 1980, Soviet leaders were inclined to be far more defensive than they had been even a year earlier. Although willing to provide a few divisions to support a crackdown coordinated from Warsaw, Moscow showed no inclination yet to mobilize a larger invasion force. If Afghanistan had shown anything, it had been that invading a united population in support of a corrupt regime virtually guaranteed a military and political catastrophe, not to mention the burden of international sanctions. To this extent the U.S. contact in the Polish embassy was again quite accurate in his suggestion that "the main deterrents to Soviet intervention . . . are the certainty of Polish resistance and the irreparable blow the intervention and its bloody aftermath would inflict on détente in Europe."[58] Therefore, the Soviets responded to the labor unrest in Poland much as they had to the spread of religious nationalism in 1978–79. Less than two weeks after receiving Vakhrameev's report, on 30 September, members of the Central Committee Secretariat drafted a number of measures designed primarily to contain the spread of antisocialist sentiments into the Soviet Union.

Bourgeois propagandists, the Secretariat argued, were using Polish events to subvert socialist principles, particularly the leading role of the Party. Because Polish censors had been too permissive, there was a considerable risk of antisocialism spreading across the border into the Soviet Union. Soviet media and propaganda organs were therefore instructed to exercise extra vigilance in addressing and reporting on the developments in Poland. Newspapers such as *Pravda, Izvestiia, Trud,* and *Komsomolskaia Pravda,* as well as Gostelradio (state television and radio) and TASS, received specific instructions detailing which policy positions their reporting was to support. They were to underscore the role of both the working class as well as official trade unions in building a socialist society. Poland's position in the Warsaw Pact alliance and CMEA was to feature highly, along with the "egalitarian, mutually beneficial character" of Soviet-Polish relations. To the extent possible, the Soviet news bureaus were instructed to follow Polish press coverage in order to "expose enemy propaganda" that might make it past indulgent Polish censors.[59] They were also encouraged to offer whatever propaganda assistance their Polish counterparts might require to combat the spread of antisocialism.[60] No effort was to be spared in mobilizing the full might of Soviet propaganda against the Polish opposition. For the time being, at least, the press was the key to Moscow's defensive perimeter, working to contain the spread of Polish influence into the USSR.

The Failure of "Administrative Measures" in Poland

Following his election to the post of first secretary of the PZPR, Stanislaw Kania spent the entire fall in an attempt to "outmaneuver the society by means of various administrative measures" short of introducing martial law.[61] However, the Solidarity opposition repeatedly frustrated his efforts. When, for instance, promised wage increases failed to materialize by the end of September, Solidarity organized a one-hour warning strike for 3 October. The day after the strike, Kania addressed the Party's Sixth Central Committee Plenum with a message intended to appease the workers. The tone of the address sounded very much like Vakhrameev's earlier conclusions forwarded to Moscow. The August strikes, he conceded, had been genuine working-class protests brought on by the mistakes of the Gierek regime. Therefore, the new government would make a few fundamental, albeit gradual, changes in the nation's socioeconomic policy. These even included greater democratization of the Party to be implemented as soon as possible at an extraordinary Party congress. Kania defended his initiative, no doubt with Moscow in mind, by asserting that "the policy of concord and cooperation is our country's only chance."[62] Hence, rather than reversing the Gdansk concessions with "administrative means," Kania's desire for peace was already leading to further compromises.

Nevertheless, the Polish leadership remained committed to halting the momentum of the union movement before Solidarity's official registration scheduled for 24 October. When Lech Walesa arrived at the Warsaw District Court on the appointed day to collect Solidarity's legal certification, he was upset to discover that the regime had attempted yet another administrative feint designed to weaken the new organization. To the statutes which Solidarity had submitted in September, the presiding judge had added a new clause stipulating that the union recognized the Party's leading role in society and that Solidarity would not threaten Poland's international alliances. Popular response was swift and indignant. "Full responsibility for sustaining social tensions around the issue of 'Solidarity's' registration," the union's National Coordinating Commission warned, "remains with the authorities."[63] Tensions throughout the country shot up overnight. Solidarity leader Bronislaw Geremek noted that the regime had "practically invited a general strike against the leading role of the Party!"[64] As Walesa debated the merits of a general strike with his advisers, Yugoslavia's *Ljubljana Delo* predicted that further weakening of PZPR authority in the standoff would precipitate a Warsaw Pact invasion of Poland.[65]

Many well-informed outside observers regarded the prospect of an invasion of Poland as very high by late October 1980. Former National Security Council (NSC) adviser to the Carter administration Zbigniew Brzezinski recalls that "toward the end of September and certainly early October, the situation [in Poland] began to look more ominous, with the portents of a possible Soviet invasion. Accordingly, I started convening the SCC [Special Coordination Committee] in order to review contingencies for a possible crisis."[66] Close to the Polish frontier, the Soviet Northern Group of Forces had indeed begun to increase its battle readiness.[67] Its presence prompted repeated declarations of loyalty to the socialist alliance from a Polish leadership eager to avoid a demonstration of socialist fraternalism in action. "Our country's participation in the system of socialist alliances is an important factor of the Polish raison d'état," read one such appeal. "Poland is a permanent factor in European security and is situated in the immediate security zone of the Soviet Union."[68] Though Solidarity claimed a membership of between 5 and 6 million workers (including an estimated 750,000 Party members), most recognized that the "geopolitical realities" of the socialist bloc necessitated careful attention to Soviet sensibilities.[69] Therefore, on 30 October, with Solidarity and the state on the brink of confrontation, Kania left Poland for consultations in Moscow.

As they prepared to receive Kania at the end of October, Brezhnev and his colleagues on the Politburo shared deep anxieties about Warsaw's early steps against the emergent opposition movement. On 29 October, with Poland on the verge of a general strike, Brezhnev voiced his concern that "a full wave of counterrevolution is now sweeping across Poland, but nothing is being said about it in the appeals of the Polish press or of our Polish comrades; nothing is being said about the enemies of the people. Certainly these are enemies of the people, the direct collaborators of counterrevolution and the counterrevolutionaries themselves are coming out against the people. How is this possible?"[70] Andropov and Gromyko seconded Brezhnev's objections, noting that the Polish leaders ought to be encouraged to focus press attacks on antisocialist elements rather than on the mistakes of previous regimes. The brazen activities and statements of Solidarity figures such as Kuron and Walesa also prompted many in the Kremlin to call for more resolute steps against the Polish opposition. Brezhnev noted with disgust that while Walesa traveled freely all over Poland spreading antisocialism from town to town, the Polish press simply remained silent.[71]

The situation had degenerated such that Brezhnev believed Polish leaders ought to consider the use of force to restore order. "Indeed," the Soviet leader suggested, "maybe martial law ought to be introduced."[72] It remained to be seen, however, whether the Kania regime would agree to a military solution. In the opinion of KGB chief Yuri Andropov, Polish leaders simply did not understand the full import of the deepening crisis. Nevertheless, Defense Minister Ustinov retorted, if martial law was not implemented, matters promised to grow far worse. The Polish army was already reeling from disturbances that compromised its effectiveness. As such, Ustinov felt that Soviet involvement would soon become indispensable to a successful restoration of order. "Our Northern Group of Forces," he volunteered, "is prepared and stands in full battle readiness."[73]

The military intervention that Ustinov had in mind was almost certainly the use of Soviet troops to support the introduction of martial law by Polish forces, not a Soviet-led, 1968–style invasion of Poland. According to military charts prepared by the East German armed forces, along with U.S. reconnaissance data, the Soviets were in the process of bringing three motorized divisions to battle readiness in the western republics of the USSR during the fall of 1980. The East German documents suggest that an additional airborne division—all of which remain in a perpetually battle-ready status—would have been available for use in Poland, had the Polish political leadership given the green light to outside intervention.[74] Added to the two divisions that constituted the Northern Group of Forces, this was still well short of the nine to twelve Soviet divisions that the Suslov Commission had estimated would be necessary to support a wholesale invasion of Poland.[75]

Clearly, then, the key to a successful resolution of the crisis lay with the Polish government itself. But as Andrei Gromyko pointed out, while Polish defense minister Wojciech Jaruzelski was a trusted ally, he had yet to offer any specific plans for the implementation of martial law.[76] Jaruzelski was still known for his assertion in 1976 that Polish soldiers would not fire on their fellow citizens. Therefore, Gromyko concluded, Moscow would have to lecture Kania and his colleagues about the importance of resolute action. His final observations resonated with the historical rationale of Brezhnev's August 1968 reprimand of Alexander Dubcek. "Concerning martial law in Poland," Gromyko concluded, "we must regard it as a measure for saving revolutionary achievements. Of course, maybe it shouldn't be introduced immediately, particularly not right after the return of Kania and Pinkowski from Moscow; let's wait a bit; but we must direct them to it and encourage them. We cannot lose Poland. The Soviet Union lost six hundred thousand of its soldiers and officers liberating Poland in the battle against Hitler's forces, and we cannot allow a counterrevolution."[77]

Gromyko's pointed argument aptly characterized the general consensus of the Soviet leadership in the fall of 1980. Anxious about the threat to "real socialism" in Eastern Europe, the Politburo concluded that Poland's opposition had to be stopped by force.[78] Once again, as in August 1968, Soviet leaders justified their concerns with emotional appeals to the high cost of liberating Eastern Europe from the Nazis. Thus far, however, Warsaw had proven unwilling even to mobilize the Polish press against such "antisocialist" elements as Jacek Kuron and Lech Walesa. Although Ustinov obviously felt that the situation warranted intervention by Soviet forces, all present at the Politburo meeting recognized that the involvement he had in mind was out of the question unless the Polish leadership chose to use force itself.

At this point in the crisis, however, the Poles were not at all inclined to take up Ustinov's offer of assistance. The extreme colors in which the Soviet Union painted the existing situation in Poland contrasted sharply with the prevailing views in Warsaw. While recognizing the seriousness of the deepening crisis, the Poles were unwilling to draw a correlation between Poland and previous East European crises. Meeting at the height of the "registration crisis" on 25 October, the Polish Politburo hardly mentioned the question of using force against Solidarity. All attention was focused on finding an acceptable political solution.[79] This position totally precluded approval of any outside military action. Indeed, as the head of the Central Committee department for liaison with socialist countries, Konstantin Rusakov, pointed out during the October 29 Politburo session, Kania was resolutely opposed to any "international assistance" from Warsaw Pact forces. Along with most of the Polish leadership, Kania ardently believed that Poland was "not a situation like those in Hungary or Czechoslovakia."[80]

Nevertheless, the talking points drafted for Kania's upcoming visit did raise the prospect of international assistance. Konstantin Chernenko, one of the members of the Suslov Commission that had drafted the talking points, explained that they had been designed to stress, above all, "the need to take decisive steps against antisocialist elements."[81] This was a sound strategy in the minds of many on the Politburo, including the young Mikhail Gorbachev. In a rare expression of opinion about the Polish crisis, Gorbachev concurred with Chernenko: "It is necessary to speak directly and decisively with our Polish friends. They are still not taking necessary measures, [instead] they are adopting a kind of defensive position that they will not hold for long; they themselves could be thrown down."[82] Gorbachev's remarks reflected the concern on everyone's mind: that the Polish communists might be overthrown if they did not take the offensive. Therefore, the need for the PZPR to use military force, possibly in conjunction with limited outside assistance, remained at the center of Moscow's talking points at the October 30 summit talks.

The matter of economic assistance also presented some difficulties on the eve of the Polish arrival in Moscow. Kania had written in the preceding days to outline Poland's economic needs. Working from his letter, the Soviet State Planning Committee, Gosplan, put together a package of emergency aid to be presented at the October 30 meeting. The package provided for additional credits amounting to 280 million rubles, along with a short-term loan of 150 million rubles. Gosplan chairman Nikolai Baibakov noted that the USSR could increase deliveries of badly needed raw materials as required, including up to 500 million rubles worth of fuel in 1981, 500,000 tons of grain, 200,000 tons of diesel fuel, and an unspecified amount of cotton. In all, the aid package offered on 30 October was worth approximately 1 billion rubles.[83]

The problem was that to increase aid to Poland, the USSR would have to cover its costs by selling more oil on the world market. This oil, Baibakov indicated, would have to be diverted from the other CMEA member-nations in Eastern Europe, who were unlikely to accept reductions with grace. "Of course," Baibakov predicted, "they will all object, that is certain. But what can you do? We don't have any other option, so we have to go with this one."[84] The other members of the Politburo agreed and ratified Baibakov's aid package before moving on to other business.

Publicly, the Soviet-Polish summit of 30 October had the look of friendly cordiality traditionally reserved for press coverage of socialist interstate relations. Smiling for the TASS photographer were Kania and Pinkowski alongside Soviet representatives Brezhnev, Gromyko, Rusakov, Premier Nikolai Tikhonov, and First Deputy Premier Ivan Arkhipov. The official press release described the spirit of amity and agreement that characterized the discussions, with Brezhnev expressing Soviet confidence in the ability of the Poles to solve their own economic and political problems. Touching on the sources of the crisis, the communiqué spoke of outside intervention by "imperialist circles" intent on subverting socialist Poland.[85]

In the quiet chambers of the Kremlin, however, a far more critical attitude permeated Soviet assessments of the visit. Shortly after the Poles' departure, on 31 October, Politburo members met to express their misgivings about Kania and his handling of the crisis. Overall, they felt, the Poles had come across as indecisive on the question of confronting counterrevolution. Kania's leading concern expressed during the summit had been Poland's mounting indebtedness. As Brezhnev observed, "The economy of Poland finds itself directly dependent on the West." Kania was consequently driven by the fear that any strain on the situation in Poland would prompt the West to refuse further credits, a move that would bring Poland "to its knees."[86] This concern was doubtlessly responsible for the fact that, of all the points discussed during the summit, Kania's only objection had been to the imposition of martial law. Should the need arise, he had argued, the state knew how to use the army as well as whom to arrest. Still, Brezhnev commented to his colleagues, the Poles gave no indication that the time had come for such extreme measures.[87]

Evidently the Poles had chosen to delay their plans for martial law. Indeed, one wonders just how much they had divulged of these plans in talks with the Soviets. As Brezhnev remarked, "We directly asked Kania whether the Party had a plan for martial law when an open threat to national power emerges." This would seem to indicate that Jaruzelski had yet to present Moscow with any clear notion of his intentions. At the summit itself, Kania simply reassured the Soviets that Warsaw would be ready if and when the time came.[88]

Though Kania's apparent reluctance to consider martial law troubled Brezhnev, it was the Polish leader's attitude toward the question of counterrevolution that most concerned him. On the one hand, Brezhnev noted that both sides had reached "complete mutual understanding both on the causes of the crisis and on the scale of the counterrevolutionary threat."[89] On the other hand, Kania and Pinkowski seemed to be "afraid to mention the word counterrevolutionary." Brezhnev recalled that Soviet diplomats in Bonn had recently reported a conversation with Polish colleagues in which the latter had spoken of the possibility of an armed insurrection in Poland. The contradiction was striking. "How can these Polish comrades fail to understand the simple truth," Brezhnev exclaimed, "that counterrevolution is afoot all around them?" While not responding to this rhetorical outburst, both Andropov and Ustinov demanded further investigation into this suggestion of armed insurrection.[90] Although discussion of Soviet intervention did not arise at the October 31 Politburo session, Ustinov did call for continuing "vigilance" toward the developments in Poland.

While the summit seems to have shelved the question of outside military assistance for the time being, the Poles had also used the meeting to express a more political concern. Kania was worried that his government might appear to be under too much Soviet control. Therefore, while promising to share Moscow's concerns with his colleagues in Warsaw, the Polish first secretary also sought to avoid the appearance of Soviet involvement in Polish affairs. "It is important for the Polish leadership not to permit talk that it acts under orders from Moscow," Brezhnev explained.[91] Yet it did not occur to the general secretary that Kania might translate this preoccupation into a disregard for Soviet recommendations. To the contrary, Konstantin Chernenko believed that the summit had opened the eyes of the Poles to the actual situation in their country. "It will help them, of course," he said, "to be more energetic in those steps which they plan to undertake against antisocialist elements as well as to defend the achievements of socialism."[92]

Meanwhile, members of the Soviet state administration had already begun to take steps in defense of Soviet state interests by shoring up the nation's informational cordon sanitaire along the border with Poland. In conjunction with the propaganda measures outlined on 30 September, the Main Administration for the Protection of State Secrets in the Press, a part of the Council of Ministers, contrived further steps in October to "control" the distribution of thirty-one Polish newspapers and journals in the Soviet Union.[93] Removed from normal circulation, these publications were permitted delivery only to institutions maintaining "special collections" of foreign literature.[94] An additional twenty-six papers and journals from Poland were to be checked for objectionable material by Soviet censors before being forwarded to subscribers or sold to the public.[95]

The Main Administration also began to "control" all correspondence sent by post from Poland, both to organizations and to individuals. This was a daunting task. Each day one thousand to twelve hundred pieces of mail from Poland reached the international post office in Moscow. Additional pieces entered the USSR through Leningrad, Minsk, Vilnius, Riga, Kishinev, Lvov, and Brest. If all this was channeled to Moscow as well for inspection, volume was estimated to exceed three thousand pieces per day. While this volume appeared unmanageable, it was also deemed unavoidable, as the regional organs of the official censorship agency, Glavlit, were considered too inexperienced and understaffed to manage foreign-language materials. Therefore, the Main Administration requested that the Politburo approve an increase in the Moscow Glavlit staff that would enable it to cope with the additional work. Ideally, it recommended, the staff should include four people with knowledge of Polish—two editors and two inspectors.[96]

The measures undertaken by the Main Administration aimed to isolate Soviet society from potentially destabilizing Polish influences. Essentially, therefore, they were once again a logical continuation of the policy begun in 1978 to contain religious nationalism in Eastern Europe. During the intervening years, the lack of PZPR diligence on censorship issues had apparently brought the socialist camp to an even more dangerous juncture. This was no ancillary concern for Brezhnev and the Soviet Politburo. During the "normalization" of occupied Czechoslovakia, Moscow had learned how damaging an unfriendly press could be. This lesson only served to cement the Soviet conviction that strict censorship was vital in the struggle against Poland's opposition movement. If Warsaw was not up to the task, then Moscow's censors would have to protect Soviet interests themselves. When, on 5 December, the CPSU Secretariat finally recommended the Glavlit staff increase to the Central Committee, it justified the request with references to Polish negligence. The consequences, it predicted, could compromise Soviet interests by allowing "Polish anti-Soviet materials" into the USSR.[97]

The Central Committee ultimately approved this assessment and its recommendation on 22 December 1980, instructing the Soviet ambassador in Poland to reassure the Polish Central Committee that the new steps were "especially temporary" in nature. The message to Warsaw contained few details of the measures under way, short of noting that Moscow was "limiting the distribution of some Polish periodicals in the USSR."[98] The objective of the steps was, after all, the preservation of *Soviet* stability, not Polish. In the same way that Kremlin leaders had acted in the late 1970s to contain Poland's Catholic activism, so now they turned to the challenge of its unionism. While part of this effort involved getting the Poles to put their affairs in order, equal attention went to separate initiatives aimed at protecting Soviet domestic stability, regardless of what happened across the border.

Yet unaware of these provisions being taken to isolate Polish unionism in Eastern Europe, Kania returned from the Moscow summit on 30 October confident that the Soviets were at least not entertaining an immediate invasion of Poland. He immediately encountered a rising storm of protest from Solidarity representatives still upset by the conditions the court had attached to their charter. Moreover, in addition to Solidarity's original statutes they now demanded an independent farmers union, greater access to the mass media, pay raises, increased availability of consumer goods, and an end to "repression" of union activists. Refusal to make these concessions, they warned, would result in a nationwide general strike on 12 November.[99] Tensions rose as Polish television broadcast footage of Polish-Soviet joint military maneuvers, a clear implication that a military crackdown was being readied with the Warsaw Pact alliance.[100] At a Solidarity rally outside the Supreme Court in Warsaw on 10 November, a dark sense of humor turned the popular chant "Solidarity today, success tomorrow" to "Solidarity today, Soviets tomorrow!"[101]

In the end, both sides again chose compromise over confrontation. The Supreme Court agreed on 10 November to drop the offending clauses from Solidarity's legal statutes. In exchange, the union agreed to add as an appendix to the charter the first seven points of the Gdansk Accords—including recognition of the Party's leading role.[102] The fear of Soviet invasion prompted Solidarity to temper its additional demands. Of course, very few Poles found this to be a welcome factor in their domestic affairs. One day after the resolution of what came to be known as the "registration crisis," on 11 November, some ten thousand Poles rallied to the Tomb of the Unknown Soldier in Warsaw to mark Poland's interwar Independence Day. Here, around the body of a soldier killed in the 1920 war with Russia, people met to discuss patriotic themes such as independence, the 1939 Nazi-Soviet Pact, and the Katyn Massacre. British historian Timothy Garton Ash was present at the rally and reflected later, "For Solidarity to limit its demands to those which did not challenge Soviet vital interests required an immense act of national denial."[103] The patriotic demonstration illustrated that anti-Soviet antagonism lay at the very center both of Poland's national rage and of its continued self-control. What remained unclear was how long it would be before the former overcame the latter.

No doubt reflecting themselves on this question, the Polish leadership and General Staff met in early November to discuss their newly drafted plans for implementing martial law. It was to be this plan that would ultimately bear the responsibility for extinguishing Solidarity when the time came for confrontation. Indeed, according to Colonel Ryszard Kuklinski, "The initial vision or concept of the imposition of martial law—insofar as it regarded postulates and wishes as to what should be suspended, prohibited, ordered, militarized, and delegalized, where should the army be dispatched and where the security forces, who should be protected and who interned—was not far removed from the final concept implemented thirteen months later."[104]

Pressure to put these plans into action was strong. Moscow repeatedly urged Warsaw to act swiftly and decisively to destroy Solidarity. Meanwhile, Western governments inadvertently contributed to the sense of urgency facing Polish communists. On 4 November, Ronald Reagan was elected president; he had promised to increase the American military budget dramatically. Later, on 17 November, the defense ministers of the NATO member-nations voted to increase military spending by 3 percent and to reiterate the threat of nuclear first use if attacked by conventional forces.[105] That same day the first round of U.S.-Soviet talks aimed at eliminating nuclear missiles from European territory ended in a fiasco. Therefore, Warsaw and Moscow viewed Western support of Solidarity as consistent with a posture of ever increasing confrontation, poised to destabilize the East-West military and political balance in Europe.[106]

Poland's domestic developments did little to diffuse the perception that the Solidarity crisis was becoming a decisive battleground of the Cold War. Less than two weeks after the settlement of the "registration crisis," on 20 November, authorities arrested two Solidarity volunteers in Mazowsze, Jan Narozniak and Piotr Sapielo, for possession of a secret state document. Issued by Prosecutor General Lucjan Czubinski to his staff, the document was titled "On the Present Methods of Prosecution of Illegal Anti-socialist Activity" and contained a surprisingly inaccurate assessment of Polish opposition activities since 1964.[107] Nevertheless, the arrests of Narozniak and Sapielo ignited widespread public furor across Poland that culminated in scattered work stoppages and another threat of a general strike, scheduled this time for 27 November. On 25 November, the new Soviet consul in Gdansk, V. Zelenov, reported an increase in threatening phone calls coming into the consulate. He added that a letter had been delivered to him on the same day as the Mazowsze arrests, supposedly from KOR, which warned Soviet representatives to clear out of Poland by 20 December.[108]

Zelenov's report offered a sharply worded assessment of Solidarity that differed in tone and content from the earlier analysis of his predecessor. Whereas Vakhrameev's reports had once stressed the legitimate grievances that Polish workers brought to the negotiating table, Zelenov now warned against underestimating the antisocialist threat in Poland. The problems facing the Poles, he argued, were *not* simply the result of genuine worker resentment but reflected a failure to recognize and confront the nation's increasingly powerful antisocialist elements. "Analyzing the situation in Gdansk in the last two to three years," wrote Zelenov, "it is possible to trace how opposition elements gradually increased the number of their organizations, and in conditions of near-total lawlessness gradually legalized their activities."[109] He alleged that the Polish opposition had received instructions from "Western ideological centers" and that KOR virtually controlled the independent union movement.[110] In so doing, his dispatch confirmed Moscow's misgivings toward the October legalization of Solidarity and the failure of Kania's subsequent "administrative measures."

Coordinated Intimidation

As a result, Soviet intimidation tactics stepped up noticeably in late November 1980. On 24 November, facing railroad strikes in Poland, Moscow publicly condemned any obstruction of the secure transportation links used by the Warsaw Pact to shuttle men and matériel through Poland to East Germany as a violation of its vital national interests.[111] Three days later, on 27 November, *Pravda* called for "urgent measures" to restore the leading role of the Party in Poland.[112] That same day, before the morning papers had yet appeared on the streets, the Polish government released Narozniak and Sapielo with guarantees for their safety. Kuron and Walesa worked fast to head off the general strike, noting to their fellow unionists the importance of bearing in mind Poland's "geopolitical reality."[113]

Soviet leaders, however, were not at all reassured by this settlement. From Moscow's perspective, government concessions in the "Narozniak affair," in conjunction with the November 10 legalization of Solidarity's statutes, had compromised Kania's regime. Ryszard Kuklinski argues that in late November the Kremlin worried that Kania might even have been "playing a double game" in his discussions with Moscow. Therefore, Kuklinski claims, "at the end of November 1980 the Soviet leadership began to organize behind the stage a new PRL [Polska Rzeczpospolita Ludowa, or Polish People's Republic in Polish] leadership team, with the active participation of its embassy in Warsaw and the Supreme Commander of the United Armed Forces of [the] Warsaw Pact Marshal Viktor Kulikov and its representative at the Polish Army, Army General Afanasiy Shcheglov." Kuklinski holds that this new collaboration aimed at ensuring a seizure of power in Warsaw by PZPR hard-liners. Supposedly, this was to have been "preceded by the introduction of large military forces of the Soviet Union and other Warsaw Pact countries into Poland." The scenario Kuklinski describes would therefore have been a repetition of the 1968 invasion of Czechoslovakia.[114]

To many observers around the world, by late November the stage appeared to be set for an encore of 1968. Secret cables received from Kuklinski prompted American intelligence to read Soviet military maneuvers as clear evidence of an impending invasion. Informed of this prospect by Washington, many Western political leaders sought to warn the Soviets against invasion. Joseph Luns, the NATO secretary-general, offered the first of these public admonitions on 21 November, followed by the governments of several NATO member-nations on 28 November and 2 December.

Nevertheless, Western impressions notwithstanding, one must carefully consider how historical assumptions colored and even misinformed Ryszard Kuklinski's interpretations of Soviet intent. Kuklinski had participated in the 1968 invasion as a member of the Special Command Center of the Polish Army in Czechoslovakia, and he readily admits that this experience strongly influenced his views on the events of 1980.[115] Additionally, Kuklinski had no entrée into Soviet intentions at any time during the entire crisis. Though he might have gleaned some understanding of Soviet strategy from his contact with Polish leaders, Kuklinski was often reluctant to solicit their impressions. For example, in describing the meetings between Jaruzelski and Kulikov in late November, the colonel recalls, "The details of these dramatic conversations are unknown to me. General Jaruzelski alone can and should reveal them. As for me, I only know of their results." He writes that the discussions left Jaruzelski "utterly devastated."[116] Kuklinski's view of what had transpired was therefore based entirely on what he was able to surmise from Jaruzelski's demeanor.

What remains the great strength of Kuklinski's account is precisely this type of insight into how the Polish leadership *interpreted* Soviet intentions. Clearly, Kulikov's visit left Warsaw in a state of panic. Immediately after the Soviets departed, on 1 December, Jaruzelski dispatched two members of the Polish General Staff to Moscow: Army Division General

Tadeusz Hupalowski and Colonel Franciszek Puchala, retired. Kuklinski asserts that the objective of this mission was familiarization of the officers with Soviet plans for a military intervention from which Polish armed forces had been excluded entirely.[117] Kuklinski writes that fear of this impending invasion "completely paralyzed the then top leadership of the Ministry of Defense. General Jaruzelski was in a state of shock, stayed behind locked doors in his office and was completely inaccessible to even his closest associates . . . the paralysis lasted throughout November 30 and December 1. Everyone was waiting for a miracle."[118]

The Polish leadership concluded that Moscow simply underestimated the strength of the opposition it faced in Solidarity. Rather than restoring order, an invasion was likely to result in even greater social unrest, perhaps even the start of a national uprising. Consequently, Kuklinski writes, Jaruzelski used his influence with Moscow to effect a shift in the proposed intervention plans. After what amounted to "dramatic bargaining" with the Soviets, he secured an agreement "to the participation of a few Polish units in implementing secondary tasks." Two Polish armored divisions were to be attached to the participating two Czechoslovak divisions, while two Polish mechanized divisions joined the one involved German division. The Soviets, for their part, were supposedly prepared to deploy fifteen divisions.[119] With any luck, the Poles hoped, the increased presence of Polish forces in the crackdown would temper the kind of patriotic response that could lead to a civil war in Poland.

Since Kuklinski first went public with these recollections in the mid-1980s, additional accounts have appeared that permit a reexamination of his story. To begin with, U.S. reconnaissance photos never revealed a trace of the fifteen Soviet divisions Kuklinski claims were to take part in the purported intervention. As Mark Kramer writes, "The Special Analysis issued by the CIA on 24 December 1980, based on the imagery obtained between 16 and 18 December, marked the first solid determination since the cloud cover had receded over the western USSR that only three Soviet divisions were on full alert."[120]

Equally as compelling have been the reminiscences of former members of the Soviet General Staff who have offered their own testimonials about the events of 1980–81. At the time of the crisis, Army General Anatolii I. Gribkov was serving as first deputy chief of the General Staff of the Soviet Armed Forces. His direct superior was Marshal Viktor Kulikov, Supreme Commander of Warsaw Pact Forces. Both have publicly rejected the notion that an invasion was under way in the late autumn of 1980.[121] In denying that an invasion was under way in the late fall of 1980, General Gribkov explains that the Soviets were exploiting previously scheduled military maneuvers to influence a resolution of the Polish crisis through fear and intimidation. The Soiuz-80 exercises, he writes, were part of a regular series of maneuvers, planned long before December 1980. Each year when joint exercises were scheduled to occur, the WTO Military Council would meet in the fall to plan them. Thus it was determined that the Soiuz-80 exercises would be held in October 1980, at the end of the summer training season and after the fall harvest.[122] Participating forces were to include the Polish Coastal and Szlask military districts, the staff of the Soviet Western Military District, two Czechoslovak army staffs along with two from the GDR, and the staff of the Soviet Northern Group of Forces along with three other Soviet army staff groups. Marshal Kulikov was appointed to run the exercises, with Gribkov as his chief of staff.[123] At Warsaw's request, however, Moscow agreed to postpone the exercises indefinitely owing to the nature of Poland's deepening crisis. The entire operation consequently went on standby, though field communications, particularly radio relay stations, which had been deployed for the October exercises, remained in place, as it was estimated to be too costly in time and materials to reposition them later on.[124]

Strangely, Kuklinski, Kania, and Jaruzelski all fail to include consideration of these preparations in their accounts of the autumn military buildup. Instead, Kania's memoirs assert that Poland's neighbors were moving steadily in the direction of intervention. He writes that "the facts mounted quickly, the collective perception of which should have elicited apprehension and concern because of the reaction of the allied nations to the development of the situation in Poland. The initial sound of these facts was not very well developed to expect the threat of intervention, but some of them were sufficiently transparent. Ever sharper assessments of the situation in our country were being formulated. The Soviet ambassador in Warsaw exhibited more and more demonstrations of a critical nature in the face of the occurrences in our country and in relations to our policy. We noted the sharper tone of the press of our neighbors on the subject of Poland, especially in the GDR and Czechoslovakia."[125]

Poland's socialist neighbors had indeed responded with serious misgivings to the growth of Solidarity. Driving this reaction was their fear that the Polish opposition movement might spread and destabilize socialist rule throughout Eastern Europe. Speaking on 21 October at a meeting of the Bulgarian Politburo, one member, Grisha Filipov, voiced the concerns of all present that "similar events, regardless of the specific conditions in the People's Republic of Poland, are possible, too, in other socialist countries, if a right political line is not consistently carried out, if the ties with the masses are not being constantly strengthened, if a class approach is not implemented in solving the urgent problems of social and economic development."[126] What was at stake was clearly the fate of socialist rule in Eastern Europe, argued Petur Mladenov at a subsequent Politburo meeting four days later. "If we leave Poland, we'll have to be ready to leave the German Democratic Republic, too, we'll have to be ready for a war on a large scale." Bulgarian first secretary Todor Zhivkov agreed, adding only, "First Romania and Yugoslavia, then the German Democratic Republic."[127]

For the Warsaw Pact states that shared a border with Poland, these concerns elicited defensive initiatives that seriously upset amicable ties with Warsaw. During Soviet Politburo discussions on 29 October, Rusakov had observed, "Poland has not been developing especially good relations with a number of neighboring socialist nations, for instance with the GDR." He had noted that the East German government wanted to begin requiring visas for travel between Poland and the GDR, despite Polish objections. Rusakov had proposed at the time that the two nations be permitted to resolve the question without Soviet interference, and no one had objected.[128] In any event, matters played out rather more dramatically than expected. On 8 November rail traffic between Poland and the GDR was interrupted, and the border was temporarily closed. All visas for Poles planning to visit the GDR were suspended.[129] The move made a deep impression on Kania, who later wrote, "This happened at the initiative of the GDR, and it is hard not to tie this decision to later events."[130] The "later events" to which he refers were the apparent preparations for a Warsaw Pact invasion of Poland in December.

Czechoslovakia also responded defensively to the political threat looming just across the border in Poland. Czechoslovak Politburo member Vasil Bilak publicly warned the Poles on 1 November not to allow "the dismantling of socialism because no sensible person will wreck the foundation of a building or its roof when changing the windows."[131] A November 6 article in *Rude Pravo* further recalled that independent trade unions had been part of the reform agenda during the Prague Spring as well.[132] These sentiments translated into policy on 18 November when Czechoslovakia introduced new currency exchange requirements that significantly reduced travel along its border with Poland.

From Warsaw's perspective, the statements and policy initiatives originating in Berlin and Prague provided a decidedly ominous backdrop for the military preparations under way along Poland's borders throughout the late fall. Kania recalls that "at the end of November I received from various sources signals about the closure of traffic of a significant part of the territory of the GDR. Additionally, forces quickly took up positions along our border. The command of the united military forces of the Warsaw Pact nations advanced with the initiative of conducting joint exercises, though without a clear definition of their size or territorial extent."[133] If, as Gribkov suggests, the plans and objectives of the exercises had been worked out by October, it is unclear why the Poles would not have known about them, particularly if they were scheduled to take place largely in and around Poland. Either the Polish government had not been fully apprised of the plans or it did not believe those given it. Considering the tone of Kania's reminiscences, the latter would appear more likely.

Warsaw Pact Summit in Moscow

As the clouds of "invasion" seemed to gather over Poland in late November, a hopeful sign arrived from Moscow. It came in the form of a phone call from Brezhnev proposing that the Warsaw Pact nations hold a summit in Moscow on 1 December to discuss Poland's deepening crisis. Because the Polish Central Committee was due to hold its plenum on the first of the month, Kania proposed moving the summit to 5 December, and Brezhnev agreed.[134] To the Poles it seemed as if they would be given a hearing before tanks began to roll into their country. Moreover, at the Seventh PZPR Central Committee Plenum, Kania would have an opportunity to put the nation's political affairs in order before going to Moscow. Thus, in the minds of the Polish leadership, there was still hope to avert the catastrophe of an invasion.

At the plenum, Kania struggled to strike a balance between the two sides of Poland's rapidly polarizing society. He declared himself in favor of "the socialist character of renewal" and denounced conservatism as an obstacle to that process. At the same time, the Polish leader condemned anarchy, counterrevolution, and cooperation with Western "centers of imperialist subversion."[135] In a nod to Moscow, the plenum removed four members of the PZPR Politburo, though none were leading reform advocates. Essentially, the regime was trying to prop up a rapidly deteriorating political center while facing pressure on the one hand from Solidarity and on the other from Moscow. Although Kania could not possibly satisfy either, at this point he was simply interested in buying some time.

It was during the Polish plenum that Moscow requested Warsaw to dispatch a member of the Polish General Staff for consultations, the results of which appear in Kuklinski's later retrospective. General Jaruzelski goes more deeply into these consultations in his own memoirs. He writes that his emissary, General Hupalowski, met in Moscow with Soviet marshal Nikolai Ogarkov, along with representatives of the Czechoslovak and East German general staffs. According to Jaruzelski, they informed Hupalowski that a large contingent of allied forces would be conducting exercises on Polish territory. When Hupalowski sought further explanation, he was unable to get one. The Warsaw Pact representatives refused to clarify their intentions, and Hupalowski simply concluded the worst. They would permit the general to make copies of the plans outlining the exercises, which he was then to take back to Warsaw. Hupalowski dutifully did as instructed and flew back to meet with Kania.[136]

According to Jaruzelski, the plans brought back to Warsaw certainly seemed to indicate preparations for an invasion. Warsaw Pact forces would enter Poland from the north, east, and west. Participating would be fifteen Soviet divisions, two Czechoslovak divisions, and one East German division. Indeed, Jaruzelski writes, no sooner had Hupalowski returned with the exercise blueprints than allied forces began closing on Poland's borders. From Warsaw it appeared obvious that an invasion had moved into high gear.[137]

Meanwhile, back in Moscow, Defense Minister Dmitrii Ustinov summoned Marshal Kulikov and General Gribkov to his office to inform them that the Soiuz-80 exercises had finally been rescheduled to begin in early December. Ustinov told his two staff officers that the decision had been cleared with the defense ministers of all participating countries: Jaruzelski in Poland, Dzur in Czechoslovakia, and Hofman in the GDR. At first, Kulikov and Gribkov objected to a December commencement, on the grounds that the Christmas holidays (celebrated in Eastern Europe) and New Year celebrations made December–January a bad time for exercises. Instead, they suggested postponing the exercises until February or March 1981. Ustinov, however, was not at all receptive to their advice and ordered them to begin the exercises in December as instructed. Politics, they realized, and not military logic, was calling the shots. "We understood that this command came not from Ustinov," Gribkov explains, "but from our highest political leadership, which was trying to exert pressure on the Polish leadership and society along all fronts."[138]

If, in fact, the December commencement of Soiuz-80 had been cleared with the East Europeans, the specific date remained to be fixed. The East Europeans, including Jaruzelski, anticipated a much later starting date than Moscow was suggesting. Gribkov recalls, "When the ministers of defense found out that the start of the exercises had been moved to 8–10 December, they were surprised."[139] Undoubtedly no one was more surprised than the Poles.[140] In advising Warsaw, Marshal Kulikov fixed the commencement for 12:00 A.M. on 8 December. The Poles, however, refused to approve what they still believed was to be an invasion of their country by Warsaw Pact forces. To begin with, Gribkov recalls, Jaruzelski was unwilling to accept the plans as drafted. As Kuklinski has observed, the Polish defense minister was unhappy with the role assigned to Polish forces and sought to redress this oversight. Meanwhile, Kania still hoped for an audience with Brezhnev at which he might convince the Soviet leader to call off the whole affair. Poland, he would argue, was perfectly capable of managing, if the need arose, with its own security forces.[141] "It seemed to me," Gribkov later observed, "that S. Kania was afraid that under the guise of the exercises in Poland allied troops would be sent in, and surely that would be the start of a catastrophe."[142] Indeed, this is *precisely* what Kania, along with most of the Polish civil and military leadership, feared.[143] The Soviet military ruse, it appeared, was proceeding as planned.

As Warsaw Pact intimidation continued to mount, at least one member of the Polish General Staff demanded an immediate imposition of martial law. Army General Eugeniusz Molczyk had been at a meeting of the WTO Committee of Defense Ministers in Bucharest, Romania, on 1–3 December when tensions reached peak levels. On his return to Warsaw, Molczyk went to Jaruzelski to demand a prompt crackdown against Solidarity. "History will never forgive us if they [the Soviets] do the job for us!" he argued.[144] Jaruzelski, however, agreed with Kania that there was still time to persuade the alliance to call off its "invasion" during the upcoming Moscow summit meeting.[145]

In the meantime, Polish authorities exploited widespread rumors of impending invasion to restore order in the workplace. On 4 December, as the Polish delegation arrived in Moscow for the WTO summit, a Polish government spokesman told foreign journalists that "Polish communists would have the right and duty to ask for assistance from other socialist countries" if the socialist system were in jeopardy.[146] Of course, nothing was further from Kania's mind, but this type of rhetoric was a compelling way of securing obedience to the state. If sufficiently cowed, perhaps Polish society would settle for Kania's relatively minor socioeconomic concessions.

From the moment that the Polish delegation arrived in Moscow, it became clear that Kania would have just as much difficulty selling this "middle road" approach to the Soviets as to KOR and Solidarity. Mikhail Suslov met the Poles at the airport and immediately raised the question of Polish additions to the summit's final communiqué, which was already being drafted. Expressing displeasure with Kania's address to the Seventh Central Committee Plenum, Suslov refused to countenance any favorable references to "socialist renewal" in Poland.[147]

Later that same day, in talks with Ustinov, Kania found the Soviet defense minister very worried about the situation in Poland. Nevertheless, he notes in his memoirs, Ustinov carefully "avoided references to the matter of intervention." He concluded gravely that Ustinov preferred to leave discussion of the invasion to Brezhnev himself. And so, at Kania's request, Ustinov arranged a private meeting with the general secretary for 5 December after the summit meetings. Though Kania had hoped to speak with Brezhnev *before* the summit, he nonetheless breathed a sigh of relief. "There is still hope," he thought as he worked through the night to refine the argument he would present at the conference.[148]

Unbeknown to Kania and the other members of his delegation, that same night the other bloc leaders met to coordinate a common position on the question of military intervention. A number of the East Europeans, especially Honecker and Husak, were strongly in favor of sending in troops.[149] Others, notably Kadar and Ceausescu, remained equally opposed.[150] Bulgaria's Todor Zhivkov was uncommitted, no doubt waiting characteristically to follow Brezhnev's lead. Consequently, the secret meeting of 4 December offered the Soviets an opportunity to assert a uniform policy for the summit meetings the following day. While the Poles could be frightened, they would not be invaded. If this was not absolutely clear prior to the secret meeting, that gathering resolved the issue. "What took place later in our presence," Jaruzelski notes, "was therefore above all a demonstration, pressure, a serious warning, and in our case, this was our first warning."[151]

What, then, of the plans to send troops into Poland? After all, both Polish and Soviet sources confirm that blueprints for such action did exist. As General Gribkov admits, "The natural question is, was there a plan to send troops into Poland? There was such a plan. Moreover, the routes of entry and regions of troop concentration had been reconnoitered, in which Polish representatives had actively taken part."[152] For the time being, however, there was little chance that the plans would be put into action either to provide military assistance to a Polish government crackdown or to invade Poland on a more massive scale. Polish authorities had displayed nothing but opposition to the first of these options, while Soviet preparations were insufficient to carry out the second at any time in late 1980. Consequently, the maneuvers conducted along Poland's borders in the late fall appear to have been precisely what they purported to be—preparations for the Soiuz-80 joint exercises. What of the fact that, in the course of 1980–81, a number of Soviet divisional commanders had convinced themselves that they were preparing for an impending invasion?[153] Gribkov explains that in the context of Soviet military doctrine, routes to the West were regularly maintained and reconnoitered for the rapid advancement of reserves in a conflict with NATO. This ongoing practice, undertaken amid the uncertainty of the Polish crisis, could well have convinced those involved that an invasion was being prepared. However, the former chief of staff points out, Soviet divisional commanders were not privy to the consultations and objectives of the Kremlin leadership, which, Gribkov assures, were against an invasion of Poland.[154]

Evidence exists that Warsaw's East European allies suspected in advance of the secret December 4 consultations that there would be no invasion. Around the time of the summit, the head of the East German secret police (Stasi), General Marcus Wolff, confided to visiting Polish communist Franciszek Szlachcic that "the Soviets won't go in."[155] Similarly, on 3 December, the premiers of both Czechoslovakia (Lubomir Strougal) and the

GDR (Willi Stoph) "voiced the conviction that the Polish working class and people, led by the United Workers Party, will cope successfully with their complicated problems and will strengthen socialism."[156] Finally, the simple fact that Nicolae Ceausescu agreed to attend the meeting, something he refused to do during the planning for the invasion of Czechoslovakia, strongly suggests that he had been assured in advance that there would be no intervention.

It was therefore an exercise in collective intimidation that took place on 5 December in a villa overlooking the Moskva River and Moscow's famous Novodevichy convent.[157] The summit began with a short, firm lecture from Brezhnev himself.[158] The general secretary remarked that he had warned Edward Gierek for many years not to tolerate opposition activities in Poland. At long last, he declared, the time had come to say "yes" to democracy and decisiveness and "no" to counterrevolution.[159] Notwithstanding Suslov's earlier rejection of Poland's "socialist renewal," Brezhnev favorably assessed the proceedings of the Seventh PZPR Central Committee Plenum. But he went on to note ominously that the USSR would consider developments in Poland in the context of bloc security, consistent with its responsibilities to the Warsaw Pact alliance. It was here that he first made a pledge that would see frequent repetition in the months to come: "The Poles will not be abandoned in distress, and we will not allow them to be harmed." The implicit meaning of these words was not lost on the Poles. "Although the word 'assistance' rings warmly when linked with 'distress,'" Kania would later write, "at the time, and afterward, it nevertheless prompted ominous associations."[160]

Following Brezhnev's introductory statements, Kania rose calmly to address the gathering.[161] He began with an admission that Poland's crisis had reached a very serious juncture. The West, he observed, was financing and otherwise supporting the national opposition movement. Moreover, that movement was closely linked to KOR and other revisionist firebrands whose goals since 1976 had been openly counterrevolutionary. However, he added, Polish authorities had already begun to arrest members of these groups and were working to create the political conditions necessary to go after KOR itself. For the time being, therefore, political solutions remained both wise and necessary. The alternative in August and September "could have provoked an avalanche of incidents and led to a bloody confrontation, the results of which would have impacted on the entire socialist world."[162] Solidarity, Kania warned, should not be underestimated. At least 5 million strong, it had shown a capacity to command widespread support within Polish society. While its strikes had taken on an obviously political character, they also rendered the independent union more powerful in its battle with the state.

Despite such a solemn prognosis, the Polish leader argued that his government could still manage to reverse these developments successfully. Already it had begun to mobilize the Party faithful, whose ranks by late December were expected to number around thirty thousand. If needed, the government planned to arm these individuals against a possible rebellion by workers. For the time being, though, its highest priority remained liberating Poland from economic dependence on the West. It was this type of assistance—the economic variety—that Warsaw most required from its allies. Meanwhile, Kania promised, the Polish Party and government would do everything it could to strengthen its position and authority in society. Should events take a turn for the worse, he implied, its measures would not be limited to politics.[163]

The allied response to Kania's presentation was not nearly as sanguine. Nevertheless, opinions did vary by degree. Todor Zhivkov did not mince his words about the damage the crisis had already caused within the socialist camp. "The developments in Poland," he said, "concern all socialist countries, the entire socialist community." He observed that the strikes had given the West cause to argue "that the political and economic system of socialism is not viable." If permitted to continue, Zhivkov cautioned, the crisis could bring about a shift in Poland's social order in the direction of liberal socialism, "which then could pose an example and provoke changes in the social order in other countries of the socialist community."[164] The only remaining domestic solution, in Zhivkov's opinion, was for the Polish state to act decisively with its army and other security forces to reimpose communist authority. "If the state or dictatorship of the proletariat should decay," Jaruzelski recalls him concluding, "then all that remains is international assistance."[165]

Hungary's Janos Kadar spoke along similar lines, albeit in a significantly less menacing tone. The crisis in Poland, he pointed out, seriously affected all the other countries of the bloc. However, Kadar continued, Hungary's official position was that "this is an internal Polish question which has to be resolved by the Poles," provided that Poland was not separated from the Warsaw Pact. He argued that "the defense of certain things has to be guaranteed—a defense by all means. And this has to become evident. This is the best way to avoid bloodshed. Because if it is clear that every means possible will be employed, bloodshed will be avoided."[166]

Erich Honecker did not permit himself such diplomatic language. The Polish events, he declared, were a repeat of the type of creeping counterrevolution witnessed in the 1968 Prague Spring. The developments of 1968 had shown how counterrevolution could come about by peaceful means. Therefore, he argued, even in the absence of open revolt in Poland, the PZPR ought to employ strict methods of societal constraint. Honecker did not attempt to conceal his unqualified disdain for the process of "socialist renewal" in Poland, observing that Dubcek also argued that the Prague Spring was "not a counterrevolution, but a 'process of democratic renewal of socialism.'" One of the leading proponents of invasion before the meeting, Honecker was not shy about expressing his readiness to commit East German forces if and when the time came. "Dear Comrades!" he declared. "We have gathered here in order to consult collectively on the possible support by the fraternal countries, which might be useful to Comrade Kania and all of the comrades in the PZPR in strengthening the people's power in Poland. Our Party and our people have great expectations with regard to this meeting."[167]

Following Honecker's forthright attacks, the comments of Romania's Nicolae Ceausescu must have come as something of a relief to the Polish delegation. As was his wont, Ceausescu played down the issue of outside intervention. Notwithstanding the meeting's goal of intimidating the Poles, Ceausescu expressed "concern and indeed the desire to have these problems resolved by the Poles themselves and to avoid them damaging the policy of détente, peace, and cooperation." Romania, he said, did not want to interfere in Poland's internal affairs. "The PZPR, the Polish working class and the Polish people, as well as all the progressive forces in Poland," he concluded, "know that they have to find the appropriate ways to overcome this situation, develop the economy, increase the standard of living, based on socialist construction and according to conditions in Poland."[168]

Whatever spirit of understanding Ceausescu might have engendered with his remarks evaporated entirely when Gustav Husak took the floor. Husak again stressed the threat posed to Czechoslovakia and the rest of the bloc by the Polish opposition, underscoring its similarities to earlier postwar insurrections. Acting as they had previously in Hungary and Czechoslovakia, he said, counterrevolutionary forces want to tear Poland from the socialist camp. The assistance of the socialist nations, he recalled of 1968, had enabled the avoidance of civil war and of Czechoslovakia's detachment from the socialist camp. "We know, dear comrades," Husak concluded, "that these problems of which I have spoken were of a different sort. It seems to me that the PZPR has a better leadership today than we in the CSSR had back then. But the question of decisiveness and determination to solve the problems energetically remains acute."[169]

Leonid Brezhnev was the last to speak. He summed up the previous remarks with an extended critique of Warsaw's apparent indecisiveness. "The crisis," he said, "hurts the entire socialist community, the international communist movement. It can have a negative impact on the general balance of power." The time had come for action, he continued. "We have to turn the course of events around and should not wait until the enemy has the Party with its back against the wall. In one word: the

Polish comrades themselves must go on the offensive against the counter-revolution and its intellectual heads." Although Moscow had been patient thus far with Warsaw's political approach to the crisis, the time had come for more forceful measures. "We do not favor taking extreme measures without extreme circumstances," Brezhnev lectured the Poles, "and we understand the caution. But this is certain: should the enemy assume power, he would not hold back like that. From experience we know that the enemy, once in power, immediately takes extreme measures in order to eliminate the Party and destroy socialism." He concluded: "Comrades. Officially the situation in Poland is not termed an emergency situation [martial law]. But in reality it is. Of course, the formal act does not matter. Hence the Polish comrades are acting correctly when they prepare for extraordinary measures. Intermediate steps have to be taken immediately since there is no time left until the start of the counteroffensive. Tomorrow it will be more difficult than today to cope with the counter-revolution."[170]

When Brezhnev concluded his remarks, the summit adjourned without reaching a formal decision on the matter of "international assistance." Still unaware that there was to be no invasion, the Poles left the meeting convinced decidedly to the contrary. Judging from accounts of the summit described in the memoirs of both Kania and Jaruzelski, its overall tone had badly intimidated the Polish delegation. "It became ever more obvious," Kania later wrote, "that our neighbors were preparing an invasion, that they would gain something like consent from us." But the Polish leader had no intention of providing that consent. He later recalled: "It remained therefore a state of peculiar suspension. Sharp judgments and pause. For this reason, the actual finale of the trip to Moscow was my fundamental conversation with Leonid Brezhnev."[171]

Kania met with Brezhnev and Rusakov on 5 December, shortly after the summit proceedings. According to his recollections of this "pivotal" meeting, the Polish leader used the opportunity to assert in no uncertain terms that armed intervention was not in the best interests of either Poland or the Soviet Union. The notion ought to be abandoned altogether, he argued, complete with a withdrawal of all Warsaw Pact forces from the Polish border.

Brezhnev listened patiently to Kania and then assumed an air of magnanimity and compromise. Still not revealing that the alliance had no intention of invading Poland, he exploited Polish anxieties as much as possible. "But all right," he began, "we won't go in." And then, after a pause, he seemed to reconsider. "But now it will become complicated, so we'll go in, we'll go in." Finally, of course, Brezhnev returned to the preordained conclusion: "But without you, we won't go in."[172] To Kania, it appeared as if Brezhnev had relented and that the "invasion" would finally be called off at the eleventh hour. Brezhnev, however, had not played his last card. As the two men parted company, he warned Kania that "if there are any complications, we will go in."[173] Intimidation, then, would continue as the key to Moscow's motivational policies toward the Polish government. As Jaruzelski later explained, Brezhnev's parting words remained an "unceasing warning" in the minds of the Polish leadership from that time forward.[174]

In the days that followed the Warsaw Pact summit, Moscow appeared initially reluctant to abandon its hard line on Poland, despite Brezhnev's "understanding" with Kania. Initial signs from Moscow were not promising. Stansfield Turner, director of the CIA, advised President Jimmy Carter on 7 December that "a joint [WTO] decision to invade was made on December 5 and can come as early as the morning or the night of the 7th. That is to say, tonight." Later that same day, NSC adviser Zbigniew Brzezinski alerted the press of this prospect and then contacted Solidarity leaders through AFL-CIO (American Federation of Labor and Congress of Industrial Organizations) channels "so that they [could] take necessary cover."[175] Meanwhile, the Soviet press continued to file reports of Poland's instability in the face of hostile opposition forces. A TASS report broadcast over Radio Moscow on the morning of 8 December spoke of counterrevolutionaries operating within the branches of Solidarity who had "turned to open confrontation" with the state and factory administrations. "These and other facts," it warned, "demonstrate that counterrevolution is leading the situation [in Poland] toward further instability and a deepening of the political struggle."[176] By evening the report had vanished from the news, prompting speculation that, with Brezhnev off visiting India, Soviet policy toward Poland remained in a state of flux.[177] However, two days later Marshal Ustinov repeated calls for "vigilance" against efforts by "reactionary" elements to undermine socialism throughout the bloc.[178]

Moscow's tough facade finally began to mellow after this final warning. In Poland, the Solidarity leadership and Catholic hierarchy issued appeals for calm on 10–11 December and openly criticized the more radical wing of the national opposition movement. Strike activity also declined considerably during this period.[179] Perhaps taking these developments into consideration, on 12 December both Radio Moscow and *Pravda* ran reports that offered the first positive commentary about Solidarity since the union's formation. Quoting Poland's *Zolnierz Wolnosci*, the Soviet press observed that "the Party, all patriots, and the vast majority of Poles . . . say yes to the process of renewal, to necessary economic reforms, to necessary changes in the trade-union movement, including Solidarity."[180] Considering the earlier commotion in Moscow over the term "socialist renewal," the report of 12 December signaled a sharp turn in Soviet policy toward the Polish crisis. Only a few days later, West Germany's *Der Spiegel* published an interview with Valentin Falin, head of the CPSU International Information Department. The interview had been conducted on 9 December, when Moscow still appeared unreconciled with Polish developments. Nevertheless, Falin was quite direct in promising that Moscow had no intention of intervening in Poland.[181] Similar sentiments appeared in the comments of Vadim Zagladin, first deputy of the CPSU International Department, during his December 9–11 visit to Rome. Sent to calm the fears of the Italian Communist Party, Zagladin expressed confidence that the Poles could work out their own problems without outside interference.[182]

While these were hopeful signs for the future of Polish sovereignty, they may have rung a bit hollow against the background of the Soiuz-80 exercises, which were held after all, beginning in early December. According to Anatolii Gribkov, the Warsaw Pact high command reopened its staff headquarters in Legnica, Poland, location of the regional communications interchange, on 10 December. Taking full account of the tensions earlier in the month, every effort was taken to avoid any suggestion of Warsaw Pact intervention in Poland. Therefore, Gribkov writes, "in the course of the exercises not one staff, not one subunit or section, not one soldier crossed the national border of a neighboring state, so as not to give the remotest cause for a provocation. Even we [the General Staff] didn't cross the Polish border in cars. We flew in by plane."[183]

The self-control of Warsaw Pact forces notwithstanding, the Soiuz-80 exercises prompted many in Poland to fear the continued prospect of invasion. On Sunday, 14 December, prayers were offered at Masses throughout Poland for national unity, expressing hope that "the institutions of our state remain secure and the sovereignty of our nation is not threatened."[184] Four days later Kania hinted that Moscow still had "deep anxiety" about the situation in Poland but assured his nation that the PZPR was capable of managing the crisis itself. In these remarks, broadcast over Radio Warsaw on the evening news, the first secretary also recognized the existence of a trend in Poland toward social democracy. He identified this trend as arising from the people's need to transform the Polish sociopolitical system.[185] In the face of a clearly popular reform movement, the Party in Poland was working hard to assert its own authority over the process of political evolution. For the time being, Moscow appeared content to stand back and see what Warsaw could manage itself, while working furiously to keep the Polish contagion out of the Soviet Union.

Conclusion

Why did Moscow elect to avoid intervention in December 1980 despite talk of an open counterrevolution in Poland? In his memoirs, General

Jaruzelski offers three compelling reasons. First, the ideological "heresy" in Poland was still in its early stages by late 1980. The Polish system continued to function, and the opposition had yet to challenge openly the Party's leading role. Second, to intervene in the affairs of a sovereign country, Jaruzelski writes, it is indispensable to have some support within the target nation, not to mention sufficient force to consolidate control afterward. Warsaw's resolute refusal to entertain offers of "international assistance" rendered the first of these conditions impossible. Moreover, it was not at all clear, in Jaruzelski's view, that the second could have been met either in December 1980. Finally, the Polish general concludes, Western warnings to the Soviet leadership played a decisive role in limiting Soviet options, particularly in the tension-filled days of late November and early December.

Each of these factors clearly played a role in the Soviet decision, as the preceding discussion has shown. The third factor of Western involvement merits special consideration, however, as its precise role has long been misunderstood. By 1980, Soviet relations with the West were in a precipitous decline. The December 1979 invasion of Afghanistan had shattered ties with the United States and left those with Western Europe on unsure footing. In February 1980, German chancellor Helmut Schmidt and French president Giscard d'Estaing issued a joint communiqué that warned that "détente cannot withstand another new blow" like the December invasion.[186] This was indeed a weighty prospect, as the Soviets had come to benefit tremendously from the political and technological dividends of East-West cooperation. A Soviet move into Poland, however, could have destroyed what little remained of these benefits.[187] Additionally, it would have given greater impetus to U.S.-Sino military cooperation along the borders of the USSR.[188]

Western concern about the fate of Poland was evident in the many official warnings presented to Moscow in the late autumn of 1980. Representatives of NATO voiced their anxieties on 21 and 28 November. Similar signals continued into the early part of December as well, beginning with an expression of apprehension concerning Soviet intentions in Poland at a summit of the European Economic Community (EEC) on 2 December. Then, on 3 December, American president Jimmy Carter warned Leonid Brezhnev that "intervention, or invasion of Poland, would be most serious and adverse for East-West relationships in general and particularly relations between the United States and the Soviet Union."[189] The president was careful to add that the United States had no intention of exploiting Polish developments in a way that would threaten "legitimate Soviet security interests."[190] Further warnings from the U.S. State Department and other American political figures followed on 4 and 7 December. Finally, the NATO member-nations issued a joint statement on 10 December reiterating their concern about events in Poland. Thus, unlike in 1968, when the United States and its allies had turned a blind eye on Czechoslovakia, December 1980 found Western attention riveted on Poland. Not only did this add the future of East-West relations to the invasion equation, but it also eliminated the element of surprise from any potential invasion scenario.[191]

Nevertheless, there does not appear to have been any point in 1980 when a majority, or even a significant minority, of the Politburo seriously considered acting on the invasion provisions contained in the Suslov Commission's August 28 memorandum.[192] As both East German and American sources reveal, Soviet military preparations in late 1980 never exceeded levels that could, at best, have rendered assistance to an imposition of martial law from Warsaw. Moreover, while it seems the Soviets might well have provided this kind of limited military assistance had Kania requested it, his persistent refusal to issue such a request ensured that allied intervention did not occur. In this respect, Brezhnev seems to have been quite sincere in his assertion to Kania that "without you, we won't go in."

This, then, was the condition of the Brezhnev Doctrine at the start of the Solidarity crisis in Poland. Although the Kremlin roundly regarded Solidarity as counterrevolutionary, it was still possible that Kania and Jaruzelski might defeat the Polish opposition with their own forces. Therefore, there was no cause to rush a final decision on the question of military intervention. As of December 1980, the provisions outlined in the August 28 Suslov Commission memorandum still remained in the realm of possibility. Did the Soviets continue, in the wake of Afghanistan, to regard the "duties" of internationalism as compatible with their long-term national interests? Would they consider an invasion if it appeared that the PZPR was incapable of acting decisively to crush the threat to communist rule in Poland? As of late December 1980, events on the ground in Poland had yet to force the Soviet leaders to address these fundamental questions.

The Collapse of Socialist Internationalism

So these princes of ours who had been for many years entrenched in
their states have no cause to complain of fortune because they have lost
them; . . . adversity caught them unprepared and their first thought was
of flight and not defense, hoping that their people would weary of the
insolence of the conqueror and so recall them. This is a good resource, to
be sure, when there is no other, but it is ill to neglect other remedies in
favor of such a hope, for certainly we should never be willing to fall simply
in the belief that someone will pick us up again. For this may not happen,
and if it does happen it does not help in your salvation, for it is a cowardly
kind of defense and not based on your efforts, and the only good, reliable,
and enduring defense is one that comes from yourself and your own valor
and ability.
—Niccolò Machiavelli, *The Prince*

AS THE SOLIDARITY CRISIS CONTINUED INTO 1981, it became increasingly obvious that Moscow had no intention of toning down its pressure on Poland. The opposition had begun to assert itself again, this time in support of Rural Solidarity, a fully independent farmers union. Although the resulting standoff brought Defense Minister Jaruzelski to the post of prime minister in February, the general proved extremely reluctant to introduce martial law in Poland, preferring instead to seek a resolution through selective intimidation. By late March this limited resort to force once again prompted Solidarity to call for a crippling nationwide general strike.

Hence, from Moscow's vantage point, the promises of the Moscow Conference dissipated completely with the start of the new year, as Poland continued to slide, unabated, into chaos. The events of late 1980 seemed to demonstrate that the only effective check to opposition assertiveness in Poland had been the threat of a Warsaw Pact invasion. Indeed, that appeared to be the only language that Polish authorities understood as well. This conviction returned Soviet troops to the field again in late March, as Poland was poised to weather Solidarity's general strike. For the first time since the start of the crisis, Solidarity backed down without receiving any significant state concessions, calling off the proposed strike in the interest of peace. But it seemed only a matter of time before the union's more aggressive elements would choose to call the Soviet bluff. Should that day come before Warsaw imposed order with its own forces, Moscow would require a response to be in place and ready.

It was the formulation of that response by mid-1981 that characterized this period as the most decisive in Soviet bloc policy since 1968. Whereas the Soviets had long been willing to send in some troops to reinforce a domestic resolution of the Polish crisis, the Kremlin had never fully resolved the question of whether to regard a wholesale invasion as a last resort. Moreover, by early 1981, Soviet perceptions regarding the nature of the crisis were beginning to shift dramatically as it became clear that the Polish government had brought the country to the verge of socio-economic catastrophe through corruption and mismanagement. It was becoming increasingly difficult to deny that the Solidarity opposition did represent the opinion of most Polish workers, not to mention a fair proportion of the Party and military as well. In whose name, then, could Soviet and other Warsaw Pact troops be sent into Poland? Moreover, what would be the consequences of such action? These questions had arisen two years earlier, before the invasion of Afghanistan. Moscow's failure to show restraint then had badly damaged the international prestige of the Soviet Union, not to mention its economic, technological, and military development. Similar action in Poland, the Soviets realized, would doubtless carry similarly devastating consequences for Soviet national interests. Therefore, by June 1981, the Soviet General Staff recommended almost unanimously that the Kremlin avoid any involvement in a Polish civil conflict at all costs. The Politburo agreed. Under no circumstances would Soviet or other Warsaw Pact forces be sent into Poland, even to support a Warsaw-coordinated crackdown.

Confronting Communist Inadequacy in Poland

For the troops participating in the December Soiuz-80 exercises, plans to celebrate the holidays would have to be canceled. Just before Christmas, unexpected orders came down from Moscow to extend the maneuvers beyond their scheduled December 21 conclusion "until further notice." Although the Soviet General Staff now had to spend all night working out additional training objectives for their troops, Kulikov and Gribkov chose not to question Ustinov again. It was clear to everyone involved, Gribkov later wrote, that the Warsaw Pact would be used to "continue the pressure on the Polish leadership and society" into the new year.[1] The protracted maneuvers had no clear military objectives, Gribkov notes frankly. Rather, "it became necessary to extend the duration of the exercise to show the Polish leadership and the Polish people that we were prepared to defend Poland from counterrevolution . . . although we were not."[2]

The issue that lay behind Moscow's decision to prolong the maneuvers was Solidarity's campaign to extend union membership to Poland's many private farmers.[3] The Rural Solidarity movement had filed an appeal with the Polish Supreme Court and on 30 December received news that its hearing had been postponed. As a result, tensions began to rise once again throughout the country. In Rzeszow, farmers staged an occupation strike in the headquarters of the defunct Provincial Council of Trade Unions on 2 January. Kania responded to the occupation a little over a week later by dismissing the very idea of a farmers union in Poland. Solidarity then turned to the Vatican for support and on 15 January, during a meeting between Lech Walesa and Pope John Paul, received the pontiff's blessing.[4]

Despite the decision to extend Soiuz-80 in response to these developments, Moscow assertively denied suggestions that it was preparing an invasion of Poland.[5] Although the military was used to maintain pressure on Poland, Moscow was careful to avoid any suggestions that might galvanize the Poles against a common enemy. Nevertheless, by January 1981 there were indications that even the Polish leadership was concerned about a possible invasion. Of particular concern was an unusually large number of reassignments in the Soviet Ground Forces high command during the months of December and January. A total of thirteen important staffing changes occurred at this time in the military districts bordering on Poland, including six generals commanding military districts or groups, four generals heading political directorates, and three higher-ranking generals of the Ground Forces.[6] While these changes seem to have been intended to provide for improved discipline among the forces along the Polish frontier at a time of great international tension, they were not seen as such in Warsaw. "Frankly speaking," Gribkov recalls, "this reshuffling elicited many unnecessary and incorrect conclusions, discussions, and hints that frightened Kania."[7] Sensing that Warsaw had drawn the wrong message from its maneuvers, Moscow began to moderate its press statements in late December and in early January.

No doubt contributing to Moscow's constraint was a growing conviction that the Polish people were not necessarily behind an overthrow of socialism in their country. This prospect was at the center of a brief analysis written by Bogomolov Institute scholar Aleksandr Tsipko following his return from Poland in December. On 20 January 1981, O. T. Bogomolov forwarded the report to Yuri Andropov at KGB headquarters.[8] Its conclusions challenged the notion that the Polish opposition was a monolithic bloc striving for the overthrow of socialism. Indeed, Tsipko noted, no one from the Church to the intellectual elite was questioning the worth of socialism in Poland. While the leaders of the Solidarity movement had begun to show signs of having political aspirations, "the majority of the rank-and-file members of 'Solidarity' avoid any political activity, not to mention activity directed against socialism."[9]

Tsipko's Polish associates went as far as to speculate that the state and Party apparatus was objectively strengthening what few antisocialist forces there were through its confrontational attitude with Solidarity.[10] One Polish scholar, the head of the Department of Propaganda and Ideology in the PZPR Central Committee Secretariat, W. Nametkewicz, blamed the rise of antisocialism on so-called Zionists. "No one in Poland is as interested in bloodletting, particularly in a military strike by Soviet forces on the local population, as the Zionists," Nametkewicz argued. Nevertheless, he warned, "there can be no doubt . . . that any external military interference in the affairs of the [Polish People's Republic] will lead to widespread armed resistance. Poles are not Czechs, and here there can be no illusions."[11] Tsipko was in full agreement. Intervention by foreign troops, he predicted, would prompt members of the Polish armed forces and many members of the Communist Party itself to revive a long tradition of underground resistance to outside invasion.[12]

The events of 1980 were fundamentally different from those which occurred in 1968, Tsipko argued. The Prague Spring had seen an openly antisocialist movement for reform sweep through the leadership of the Party while having a minimal impact on ordinary workers. In Poland, on the other hand, the agent of political transformation was the working class, "which from the very start defined its attitude toward the fundamental principles of socialism in [Poland], as toward the alliance responsibilities of its nation, in a positive manner." Indeed, Tsipko suggested, it had been the corruption of socialist values that had prompted worker unrest in the summer of 1980. He quoted Zbigniew Sufin, the deputy director of the Institute for Fundamental Problems, as arguing in this context that "at the base of the present movement of the Polish working class lies its legitimate discontent with the socialist candidates of the last ten years."[13] Everyone in Poland recognized that the nation's socioeconomic crisis was essentially the fault of Gierek's mismanagement in the 1970s. Consequently, Tsipko wrote, the most important step toward stabilization in Poland would involve restoring the moral authority of the PZPR leadership in the eyes of its people. It was not special talent that was needed in government, his Polish contacts assured him. Poland merely needed to find an honest man who kept his word and did not deceive his fellow Poles.[14] Should the Party begin to deal fairly and legally with Solidarity, Tsipko's report concluded, it would undermine the notion of a common enemy that was holding the union together. In its absence, the opposition movement was certain to fragment in time and collapse. The key was simply to act responsibly and wait for this to occur.[15]

Andropov might well have dismissed Tsipko's findings as exceedingly revisionist were it not for the fact that a member of the Soviet Politburo, L. M. Zamiatin, returned from his own visit to Poland in January 1981 with a number of similar impressions. In a January 22 briefing presented to his colleagues in the Kremlin, Zamiatin admitted that "the difficulty in Poland consists in the fact that not only is an enemy operating there with whom one must struggle decisively, but also that under pressure of past

The Collapse of Socialist Internationalism

mistakes, the Party has lost actual creative links with the people. The working class has many reasons for dissatisfaction."[16] Of course, Zamiatin did not condone the activities of the Polish opposition. He spoke with deep concern about the PZPR facing what amounted to de facto political pluralism in Poland. "Solidarity is now essentially a political party," he reported, "and is very openly hostile toward the PZPR and the state."[17] Zamiatin estimated that the forty-member KOR contingent on the Solidarity steering committee constituted the leading force of counterrevolution in Poland. He felt that these individuals were planning to seize power from the Communist Party, though PZPR initiatives seemed certain to thwart their efforts.[18] "We believe that you will be able to solve your problems yourselves," he had told his Polish interlocutors, "because although some persons in your party have committed mistakes, the party itself is pure and strong."[19]

Not all members of the Soviet leadership shared Zamiatin's optimism toward the Polish Communist Party. After listening to Zamiatin's report to the Politburo on 22 January, Foreign Minister Gromyko expressed continued misgivings with the way Kania's government was managing the crisis. "Our Polish friends do not want to take emergency measures," he said, "despite our recommendations; it would seem that this notion hasn't occurred to them."[20] The question before Moscow clearly remained how best to influence Warsaw toward adoption of more decisive policies. "We have a lot of influence over our Polish friends," Konstantin Rusakov reflected. "It has to be said that Leonid Il'ich [Brezhnev] talks with Kania nearly every week about all these problems. It seems to me that this is very important, as Leonid Il'ich touches tactfully on all these questions in conversation and lets Kania know how seriously he ought to act." All that remained was to exploit this influence institutionally. Rusakov recommended that "our organizations, the Ministry of Foreign Affairs, the KGB, the Ministry of Defense, should appoint representatives with whom we can work constantly to solve the problem in Poland."[21]

On behalf of the Ministry of Defense, Dmitrii Ustinov was quite willing to manipulate military tensions as a check to "counterrevolution" in Eastern Europe. Marshal Kulikov had recently returned from Poland with the impression that there had still been no reversal in the situation there, despite the dramatic events of the preceding December. Therefore, Ustinov proposed using additional exercises in the spring to ratchet up existing tensions. "In March we are scheduled to conduct maneuvers in Poland," he noted. "It seems to me that we should elevate these maneuvers a bit, that is to say, to let them know that our forces are in readiness."[22] If the events of December were any indication, this maneuver would convince the Poles, both opposition and authorities, that the possibility of intervention still hung on their political choices.

Mikhail Suslov cautioned that while pressure was important, so was continued cooperation with the Polish authorities. Moscow, he felt, should focus on how best to *support* the Polish leadership against Solidarity rather than on persistently coercing it.[23] After all, the collective will of the Soviet Politburo had not seriously prepared for an invasion of Poland since the start of the crisis. Rather, it had always hoped to see the Polish authorities crush the national opposition with a minimum of allied assistance. Therefore, it would be unwise to adopt a stance that appeared to be uncompromising or excessively menacing, particularly with respect to the PZPR itself. The day might soon come when Moscow had to back its words with action, and then what?

Soviet press coverage of Poland at this time keenly reflected Suslov's cautious approach. When, for instance, the Soviet military daily *Krasnaia Zvezda* reported on the continuing Warsaw Pact exercises in and around Poland, it was careful to point out that these were small-scale maneuvers.[24] A week later, in response to suggestions appearing in the *Los Angeles Times*, Radio Moscow flatly denied that the Soviet Union was preparing to crush Solidarity.[25] Eventually even Western analysts started to take such claims at face value. A secret CIA National Intelligence Estimate from 27 January concluded in part that "the Soviets' reluctance to intervene militarily [in Poland] derives above all from the enormous costs they probably anticipate in eliminating Polish armed and passive resistance, and in reestablishing a politically and economically viable Poland. Additional disincentives are the political and economic price they anticipate they would pay in their relations with Western nations, with the Third World, and within the international Communist movement."[26] Later, writing in early February for Radio Liberty, political analyst Yakov Samoilov suggested that it would cost Moscow roughly 10 billion rubles per year to occupy Poland. Considering the Soviets' own economic difficulties at that time, Samoilov argued, this was simply too large a sum to consider seriously.[27]

Caution dictated that it was far wiser to threaten Polish society, while cooperating with communist authorities, in order to ensure the purely domestic resolution desired from the beginning. Suslov remained convinced that the key to this approach lay in communist control of the media. "This is their weakest point," he complained to the Politburo on 22 January, "and it is here that we must assist them."[28]

Suslov proposed sending a delegation of top Soviet specialists to Warsaw to prepare the PZPR for its upcoming Party congress. His idea, which met with unanimous approval, was to use Soviet oversight as a firewall against Party reformers sympathetic to the Solidarity movement. Zamiatin was chosen to lead the delegation, which would leave for Poland in late January. In addition, the leadership approved Rusakov's suggestion to solicit input from the Ministries of Foreign Affairs and Defense, as well as from the KGB, on how best to influence the course of events in Poland.[29]

The Rise of Wojciech Jaruzelski: Martial Law at Last?

Had Tsipko and Zamiatin correctly identified Solidarity at this juncture as a moderate, essentially socialist reform movement? Timothy Garton Ash writes about an interview that he conducted that winter with the farmers staging an occupation strike for Rural Solidarity in Rzeszow. He quotes one of the men as speaking very frankly about the "need for free and secret elections, the right to buy and sell and inherit land, to speak out about violations of human rights." When Garton Ash commented to the farmer that this could mean the end of the communist system, the fellow reportedly lit up and enthusiastically exclaimed, "But of course!"[30] Not long afterward, another supporter of Rural Solidarity, a historian of the Polish peasant movement, told the visiting Englishman directly, "What we are saying now is: the last thirty-five years have been a catastrophe. Let us start again in 1945."[31]

This type of sentiment had begun to transform into decidedly political demands during the early months of 1981. Though Solidarity had not called for Poland's removal from the Warsaw Pact or for an end to communism, it had issued demands for the resignation of district governors, mayors, and other political officials in many parts of Poland.[32] It also made significant demands on social issues, including government concessions on the matter of work-free Saturdays, as well as recognition of Rural Solidarity as an alliance of the nation's independent farmers.[33]

These developments are all the more interesting when one considers that they culminated after General Wojciech Jaruzelski assumed the post of prime minister at the Eighth PZPR Central Committee Plenum of 10 February. In a country very proud of its military tradition, Jaruzelski came to the position as one of the nation's most widely respected public figures. As a young man Jaruzelski had been deported with millions of other Poles to Siberia in the opening months of World War II. Following the German invasion of the USSR, he attended the Soviet officers' training school in Riazan and participated in the wresting of Poland from the Nazis. After the war, he joined the PZPR and by 1960, at age thirty-seven, had become the Polish army's chief political commissar. Five years later, Jaruzelski continued his rise through the ranks to become chief of staff, and then, in 1968, minister of defense, just in time to oversee Poland's participation in the invasion of Czechoslovakia.

During the riots of 1970, Jaruzelski became a candidate member of the PZPR Politburo and was responsible for giving the order to fire live ammunition at the strikers in Gdansk.[34] Later, when compelled to explain his actions, Jaruzelski said, "Do you want [an army] that would overthrow the government whenever it disliked a particular decision of this legally elected [party] leadership? No! Our soldier will always defend our people's government. Together with you he will defend the party!"[35] This type of loyalty did not go unrewarded. A year after the riots, he was elevated to full membership on the Politburo. As already noted, however, when workers began to demonstrate against the Party again in 1976, Jaruzelski ordered the army to remain uninvolved, pointedly refusing Gierek's request for military assistance. It was then that he reportedly told the astonished first secretary, "Polish soldiers would never fire at Polish workers."[36] In light of the events of 1970, this hardly represents a statement of general principle, not to mention verifiable truth. More likely it was a reflection of Jaruzelski's recognition that Gierek's political fortunes were on the wane in Poland amid the nation's rapidly declining economic conditions. Jaruzelski therefore seems to have made the shrewd decision not to involve himself in the repression of civil discontent, lest he unwisely attach his own career to Gierek's decline.[37] In any case, despite his motives, the general's refusal to use force in 1976 soon garnered him tremendous popular acclaim within Poland's emergent civil society, a reputation that he continued to enjoy in 1981.[38]

But Jaruzelski's appointment as prime minister was only part of the reason that many came to regard the Eighth Party Plenum as a turning point for the PZPR. The meeting also marked the start of the Party's retreat from its earlier positions embracing "socialist renewal" in Poland. Rather, Kania now spoke powerfully about the need to exterminate "counterrevolution in the egg."[39] In conjunction with Jaruzelski's nomination, this statement might have seemed to signal that the Party had shifted toward martial law. However, as if to justify his reputation as a moderate, the new prime minister promised to grant Solidarity a permanent committee for relations with the government in exchange for a ninety-day moratorium on strikes throughout Poland. He explained that the government would make use of this period to stabilize the nation's flagging economy.

Though Jaruzelski's diplomatic overtures toward the opposition upset the Soviets in Moscow, the latter were content for the time being to contain any show of public disapprobation. A confidential PZPR assessment from 18 February of official talks with Zamiatin and his delegation noted that the "nomination of Gen. Jaruzelski as Prime Minister of the Polish government has been received with hope. This is a familiar and deeply respected man in the USSR."[40] The following day, Moscow approved an agreement with Poland extending further credits while freezing payment of interest on outstanding loans granted in the preceding four years.[41] Later that month, at the Twenty-sixth CPSU Party Congress, Brezhnev even admitted that the crisis showed the importance of effective dialogue with the masses.[42] When Polish and Soviet leaders met for talks after the congress, their final communiqué jointly declared that "the socialist community is indissoluble, and its defense is a matter not only for every single state, but for the entire socialist coalition. The Soviet leaders declared that the USSR, together with the other fraternal nations, has rendered, and will render, every necessary support to socialist Poland and the Polish communists in their strenuous effort to bring about the fundamental normalization of the situation in the country."[43] This was very strong language that seemed to suggest that Warsaw and Moscow saw eye to eye on the matter of socialist internationalism and "international assistance," should matters continue to deteriorate.

In fact, the Soviets found little about which to agree on with the Poles during their closed-door meetings in early March. Their final communiqué suggested a common view that simply did not exist. The Moscow leadership was furious about the concessions that Jaruzelski's government had finally made to the Rural Solidarity movement in Rzeszow on 18 February. How, they wanted to know, could the Polish Communist Party offer guarantees on the private ownership of land?[44] For years Brezhnev had been pushing for an end to private agriculture altogether in Poland. This was, after all, one of the cornerstones of Soviet-style socialism, and it characterized every economy in the bloc except Poland's. One can only imagine, therefore, the ire with which the Rzeszow Agreement was met in Moscow, as well as the tension this created between the Soviets and their Polish guests.

Nevertheless, Kania and Jaruzelski had come to Moscow prepared to offer proof that Warsaw was preparing to take resolute action against the opposition. Weeks earlier, on 16 February, forty-five members of Poland's Ministries of Defense and Internal Affairs had met at the Inspectorate of Territorial Defense and Internal Defense Troops to work through a mock-up scenario of introducing martial law.[45] Here the Polish General Staff and its Soviet advisers had approved a list of roughly six thousand Solidarity activists who were to be interned at the outset of military rule. Additionally, they decided not to advise the Sejm in advance of the impending declaration, lest the opposition receive word and take defensive measures. On 20 February, the General Staff presented its conclusions to Prime Minister Jaruzelski, who approved them with few revisions. The general was, therefore, in a position to assure the Soviets at the Twenty-sixth CPSU Party Congress that the PZPR, "being aware of the support of the Allies, is resolved to resort to this measure of defending the country from counterrevolution."[46] In this light it is intriguing to note again the very menacing tone of the joint communiqué published after the Soviet-

Polish summit, with its clear insinuation that a Polish crackdown could well involve outside assistance from the Warsaw Pact.

The problem was that the Polish leadership had no intention of implementing its plans for martial law anytime soon. As Colonel Ryszard Kuklinski later recalled, "In the Spring of 1981 [martial law] was neither realistic nor even possible, because the authorities had at their disposal a partially disintegrated MSW [Ministry of Internal Affairs], an army of doubtful loyalty, and a handful of hard-liners in a disintegrating PZPR, while on the other side they were opposed not only by the millions of Solidarity members but also by nearly the entire hostile society. Given such a ratio of forces, the success of the coup was doomed in advance."[47] The Poles made no secret of this conviction. Jaruzelski explained again and again to the Soviet leadership the need to hold off implementation of his plans for a while until the ratio of forces in Poland improved to favor the Party.[48] For their part, the Soviets also seemed content to take this one day at a time. That the plans had been drafted and approved constituted a major step forward in Moscow's perspective. It appeared that the crisis had finally turned a corner in the direction of a decisive resolution. At last, in early March, the military exercises that had begun in December as Soiuz-80 came to an end.[49]

Warsaw's Campaign of Intimidation Backfires in Bydgoszcz

Kania and Jaruzelski returned from Moscow clearly at pains to convince the Soviet leadership that its confidence had not been misplaced. State action, while not decisive, was indeed swift. On 5 March, only one day after the summit discussions in Moscow, Polish police arrested KOR leader Jacek Kuron in Warsaw. Kuron was charged with slandering the state, an offense punishable by up to eight years in prison. However, after only six hours in custody, Kuron was allowed to go free. The following day authorities attempted to seize yet another KOR luminary, Adam Michnik, in Wroclaw, but Michnik simply refused to allow himself to be taken. He received a workers guard from the local Solidarity organization to protect him from further attempts of this sort, a move that curiously seems to have daunted the weak efforts of the Wroclaw police. Meanwhile, four members of the Confederation for an Independent Poland, another opposition group, suddenly found themselves facing charges of antigovernment activities.[50] Elsewhere, in Warsaw, government-issue tear gas canisters were tossed into a shop whose personnel regularly wore armbands in support of Solidarity. In Poznan, delegates to the upcoming Rural Solidarity National Congress received warnings not to attend from unidentified individuals. In Novy Sacz, a local Solidarity chairman was found hanged to death under mysterious circumstances. Finally, on 10 March, with Lech Walesa scheduled to meet Prime Minister Jaruzelski for the first time, eighty-six-year-old Antoni Pajdak, a senior member of KOR, was attacked by an unknown assailant armed with a tear gas canister.[51]

Clearly the government had gone on the offensive, hoping to intimidate KOR and its allies in Solidarity. The police received direct instructions from PZPR Politburo member Andrzej Zabinski to subdue the opposition as best they could. Zabinski had not minced his words. "The aim of the struggle is to divide the leading KOR people from the factories," he said, which means also "to destroy the new union structure and impose a branch structure on them. . . . Then we will have an easier game."[52] Consistent with Jaruzelski's promise to the Soviets, the Polish authorities were working to divide and conquer the opposition. In particular, they sought to undermine the alliance between the workers and the intelligentsia in order to improve the "balance of forces" in their favor. Only then could the plans for martial law prove useful in resolving the national crisis.

Ironically, the Soviet Politburo gave little indication that it even noticed what Kania and Jaruzelski had just begun in Poland. Rather, meeting on 12 March, its members expressed nearly universal dismay over the way the Poles had chosen to resolve their situation. Brezhnev's meeting with Erich Honecker during the Twenty-sixth Party Congress had reinforced the Soviet leader's conviction that "we are all clearly united on the fact that the Polish comrades must be set to more positive [that is, offensive] measures in order to bring the country to order and establish strict stability."[53] As Konstantin Rusakov observed, "Even after the famous conference of the fraternal nations [the December 5 Warsaw Pact summit] the Polish friends nevertheless did not arrive at the need to realize a set of cardinal measures for putting the country in order."[54] If the Kremlin had noticed Warsaw's new intimidation campaign, it did not regard it seriously.

Despite Warsaw's tough new initiatives, Polish society continued to stage its own high-profile offensives. On 16 March a group of private farmers occupied the Bydgoszcz headquarters of the United Peasant Party, one of the nation's two noncommunist political parties with seats in the Sejm. The farmers resurrected earlier demands for a full recognition of Rural Solidarity as an official independent union and declared the start of an extended occupation. Unlike the long standoff at Rzeszow, however, the occupation in Bydgoszcz ended swiftly in a violent clash between the state and society—the first since the crisis had begun the previous summer. Two hundred police entered the occupied headquarters and gave the protesters fifteen minutes to finish drafting their final communiqué. When this intimidation failed to dislodge the farmers, uniformed police and plainclothesmen set upon them with rubber truncheons. Three people were badly hurt in the melee as the authorities brought the ill-fated sit-in to a sudden, tumultuous conclusion.[55]

The crackdown in Bydgoszcz instantly intensified popular expectations of nationwide military action, and all heads turned to Jaruzelski for confirmation. As fate would have it, the previously scheduled Soiuz-81 Warsaw Pact maneuvers had just begun the same day that the Bydgoszcz incident occurred; thus Prime Minister Jaruzelski was unavailable for an immediate public response.[56] Ultimately, the general returned to Warsaw in time to veto an attempt by Polish hard-liners to use the event as an excuse to introduce martial law on 23 March.[57] Consequently, Warsaw's official response to the Bydgoszcz incident was merely a statement asserting that "the authorities in Bydgoszcz had acted legally in the interest of law and order."[58]

Predictably, the Polish opposition was not at all receptive to this explanation of the government's resort to violence. Meeting on 23 March, advisers from Solidarity's National Coordinating Commission counseled Walesa against acting rashly. Jaruzelski, said the journalist Tadeusz Mazowiecki, was "the last chance for a peaceful solution in Poland." Bronislaw Geremek agreed completely. If the union called for a general strike now, he warned, it would amount to a national insurrection.[59] No one doubted that the inevitable result of this would be a Soviet-led invasion of Poland. On the other hand, if the union did nothing, it would gradually lose hard-won ground to the new government offensive. Therefore, the commission chose a graduated response that would leave the state some room to maneuver before playing its trump card of a general strike: It would call a four-hour nationwide warning strike on 27 March. If demands were not met, this would then become a general strike four days later. These demands included punishment of those responsible for the violence in Bydgoszcz, recognition of Rural Solidarity as a fully independent union, guarantees for the security of Solidarity members, full pay for striking workers, and the dismissal of all criminal charges against members of the opposition.[60] It was an unlikely ultimatum that virtually guaranteed eventual recourse to a general strike. Thus the leaders of Solidarity prepared to face a Soviet military intervention.

As in the previous December, the sense of impending invasion was far stronger in Poland than it was in Moscow. Indeed, as they met on 26 March, only one day before the four-hour warning strike, there is no indication that Soviet leaders even considered the prospect of an armed intervention. Believing the Polish authorities to be on the verge of a crackdown, they busied themselves almost exclusively with the difficulties of meeting Poland's mounting economic needs. Vice President Jagielski of Poland's Council of Ministers had recently forwarded an urgent demand for additional oil, metal, cellulose, light industrial raw materials, and other products to the Kremlin's attention. However, as Ivan Arkhipov was quick to point out, the Soviet Union was already giving nearly as much economic assistance as it could afford. While the USSR was anxious to provide what it could to Poland's deeply mired socialist economy, certain items, such as light industrial raw materials, were simply not available for export.[61]

Jagielski painted the situation in particularly dark hues. Although plan targets for 1981 had been set a full 20 percent lower than those of the preceding year, the Polish economy was unlikely to meet even these lowered expectations. Coal production, the nation's leading source of hard currency revenue, was now forecast to top out at 170 million tons, 10 million tons short of its quota. The situation was no better for consumer goods. Meat production was down 25 percent, while sugar production was probably going to fall 550 million tons shy of its targeted 1.5 million tons. Jagielski concluded this litany with the apocalyptic prediction that bread and flour were liable to be the next casualties of the economic slide.[62] This was doubtless intended to frighten Soviet leaders into conceding to Warsaw's requests, mindful that the 1917 Russian Revolution had begun with bread riots.

Against this bleak economic forecast, Poland's international debt appeared inescapably debilitating. As of March 1981, the country owed a total of $23 billion to foreign investors. This included $9 billion in guaranteed loans owed to foreign governments, and $14 billion in private loans from four hundred foreign banks. Though it required $9.5 billion in new imports, Poland's export earnings amounted to only $8.5 billion. Moreover, it was obliged to pay $1.5 billion in interest to its increasingly impatient creditors that year. The government, therefore, would continue to rely on Western financial markets in order to meet its economic needs.[63]

Jagielski shrewdly sought to use this ideological risk to lever his substantial request for $700 million in aid from the Soviet government. Although the Kremlin leadership was certainly moved by his argument, it also received assurances from Arkhipov that the Soviet economy simply could not afford to deliver such assistance. Moscow could, and would, provide hasty deliveries of oil, gas, iron ore, and other products, but $700 million was simply too great a burden for the Soviet Union to withstand.[64]

The realization that the economic might of the Soviet "colossus" had reached its limits did not come easily to some members of the Politburo. Andrei Gromyko was especially impatient with the Polish request. The Poles, he felt, just did not seem to appreciate the extent to which Moscow was already supporting their economy. "They consider this a trifling matter," he complained. "But in fact it is certainly the case that all of the cotton they have is ours, the ore is completely ours, as is the oil."[65] Arkhipov agreed that the Poles were not making the best use of Soviet assistance. Poland had been receiving oil from the USSR at 90 rubles per ton at a time when it was selling on the world market for 170. Therefore, if Warsaw merely resold a portion of Moscow's generous deliveries in the West, it would net a financial windfall.

Hence, when the Politburo adjourned on 26 March, it remained opposed to meeting the full Polish request. Arkhipov would see to increased deliveries of the products he had indicated were available. But the Soviet economy simply could not shoulder the type of subsidization that the Polish government required, no matter what the political cost. Soviet national interests, now defined as distinct from those of Eastern Europe, had to take precedence. The domestic stability of the Soviet Union, itself now in danger, had to be protected from following Poland into sharp decline.

This is not to suggest that the Soviets had resigned themselves to the collapse of socialism in Poland. On the contrary, the Kremlin fully expected in late March that Polish authorities were finally about to declare martial law against the opposition. Despite Jaruzelski's threat to resign—or perhaps because of it—a Soviet delegation arrived in Warsaw on 27 March to review Polish preparations for the anticipated crackdown. Led by Marshal Kulikov, the delegation was made up of roughly thirty officials from the KGB, Gosplan, and the Soviet Ministry of Defense. It came prepared with extensive recommendations from Moscow. Martial law ought to begin, they argued, with the internment and summary courts-martial of leading opposition figures approximately fourteen hours before publicly notifying the nation of the new regime. Following the suspension of Poland's constitution, all state authority was to be transferred to the nation's Supreme Military Command. Once martial law had been officially declared, Polish army and security forces would move to crush any resistance strikes. Although Soviet forces would play no formal role in the crackdown, the delegation suggested that Polish staff and local officers accept the assistance of Soviet advisers.[66]

Meanwhile, the Soviet press began to promulgate an effective tale of rampant revolt in Poland, timed to coincide with the Soviet visit. Poland was on the brink of anarchy, Radio Moscow reported on 26 March, and the opposition was preparing to take over the government by force.[67] The military daily *Voennyi Vestnik* carried a similarly menacing tone with its assertion that Polish events were comparable with those of the 1968 Prague Spring.[68] Radio Moscow kept the pressure on Poland the following day with accusations that KOR had taken over the Solidarity leadership. It alleged that KOR planned to use the four-hour warning strike to create chaos and anarchy in Poland as a lever against communist rule.[69] Thus, by the time Kulikov's delegation met with Polish authorities, the Soviet press had already presented an extensive justification for the expected use of military force against the opposition.

The Soviet propaganda offensive did not go unnoticed in Poland. Following the uneventful four-hour warning strike, Solidarity's rank and file readied itself for the escalation that had been prefigured from the start. Numbering roughly 9.5 million of Poland's 12.5-million-person workforce among its members, Solidarity was emboldened to take on any possible contingencies. Its central leadership passed down directives on how members ought to respond to everything from a general strike to an invasion. In the case of the latter, Poles were instructed to carry out passive resistance similar to that of the Czechs and Slovaks in 1968. Signposts were to be changed or obliterated, and food requisitioning was to be rendered impossible. Few doubted that invasion lay in store for Poland; thus expectation filled the air. Despite the tension of the moment, however, Poles hung on to their laconic sense of humor. In Warsaw, for instance, new resistance posters showed a map of Poland with a construction site sign that read, "No Entry! Building in Progress."[70]

Judging from the feverish pitch that Soviet propaganda reached in late March, Moscow clearly presumed that the final decision to declare martial law would come at the Ninth PZPR Central Committee Plenum, scheduled to meet on 29 March. When that day arrived, the Soviet press charged that rebels had spilled into the streets of Poland, setting up roadblocks and destroying street signs all over the country. In Warsaw, Solidarity supporters had purportedly seized a television transmitter and were planning to take over enterprises and communications centers while preparing attacks on members of the militia and state security forces.[71] Against the background of the Soiuz-81 exercises already under way in and around Poland, this type of rhetoric set off alarm bells from the river Bug to the river Potomac. In Washington, on 27 March, the Defense Intelligence Agency issued a secret Information Report cautioning in part that "the weekend of 28–29 March will be ominous for Poland. Force may be used to achieve a settlement. Warsaw Pact game plan is for Polish units to suppress the dissident elements of Polish Society. Warsaw Pact support, if needed, will be provided by Russian, Czech and GDR forces. Such external support will however be very discreet."[72] Once again, as it had in December, the American government issued public proclamations warning against an invasion of Poland.[73]

It is difficult to say how long Jaruzelski could have held out against such intense pressure to introduce martial law had Solidarity gone ahead with the planned general strike. In any event, Lech Walesa rendered the question hypothetical with his decision to cancel the strike in the interest of peace. As it turned out, his advisers successfully convinced him that playing the union's trump card would amount to a declaration of civil war in Poland and loss of what the opposition had achieved there.[74]

While some felt that this was a wise move, others equated caution with cowardice, complaining of the advisers that "they were frightened by the tanks!"[75] The result was a fragmentation of the union and a loss of its singularity of purpose. For the first time since August 1980, Walesa began to face assertive challenges to his leadership. The resulting divisions predictably weakened him in dealings with state authorities, particularly in his ability to threaten another general strike. As Timothy Garton Ash notes, "The decision of Walesa and his advisors dealt a fatal blow to the credibility of Solidarity's ultimate deterrent."[76] In his own defense, Walesa suggested that there was no way to know whether a general strike would have led to civil war or a Soviet invasion. He pointed out that "the Pope wrote to us, and the Primate, pleading for reason and reflection. Tomorrow we may achieve more, but we may not go to the brink. At the same time, I know that what is good today may turn out tomorrow to be bad. And the historians, when they come to judge, may say: but he was crazy, the authorities were bluffing, they were weak, their bark was worse than their bite, it would have been possible at last to put the country straight, they could have won, and they flunked it. They can judge me like that in 10 or 50 years. And we don't yet know if I was right, or those who took another view. In my opinion, the risk was too great."[77]

Two decades later it is still difficult to say what response the general strike would have elicited from Polish authorities. Later assertions from Polish ambassador Ruarz (following his defection to the West) that martial law would have followed such a serious development suggest that some circles in Warsaw were quite confident that Jaruzelski's threat to resign could be surmounted. As for the Polish leadership itself, new evidence indicates that it was working hard at the end of March to ensure that the threat of an outside invasion would temper union initiatives decisively. Following discussions with Marshal Kulikov in April, the East German Defense Ministry issued a report stating in part that the "prolongation of the exercise 'SOIUZ-81' came explicitly as a result of the requests of comrades Jaruzelski and Kania. They wanted to utilize the exercises to strengthen their position. Simultaneously they hoped to exert a positive influence on the progressive forces in Poland and show 'Solidarnosc' and 'KOR' that the Warsaw Pact countries are prepared to render Poland help all around. Thereby a certain pressure should also be exerted upon the leadership of 'Solidarity.' "[78] What is certain is that, as of late March 1981, Solidarity's power had begun to give way, if ever so gradually, to the combination of Warsaw's intimidation and Moscow's military maneuvers.

Brest

Notwithstanding the psychological edge that Polish state authorities enjoyed over Solidarity after the Bydgoszcz incident, relations between Moscow and Warsaw actually worsened after Walesa's tactical retreat. When it had become clear that the PZPR would not have to declare a state of emergency, the Soviet leadership allowed its frustrations with Kania and Jaruzelski to show publicly for the first time since the start of the crisis. On 2 April a bulletin appeared in *Pravda*, as well as over TASS and Radio Moscow, with complaints that Party organizations had done nothing to crush a recent counterrevolutionary demonstration at Warsaw University.[79] This unprecedented expression of open impatience with the Polish government accurately reflected the mood of the Soviet leadership in private as well. Speaking to the Politburo on 2 April, Brezhnev summed up the general attitude toward Warsaw. "We all have a great concern for the further course of events in Poland," he said. "Worst of all is the fact that our friends listen, agree with our recommendations, but do practically nothing. And the counterrevolution is advancing on every front."[80] "How many times have we told you," Brezhnev continued as if addressing the Poles themselves, "that you have to take decisive measures, that you cannot endlessly surrender ground to 'Solidarity'? You go on about a peaceful way, not understanding, or not wanting to understand, that this 'peaceful way' to which you cling could cost you in blood."[81]

Brezhnev felt that the time had come to sit down and talk very directly with Kania and Jaruzelski, to apply pressure in a way that would convince them once and for all to introduce martial law in Poland. Accordingly, he proposed that Andropov and Ustinov meet secretly with the two Poles just outside the city of Brest, not far from the Soviet-Polish border. There the KGB chairman and minister of defense might "review the situation" with their Polish guests, setting forth in a convincing manner Moscow's demands for decisive action against Solidarity. Should this fail to make the desired impression, Brezhnev added, Moscow could hold in reserve yet another Warsaw Pact summit, similar to that of 5 December 1980.[82]

Both Andropov and Ustinov enthusiastically supported Brezhnev's suggestion. Each felt strongly that the situation in Poland warranted leaning more heavily on the Polish government to heed Moscow's concerns. As Andropov put it, "The question we face now is how to assert greater influence, more pressure, on the leadership of our friends." Somehow the Poles had to be made to introduce martial law themselves so that the Soviet Union would be spared a costly intervention. Even Ustinov supported this as the wisest option in Poland. "Leonid Il'ich [Brezhnev] spoke rightly in his proposals that a convocation of the seven nation-states of the Warsaw Pact must be held in reserve," he said, "and to take now all necessary measures so that the Polish friends act independently."[83] Indeed, members of the Politburo indignantly regarded Western warnings of an impending Warsaw Pact invasion as fabricated. Observed Andrei Gromyko: "A lot is being said about the Soviet Union, as if to warn us that the Soviet Union should not interfere in Polish affairs with its armed forces. But this is clearly the case that bourgeois propaganda has always taken hostile positions with respect to the Soviet Union and so will give this information . . . in a biased way."[84]

The problem with relying on the Poles, however, was that it was not yet clear whether they were willing to handle the job themselves. Jaruzelski, the man on whom Moscow had pinned its hopes, was confused about what to do next in dealing with the popular opposition movement. Additionally, it was not certain that the Polish army and security forces would obey an order to impose martial law if Jaruzelski gave it. Consequently, Gromyko proposed that Soviet military observers conduct a serious analysis of this question before any further steps were taken to impose martial law in Poland.[85]

Not everyone shared Gromyko's cautious attitude. Defense Minister Ustinov, for instance, was far more sanguine about the reliability of Polish forces. He pointed out that it had been the Polish *leadership* that had thus far proven reluctant to act, even in the face of a nationwide general strike. Its desire to avoid widespread bloodshed would prove its undoing, the defensive minister warned. "I think bloodshed is unavoidable—it will occur," he assured the Politburo. "And if they fear this, of course they will have to give up position after position. In this way they could lose all the achievements of socialism." General Jaruzelski, he continued, was beginning to prove a major disappointment. Once considered a man of action in Moscow, Ustinov now suggested that he "actually turned out to be weak."[86]

The Poles had to be made to understand that martial law was both necessary and unavoidable, regardless of the bloodshed. The secret meeting with Andropov and Ustinov on the outskirts of Brest would afford an opportunity to get this point across in no uncertain terms. "We are speaking to them about taking military measures," Andropov complained, "administrative, judicial measures, but they constantly limit themselves to political steps." From where he sat, it seemed certain that the results of this practice would be a bloodless coup that would leave Solidarity in control of Poland.[87] Brezhnev agreed. At the meeting in Brest, he said, Andropov and Ustinov would have to make it clear that when Moscow demands "decisive measures," it means very decidedly the introduction of martial law. This, he said, would have to be explained in a sensible way, so that there could be no misunderstanding. "Right," Andropov replied, "we have to say that the introduction of martial law means establishing a curfew, limited movement on city streets, strengthening security of state and Party institutions, and of enterprises, etc."[88]

The KGB chairman directly identified the domestic causes of his anxiety over the Polish crisis lest his colleagues lose sight of what was most fundamental in their deliberations. "I want to say something about the fact that the Polish events are having an influence on the state of affairs in the western oblasts of our country," he announced. "Polish radio and television are received in many villages of Belorussia. Additionally, I have to say that spontaneous demonstrations have flared up in parts of Georgia, groups of people shouting anti-Soviet slogans have gathered together, etc. So we have to take strict measures here as well."[89] From Andropov's perspective, as from that of many in the Politburo, the Solidarity crisis marked the culmination of the Polish nationalist threat to Soviet domestic stability begun years earlier. Yet it was more than simply an intensification of those elements that had concerned the Kremlin since Poland's Catholic renaissance began in the late 1970s. Poland now amounted to an economic and political anchor tied around Moscow's neck and threatening the survival of communism throughout the bloc. Efforts to prop up its socialist economy were beginning to tap the very limits of Soviet resources. On the other hand, an intervention promised to be far costlier, both economically and politically. So far Moscow had focused the bulk of its attention on the situation in Poland itself. But, as Andropov realized, the time had come to worry about the impact of the crisis on Soviet domestic stability. Soon a choice would have to be made on how best to protect that stability; in the KGB, the reevaluation had already begun in earnest. For the time being, however, Soviet leaders agreed to send Andropov and Ustinov to Brest the following day in a desperate attempt to hold the bloc together through force of Polish arms.[90]

The Brest meeting came together very hastily when, shortly after the Politburo had adjourned, Defense Minister Ustinov contacted General Gribkov in Poland and ordered him to arrange matters with Kania and Jaruzelski. Only days after they had failed to introduce martial law at Moscow's request, the Poles worried about leaving the relative security of their native soil. They nervously proposed that the meeting take place in Poland, just outside Warsaw. When this proved unacceptable, they reluctantly agreed to fly secretly to Brest by way of a Soviet military base in Poland. The meeting was set for the evening of 3 April 1981.[91]

The Poles arrived at the Soviet military base in an exceedingly agitated state. Mindful of what had happened to Imre Nagy and Alexander Dubcek, prior to leaving Warsaw, Jaruzelski had asked a friend, General Michal Janiszewski, to take care of his wife and daughter if anything should happen to him. In addition to Kania, Jaruzelski traveled with a single aide, to whom he had given a pistol and a poison-gas hand grenade.[92] At approximately 7:00 P.M., General Gribkov escorted the three men to an unmarked Soviet Tupolev 134 and tried to assuage their fear. "They thought it would be like 1968 with the Czechoslovak leadership," Gribkov later recalled, "when they were taken to Moscow and arrested."[93]

Perhaps concerned that the plane was doomed never to arrive at its destination in one piece, Kania and Jaruzelski tried to convince Gribkov to accompany them to Brest. Gribkov declined, but promised them that he would meet them the following morning when they returned. With that, he ordered them drinks and refreshments and bid them a good flight.[94]

When the Tu-134 touched down in Brest, there were three Volgas waiting on the runway with curtains drawn and no license plates. The three Poles got into the first car and traveled down a small, unpaved road that led to a large brick building in the middle of nowhere. Jaruzelski remembers that "in that moment I told myself: this could be a one-way trip. Without saying a word I turned toward Kania who was clearly having the same thought."[95] When the cars came to a halt, there, in the beam of the headlights, stood three Soviet railroad cars, from which Andropov and Ustinov emerged to greet their guests. Upon entering the railroad cars, the Poles found that they had been tastefully outfitted, complete with a long rectangular meeting table, armchairs, sofas, and an impressive buffet. Amid this congenial atmosphere, the two sides sat down and began a frank exchange on Poland's future.[96]

The discussions went on for six hours, starting at 9:00 P.M. According to the report that Andropov and Ustinov later delivered to the Politburo on 9 April, Kania began the meeting with a long string of excuses for his government's hesitancy in dealing with the opposition.[97] The PZPR, he explained, was under a tremendous amount of pressure from Solidarity and other antisocialist forces. The fallout from the Bydgoszcz incident had demonstrated that the counterrevolution was, for the time being at least, stronger than the state in Poland. Consequently, the government feared a confrontation and was doing everything possible to avert a general strike.[98]

The Soviets dwelled on the need to confront the opposition forcefully and decisively. Argued Ustinov, "In many countries, no sooner does an uprising flare up or some kind of confusion start, than extraordinary measures are taken or martial law introduced. Take Yugoslavia: there was a demonstration in Kosovo, they introduced martial law, and nobody said a word about it. We don't understand why the Poles are afraid of introducing martial law."[99]

In conjunction with their resistance to declaring martial law, the Poles made it clear that they still objected to the notion of allied intervention in Poland. "Concerning the introduction of troops," Andropov later reported to the Politburo, "they said directly that it is absolutely impossible, as is the introduction of martial law." They said the Poles "underscored at the meeting that they will restore order with their own forces." The move against Solidarity would begin after the election of a new Central Committee at the upcoming Ninth PZPR Party Congress. Contrary to the union's expectations, Solidarity would not be permitted to run candidates in the Central Committee elections.[100] Presumably this would permit the Party to consolidate itself before then moving aggressively against the opposition.

This struck the Soviets as entirely inadequate. They stressed that the opposition had already assumed the upper hand in Poland, rendering military measures absolutely unavoidable.[101] Andropov and Ustinov therefore demanded at Brest that the Poles sign off on the final plans for martial law. Despite the high command's resolution of 16 February to keep the impending declaration a secret, Kania and Jaruzelski objected that the documents had first to be approved in the Sejm.[102] However, the Soviets would not stand for any further stalling. According to Andropov, "We said that there is no need for any passage through the Sejm; this document, according to which you will be acting when you introduce martial law, must be signed personally by you, comrades Kania and Jaruzelski, so that we know that you are in agreement with the documents, and you will know what you have to do in time of martial law. If it comes to introducing martial law, then you will have no time to deal with working up measures for introducing martial law; they must be prepared earlier."[103]

Either the Poles signed on to introduce martial law at a specified time, or the Soviets would no longer trust that Polish forces could handle the job. Of course, the unspoken implication here was that the Warsaw Pact would impose order if the Poles could not. Jaruzelski was keenly aware of this risk, as he later recalled: "I had my own experience from the previous December, which I studied very carefully, [and] from the Soviet intervention in Hungary and Czechoslovakia. I knew that decisions are made in the last five minutes, and nobody foresees them. I felt that the most important thing now was to properly judge the situation, the circumstances, the logic of events. 'We cannot agree to the dismantling of a state which is part of the Warsaw Treaty,' they said."[104] The Soviets underscored their threat with reference to Brezhnev's promise to send in troops if matters in Poland got worse, along with the now famous declaration that Poland would not be abandoned in time of trouble.[105]

It was all more than the Poles could bear. Indeed, at one point Jaruzelski again voiced his desire to resign rather than introduce martial law against the Polish people. He respectfully requested that Moscow release him from his post as prime minister. However, Andropov and Ustinov refused to accept his resignation, explaining that it was essential that he remain at his post and serve with distinction. With the opposition preparing to seize power, they said, Jaruzelski's resignation would not help state initiatives.[106] Thus, with no alternative remaining, Jaruzelski and Kania promised that the final plans for martial law would be signed the following week, by 11 April.[107]

As if their military compulsion was not sufficiently convincing, Andropov and Ustinov also brought economic pressures to bear. They stressed the degree to which Poland had become dependent on Soviet assistance. Should shipments of oil, cotton, or iron ore be cut off, they speculated, what would happen to Poland's economy? Certainly this prospect ought to be presented to the Polish workers in terms they could understand. If properly utilized, it could amount to a powerful weapon against Solidarity.[108] Additionally, the Soviets inquired, why had Warsaw so far failed to blame the nation's continuing economic crisis on Solidarity? After all, each time the union called a strike it cost the country millions of zlotys.

In terms of galvanizing Polish society, the Soviets stressed the priority of ensuring unity within the PZPR. Ultimately, it was hoped, a unified Party would be capable of more decisive action, and resolute steps would win the day for communism. Throughout the course of the six-hour meeting, the Soviets never tired of repeating this point. "We told Kania directly," Andropov later said, "that you retreat every day, but you must act; you must solidify military measures, and you must solidify emergency measures."[109]

"Discussion" went on in this manner at the Brest negotiations until 3:00 A.M. on 4 April. Nevertheless, when the Poles met General Gribkov that morning on their return to Poland, they appeared in better spirits. No doubt aware that Gribkov would be reporting their every word back to Moscow, Kania and Jaruzelski spoke quite favorably about the meeting. It had provided a good exercise in business and politics, they said, not to mention moral support for the Polish leadership.[110]

From the Soviet side, the decision to end the Soiuz-81 exercises on 7 April seemed to suggest a degree of satisfaction with the Brest discussions. Actually, however, Andropov and Ustinov had returned from Brest with contrasting proposals. When Andropov offered his report to the Politburo on 9 April, he went as far as to raise the possibility of secret cooperation with the Polish conservatives as an alternative to the Kania regime. In Andropov's words, "Other members of the [PZPR] Politburo, comrades Olszowski and Grabski, occupy some excellent positions, firmer than the leadership. We should work with them." The KGB chairman described how these conservatives in Warsaw proposed to "organize an underground Politburo and undertake work." Apparently the Polish conservatives had received advice from Bulgaria's Todor Zhivkov to try this, a rumor that Andropov had not yet confirmed. While not necessarily willing to champion the idea himself, Andropov saw no reason to discourage it. In his view, "If the leaders of the fraternal parties give the Polish friends these kinds of recommendations, then we, of course, will lose nothing, but stand to gain from it."[111]

Defense Minister Ustinov, however, was not as open to the kind of dual-track approach that Moscow had used in dealing with the Czechoslovak quislings in 1968. Kania and Jaruzelski were not involved with the opposition the way Dubcek and his allies had been. Therefore, although there had been a reasonable political motivation for circumventing Dubcek, the same could not be said for Kania or Jaruzelski. The idea might be kept alive through other East European leaders, but Ustinov felt that Moscow ought to keep it at arm's length for the time being. Kania and Jaruzelski seem embattled, he observed, but the Soviet Union should persist in supporting them, as well as in fostering good relations between them.[112]

Eventually it was decided, with Brezhnev's requisite approval, to take up the question with the East European allies. However, these consultations were to refrain from revealing the full measure of Soviet thinking on Poland. Gromyko noted, for instance, that "under no circumstances should it be mentioned that the [Brest] meeting has taken place." Andropov seconded this, underscoring that "we must absolutely not talk about the meeting."[113] And so the details of Moscow's pressure tactics would remain closed to the other socialist parties of the bloc.

In the days that followed, the Polish leadership gave Moscow considerable cause for reevaluating its support of Kania and Jaruzelski. On 13 April, two days after the agreed date for signing the final plans for martial law, Marshal Kulikov and his deputy for allied fleets, Admiral Mikhailin, requested a visit with Prime Minister Jaruzelski. The Polish general did what he could to avoid the meeting, as he still could not bring himself to fix a date for the imposition of martial law. Speaking to his aides, Jaruzelski repeated his anguish at the very thought of it. "Even in my blackest imagination," he told them, "I could not conceive our doing anything like that. I would rather be no longer Prime Minister when these documents have to be signed and implemented. But the situation is such that bloodying three noses in Bydgoszcz has led us to the edge of the abyss."[114] Ultimately, of course, Jaruzelski received Marshal Kulikov and his deputy that same day with the news that he had yet to fulfill his promise of setting a date for the start of emergency rule.

"Maintaining the Correct Tone": Evolving Soviet Perceptions

As if Jaruzelski's refusal to meet his agreement with the Soviets were not disquieting enough, two days later, on 15 April, an independent Party forum made up of 750 members of the PZPR from thirteen provinces convened in Torun to discuss the dismantling of democratic centralism at the upcoming Party congress.[115] The forum called instead for the introduction of genuinely democratic proceedings, prompting conservatives throughout the bloc to suggest that the PZPR was about to lose its very identity as a communist organization. The following day warnings began to appear on Czechoslovak television that Polish revisionists were prepar-

ing "for the transformation of the PZPR into some kind of social democratic party."[116]

Speaking with Kania on 15 April, Brezhnev found the Polish first secretary more self-confident, yet fully alive to how serious the political
situation had become. In his assessment of the conversation, which he
presented the following day to the Politburo, Brezhnev stressed the importance of maintaining "the correct tone in relations with our friends."
He reflected that, "on the one hand, it isn't worth bothering them un-
necessarily or making them nervous, so that their hands are not free. On
the other hand, we should assert continual pressure in such a way as to
direct attention to miscalculations and weaknesses in their policy and in a
comradely fashion advise them what they should do."[117]

Rather than micromanaging the situation for the Poles, Brezhnev was
now suggesting a comparatively laissez-faire policy, lest excessive pressure
obstruct Warsaw's ability to handle the crisis itself. What was needed at
this point, he felt, was a clearer estimation of where recent events were
liable to lead Poland in the long run. As such, Brezhnev proposed that, in
addition to the ongoing work of the Suslov Commission, the Central
Committee ought to undertake "a broader, so to speak, strategic analysis which would call us to turn from the current events and evaluate a
more distant developmental perspective on the situation in and around
Poland."[118]

Meanwhile, although profound changes were afoot in Poland that
could alter the entire strategic balance in Eastern Europe, there seemed
to be little chance for the Soviets to influence a satisfactory political
shift there. By mid-April, Moscow abandoned any hope of sidelining
Kania and Jaruzelski in favor of Polish conservatives. There were not
enough "healthy forces" in Poland to halt the slide toward a Yugoslav- or
Eurocommunist-style system, asserted a pair of Suslov Commission reports delivered to the Politburo on 16 April.[119] While the existing team of
Kania and Jaruzelski was admittedly moderate in its political leanings, no
viable alternative to their leadership could be found within the PZPR.[120]
Fortunately, the commission conceded, both remained loyal to Moscow
and the Warsaw Pact alliance.

The problem was that this regime seemed to have lost all control over
the course of developments in Poland. According to the commission's
report, " 'Solidarity' has been transformed into an organized political
force, which is able to paralyze the activity of the [Party] and State organs
and take de facto power into its own hands. If the opposition has not
yet done that, then it is primarily because of its fear that Soviet troops
would be introduced, and because of its hopes that it can achieve its aims
without bloodshed and by means of a creeping counterrevolution."[121]
Whereas previous assessments had sought to differentiate between KOR

extremists and the rest of the Polish opposition as the source of this counterrevolution, the commission now blurred this division. "Even if there was to be a schism between Walesa and the extremists from [KOR-KSS], Walesa himself and the Catholic clergy who back him have not the slightest intention of easing the pressure on the PZPR." The commission felt that in the near future extremists might well seize control of the union, "with all the consequences that would ensue."[122]

Consequently, from the commission's point of view, the PZPR was fated to fail in its efforts to reach an agreeable political solution with the national opposition. Should Walesa maintain control of Solidarity, the future looked bleak. Should the extremists take control of the union, it looked even bleaker. "Despite realizing that Poland's geographical situation deprives them of the opportunity to obstruct the country's participation in the Warsaw Treaty Organization," the reports observed, "or to encroach on the principle of the leading role of the Communist Party, these forces have clearly decided to undermine the PZPR from within, to bring about the party's rebirth, and thus to seize power 'on a legal basis.'" In other words, Moscow accepted that the "counterrevolution" it perceived in Poland was the result of domestic forces, rather than Western provocateurs. Moreover, it saw the attempts to introduce greater democracy at the upcoming Party congress as an essential step in Solidarity's seizure of power. If it was able to infiltrate the Party from within, the opposition would then be able to bring about reform from above, as Dubcek had in 1968. The PZPR would then be stripped of its Marxist-Leninist character, and the result would be a bloodless coup. Indeed, the commission's report suggested, existing preparations for the upcoming Polish congress suggested that this process was already well under way.[123]

The difficulty with supporting Polish conservatives was that they, like the Czechoslovak quislings twelve years earlier, failed to take account of Solidarity's broad base of popular support in Poland. Concerned about the trend toward social democracy, such conservative leaders as Tadeusz Grabski, Andrzej Zabinski, Stefan Olszowski, and Stanislaw Kociolek appeared to be strongly in favor of outside intervention. "One gets the impression," the commission reported, "that they believe the solution to the crisis will come only through a frontal attack on 'Solidarity' without taking account of the current correlation of forces. In espousing this view, they do not believe there is a possibility of rectifying the situation without the introduction of Soviet troops."[124] Clearly, then, the shift toward cooperation with Polish conservatives would have amounted to a shift in favor of military intervention. The question was, how much intervention would they require? Collaboration with Grabski, Zabinski, and the other conservatives in Warsaw could well require Moscow to commit far more than it felt it could afford for the sake of stability in Poland. After months of listening to Kania and Jaruzelski speak about the correlation of forces, the Soviets were beginning to believe them. Against this backdrop, the Polish hard-liners seemed to be advocating a decidedly reckless option in their bid to retain power.

Of course, this did not mean that the commission had softened its stand against the reform-oriented right wing in the PZPR. The report painted these individuals as collaborators in counterrevolution, working to introduce a new political system in Poland. "Ideologically," it declared, "they are close to some of the leaders of 'Solidarity' in their support for a transformation of the socioeconomic structure of Poland along the lines of the Yugoslav model. In the political sphere they support a position coinciding with the 'Eurocommunists' and the social democratic ideas of pluralism."[125] Politically, then, Moscow saw itself in a struggle against the creation of a liberal communist or even social democratic state in Poland. It was to avoid this type of transformation that "healthy forces" in the PZPR had to control the upcoming Ninth Party Congress.

The Kremlin had finally come to terms with the popular strength of the Polish opposition movement. Warsaw had long spoken of the need to use political maneuvers in redressing the "balance of forces" before launching a military crackdown. Soviet observers, including Consul General Vakhrameev, Aleksandr Tsipko, and L. M. Zamiatin, had each come to accept this as well. By spring 1981, with the drafting of the aforementioned commission reports, most of the Politburo finally agreed.

But how were Polish communists to cope with the challenge of the popular opposition movement? The commission's report recommended taking advantage of both the fragmentation of Solidarity's leadership structure and the worry about the possibility of an outside invasion. The latter tactic would enable Polish authorities to "exploit the fears of internal reactionaries and international imperialism that the Soviets might send troops into Poland." If managed effectively, this approach would then enable Warsaw to "disrupt the anti-socialist and anti-national activity of KSS-KOR and its leaders and bring about the isolation of these counter-revolutionaries."[126] It was essential, therefore, that Moscow continue to posture menacingly along Poland's borders. As long as it did, the Polish government could wield Brezhnev's promise not to abandon Poland in time of trouble as an implicit threat against the opposition. For its part, Moscow would continue doing what it could to support the Polish economy while making certain that the Poles recognized their dependence on the USSR.

In the meantime, the commission recommended the dispatch of representatives from the Central Committee's Department for Organizational-Party Work to help the Poles prepare for the upcoming Ninth PZPR Party Congress. Soviet advisers were to review and approve the draft PZPR statutes and other documents for presentation at the congress. This action would hopefully check efforts by the Polish revisionists to seize control of the Party through gradual infiltration. Additionally, ideas would be solicited from Komsomol (Young Communist League) and other officials on how best to influence Polish youth, unions, writers, and other influential sectors of Polish society.[127]

These efforts to influence the Polish congress continued throughout the month of April and included a visit by Suslov and Rusakov to Warsaw. Press coverage of their return to Moscow made no secret of their displeasure. Revisionist elements had begun to threaten the integrity of the PZPR, a TASS bulletin reported on 25 April. It was the first time since the start of the crisis that the Soviet press had leveled an accusation of revisionism against members of the PZPR. The disparaging remarks that had begun in the wake of Bydgoszcz were now becoming ideological attacks on the Polish Party, a clear reflection of Moscow's deep frustration. Of particular concern was the opposition's attempt to introduce horizontal structures into the traditionally vertical hierarchy of democratic centralism. Speaking to the Politburo on 30 April, Suslov cautioned that this trend, if allowed to continue, would inevitably lead to the destruction of the Polish Communist Party. Defense Minister Ustinov agreed, arguing that horizontal organization would ipso facto undermine the structural principles of a Marxist-Leninist party.[128] Suslov responded by firing off a demand to Warsaw that Polish conservatives, although a minority voice, receive ample influence at the upcoming congress. Kania promised to engineer this as best he could.

Suslov recommended that Moscow accept this assurance in good faith. It had to display a willingness to work with, rather than against, the Polish government, if the PZPR was to hold itself together. There had to be some faith on both sides of the table. Brezhnev offered the voice of skepticism. "Generally," he replied, "there is little faith in them because, although they listen, they don't do as we advise." Rusakov offered that phone calls and visits from Moscow did seem to constitute a very important check on the activities of the Polish opposition.[129] Brezhnev had to concede this point, as he himself had opened the meeting with the proposal that Moscow exploit more opportunities to meet privately with the Polish leaders as it had in Brest. From his perspective, these discussions had been undeniably useful and offered a model for handling the Poles in the future.[130] Perhaps, then, it was worth investing a greater degree of trust in Warsaw.

In the weeks that followed, however, the search for a bridge between state and society in Poland led Kania ever farther down the road of decentralization and liberalism. Despite its effort to invest more trust in the PZPR leadership, Moscow could not conceal its disapproval. On 8 May,

Pravda ran an article that contrasted "real socialism" with more subjective, idealistic models of socialism, untried, yet "passed off as 'genuinely socialist.' "[131] Amazingly, on 18 May, Kania responded with a speech that expressed undisguised defiance to Soviet attacks. Appearing on Polish television, he declared to the nation: "There can be no retreat from . . . no turning back from" the path of reform in Poland.[132]

The reform battle soon moved onto the pages of the Polish press. On the eve of a meeting between Marshal Kulikov and the Polish leadership in late May, *Sztandur Mlodych* ran an article calling on the PZPR Central Committee to take decisive steps against the threat of counterrevolution in Poland. It was signed by a conservative front calling itself the Katowice Party Forum.[133] In reply, the official Polish Press Agency (PAP) Maritime Service berated the "dormant antediluvian dinosaurs" that were, "encouraging the Party authorities to repeat the Czechoslovak experience and to ask for help from the USSR."[134] Moscow predictably favored the Katowice Party Forum in a rejoinder published in *Pravda* on 2 June. Kania's government ought to be turning to "universal methods" of constructing socialism, the *Pravda* article asserted, rather than searching for some type of uniquely Polish variant.[135] In other words, there could be no return to the "separate roads" to socialism that had spawned revolutions in Hungary and Czechoslovakia. Soviet norms had been the golden mean of socialist construction since 1968, uniting all that national custom had divided, and would remain such for the foreseeable future if Moscow had any say in the matter.

With faith in the Polish Party leadership fading quickly, the Soviets sent an open letter to the Polish Central Committee warning against revisionism at the upcoming congress. Horizontal structures and other reformist trends, the letter asserted, threatened to split the PZPR into factions, weakening it fatally. "The possibility cannot be excluded," it declared, "that an attempt might be made at the Congress itself to defeat decisively the Marxist-Leninist forces of the Party in order to liquidate it."[136] "Respected comrades," it continued, "in writing to you we not only have in mind our anxiety about the situation in fraternal Poland and the conditions and the future prospects of Soviet-Polish cooperation. Like other fraternal parties, we are also concerned that the anti-socialist forces, the enemies of the People's Republic of Poland, are menacing the interests of our entire community, its cohesion, its integrity and the security of its frontiers—yes our common security! . . . We believe that a possibility of avoiding a national catastrophe still exists. . . . Our point of view was expressed with precision in the declaration of Comrade L. I. Brezhnev to the Twenty-sixth Congress of the CPSU. We will not permit any attack on socialist Poland and we will not abandon a fraternal country in distress."[137] All the formulas that might have suggested an impending invasion under the terms of socialist internationalism and the Brezhnev Doctrine were present. Perhaps now, the Soviets doubtlessly hoped, pressure from the PZPR Central Committee might be sufficient to coax Kania and Jaruzelski to introduce martial law.

In fact, the shaken Central Committee tried to remove Kania from his post at its plenum of 9–10 June with a vote of no confidence. However, the wily first secretary managed to evade the effort by demanding that every member of the Politburo face the same vote, a prospect that few were willing to chance. Jaruzelski's support also undoubtedly played an important role in Kania's favor, as the nation's military leaders all voted with their commander.[138] Ironically, therefore, the upshot of the whole affair was that Kania emerged looking like a Polish patriot standing again in defiance of Big Brother in Moscow. Some observers even speculated that the Soviets might have intended the letter to strengthen Kania's standing in Poland, not to mention Jaruzelski's.[139]

Thus, while profoundly disquieting, the June letter did little to curb the enthusiasm for reform spreading within the PZPR. In the weeks that remained before the congress, pro-reform Central Committee member Tadeusz Fiszbach continued to argue that "an historic union is taking place between democracy in the Party and the independence of the trades union organization of the working class. In the long run, none of these important factors can function independently. . . . I think the trades union must be guaranteed the right to co-participation in taking strategic decisions."[140] Statements such as these convinced the Soviets more than ever that the counterrevolutionaries in Poland were on the verge of executing a bloodless coup d'état. From Moscow, General Gribkov recalls, it appeared that "the Polish United Workers Party had lost its position in society once and for all."[141] With communism seemingly about to collapse in Poland, the Soviets felt that they had reached the fail-safe point. The time had come to consider whether or not to intervene militarily.

"Under No Circumstances . . ."

With their political options nearly exhausted, Soviet military and political leaders met separately in mid-June for the express purpose of reaching a decision on the matter of armed intervention.[142] The military consultations took place at the Soviet Ministry of Defense at the initiative of Defense Minister Dmitrii Ustinov. In attendance were First Deputy Ministers of Defense H. V. Ogarkov, V. G. Kulikov, and S. L. Sokolov; the head of the military's Main Political Administration, A. A. Epishev; first deputy chief of the General Staff, Army General S. F. Akhromeev; the head of the Main Operational Administration, Colonel General V. I. Varennikov; and first deputy chief of the General Staff, Army General A. I. Gribkov.[143]

At the start of the meeting, a map was brought out indicating the concentrations of Warsaw Pact forces in and around Poland. These included Polish, Czechoslovak, and East German divisions in addition to those of the Soviet Union. Deputy Minister Ogarkov began with an assessment of the sociopolitical situation in Poland, along with consideration of how Soviet forces might participate in a hypothetical intervention. Not yet a solidified plan of battle, Ogarkov's comments amounted only to an estimation of how an invasion might take shape if the need arose. Indeed, Ogarkov was not in favor of such an option, fearing that the Soviet Union would be drawn into a Polish civil war if it sent in troops. He had simply cobbled together what Gribkov calls a "hint" of a plan in response to a direct order from Ustinov. In fact, he spent the majority of his presentation discussing how to prevent the Soviet Northern Group of Forces from being drawn into an internal conflict by Polish extremists.[144]

When the floor opened to opinions and comments, the only person in attendance who still expressed a desire to intervene in Poland was Marshal Kulikov. Aware that he was outnumbered, he castigated his colleagues: "Without sending in troops, we will never restore order in Poland. We must send in troops."[145] His position differed sharply from the majority view that invasion would be unwise, and even potentially disastrous.

Among those who felt this way was Kulikov's chief of staff, General Gribkov, who offered an impassioned argument against Warsaw Pact involvement. Like Aleksandr Tsipko before him, the general stressed that significant differences existed between the 1968 Prague Spring and the Polish crisis. "In Czechoslovakia," he said, "events developed beginning with the highest echelons of power. In Poland, on the other hand, it is the people rising up who have all stopped believing in the government of the country and the leadership of the Polish United Workers Party." Consequently, Moscow could not "normalize" the crisis in Poland merely by replacing the Party leadership as it had in Czechoslovakia. This time, as in Afghanistan, Moscow would have to contend with an entire nation galvanized to resist the reimposition of Soviet-style norms. Unlike in Czechoslovakia, Warsaw Pact units entering Poland could expect to face heavy armed resistance. "The Polish armed forces are battle-ready and patriotic," Gribkov argued. "They will not fire on their own people. In the case of an entrance of allied forces into Poland, the leadership of 'Solidarity' will raise the people against us and the other troops. A civil war could start."[146]

The general suggested that the Polish government had yet to exhaust all measures that might enable an avoidance of outside intervention. It still had not attempted sincerely to reach a serious, long-lasting agreement with Solidarity. Moreover, should a negotiated solution prove unfeasible, it was entirely possible that Polish forces could successfully introduce martial law in Poland. Gribkov had just returned from Poland himself and offered the impression that "the Army, MVD [Ministry of Internal Affairs], and security [forces] are still fulfilling their functions in the interest of the state."[147] Consequently, before the Warsaw Pact began a costly invasion, it ought to permit Polish authorities to impose order themselves.

Ultimately, however, these military arguments paled in Gribkov's estimation when compared with the impact an invasion would inevitably have on Soviet national interests and international prestige. If over one hundred nations had condemned the Soviet Union in the United Nations General Assembly for its invasion of Afghanistan, he reasoned, then entry into Poland was certain to incite the ire of the entire world.[148] Gribkov emphatically concluded: "Under no circumstances must troops be sent into Poland. Such an action would be unpredictable in its consequences. We will lose our authority and many friends throughout the world. The West won't look at our action through their fingers, it will act." The Polish authorities, he reiterated, should be permitted to manage the situation themselves. "If they don't agree on anything around the negotiating table then they have a plan for martial law all worked out."[149] Let them put it to use without Soviet assistance.

After Gribkov had finished, both Sokolov and Epishev rose to echo his conclusions as well as his recommendation not to send in troops under any circumstance. An invasion, they asserted, would amount to nothing short of "military-political adventurism" inconsistent with the best interests of the USSR. General Akhromeev agreed and lent his voice to the growing chorus against intervention. In the end, Kulikov remained the only member of the Soviet General Staff in its favor. Defense Minister Ustinov had received a very clear message from his officers. He thanked them for their input and hurried off to present his findings to members of the Politburo.

After Ustinov had left, Kulikov was not shy about expressing his displeasure with Gribkov's impassioned argument against intervention. Standing in the hall outside Ustinov's office, the marshal sought an explanation for Gribkov's behavior. "What's wrong with you?" he demanded. "The commander in chief is for the introduction of troops, and the chief of staff is against the introduction of troops!" Gribkov stood his ground. "This was a question of big politics," he replied. "You are mistaken. You cannot do this, no matter what. You cannot send in troops."[150] With that the two men went their separate ways to await Ustinov's return and the Kremlin's final word on the matter.

Approximately two hours later Ustinov returned to his office at the Ministry of Defense and reconvened the General Staff. "A meeting of the Politburo has just taken place," he began. "The Polish question was discussed in detail. I reported on our conversation and on the conclusions and proposals that you offered. Other members of the Politburo spoke as well. At the conclusion of the meeting, M. A. Suslov spoke. He said that under no circumstances, even if the Polish leadership requests, will we send Soviet and other troops into Poland. If a new leadership comes to power, we will cooperate with it. We cannot subject our country to international condemnation yet again." Suslov, who had chaired the meeting in Brezhnev's absence, agreed that the Poles ought to be permitted to handle their own affairs, regardless of the consequences. Moscow would do what it could, short of military assistance, to help Warsaw, especially in its efforts to strengthen Party unity in Poland. However, there could be no further consideration of military intervention. "Under no circumstances must troops be introduced," Suslov concluded. "Introduction of troops would be a catastrophe for Poland and, yes, for the Soviet Union."[151] With one firm tug, Moscow's leading ideologue and head of the Commission on Poland pulled the rug out from under the already tottering principle of socialist internationalism and its derivative Brezhnev Doctrine.

According to Gribkov's account, the Soviet leadership was well aware that a successful counterrevolution would certainly replace Polish communism with some form of social democracy. Moreover, this action would undoubtedly transpire under the watch of a Solidarity-led government.[152] Nevertheless, ideological considerations now took a back seat to Soviet international standing and internal stability.[153] The Kremlin would indeed continue to rattle its saber loudly in a bid to cow Poland's bold opposition and its reformist collaborators in the PZPR. However, should that opposition have the courage to call Moscow's bluff, it would discover, in effect, that the Soviet bark now far exceeded its bite.

After their briefing with Ustinov, the Soviet officers were dismissed and began filing out of the defense minister's office. As they left, Gribkov took the opportunity to remark to Kulikov, in reference to their earlier conversation, "You see what they decided at the Kremlin, not to send in troops under any circumstances." No doubt stung in his defeat, Kulikov merely blustered, "All the same, we will send them in."[154] Yet like the doctrine itself, Kulikov's was now an empty threat. With the decision to make a clear distinction between Soviet national interests and the defense of East European communism, socialist internationalism had ceased to be a central tenet of Soviet foreign policy.

Conclusion

The moderation of Soviet policy toward Poland in early 1981 occurred gradually, consistent with the fundamental shift of perception that informed it. When the year began, threats of military intervention seemed to provide the only viable deterrent to counterrevolutionary initiatives in Poland. Despite official denials of an impending intervention, Warsaw

Pact units participating in the Soiuz-80 maneuvers remained in the field more than two months longer than originally scheduled. Then, only a few weeks after the conclusion of Soiuz-80, in early March the Soiuz-81 exercises sufficiently reinvigorated fears of allied invasion to prompt Solidarity to retreat from its proposed general strike.

Meanwhile, Soviet observers such as Aleksandr Tsipko and L. M. Zamiatin awakened the Kremlin to the genuine popularity of Solidarity's complaints against the Polish authorities. Although Soviet discussions had repeatedly condemned attempts to resolve the crisis through political measures, both Tsipko and Zamiatin now supported redressing the political balance in Poland before moving to a military solution. If only the government dealt fairly and legally with society, Tsipko reported, the opposition alliance would very likely fall apart for lack of a common enemy. For his part, Zamiatin stressed Solidarity's emergence as a de facto political party capable of challenging communist control in Poland. He urged the Party to reassert its authority over the Polish press in a bid to win back the hearts and minds of the Polish nation.

Consistent with the gradualism of these two perspectives, by early 1981 Soviet policy toward Poland took on a much stronger political tone than it had previously displayed. The powerful influence of reform ideas within the Party prompted serious concern that communists in league with Solidarity were preparing to take control of the PZPR at its upcoming Ninth Congress. The Soviet leadership had no doubt but that the resulting transformation of Polish communism would result in a Eurocommunist or social democratic alternative. It nonetheless balanced demands for "decisive action" with political recommendations aimed at thwarting revisionist control of the Ninth Party Congress. No longer did the Soviets insist on the immediate declaration of martial law in Poland. Indeed, the Suslov Commission's important report of 16 April criticized Polish conservatives for their desire to launch a "frontal attack on Solidarity" without first redressing the national "correlation of forces." Inasmuch as this option could succeed only with allied military assistance, the commission regarded it as rash and undesirable.

Still, the military element in Soviet policy remained paramount, as a means not only of intimidating the Polish opposition but also in securing Warsaw's compliance with Kremlin dictates. Certainly the threat of invasion was decisive in averting the general strike planned for late March. But it was no less important in the Brest meeting of early April or in the Soviet letter to the PZPR of early June. While economic levers also came into play in Moscow's dealings with the Polish government, all roads ultimately led back to military pressure. Moscow had not sent the head of Gosplan to meet with the Poles in the dead of night—it had sent the head of the KGB and minister of defense. Similarly, the June letter did not dwell on Poland's need for Soviet aid but rather on its responsibilities to the common security of the socialist alliance. Again and again, Soviet statements rang with Brezhnev's earlier promise not to "abandon a fraternal country in distress." All the formulas were present, in both word and deed, to indicate that the Brezhnev Doctrine remained alive, well, and poised for action. And yet, following the decision of 4 December to put off an intervention for the time being, Moscow had still not formally resolved what it would do should events in Poland run out of control. Until mid-1981 there had been sufficient cause to assume that, eventually, Polish authorities would use their own forces to crush the counterrevolutionary opposition with limited outside assistance.

The developments of May and early June raised for the first time the prospect that this was unlikely. With Moscow now convinced that the opposition was making inroads into the Party itself, Kania's undisguised defiance of Soviet criticism did little to restore confidence. To make matters worse, only weeks thereafter Jaruzelski and the military elite had stepped in to prevent the Kremlin's June letter from toppling Kania. Suddenly it became hard to say whom the Soviets could trust to "normalize" the situation in Poland. Nationalist opposition to Moscow, it appeared, would soon extend from factory picket lines to the very corridors of power in Warsaw. Clearly it was this conviction that prompted the Kremlin to rule once and for all on the question of military intervention.

The Soviet General Staff's virtually unanimous vote to reject this option, regardless of the political circumstances, shows the degree to which considerations of national interest had transformed bloc policy since 1968. Suslov had made the point most clearly when he reportedly declared, "If a new leadership comes to power, we will cooperate with it. We cannot subject our country to international condemnation yet again." The Soviet leadership, both military and civilian, had learned a number of expensive lessons from the war in Afghanistan. It could not afford to make the same mistakes again, even if this meant an opposition victory in Poland. Ultimately, of course, this was only a worst-case scenario. As the balance of Suslov's comments indicate, Moscow had not yet concluded that it could no longer work with Warsaw. If anything, the decision to reject the option of military intervention only strengthened existing efforts to look after the political fortunes of the PZPR. After all, a palace coup in Warsaw would invariably expose the emptiness of Moscow's guarantee in Eastern Europe and so could endanger communist rule throughout the bloc. In time, Moscow would have to address the implications of this new vulnerability in allied affairs. Until then, the Soviets would continued to rattle a rusted saber, desperate to hide the reality of their own impotence.

7 Staring into the Abyss

> The theory of "no conflict" did not permit an understanding of the nature
> and sources of contradictions and crises in the framework of socialist
> cooperation, not to mention creation of mechanisms and procedures for
> their timely disclosure, prevention, or elimination. This led to erroneous
> decisions which led to the deformation of relations between socialist states.
> —V. I. Dashichev at a 1989 roundtable discussion on Eastern Europe

> We were not victorious
> but we fought.
> We could not get rid of the tyranny,
> but stopped its course.
> We did not rescue our country,
> but defended it.
> And if history will be recorded one day
> we will be able to say
> that we resisted!
> —Lajos Kossuth

ONCE THE SOVIET LEADERSHIP had circumscribed its options in
Poland, a renewed urgency regarding martial law returned to its relations
with Warsaw. Moscow quickly perceived that the fate of communism in
Poland, and quite possibly throughout Eastern Europe, now depended
entirely on a domestic resolution of the Solidarity crisis by Polish forces.
Should Warsaw prove unequal to this task, the alliance would look to the
Kremlin for evidence of its commitment to socialist internationalism.
When, instead, Moscow moved to stabilize its relations with the new
opposition government, the full bankruptcy of Soviet bloc integration
would be exposed for all to see. As the revolutions of 1989 would later
show, the consequences of such a revelation would be politically catastrophic. Hence, Warsaw simply had to be made to realize that its responsibilities to the rest of the socialist camp prohibited any further concessions. The time for adjusting the "correlation of forces" was past. Martial
law was needed swiftly and decisively.

However, Kania's ability to survive the political fallout of Moscow's
June letter did little to encourage Soviet faith that Warsaw would soon
take action against Solidarity. Nor did it augur well for the resurgence of a
pro-Soviet, conservative Party platform at the Ninth PZPR Congress, now
scheduled to convene in July 1981. Although Soviet military leaders, in
coordination with leading press organs, could increase the level of tension along the Polish-Soviet frontier, only time would tell how long the
Poles would remain intimidated by empty threats.

When the Polish congress finally convened in early July, Prime Minister Jaruzelski challenged the hours of pro-reform speeches with a warning that the government would enforce limits on opposition activity. In the months that followed, as hunger marches and public demonstrations threatened to overwhelm communist authorities, Jaruzelski provided the only promise of a counteroffensive against the Polish opposition. When Solidarity met in September for its first national congress, its obviously political aspirations suggested that little time remained to head off a wholesale transformation of Poland's sociopolitical system. Jaruzelski would clearly have to act quickly if he was to check Poland's evolution into a Western-style social democracy.

October marked the start of a decisive shift in this direction. The combination of Moscow's continued intimidation and political maneuvering finally took its toll on the Polish Party leadership, prompting it to sack Kania in favor of General Jaruzelski. This left the general simultaneously in charge of the Party, the government, and the military. Never since the dictatorship of Józef Piłsudski in the 1920s had one man commanded so much power in Poland. Soon the Polish military machine moved into high gear. By late fall, everything was in place for the introduction of martial law. November saw the PZPR Central Committee approve the decision to act. All that remained was to set a date.

For Jaruzelski, these last days leading up to the declaration were agonizing in every respect. After a year of insisting that Poland be permitted to handle the crisis itself, Jaruzelski appears to have undergone a change of heart in the fall of 1981. While hope had remained for a negotiated settlement with Solidarity, both Jaruzelski and Kania had resolutely opposed the use of force on a wide scale. Equating martial law with the introduction of allied troops into Poland, the two men had resisted both options. However, by September their hope of avoiding open conflict with the opposition evaporated in the wake of the union's first national congress convened in Gdansk. As union delegates excoriated Poland's communist system and issued appeals to the workers of Eastern Europe to join their movement, the Polish government concluded that further negotiations were pointless. Martial law would have to be implemented or Party rule in Poland would collapse. And so the man who had always linked martial law with Soviet military intervention turned to Moscow with a request for Warsaw Pact assistance. Yet in the face of a plea that Poland would be lost to the alliance if Warsaw had to face Solidarity alone, the Soviets flatly refused to intervene militarily. Indeed, the Soviet discussions that immediately preceded the declaration of martial law in Poland provide the most revealing evidence we have regarding Soviet perceptions of the Solidarity crisis. They demonstrate convincingly that by December 1981, conflicting national interests had completely eclipsed the commitments of socialist internationalism in Soviet bloc policy.

Kania as Persona Non Grata

The day that followed Moscow's June decision not to intervene militarily in Poland for any reason found Marshal Kulikov and General Gribkov again in the office of the Soviet defense minister. Ustinov had summoned them for the purpose of discussing the limited military options that remained open to the Kremlin. Although intervention was now out of the question, military exercises remained an effective means of bringing pressure to bear on the Poles. The next set of tactical maneuvers involving Soviets, Poles, Czechoslovaks, and East Germans was scheduled for October. Participating East European nations would be sending their ministers of defense to observe the proceedings, affording an opportunity to lean collectively on Jaruzelski, his chief of the General Staff General Florian Siwicki, and other Poles in attendance. Although Ustinov himself was not planning to attend the exercises, he would rely on Kulikov and Gribkov to keep the heat on Jaruzelski. The PZPR must be encouraged to act on its own rather than rely on "an uncle who will come and do everything for them." Now that the prospect of military intervention had been ruled out, Moscow could not risk the possibility that Jaruzelski was biding his time in expectation of outside assistance.[1]

This focus on Prime Minister Jaruzelski to the exclusion of Kania had become, by mid-June, a fundamental facet of Soviet policy toward Poland. For days after the letter of 5 June had failed to bring about Kania's removal, Brezhnev refused to take any calls from Warsaw. When he finally relented on 16 June, the two men held a decidedly terse conversation. "I had not wanted to talk to Kania for a long time," Brezhnev told the Soviet Politburo on 18 June, "but he tried hard to secure this conversation: he called me every day from Friday to Monday. Therefore, on Tuesday, 16 June, it was no longer comfortable to avoid the conversation, and I connected with him, as stipulated, when he was with the members of the [Polish] Politburo."[2]

Kania opened the discussion by thanking Brezhnev for the June 5 letter, taking care to recognize its legitimate concerns. However, Brezhnev had exhausted his patience with Polish rhetoric. "Comrade Kania," he bellowed, "how many times have I told you about this from the very start of all this business? I told you constantly what should be done, and that you cannot answer counterrevolutionary demonstrations with words."[3] In an effort to calm the Soviet leader, Kania agreed that one had to respond more aggressively to counterrevolution. However, he noted to Brezhnev that, since the Ninth Party Plenum, Solidarity had offered very little resistance to state authority. Moreover, he promised that a number of key personnel changes were planned to take effect in the coming days, including removal of the head of the Central Committee's Department of the Press, Radio, and Television.[4]

Turning to the topic of the upcoming Ninth PZPR Party Congress, Kania assured Brezhnev that this event would be characterized by a spirit of unity and discipline which did justice to Marxist-Leninist norms. The Soviet leader left no doubt that he was counting on the Poles to do precisely this. The very existence of communism in Poland was in jeopardy, Brezhnev said, and thus "difficulties at the Congress could well prove fatal for the PZPR." He cautioned: "If you don't succeed in securing a reversal in the political situation by the time of the congress, you will ruin the congress, and the Party itself, and with your own hands surrender power to the opposition—this is how the matter stands today. It is time you finally understood this. I am telling you this as a comrade."[5] Kania sought to conclude this unpleasant exchange with additional assurances that he would fulfill Brezhnev's requests if at all possible. The Soviet leader responded simply that "actions would show."[6]

Certainly the call had been tense. However, one wonders if Kania was able to see past this to notice that for the first time since the crisis began, Brezhnev had failed to link the collapse of Polish communism with the interests of the entire socialist community. As Ustinov's discussion with Kulikov and Gribkov had suggested, Moscow was attempting a new strategy in dealing with the Poles. Rather than rely exclusively on Polish fears of invasion, Soviet leaders now conveyed that if events began to overwhelm the PZPR, they *would not* step in to save it. The guarantees of socialist internationalism were now implicitly defunct. If the Poles failed to live up to their responsibilities, so might the Soviets. Assuming a philosophical outlook on the question, Brezhnev speculated to his colleagues, "Maybe they will at least reconsider and act more decisively. We will see."[7]

The Ninth PZPR Party Congress

In the weeks that followed, Soviet rhetoric continued to stress the Polish Party's tenuous grip on power in the run-up to its scheduled July congress. Seeking to encourage more aggressive ideological work, one televised assessment by Leonid Zamiatin cautioned on 20 June that "the situation in Poland is not only not improving, not only not stabilizing, but the crisis has encompassed the economic field and now the political sphere in the country is experiencing a crisis as is the ideological sphere." Zamiatin called on the Polish government to take immediate action to "lead Poland out of a catastrophic situation."[8] Meanwhile, war games in East Germany, the activation of a Hungarian brigade, the resumption of intensive training in the Western Ukraine, and the conduct of high-profile Soviet maneuvers in Silesia illustrated that Moscow's new "hands-off" tactic was reserved for relations with the Polish leadership. Publicly the Soviets would maintain its menacing tone toward the Polish opposition.[9] When, on 3 July, Soviet forces ended their maneuvers in Silesia, Soviet foreign minister Andrei Gromyko arrived in Warsaw for consultations with Polish leaders. There he received assurances from both Kania and Jaruzelski that "Poland was and would remain a socialist state and that the Party, despite the difficult situation in the country, would not permit the government's authority to be taken over by anti-socialist forces."[10] The final communiqué of Gromyko's visit, issued on 5 July, echoed this tone, promising that reform advocates would not control the upcoming congress agenda. Radical democrats, the communiqué declared, would not be permitted to "discredit the socialist system, notwithstanding the best efforts of the West." Though both governments still opposed the use of a Warsaw Pact invasion, they nevertheless pledged publicly that the fate of Poland was linked indissolubly to the interests of the entire socialist bloc. With luck and a healthy element of Soviet bravado, Poland's "self-limiting revolution" would continue to hobble itself until Warsaw could introduce martial law itself.

The long-anticipated Extraordinary Ninth PZPR Party Congress finally convened in Warsaw on 14–18 July. After agonizing over its preparation for months, Moscow's response to the event itself exhibited a healthy sense of skepticism and wariness. *Pravda*, for instance, censored more than a dozen passages from its translation of Kania's opening speech. These included expressions of support for Solidarity as a workers' lobby; rapid promotion of young, well-educated people within the government; truth in the media; bureaucratic and wage reform; educational opportunities for the children of workers and farmers; and tributes to both the Catholic Church and Polish socialist theory.[11] Another important address, that of leading reformer and Deputy Prime Minister Mieczyslaw Rakowski, received no attention at all from the Soviet papers short of oblique references to the "discord" of several "revisionist" speeches.[12]

Representing the CPSU at the Polish congress was Soviet Politburo member and Moscow Party boss Viktor Grishin. Grishin had spent years suppressing dissident intellectuals in Moscow and brought the same attitude with him to Warsaw. His address to the Poles stressed adherence to the Soviet model of socialism, particularly as it pertained to public ownership and the Party's leading role in society. Should the PZPR abandon these "objective laws of Marxism-Leninism," he declared, Poland would surely witness a restoration of capitalism within its borders. Grishin implied that Moscow would consider the use of economic sanctions to ensure Polish compliance if necessary, while nevertheless expressing his hope in a successful normalization of the national crisis.[13]

As if to justify Grishin's hope, Prime Minister Jaruzelski appeared before the congress on 18 July with words of conviction and determination. The Soviet press was duly attentive to Jaruzelski's pledge that he would stand up to the national opposition once and for all if it failed to moderate its demands. "There are boundaries which must not be overstepped," he intimated. Should the independent union press too hard, it would force the government to respond decisively and with force. "It would be disastrous for the nation, for the state," the general predicted. "We must not allow this to happen. This is the patriotic duty of every citizen and, above all, the duty of the people's authorities. In the name of superior reason, when the situation justifies it, the authorities will be forced to carry out with determination their constitutional duties in order to save the country from disintegration and the nation from catastrophe."[14] While still only a promise of action, Jaruzelski's address stressed a willingness to act with Polish forces if compelled by the opposition. As such, the prime minister seemed to be moving in precisely the direction that Moscow had long favored.

Ultimately, however, the conclusion of the congress suggested a decisive victory for reform advocates whose agenda vis-à-vis Solidarity was far less confrontational. Proponents of democracy managed to drive through a number of innovations in Party life, including multiple candidates for all positions and the use of secret ballots. A full 90 percent of the 270 Central Committee deputies elected in accordance with these altered procedures were new candidates. Forty of them openly expressed their loyalty to Solidarity.[15] Though he too faced the tyranny of the ballot box, Kania handily defeated his only opponent for the position of first secretary in a vote that, for the first time, included the entire congress.[16] However, he found himself surrounded by many new faces in the top leadership, as only four of the fifteen members from the former Politburo managed to hold on to their positions. Significantly, two of the four were Moscow favorites Olszowski and Milewski, though their conservative allies Grabski and Zabinski failed to be reelected. The fact that *Pravda* refused to publish the names of the new PZPR Politburo and Central Committee Secretariat revealed Moscow's predictable aggravation with these results.[17] Speaking with Kania after the elections, Brezhnev noted, "We think that the Congress was a serious trial of strength for both the Party and you personally. It clearly cast light on the extent of opportunism and the threat represented by opportunists. If they had been given a free hand they would have diverted the party from Leninism to social democracy. . . . In spite of this, the final outcome of the Congress and the fact that the highest party authority chose you for the post of First Secretary, create a reliable basis for resolute and consistent measures for the solution of the crisis and the stabilization of the situation."[18] Despite its exasperation with Kania's ineffective leadership, Moscow was clearly at pains to make the best of an increasingly desperate political situation.

Popular Demonstrations and the Question of "Counterrevolution"

While the spirit of reform was beginning to democratize Party politics at the congress, it did not offer any new solutions for resolving the nation's socioeconomic crisis. Consequently, as Party reformers were congratulating themselves for their accomplishments, the nation's standard of living continued to plummet. July brought an announcement from the government that monthly meat rations would be cut from 3.7 to 3.0 kilograms per person in August and September. This in turn touched off rumors that the Party was diverting food either to secret underground storage bins or Soviet shops in order to weaken popular resistance in Poland.[19] Hunger marchers took to the streets, beginning demonstrations that lasted into August.

Popular political sentiment grew steadily more radicalized, unimpressed with the reforms under way within the PZPR. One interfactory group involving three thousand enterprises had been calling since March for a reinterpretation of "social ownership." Society, it argued, and not the state ought to control the country's means of production. By July, this group had begun to advocate the preparation of political parties in anticipation of local elections scheduled for February 1982. It saw these as a stepping-stone to its goal of transforming Poland into a "self-governing state."[20] Of course, it was not very difficult to discern that a "self-governing state" would reflect the philosophy of Poland's self-governing trade union, Solidarity.

However, it was not clear where the union itself stood on the question of Poland's political future. Solidarity advisers Geremek and Kuron asserted that it was too early to consider the creation of new political parties. Instead, Kuron continued to support the formation of self-government clubs to instruct society in the vagaries of democracy.[21] Thus, by midsummer, the national opposition had become badly split over the pace of political reform in Poland. While most envisioned a common goal of greater popular participation in government, what form this would take was uncertain.

So did Solidarity aim to overthrow communism in Poland as Soviet propaganda continued to assert? The divisiveness within the union membership renders it difficult to answer that question. Timothy Garton Ash argues from his observations on the scene that it did not. He suggests that the "Polish revolution" remained self-limiting, even at this later point in the crisis. Granted, he admits, it did desire a share alongside the Party in social and economic decision making. Nevertheless, he writes, "the National Commission had no intention of overthrowing the Party, or of laying a finger on foreign and defense policy, which 'fundamentalists' and 'pragmatists' alike still recognized as Soviet vital interests in Poland."[22] On the other hand, Moscow had demonstrated in 1968 that Soviet-style communism was inconsistent with the type of social and economic influence to which Solidarity aspired. While the union might well have been resolved to seeing the PZPR remain in power, the present system differed fundamentally from that which had existed since 1945. Therefore, to Moscow, as well as to Polish conservatives, even this "self-limiting" option was decidedly "counterrevolutionary."

Nevertheless, Solidarity sought to limit the degree to which its rhetoric permitted this conclusion. For instance, speaking at a meeting of the union's National Coordinating Commission on 24–26 July, Jacek Kuron declared that "the hitherto existing system of power in Poland has ceased to exist, the government is not able to rule. The government lacks a democratically elaborated program and cannot refer to anybody, since the government also does not represent society. A revolution is being executed in which the existing order has been overthrown and no attempt has been undertaken to construct a new system." At the same time, he was careful to add that Solidarity could not create that new system. "Such system must be constructed by the whole society," he said, "hence there are clamorous demands for a political party." This process should remain self-limiting, he continued, "since the USSR will definitely march in, if it acknowledges that its military domination in Poland is imperiled. . . . If we have not decided to overthrow the authorities, we should not take any activities which are important only with respect to the maximum goal. . . . So since the Union does not want to overthrow the system, it is necessary to support the self-government initiatives movement, which is the only power able to present a credible program for overcoming the crisis."[23]

By late July, however, it appeared that Solidarity might soon realize its vision of a new Polish system and without any sort of dramatic uprising. The Party had begun to democratize its operations, and Kania seemed committed to the path of "socialist renewal." In addition to the new democratizing of the Party's internal policies, on 31 July Poles saw the new Censorship Act promised in the Gdansk Accords finally written into the law books. The new law overturned the so-called special decree of 1946 that had given state authorities the right to censor any and all published materials. It stipulated that certain publications and artistic performances would now be exempted from prior government review. Those which were not exempted would now receive the right of appeal in administrative courts.

Poland's new Censorship Law was especially significant for what it revealed about the shift in Soviet bloc policy. A similar development had been instrumental in bringing the Warsaw Pact into Czechoslovakia to crush the Prague Spring in 1968. During the normalization that had followed, control of the Czechoslovak media constituted a fundamental element of Soviet occupation policy. By contrast, the Soviet press brought very little pressure to bear on the Poles for the Censorship Act of 1981. Certainly, the Kremlin remained concerned about control of the Polish media; the Suslov Commission report of 16 April had taken a firm stance on this point. But once the Politburo decided that an intervention was out of the question, its options in Poland became sharply restricted. Barring a reversal of this decision, all the Soviets could do was to hope that martial law would strike down the new law.

Additionally, when the law was enacted, Soviet attention was otherwise occupied with the outbreak of hunger marches in Poland. Convinced as it was that the national opposition was preparing its seizure of power in Poland, the Kremlin regarded the marches as an opening salvo. Although Soviet press coverage carefully avoided reporting on the details of the marches, on 5 August *Pravda* spoke of the opposition's attempt to move popular discontent out of the factories and into the streets.[24] Expecting the Polish authorities to respond immediately with a declaration of martial law, Moscow, Berlin, and Prague offered whatever technical or material assistance Kania and Jaruzelski might require.[25] On 8 August Marshal Kulikov met with Prime Minister Jaruzelski to discuss the combat readiness of the Polish armed forces. His presence worried some Polish authorities. Did the Soviets still have faith in the PZPR despite what appeared to be a steadily worsening sociopolitical crisis? Deputy Defense Minister Tadeusz Tuczapski raised this question at the Party's Central Committee plenum of 11 August. "Our membership and place in the socialist community," he said, "indicate that we must be an authoritative partner who is worthy of trust, is politically strong and has a defense force that corresponds to our economic potential and the jointly agreed pledges. We have still not regained that trust."[26] A week later the Soviet leadership appeared to justify Tuczapski's concern following a brief visit by Kania and Jaruzelski to the Crimea for consultations. Unlike earlier statements of this kind, the final communiqué issued at the conclusion of the visit did not express Soviet confidence in the Polish leadership and its capacity to resolve its mounting crisis.[27]

Solidarity Holds Its First National Congress

By late summer, Solidarity's increasingly political demands had given the Soviets plenty of grist for their propaganda mills. On 12 August its National Coordinating Commission called on Poles to support "territorial self-government; the transformation of local councils and the Sejm, by way of democratic elections, into authentic representatives of society with increased powers over the state administration."[28] This was a program that many found an attractive alternative to the reforms under way within the PZPR Party Congress. Even the Catholic Church became involved, instructing its priests to read a statement of support for worker self-government from the nation's pulpits at Sunday Mass on 16 August.[29] Granted, these aspirations remained vague, defined largely by Jacek Kuron's "Clubs of Self-Government Initiatives, which would prepare regional self-government under the organizational and personnel patronage of 'Solidarnosc.'"[30] However, Solidarity's first congress was scheduled to meet in Gdansk beginning on 5 September and would afford an opportunity for the union to lay out a common vision for the future of Poland.

Worried that a new sense of purpose might well render the opposition impervious to state initiatives, Warsaw offered promises of emergency measures if the upcoming congress went too far. At the PZPR Central Committee plenum of 2–3 September, Kania issued a warning that any attempt to use civil disturbances against the state would be met with a declaration of martial law. "I would like to state with full emphasis and calm," he announced, "that in order to defend socialism the authorities will resort to all means necessary. We do not want this and do not threaten the use of this weapon [martial law]. Our declaration aimed at agreement signifies an offer of alliance with all those who are not against socialism."[31] Ironically, this warning managed to upset the Kremlin, as it had been a long time since Soviet communism had espoused the principle of "anyone not against us is with us." Still, the Soviet press was not above altering the sense of Kania's statements to fit its more rigorous views. Accordingly, all articles addressing the Polish plenum speech reported that Kania had supported an agreement only with "forces *standing in defense of the gains of socialism.*"[32]

Lest Kania's warning not amount to a sufficient deterrent, Moscow launched the largest military exercises in Warsaw Pact history on 4 September. U.S. Air Force analysts estimate that the Zapad-81 maneuvers had been planned for a long time. But the fact that they were timed to start on the eve of the Solidarity congress was a clear indication of their political content. For eight days Poland's allies mobilized and trained in Belorussia, the Baltic republics, and along the Polish coast, raising once again the specter of invasion. Consistent with the Suslov Commission report of mid-April, Moscow hoped the maneuvers would prevent radical voices from prevailing on the congress to launch an open rebellion against the government.

This time the looming presence of Warsaw Pact forces did little to temper Solidarity's initiatives. Strengthened by shared ideals and confident of international support, congressional delegates issued an unprecedented appeal to the workers of Eastern Europe. Whether Albanian, Bulgarian,

Czechoslovak, East German, Hungarian, Romanian, or even Soviet, this historic entreaty declared, the time had come to follow Poland along the road of social reform. With words resounding with Marxist irony, the Solidarity delegates proclaimed: "As the first independent self-governing trades union in our post-war history we are profoundly aware of the community of our fates. We assure you that, contrary to the lies spread in your countries, we are an authentic ten-million strong organization of workers, created as a result of workers' strikes. Our goal is to improve the condition of all working people. We support those among you who have decided on the difficult road of struggle for free trades unions. We believe that it will not be long before your and our representatives can meet to exchange our trades union experiences."[33]

There could be no denying that Solidarity had adopted a decidedly political agenda, full of implications for the broader socialist community. While delegates made no attempt to offer a distinct alternative, the word "socialism" never once appeared in the Solidarity program drafted at the congress. Indeed, one delegate, Professor Edward Lipinski, delivered a lecture to the convocation which asserted in part that after World War II, "what was created . . . was a socialism which meant a rotten, inefficient, wasteful economy. It was precisely the socialist economic system which led not to economic crisis, but to an economic catastrophe without parallel in the history of the last one or two hundred years."[34] Lipinski went on to challenge those who would characterize the Solidarity movement as "counterrevolutionary." The union was not interested in a restoration of capitalism, he observed: "Only those who demanded a privatization of heavy industry would be counter-revolutionary. In Poland there are no such forces. But there are forces who demand freedom, who demand conditions of normal life for the Polish nation. [Applause] And those are not anti-socialist forces."[35] Hence, the professor offered a patently political attack on the existing system under the guise of an undeniably economic reality. This was a style of brinkmanship that the congress was willing to accept as distinct from a blatant refusal to recognize the leading role of the Communist Party in society. At the conclusion of Lipinski's lecture, the delegates applauded appreciatively.[36] The world seemed to be witnessing its first genuinely proletarian revolution ironically preparing to overthrow communist rule throughout the bloc. Indeed, the Solidarity leadership made no secret of this. As Lech Walesa admitted openly at the time, the union was merely echoing the words of Karl Marx's *Communist Manifesto*: "Workers of the world, unite!"[37]

Nevertheless, while anxious to generate a groundswell of support all over Eastern Europe, the Solidarity leadership still trod very cautiously around explicitly political demands. Even among the union's more assertive factions there was little desire to initiate a confrontation with government forces. For instance, when one delegate from Gdansk proposed that Solidarity withdraw its recognition of the Party's leading role, he received a decidedly cool response.[38] Indeed, the congress went as far as to recognize explicitly the postwar division of Europe, as well as Poland's responsibilities to the socialist bloc. "We want to continue the work of the great change initiated by us without violating international alliances," it stated in one press release.[39]

Despite such expressions of self-control on the part of the union, Warsaw's response to the proceedings in Gdansk was predictably grave. Even reform advocates within the government regarded the Solidarity congress with shock and disappointment. The noted revisionist Deputy Prime Minister Rakowski, who had been the state representative in negotiations with Solidarity, saw no point in any further discussions with it. From his perspective, the "programmatic objectives outlined in the documents already adopted in Gdansk annihilate the spirit of partnership which has been replaced with a spirit of struggle with the government, or, to put it more precisely, with the [PZPR] and the people's power above all."[40] The congress had been the last straw. By late September there were few in the Polish government who still believed the situation could be resolved through negotiation. It would be more than two months before the government would sit down again for talks with Solidarity, but then only in an effort to distract it from the preparations under way for the introduction of martial law.

The Gdansk proceedings elicited similar condemnation from Moscow and its socialist allies. Predictably, what most upset the Soviets was Solidarity's attempt to disseminate counterrevolutionary ideas throughout the bloc with its "Appeal to the People of Eastern Europe."[41] At the height of the Brezhnev Doctrine in years past, this alone would have been sufficient justification for an allied invasion. Socialist internationalism would have dictated that the Polish trades union had become a threat to communism everywhere. But with the option of intervention now abandoned, the Kremlin was not certain how most effectively to register its displeasure. Addressing the Politburo on 10 September, Brezhnev condemned the appeal as a "dangerous and provocational document" that sought to generate unrest all over the socialist world. He recommended that the Suslov Commission work with three or four of the largest enterprises in the Soviet Union to target Solidarity with a letter-writing campaign. Soviet workers, he asserted, must go on record rejecting the "demagoguery" of the Polish opposition. Both Gorbachev and Grishin extolled the merits of this idea, with the latter commenting that collectives in the Zil, Serp, and Molot factories were already being prepared for a media blitz. Zimianin confirmed this to be the case. TASS, he explained, was preparing press releases that accused the Solidarity leadership of worsening Poland's national crisis. Additionally, Soviet propaganda would soon launch appeals to the collectives of several Polish enterprises.[42]

When it was suggested that Brezhnev phone Kania to discuss developments in Gdansk, many questioned whether the call would do any good. After all, Gromyko pointed out, while phone calls remained a useful lever for exerting pressure on Warsaw, Brezhnev had just spoken with Kania and Jaruzelski during their trip to the Crimea. Brezhnev agreed, adding: "Frankly speaking, as it seems to me, there is neither a desire nor any use in speaking with Kania now."[43]

Elsewhere in the socialist world, frustration with the Polish leadership was similarly grave. In talks with Cuban leader Fidel Castro on 13 September, East German general secretary Erich Honecker complained that both Kania and Jaruzelski had proven very disappointing in their inability to manage the crisis threatening their country. "In Poland," he said, "the situation these days is such that if there was no socialist environment, the counterrevolution would already have built a government." Insisting that a restoration of order was desperately needed, he added, "We are prepared for any kind of assistance." Honecker expressed his conviction that the Soviets would ensure that the crisis would be resolved in favor of socialism by any means necessary. "Under no circumstances will Poland be given up," he said, "because that would change the power relationships in the world. The US understands this of course, and only for this reason do they hold the counterrevolution back. They fear our intervention."[44] Honecker, it appears, was not aware of the degree to which Moscow had already permitted the Polish crisis to assume its own course, for better or for worse.

Moscow Raises the Stakes

With each passing week, the Polish first secretary frustrated Soviet hopes still more. In his desire to reach a compromise agreement with the "anti-socialist" opposition, Kania even seemed willing to overlook attacks on Soviet might and prestige in Poland. When monuments to the USSR were vandalized and Soviet Politburo members were lampooned in the press, Prime Minister Nikolai Tikhonov complained bitterly, "They are laughing at us! It seems to me that we can no longer remain silent, and that either through government or other channels, we must lodge a protest with the Polish government about this. In my opinion, we must not fail to react." Andrei Gromyko counseled restraint, reminding Tikhonov and the rest of the Politburo that they were, in fact, talking about a friendly nation. Clearly the foreign minister was right; self-restraint would have to be the watchword of Moscow's response. The Polish government was its only hope for the future of communism in Poland—perhaps in Eastern Europe. Alienating it could only prove counterproductive. Accordingly, the Politburo resolved on 10 September to have the Central Committee's Liaison Department and Foreign Ministry simply contact Warsaw to address "hooliganism" against Soviet interests in Poland.[45]

A letter to the Polish leadership went out that same day. Soviet ambassador Boris Aristov received the telegram and delivered it personally to Kania. It read in part: "The CPSU Central Committee and the Soviet government feel that further leniency shown to any manifestation of anti-Sovietism does immense harm to Polish-Soviet relations and is in direct contradiction to Poland's allied obligations. . . . We expect the [PZPR] leadership and the Polish government immediately to take determined and radical steps in order to cut short the malicious anti-Soviet propaganda."[46] While perhaps a more mild treatment than Tikhonov would have preferred, the letter did carry the character of a Soviet ultimatum to the Polish government. Moreover, its dissemination through PAP, Poland's official press agency, exposed Moscow's differences with Warsaw to the entire nation. Moscow also made the letter public, publishing it as an editorial in both *Pravda* and *Izvestiia* on 19 September. The time for backroom negotiations between allied parties had passed. Convinced that Kania's leadership was leading Poland down the road to ruin, Moscow was now willing to air its grievances with Warsaw in strikingly open terms. Once again the Polish authorities assumed a state of panic. Unsure of the letter's full implications, the members of the PZPR Politburo reportedly discussed the prospect of declaring martial law in Poland without delay.[47]

Moscow's open confrontationalism met with approval from a number of East European leaders who had long pressed for more assertive measures to contain the spread of Polish unionism. Because of the political threat its opposition movement posed to the entire Soviet bloc, Poland had become a pariah state in the socialist community. Many of its neighbors repeatedly petitioned Moscow to take action against the prospect of an international counterrevolution. Meeting with the Politburo on 17 September, Brezhnev addressed their fear that the situation in Poland was out of control.[48] Recent discussions with the socialist allies indicated that Honecker, Husak, and Zhivkov all agreed with Moscow's frank treatment of the Polish government. All felt that Kania had been "displaying unacceptable liberalism," for which the Soviets ought to "press him strongly." Honecker, as was his wont, had been the most aggressive of the three. In his opinion, the leaders of the Warsaw Pact nations ought to hold another summit in Moscow where they might sack Kania in favor of the conservative Olszowski.

While the Soviets were unwilling to intervene that openly in Poland's political affairs, they did recognize the need to become more assertive with the Poles. The question was how. All eyes would soon turn to the question of military intervention if a political resolution proved ineffective. As Hungarian ambassador Jozsef Garamvolgyi would write from Warsaw after a September 18 meeting with Kania, "Polish communists have assessed their forces. For such action [as martial law] their resources would be insufficient and thus the support of allied forces would be necessary." Yet the Hungarian ambassador recognized at the same time the predictably grave fallout of such a response. "The consequences of this would, however, set back the development of socialism by decades," he warned.[49] Of course, the Soviets had already concluded this months earlier in their decision to forswear military intervention in the Polish crisis. Still, they were not ready to admit that they had lost all control over the situation in Warsaw. Hence, the Politburo session of 17 September concluded with the resolution to have the ministries of defense and foreign affairs work with the KGB to determine what options remained open to Soviet influence.[50]

The press remained central as ever to this effort, and Moscow continued to use it for the purpose of attacking both Poland's opposition elements and its organs of state control. The union was preparing to hold the second part of its two-stage congress 27 September–8 October, and *Pravda* continued to charge that counterrevolutionaries had begun an "anti-Soviet orgy" in Poland. The challenge to Soviet interests was implicit but unambiguous, and Solidarity wasted no time in responding. "We do not want the power," declared delegates of the enterprise KWK Lenin in Myslowice-Wesola in a meeting on 17 September. "We do not want to change the socialistic order, every thoughtful person knows that that is unrealistic. What we want is to make justice under this system, we want a single law equal for everybody."[51] "We demand a halt to threats and menaces of losing independence," stated another meeting of Solidarity delegates at ZMB Zremb in Ciechanow on 19 September. "Taking into account the fact that our country borders only with the friendly nations, we deem such actions as contrary to the Polish reasons of state and aimed at undermining our political and military alliances. If our evaluation is wrong, we demand that the state be pointed out, from among those neighboring Poland, which would be ready to violate its sovereignty and independence."[52]

Indeed, the Solidarity leadership thought enough of the rhetoric coming out of Moscow that it passed a resolution during the second stage of its national congress recognizing the alliance with the Soviet Union as integral to Poland's national interest. The last thing that the union wanted was the government in Warsaw to feel that its failure to implement martial law constituted an abrogation of the Warsaw Pact treaty of alliance.

Unfortunately for Solidarity, the time for such concessions had passed. The government had already begun accelerating preparations for the introduction of martial law, which it now saw as virtually unavoidable. Military and security forces brought their units up to full battle readiness. Work stations and special communications equipment were becoming operational. Measures drafted months earlier in response to Soviet pressures finally came to life. On 13 September, Kania attended his first meeting of the National Defense Committee, where he found that virtually the entire body supported the immediate imposition of martial law. As Colonel Ryszard Kuklinski reported two days later to American intelligence officials, "It seems that the tenor of the meeting surprised Kania. Although he did not question that such a development was inevitable, he reportedly said, in these precise words, that 'a confrontation with the class enemy is unavoidable. This involves first a struggle using political means, but if that should fail, repression may be adopted.'"[53] However, Kuklinski later recalled, the time for political maneuvering had clearly come to an end by early fall 1981. "After almost a year of preparations for imposing martial law," he told one interviewer, "I became accustomed to pouring plans onto paper. But in September the first collisions between these plans and the human element commenced. I felt sickened, listening to the representative of the Propaganda Department under the PZPR Central Committee who was commenting to me on his vision of shutting down weeklies and newspapers which I used to read and even value or when he began to name columnists and journalists whom I liked to read or listen to and whose voices were soon to be quenched."[54]

By the end of September, Polish forces were reportedly ready to move against society whenever Jaruzelski gave the order.[55] With the collapse of negotiations between the government and Solidarity, Warsaw began a gradual militarization of society. On 24 September, Prime Minister Jaruzelski informed the Sejm that units from the Polish military would henceforth assist the Interior Ministry in keeping order throughout the country. At the same time, he offered the hope that some common ground might be found with Solidarity in order to avert a national catastrophe. "Now is the moment of decision," he told the legislature. "Preserving the readiness to defend the socialist state, we are waiting for an answer from the leadership of Solidarity, and a change in the line decided by the first round of the congress. The future course of the country and the people depends on whether Solidarity honors its commitments contained in the agreements of 1980."[56]

Soviet press coverage, meanwhile, inflamed existing tensions by continuing to remind the Poles of their obligations to the Warsaw Pact alliance. Articles appearing in *Pravda* in early October accused Solidarity of plotting to withdraw Poland from the alliance, its proclamation to the contrary notwithstanding.[57] On 14 October, *Pravda* ran an editorial from Mikhail Suslov which declared that Warsaw's communists could "firmly count on" the support of Moscow and its allies in time of crisis.[58] While merely a reaffirmation of Brezhnev's now famous promise from the Twenty-sixth CPSU Party Congress, Suslov's article reflected the Kremlin's perspective that the "time of crisis" had arrived.

The "support" Suslov had in mind was not martial in nature, but economic and moral. While intimidating rhetoric had its place, some means had to be found to ensure that Warsaw acted on its own—and soon. As Kania seemed incapable of resolute action, the Soviets sought out an opportunity to remove the Polish first secretary and replace him with Jaruzelski. The October plenum of the PZPR Central Committee afforded the earliest and most favorable occasion to act while the Poles were still reeling from the Kremlin's September letter. As the plenum began on 16 October, however, Moscow received word that Jaruzelski was prepared to reject any attempt to elect him first secretary of the Party. Word would have to be relayed to the prime minister instructing him that refusal was not an option. Unfortunately, once the plenum had begun, the Soviets found it nearly impossible to contact Jaruzelski without appearing to meddle directly in Poland's internal affairs. Somehow someone had to slip a message quietly to the general indicating Moscow's wishes, but how?

Military channels appeared to offer the best hope for success, considering Jaruzelski's many contacts with the Soviet armed forces. Defense Minister Ustinov accordingly placed a call to General Gribkov and ordered him to use all means at his disposal to get through to Jaruzelski. He was to instruct the prime minister that under no circumstances could he turn down the promotion. He, not Kania, enjoyed the Kremlin's full trust and support. Gribkov made several copies of Ustinov's message and sent them all to Jaruzelski by a variety of routes, hoping that at least one would reach him in time. One went by closed channels to the senior Soviet military chairman in Warsaw, Army General Shavelov. Another went to General Kornienko, then Soviet military attaché in Warsaw. It was Kornienko who managed to notify Jaruzelski through a network of personal contacts. Subsequently, though he had initially been opposed to the idea, Jaruzelski assumed the top post of first secretary in the PZPR on 18 October.[59]

For the first time in months, Moscow was pleased with the news from Warsaw. The Polish Central Committee had finally sacked Kania and installed a soldier who might act swiftly to restore discipline and order in Poland. The official Soviet statement congratulating Jaruzelski on his new appointment expressed trust that the Polish general would use his "great prestige" to roll back "encroachments of counterrevolution" in Poland.[60] Privately, in their first conversation after Jaruzelski's election, Brezhnev told the new Polish leader, "It was appropriate of you to give your consent to such a decision. In the PZPR right now there is no other individual whose authority is equal to yours; this is evident from the results of the vote at the plenum." He expressed Moscow's conviction that Jaruzelski would cope effectively with the "difficult tasks" that stood before him. Lest there be any delay, Brezhnev was careful to note how important it was, "without wasting time, to take the decisive measures you intend to use against the counter-revolution."[61]

Jaruzelski's reply bore witness to the Soviet role in his decision to accept the Party's highest position. "I want to tell you frankly," he said, "that I had some inner misgivings about accepting this post and agreed to do so only because I knew that you support me and that you were in favor of this decision. If this had not been so, I would never have agreed to it. This is a very burdensome and very difficult task in such a complicated situation in the country, in which I now find myself both as prime minister and as minister of defense. But I understand that this is proper and necessary if you personally believe so." The general also spoke of the increasing militarization of Polish society already under way in preparation for martial law. The army, he explained, was in the process of integrating itself "in all spheres of the life of the country." He had already advised the first secretaries of Poland's provincial Party committees accordingly. Moreover, military officers would soon begin meeting with Polish workers in an effort to "exert direct influence on the workers and shield them from the influence of 'Solidarity.'" In the meantime, the PZPR would "be combating the adversary and, of course, doing so in such a way that it will produce results."[62] Brezhnev was satisfied and concluded the conversation by wishing the new first secretary success in all his efforts.[63]

Jaruzelski soon made good on his promises. On 23 October, less than a week after his election, the Polish government announced that it was dispatching army units throughout the countryside to help local authorities protect food supplies and maintain order. Jaruzelski also extended the period of national military service for two-year conscripts, scheduled to end soon, by two months.[64] Military units began arriving in nearly two thousand Polish villages on 25 October. For the next four weeks, the army acquainted itself with the local administrations they would be controlling under martial law. They would remain in the villages until the end of November, at which time they would be transferred to Poland's larger towns and cities. There they would await Jaruzelski's declaration of emergency.[65]

The question in both Warsaw and Moscow continued to be the same as it had been for months: When would the Polish government actually make the declaration? In late October, the Poles remained reluctant to move too fast. Following a one-hour general strike staged by the union on 28 October, members of the PZPR Politburo demanded that Jaruzelski move to outlaw strikes in Poland. However, the general preferred to adhere to proper constitutional procedures. Speaking before the Sejm on 30 October, Jaruzelski announced submission of a draft law "on extraordinary means of action in the interest of the protection of citizens and the state."[66] Until it was approved, he was reluctant to act.

At this point further Soviet coercion might well have seemed needless and perhaps even disadvantageous. From Moscow's perspective, however, Warsaw had a long history of promising decisive steps that it later failed to take. Consequently, the Kremlin intended to maintain the pressure on Warsaw until Jaruzelski initiated martial law. As fate and careful planning would have it, late October afforded the opportunity that Ustinov had discussed with Kulikov and Gribkov in June. Military maneuvers scheduled to run through early November brought the Soviet General Staff together with Polish, East German, and Czechoslovak military leaders. The array of officials in attendance included virtually the entire Polish General Staff, from Jaruzelski on down, with the exception of General Siwicki.[67] In addition to Kulikov and Gribkov, the ministers of defense from East Germany (Hofman) and Czechoslovakia (Dzur) were also present.[68] As Ustinov had foreseen, this arrangement offered the allies ample time in which to wheedle Jaruzelski and his staff on the matter of martial law.

Discussion ranged over the many obstacles facing Poland in the fall of 1981. Using the most diplomatic language they could muster, the Soviet generals, Hofman, and Dzur worked to convince the Poles that they had essentially two options. They could either consider bringing members of Solidarity into the government, or they could declare martial law. Should Warsaw choose the latter, Jaruzelski would have to convince the nation that extreme measures were necessary to stabilize Poland's socioeconomic condition. After all, martial law would perforce involve many unpopular limits on society. Poland's borders would have to be closed to prevent outside literature or Western ideological centers from spreading further counterrevolutionary propaganda. Closure would also prohibit the opposition from importing printing equipment, radio apparatus, and weaponry that it might use in its struggle against the state. Additionally, the government would have to crack down hard on Poland's independent media to ensure the reimposition of strict nationwide censorship.[69]

The Poles listened attentively to these arguments, occasionally raising a number of concerns pertaining to the imposition of martial law. However, on the whole, Jaruzelski conveyed his full confidence that, when the time came, Polish forces would successfully introduce emergency rule. He offered further assurances that, come what may, these Polish army and security forces would remain firmly under state control. Should Solidarity move to seize power, Warsaw would be ready to defend communist rule in Poland. While this essentially surrendered the question of timing to the opposition, discussions remained cordial, and the question of outside intervention never arose. The realization that Warsaw was on its own now seemed evident to all present. Nevertheless, Jaruzelski's confidence was infectious, inspiring hope that Polish forces would achieve what they set out to do. Therefore, when the allied leaders got together over dinner toward the end of the maneuvers, they expectantly raised their glasses to a successful resolution of Poland's political and economic crises.[70]

The Limits of Socialist Internationalism in Practice

While Hofman and Dzur were participating in the Zapad-81 exercises, Moscow dispatched Konstantin Rusakov to the capitals of Eastern Europe to discuss the economic ramifications of the coming crackdown in Poland.[71] As expected, East European response was mixed. All expressed their approval of Moscow's conclusions regarding the need to provide whatever material resources it could to support socialism in Poland. But none was initially willing to countenance diversion of those resources, particularly oil and gas, from their own contracted deliveries. Ultimately, Kadar, Husak, and Zhivkov relented in the interest of socialist internationalism. Honecker, on the other hand, adamantly refused, arguing that such a move would seriously undermine the East German economy. The GDR was already suffering from a reduction of Polish coal deliveries, he pointed out. Moreover, the country had begun to experience a rapid decline in its standard of living which the government could not adequately explain. State economic officials were already reconsidering the feasibility of existing plan targets. Reduced imports of Soviet energy products would therefore come as a severe blow to East German economic stability.[72]

On 29 October, the Soviet Politburo addressed itself to these complaints. In his conversation with Rusakov, Honecker had implied that Berlin might respond to any diversion of Soviet oil and gas by curtailing its own deliveries of East German uranium to the USSR.[73] On the basis of this warning, he suggested that Moscow reconsider its decision and then reply to him in writing of its final resolution. Clearly he believed that Moscow would concede and forward East Germany's full complement of energy products. However, as Ivan Arkhipov was quick to point out, uranium deliveries from the GDR made up only 20 percent of that utilized in the Soviet Union. In short, there were alternatives to East German ore if Honecker tried to play hardball. Moreover, Arkhipov continued, East Germany relied on the Soviets to build its atomic power plants. "That is a big deal," he asserted, implying that Honecker ought to factor this assistance into his dealings with Moscow.[74] Brezhnev told his colleagues to go ahead with the planned diversions. Lest there be any lingering doubts, he proposed meeting with the East European leaders as soon as possible for consultations. The Polish economy teetered on the point of collapse and had to assume top priority.[75]

Moscow was also quickly approaching the limits of what it could afford to give its allies by way of assistance. The Soviet economy was experiencing its own trials, which the crisis in Eastern Europe threatened to exacerbate. Mikhail Gorbachev would later write of this period: "Economic growth had virtually stopped by the beginning of the 1980s and with it the improvement of the rather low living standard. The real *per-capita* income of the USSR was among the lowest of the socialist countries. . . . We were faced with the prospect of social and economic decline. Finances were in disarray, and the economy was out of balance and in deficit. There was a shortage not only of foodstuffs and industrial goods, but also of metals, fuel and building materials, i.e., everything that was produced in enormous quantities."[76] Several important sectors were unlikely to meet their plan targets for the year. Coal production had already fallen short by 10 million tons, which Moscow would doubtless have to make up either through imports from Poland or with hard currency purchases on the world market. Sugar and vegetable oils would also have to be found abroad. Inasmuch as the oil industry had not exceeded its projected output, Moscow could not make up for these shortfalls, not to mention increase deliveries to Eastern Europe.

In fact, Moscow continued to hope that relations with Poland would soon assume a more mutually beneficial character.[77] Ideally, the Soviet leaders wanted to link increased deliveries of oil and other products to Poland with Polish exports to Moscow, in accordance with the bilateral norms of Soviet bloc trade. Theoretically at least, this could mean that Warsaw's failure to respond with increased deliveries of coal and other exports would result in a curtailment of its oil deliveries. But, as of October 1981, it was still premature to consider mutually beneficial trade with Poland. Only two months earlier, the Bogomolov Institute had forwarded a report to the CMEA which had warned that "refusal by the USSR to provide assistance to Poland for solution of this [economic] problem will be linked with seriously negative consequences. Either the West will assume the role of savior to the Polish economy, with all of the resulting economic and political consequences, or the Soviet Union will be forced to assume the remission of Polish indebtedness upon itself."[78] Hence, for the time being, Moscow would simply continue to offer what little aid it could to prevent this from coming to pass.[79]

It should be noted that Soviet support of the Polish economy was not connected to any particular satisfaction with Jaruzelski's early policies as head of the PZPR. Initial impressions of the new first secretary were decidedly mixed. "I don't believe that comrade Jaruzelski has done anything constructive," Brezhnev remarked to the Politburo on 29 October. "It seems to me that he is not a strong person." Andropov agreed that the Polish general had so far done very little. However, he continued, Jaruzelski was still new to the job and deserved more time to prove himself.[80]

Confusion regarding Jaruzelski's Policies

What concerned the KGB chief most that October was the general's apparent change of heart regarding outside military intervention. He and other members of the Polish government had begun inquiring repeatedly about the prospects of a Warsaw Pact intervention in Poland. "The Polish leaders are talking about military assistance from the fraternal nations," Andropov reported to his colleagues on 29 October. Could it be that they were trying to relinquish responsibility for the crackdown against Solidarity? If so, then there could be no question regarding Kremlin policy. Soviet interests had to be preserved above all. Moscow was in the process of implementing this line secretly in Afghanistan according to former first deputy foreign minister Georgii Kornienko. "In the fall of 1981," Kornienko writes, "the Politburo approved a proposal prepared at the initiative of the MFA [Ministry of Foreign Affairs] and with the support of Andropov and Ustinov to organize a diplomatic process aimed at such a regulation of the situation around Afghanistan that it would permit the withdrawal of Soviet forces from that country."[81] The Soviet leadership was not about to walk out of one conflict and into another. Should a conflict arise between Soviet interests and communist rule in Poland, Andropov insisted, Moscow was duty-bound to choose the former over the latter. Regardless of the political ramifications, he concluded, "we should adhere firmly to our line—not to send our troops into Poland." Defense Minister Ustinov concurred: "In general it must be said that it is impossible to send our troops into Poland. They, the Poles, are not prepared to welcome our troops."[82]

Only weeks earlier, Jaruzelski had not raised the question of foreign intervention with Kulikov or Gribkov during the Zapad-81 exercises. Was it possible that he now genuinely relied on it as a fail-safe option? Considering the confidence with which he regarded his own armed forces in discussions with the Warsaw Pact allies, one might well question whether Jaruzelski ever even considered this alternative. And yet members of the Soviet leadership were becoming convinced not only that he had considered outside intervention but also that he might now be relying on it.

On the other hand, it was becoming increasingly difficult to make sense of what Jaruzelski was attempting to do in Poland. While obviously readying the country for an imposition of martial law, the general also pursued further talks with the Church and with Solidarity. On 4 November, for instance, he met with Joseph Cardinal Glemp and Lech Walesa to explore the matter of ending all strike activity in Poland. The meeting led to a brief restoration of negotiations between the two sides beginning on 17 November, the first since before the Solidarity congress. Was the general merely working to lull the union into dropping its guard before the state coup de grace? It was not clear from Moscow's vantage point.

Consequently, the Kremlin was by no means a silent spectator to the drama building in Poland. As early as late October the Soviet press began carrying a steady diet of commentary framed in extremely provocative language. On 30 October, the Soviet military daily *Krasnaia Zvezda* alleged that the Polish opposition was preparing to seize power. It therefore urged the Polish government to take immediate action in its own defense.[83] Timed to coincide with Jaruzelski's request for emergency powers in the Sejm, the article indicated a strong belief in Moscow that the Poles were on the verge of declaring martial law. As the days passed and the Soviets came to recognize that the declaration was being delayed, the Kremlin began to turn up the heat. Counterrevolutionaries would never overcome socialism in Poland, Defense Minister Ustinov declared with conviction on 7 November, the anniversary of Russia's 1917 Bolshevik Revolution.[84] Less than a week later, on 11 November, an editorial in *Pravda* warned that Solidarity was preparing shock troops for use against the government, adding that the PZPR would take "appropriate security measures" to avoid being caught by surprise.[85] As far as the Soviets were concerned, the final battle for the fate of communism in Poland was brewing. Negotiations be damned, Moscow clearly expected the crisis to come down to a test of strength between Jaruzelski's troops and Solidarity's largely unarmed millions.

Lest there be any confusion among the broader Soviet leadership, a closed plenum of the Soviet Central Committee held on 16 November offered a confidential opportunity for ideology chief Mikhail Suslov to explain the lack of outside intervention. He laid the blame for the crisis squarely at the feet of the PZPR. "The Polish Crisis," he said, "is the direct result of the Party's ideological and organizational weaknesses, of a serious violation of the Leninist principles of Party construction over many years."[86] Suslov described the Soviet response since the start of the crisis, touching even on the secret meeting in April 1981 between Andropov, Ustinov, Kania, and Jaruzelski. Nowhere in the address, however, did he mention plans for the use of outside military intervention.

Rather, he leveled sharp criticism at the West, particularly the Reagan administration, for allegedly provoking a showdown over Poland. "Pushing the Polish counterrevolution toward extremist acts," Suslov claimed, "they [Western 'imperialists'] openly provoked the socialist countries, counting on us to lose our nerve. They provoked direct interference in Poland and tried to find a reason to blame the Soviet Union and the socialist countries for such intentions." He cautioned that this situation "demands particular self-control and vigilance on our part. . . . We cannot allow imperialism to take advantage of our actions and organize an economic blockade of the fraternal nations. We cannot allow it to deepen the arms race and land the world in another war." Accordingly, Suslov assured the Central Committee, "throughout the entire evolution of the crisis in Poland the Soviet government has searched for a *political* means of resolving the conflict." Moreover, he continued, "our allies in the Warsaw Pact have shared this position."[87]

Once again, the specter of Western sanctions arose in the discussions of the Soviet leadership in the context of explaining the failure to intervene in the Polish crisis with Warsaw Pact forces. The Poles would have to do the job with their own forces when the political, economic, and social initiatives had been exhausted. Increasingly, however, it had begun to look as if Jaruzelski himself lacked the will to act.

As such, by late November a tone of conspicuous impatience permeated interparty correspondence between Moscow and Warsaw. Shortly after his installation as first secretary, Jaruzelski had contacted Brezhnev to request an audience for consultations. Brezhnev used his reply in a letter dated 21 November as an opportunity to upbraid the Polish leader for failing to justify Moscow's confidence in him.[88] "The anti-socialist forces," he complained, "not only are gaining sway in many large industrial enterprises, but are also continuing to spread their influence among ever wider segments of the population. Worse yet, the leaders of 'Solidarity' and the counter-revolutionaries are still appearing before various audiences and making openly inflammatory speeches aimed at stirring up nationalist passions and directed against the PZPR and against socialism. The direct consequence of this hostile activity is the dangerous growth of anti-Sovietism in Poland."[89]

Brezhnev also implied that Jaruzelski's ongoing talks with the Church and Solidarity toward creating a national accord would only weaken state control over Polish society. "Indeed," he said, "aren't the class enemies trying to instill the 'Front of National Accord' with political content that would bolster their idea of, at a minimum, attaining a division of power among the PZPR, 'Solidarity,' and the Church with the result that socialism would collapse? It is also clear that they are exploiting their current influence among the masses to establish a huge advantage in the upcoming elections for national councils, thus continuing their path toward the legal seizure of power in the country."[90] Therefore, Brezhnev argued, the Party ought instead to work toward strengthening its role in the Front of National Accord by forcing the Church and Solidarity to recognize Poland's socialist constitution, its socialist system, and the inviolability of its alliances. "We are not opposed to agreements," Brezhnev pointed out. "But such agreements must not make concessions to the enemies of socialism."[91]

As expected, the Polish opposition would consider these conditions totally unacceptable. And so, realistically speaking, force was the only means of resolving the crisis without any state concessions to Solidarity. "It is now absolutely clear," the Soviet leader continued, "that without a resolute struggle against the class enemy, it will be impossible to save socialism in Poland. The essential question is not whether there will be a confrontation or not, but who will begin it and by what means it will be carried out, as well as who will seize the initiative." Solidarity, he suggested, was merely biding its time until new conscripts sympathetic to the opposition were inducted into the army. Consequently, the government's "failure to take harsh measures against the counter-revolution right away" was costing the regime precious time. The longer it delayed, the greater its chances of defeat.[92]

Brezhnev concluded this diatribe with the suggestion that Moscow target PZPR conservatives for support against their revisionist critics. Revisionism, he claimed, was weighing down the Polish Party, "like a heavy burden." In the end, it would be Party conservatives, and not revisionists, who would take up the gauntlet against Solidarity. And so it was these "healthy forces" who most deserved the Kremlin's support. Importantly, however, Brezhnev did not resurrect earlier suggestions of secretly siding with a "shadow Politburo" consisting entirely of conservatives. Despite his disappointment with Jaruzelski, the Soviet leader was evidently not prepared to make the same mistake he had condoned in 1968 with the Czechoslovaks. There was truly no alternative to Jaruzelski in the PZPR. No one commanded as much authority in both government and society. Therefore, there could be no search for Polish quislings as an alternative to the existing leadership. At most, the Soviets could only hope to side with Polish conservatives in an effort to champion adherence to traditional communist norms. It was hoped that Brezhnev's letter of 21 November would further this effort.

Shouldering Responsibility

Warsaw did not disappoint. On 22 November, a day after Soviet ambassador Aristov had delivered Brezhnev's dispatch from Moscow, police raided the apartment of KOR luminary Jacek Kuron. An official statement from the authorities explained that Kuron had been engaged in setting up an alternative political organization with his Self-Governing Republic clubs. State propaganda depicted these as the Jacobin clubs of the Polish revolutionary movement: small groups of conspirators pushing Solidarity ever more in the direction of radical political demands. Police inspectors did not have to search very long for evidence of these claims. As it turned out, the public Founding Declaration of the clubs described them as "the nuclei of future political parties in a democratic state," a claim that ipso facto implied a plan to overthrow the communist system in Poland.[93] This gave the government whatever ideological excuse it might have needed to justify an all-out offensive against KOR and its allies in Solidarity. Moreover, developments were beginning to indicate that this offensive was not far off. Indeed, the very next day, Jaruzelski's government announced that the military operational groups that had been in Polish villages since late October would now take up position in the nation's cities.

Soviet military personnel did what they could to encourage this trend. While political leaders addressed the prospect that Jaruzelski now desired outside intervention, Ustinov and Kulikov remained convinced that only the threat of an invasion would guarantee a favorable resolution of the crisis in Poland. And so, at a November 24 meeting with Polish military leaders, Marshal Kulikov warned that the troubles in Poland were jeopardizing Soviet security interests. The crisis, he complained, had started to become "projected on the military and political interests of the Warsaw Pact. The functioning of the Northern Group of Forces of the Soviet Army is being hindered." The Polish strikes, which were creating problems for the delivery of provisions and energy supplies to Soviet troops, were of particular concern. Additionally, profligate anti-Sovietism had reached unprecedented levels that threatened to provoke a Soviet response. When the time came to act, he declared, his hand would not shake.[94]

With Kulikov's words still ringing in his ears, General Jaruzelski appeared before the Sixth PZPR Central Committee Plenum on 27 November to announce that he planned to ask the Sejm for a law banning strikes. Echoing Brezhnev's cynical view of the quest for national accord, he argued that Poland had first and foremost to secure peace and order. The Politburo vote had been unanimous. The moment had arrived to act in defense of communist rule in Poland. By the end of the plenum, this realization manifested itself in a final resolution to introduce martial law in the coming weeks.[95]

Hence, as one Western journalist later observed, the doors to a national agreement in Poland closed as of the Sixth PZPR Central Committee Plenum.[96] If there had ever been any inclination in Warsaw to pursue negotiations with the Church and Solidarity after the Solidarity congress, Brezhnev's letter of 21 November appears to have undermined it decisively. Though talks continued, the limited package of reforms that the government presented to the Sejm on 1 December contained none of the concessions Solidarity had been demanding. As if to flout this snubbing, riot police from the Mechanized Units of the Citizens Militia (ZOMOs) on

2 December used force to end a student occupation of the Warsaw Fire Officers Academy. Battle lines were now drawn up, and Jaruzelski was testing the feasibility of open confrontation for the first time since Bydgoszcz. The test was a success. The students were removed from the building, and the occupation ended without any of the immediate repercussions that had followed the Bydgoszcz incident in March. Party conservatives were emboldened, with Stefan Olszowski assuring colleagues that the long-running crisis would be resolved before Christmas.[97] Members of the diplomatic corps received word that the government was preparing a military operation for December.[98] Similar notification also seems to have circulated to Poland's allies at a number of blocwide conferences convening at this time.[99]

Of course Solidarity's National Coordinating Commission was not about to allow the use of force in Warsaw to pass by without protest. As it convened in Radom to discuss an appropriate response, tempers were high, prompting many to advocate unusually confrontational action. When government agents managed to tape the proceedings, authorities were able to use especially damning statements in their official propaganda. And so, for instance, Poles heard someone alleged to be Jacek Kuron argue that "the ground must be well prepared to overthrow the authorities." Other voices called for the creation of a workers militia armed with helmets and batons to defend the union against further violence. Even Walesa was heard to say that "confrontation is inevitable, and it will take place."[100]

The final communiqué of the Radom meeting accused the state of shattering any hope for a national accord with its recent policies. Jaruzelski's request in the Sejm for emergency powers, the commission felt, would infringe on the rights Solidarity had fought hard for since August 1980. The new program of economic reforms scheduled to begin on 1 January 1982 only confirmed that the government planned to ignore union demands. Moreover, the ZOMO action in Warsaw suggested that the authorities were quickly moving in the direction of increasing force. Therefore, the commission warned, should the Sejm approve Jaruzelski's request for emergency powers later in the month, Solidarity would call a general strike along with unprecedented public demonstrations against the government.[101]

Deputy Prime Minister Rakowski would later assert that the government had moved to declare martial law only after the National Coordinating Commission's meeting of 3 December, arguing that "Radom simply scared us."[102] In fact, this assertion was far more the stuff of justification than of explanation. As the archival evidence cited above now reveals, the PZPR Central Committee had already resolved to declare martial law (which had come to be known as Operation X) nearly two weeks before Radom. Nevertheless, despite Jaruzelski's intensive preparations, Moscow continued to view the Polish leader as diffident and unsure of his policies. Although Jaruzelski had the approval of both the PZPR Central Committee and its Politburo, he continued to regard the decision to act as reversible up until the last moment. Because the Soviets sensed this, their conversations with him were filled with ominous warnings about the future of socialism in Poland.

On 7 December, Brezhnev admonished Jaruzelski that counterrevolutionaries had the PZPR by the throat. If Polish communists did not act immediately to crush the opposition, he warned, it would be too late. Indeed, it was quite possible that this fate could befall the entire socialist community. Ustinov adopted a similar tone that same day during a call to General Siwicki. In response, the Poles assured Moscow that, when the time came, they would have sufficient determination to prevent a counterrevolutionary reversal in their country. However, Jaruzelski told Brezhnev, Poland was certain to require further economic assistance if and when martial law was finally declared. He subsequently requested a meeting with state economic planning chairman Nikolai Baibakov to discuss what Warsaw might be able to expect by way of additional aid from the Soviet Union. Jaruzelski was justifiably worried that the West would respond to a declaration of martial law with an economic blockade; he therefore wanted a guarantee that Poland's allies would come to its rescue.[103]

Jaruzelski's requests turned out to be far more than the Soviet leaders felt they could spare. Baibakov returned from Poland with a list of some 350 separate items worth approximately 1.4 billion rubles. This included 2 million tons of grains, 25,000 tons of meat, 625,000 tons of iron ore, and much more. If added to what the Politburo had already approved for delivery in 1982, Moscow's total aid package would have come to a staggering 4.4 billion rubles. Moreover, inasmuch as the Polish economy was in a veritable state of collapse, the prospects for "mutual economic ties on a balanced basis" were nonexistent. Moscow would have to make up its shortage of coal on the more expensive Western markets. The only way the Poles could consider compensating the Soviet Union for its exports would be to declare a moratorium on repayment of debt to the West and channel their interest payments to Moscow.[104] If it did this, however, the Soviets stood to take the blame for Poland's economic collapse. And so the Kremlin sat, in the words of a Russian proverb, between a hammer and an anvil. If it did not provide the goods Poland required, it could be accused of abandoning its ally in time of need. Yet if it requested payment in exchange for added deliveries, then it would be responsible for Warsaw's decision to default on Western loans. Andropov saw this as an intentional setup. "But again I want to say," he complained, "that the mere posing of the question of the apportionment of goods supplied as economic assistance is an insolent way to approach things, and it is purely so that if we refrain from delivering something or another, they'll be able to lay the blame on us." In fact, the KGB chief pointed out, it was extremely unlikely that Gosplan would be able to meet all Jaruzelski's requests.[105] For the time being, therefore, the matter was tabled pending further examination by Prime Minister Tikhonov and Central Committee secretaries Andrei Kirilenko, Nadimir Dolgikh, Arkhipov, and Baibakov.[106]

Moscow was now convinced that Warsaw was planning to share the blame for imposing martial law by requesting outside intervention from its Warsaw Pact allies in the uncertain days to come. Konstantin Rusakov addressed this issue in his December 10 report to the Politburo, shortly after returning from Warsaw. According to this report, Jaruzelski had told him "that if the Polish forces are unable to cope with the resistance put up by Solidarity, the Polish comrades hope to receive assistance from other countries, up to and including the introduction of armed forces on the territory of Poland." Rusakov felt that Jaruzelski had come to rely on Kulikov's November implication that the USSR and its allies would provide military assistance if necessary. However, he noted, to his knowledge Kulikov had offered no such promise directly "but [had] merely repeated the words voiced earlier by L. I. Brezhnev about our determination not to leave Poland in the lurch."[107] Therefore, in Rusakov's estimation, Jaruzelski was simply trying to pull the wool over Moscow's eyes for reasons about which he could only speculate.

These suspicions only deepened as Jaruzelski continued to push back the scheduled commencement of martial law. Jaruzelski had begun by fixing the declaration for the night of 11–12 December. Then he had moved it to 12–13 December. By 10 December, he was considering a further delay until 20 December. No doubt eager to share the burden of responsibility, Jaruzelski insisted on receiving approval from the Sejm before he took any further action; its next session was scheduled for 15 December. But when the agenda for this session appeared on 10 December, the topic of martial law was notably absent. In fact, Jaruzelski repeatedly suggested that he would "resort to Operation X when Solidarity forces us to do so." Such words left the Soviets confused and doubtful of Jaruzelski's true intentions. Reporting to his exasperated colleagues in the Kremlin, Rusakov admitted that "everything has become very complicated."[108]

Abandoning Poland to Its Fate

The Soviets were beginning to believe that Jaruzelski might not resort to martial law at all. Andropov in particular had come to believe that the Polish leader was attempting "to find some way of extricating himself" from his responsibility to execute the will of the PZPR Central Committee. Although it had seemed that the late November resolution had been decisive, now, Andropov suggested, "it would seem that either Jaruzelski is concealing from his comrades the plan of concrete action, or he is simply abandoning the idea of carrying out this step." His attempts to link implementation of the resolution with excessive demands for Soviet economic aid reinforced this impression.[109]

In any case, the KGB chief asserted unequivocally, a military intervention in Poland remained out of the question. "We can't risk such a step," Andropov underscored. "We don't intend to introduce troops into Poland. That is the proper position, and we must adhere to it until the end. I don't know how things will turn out in Poland, but even if Poland falls under the control of 'Solidarity,' that is the way it will be."[110] Soviet national interests now diverged sharply from Moscow's earlier commitment to guarantee communist rule in Eastern Europe. The promises of socialist internationalism threatened to undermine Soviet stability at home and abroad and thus had to be abandoned in practice, if not in theory. A military intervention was certain to elicit a coordinated response from the West that would hurt the Soviet Union, both politically and economically. As Andropov observed, "If the capitalist countries pounce on the Soviet Union, and you know they have already reached agreement on a variety of economic and political sanctions, that will be very burdensome for us. *We must be concerned above all with our own country and about the strengthening of the Soviet Union. That is our main line.*"[111]

Andropov could hardly have been more explicit. With this statement, the KGB chief proclaimed the bankruptcy of the Brezhnev Doctrine. Its fundamental principle—that the fate of socialism in one country is inseparable from the fate of the entire bloc—had crumbled under the weight of divergent national interests. There was a limit to what the Kremlin was willing to pay to prop up the socialist governments of its client-states, and that limit had been reached. Its earlier commitments were reduced now to empty bluffs, relying on the memories of Hungary, Czechoslovakia, and Afghanistan for their power to convince and influence. Backs against the wall, with a clear and present danger looming over their own national stability, the Soviet leaders prepared to blink first.

Of course, the full significance of this decision would not become apparent for a number of years. As they considered the prospects of an opposition victory, the Soviet leaders did not anticipate that they might lose all influence in Poland. Soviet military doctrine still considered it essential to the defense of both Eastern Europe and the Soviet Union. Nearly all lines of communication between the USSR and what would become the western front in a war against NATO went directly through Poland. Consequently, Andropov argued, "as concerns the lines of communication between the Soviet Union and the GDR that run through Poland, then we of course must do something to provide for their safekeeping." Ustinov confirmed that Soviet garrisons in Poland were already being fortified against the possibility of attack.[112] While the Kremlin was prepared to accept the collapse of Polish communism, it was also ready to resist with force any attempt to compromise its military interests. That it did not seriously anticipate having to do so may be attributable to the many Solidarity declarations that had recognized the nation's commitments to the Warsaw Pact.

It will also be remembered that the Soviets did not foresee a Solidarity victory leading necessarily to the restoration of Western-style capitalism in Poland. Rather, they expected the establishment of a reform communist or social democratic government, similar to the type advocated in Yugoslavia and among the Eurocommunist parties. The Politburo discussions noted above clearly indicate that it never even occurred to them that Poland might someday petition to join NATO. As such, the consequences of a communist collapse, while certainly undesirable, seemed at least strategically manageable.

Nevertheless, the decision to abandon Poland to its political fate was not at all an easy one for the Soviet leadership to justify. Ultimately, what overcame any lingering doubts was Moscow's relentless obsession with vital Soviet interests, particularly Soviet prestige in the international community. Gribkov had raised this point in his June argument against intervention. Now, six months later, it remained central to Moscow's justification. "We've done a great deal of work for peace," Suslov reminded his colleagues, "and it is now impossible for us to change our position. World public opinion will not permit us to do so. We have carried out via the UN such momentous diplomatic actions to consolidate peace. What a great effect we have had from the visit of L. I. Brezhnev to the FRG and from many other peaceful actions we have undertaken. This has enabled all peace-loving countries to understand that the Soviet Union staunchly and consistently upholds a policy of peace. That is why it is now impossible for us to change the position we have adopted vis-à-vis Poland since the very start of the Polish events. . . . *If troops are introduced, that will mean a catastrophe. I think we have reached a unanimous view here on this matter, and there can be no consideration at all of introducing troops.*"[113]

What remained, then, was to communicate this position to Jaruzelski so that he realized that the responsibility for defending socialism in Poland rested entirely with him. Moscow's position on this had to be clear, Andrei Gromyko argued, to "dispel the notions that Jaruzelski and other leaders in Poland have about the introduction of troops into Poland." The foreign minister suggested instructing Ambassador Aristov to communicate Soviet intentions clearly and precisely to the Polish leaders, so that there could be no further misunderstandings. The Poles were on their own. They must realize this and act accordingly. Of course, such communication would entail considerable difficulties, particularly in relations with the West. Western creditors would doubtless cut off access to further credits and other economic assistance following the imposition of martial law. Consequently, Gromyko urged his colleagues to give serious consideration to Jaruzelski's latest request for economic assistance. Resolved to make the conclusions of this discussion the basis of all future relations with Poland, the Politburo then moved on to other business.[114]

The "working notebook" of Lieutenant General Viktor Anoshkin, Kulikov's assistant and a liaison to the Polish military, offers extraordinary insight into the impact of this news in Poland.[115] Anoshkin records that on the morning of 10 December, Defense Minister Ustinov contacted Marshal Kulikov in Poland with the following instructions: "When you hold negotiations with the Polish side, it is essential to emphasize that 'the Poles themselves must resolve the Polish question. We are not preparing to send troops onto the territory of Poland.'"[116] It was the first the Poles had heard of the decision taken six months earlier, and the rebuff came as a crushing blow to General Jaruzelski and his high command. Meeting with Marshal Kulikov on 11 December, Jaruzelski's deputy, General Florian Siwicki, pleaded that "if there will be no political, economic, and *military* support from the USSR, our country might be lost for the WTO."[117] The Soviet commander in chief steadfastly stood by Ustinov's instructions, reminding Siwicki that, in the past, "you insisted that Poland is able to resolve its problems on its own. . . . Why has the question of military assistance arisen? We already went over all aspects of the introduction of martial law."[118] Anoshkin's description of this encounter concludes with the observation that "Siwicki left here dissatisfied. He got nothing new and heard nothing new from V. G. [Viktor G. Kulikov]. The Warsaw Pact Commander-in-Chief has been restrained by Moscow!!"[119]

Last Minute Posturing

Even as members of the Politburo reasserted their collective decision not to send troops into Poland, the Soviet press continued to keep alive rumors of impending invasion in its sustained effort to check an offensive against the Polish government. The December 10 edition of *Pravda* remained riveted to the possibility of a Solidarity uprising following the decisions of the Radom summit. Detailed plans and preparations were already under way, it submitted. Workers identifying themselves with the Polish Home Army of the 1940s had allegedly taken to the streets to foment "counterrevolution." By 17 December they were to seize radio and television stations. Four days later they would undertake a coup d'état against the government in Warsaw. As if this were not enough, the *Pravda* article resurrected claims that Solidarity planned to pull Poland out of the

Warsaw Pact.[120] It was the bleakest scenario that had yet appeared in a Soviet publication since the start of the crisis. Moscow could not level accusations such as these without arousing expectations of immediate action on someone's part against the opposition. "The critical situation caused by the rampage of counterrevolution is prompting authorities to take further steps to protect the constitutional foundations of the state," the December 10 article read in part. Though it remained unclear when, and even if, Jaruzelski would act, *Pravda* was content to announce to the world that a Polish crackdown was imminent.

On the other side of the standoff, 10 December found the leaders of the Polish opposition scrambling to muster international indignation against the growing threat of martial law. The handwriting had been on the wall in Poland since late November, so recent statements in the Polish and Soviet press only underscored previously conceived misgivings. A storm was about to break over their heads that could well mean an end to all they had achieved for the reform of Polish society. The authorities, Lech Walesa told reporters, were trying to provoke a confrontation that would prove bloodier than the events of December 1970. The notion that Solidarity was preparing a coup d'état was ridiculous. After all, he continued, the only weapon that the union had at its disposal was the strike. What good was that if the government was prepared to counter with bullets? The following day, on 11 December, Walesa spoke again from the Lenin Shipyard in Gdansk. "I declare with my full authority: we are for agreement . . . we do *not* want any confrontation. The National Agreement must become a reality."[121]

However, indications were that not everyone in the union was as eager as Walesa to avoid confrontation at all costs. A poll taken in Lodz, for instance, saw 88.3 percent of those interviewed "in support of the union leadership, whatever the dangers involved," even if this meant that Solidarity "decides on action to confront the authorities for the purpose of achieving the demands of August 1980."[122] The workers had come too far to allow negotiations with Jaruzelski to undermine their hard-won victories. If necessary, they were willing to fight.

Confrontation, as Walesa had predicted in Radom, apparently had become unavoidable. Jaruzelski therefore chose this moment to act. According to former deputy prime minister Rakowski, Jaruzelski made the final decision to introduce martial law in Poland on Friday, 11 December. The prime minister summoned Rakowski to his office that afternoon. "Jaruzelski looked very serious," Rakowski later recalled, "more serious than ever. He raised his eyes and said: 'The day has come. It's for the day after tomorrow, the 13th.' I answered, 'I understand.' There was nothing to add." Like his boss, the leading revisionist had become convinced that decisive action was now a necessity to avoid a conflagration in Poland. In his opinion, "Blood would have flowed like rivers if we hadn't imposed martial law on December 13."[123]

Before issuing the order that would set the crackdown in motion, Jaruzelski placed one last call to Moscow. Inasmuch as Brezhnev was ill, Jaruzelski spoke briefly with Mikhail Suslov, inquiring about what type of response Warsaw could expect from its allies if matters became "complicated." Not feeling well himself, the Soviet ideologue replied simply, "Well, you always said that you could manage with your own forces."[124] Some hours after Jaruzelski's conversation with Suslov, Defense Minister Ustinov phoned back with the intention of stiffening Polish resolve.[125] In ironic contrast to Moscow's use of threats as a means of motivation, the defense minister now implied that "fraternal assistance" might well be an option if Polish events continued "to threaten the interests of the socialist community."[126] Perhaps comforted by this suggestion that Moscow might still reconsider the question of military assistance if matters ran out of control, at 2:00 P.M. Jaruzelski gave the order to proceed with Operation X.[127] Martial law was finally under way.

Martial Law

Solidarity took notice of the government's final preparations immediately. As the National Coordinating Commission sat in Gdansk debating the use of public demonstrations, messages began to pour in from local branches around the country. Polish security forces were on the move, they reported, sealing off Solidarity headquarters nationwide.[128] Hastily placed phone calls to the chief of the Gdansk militia received a deliberately misleading response. Don't worry, the official told them, the police were merely undertaking a large-scale crackdown on crime.[129] The members of the National Coordinating Commission were not convinced. However, they failed to perceive the full gravity of what was happening around them, spending the remainder of the meeting adopting a resolution that called for a national vote of confidence in the state authorities to be held the following February. Should the government fail to win sufficient support in the referendum, they asserted, Solidarity would then organize a provisional government and assume power in Poland.[130] There could be no doubt of it now: Solidarity was planning to overturn the communist government in Poland through a peaceful, democratic maneuver.

No sooner had the National Coordinating Commission approved this revolutionary measure than Walesa received word that telephone and telex lines to the assembly hall had been cut. The union leader had an immediate premonition of what was to come and decided that resistance was pointless.[131] "Ladies and Gentlemen," he announced, "we have no communications with the outside world. Perhaps they will be restored tomorrow, perhaps not. In connection with this I wish you good night."[132] With that, Walesa turned, left the hall, and went home to his apartment as usual. The other members of the commission soon followed. As they filed out into the snowy night, many joked among themselves about the steps the government might take against them in the coming hours. Most remained convinced that the government would have to be crazy to risk eliciting a prolonged general strike.[133]

Obviously this impression was mistaken, born as much of naïveté as of overconfidence. Events quickly revealed that the government still possessed the strength and the determination to impose its will on Polish society. As the delegates were returning to their hotel rooms and apartments in Gdansk, ZOMO security forces were aggressively rounding up and incarcerating Solidarity advocates from all walks of life. To put a balanced face on the crackdown, they also interned a number of leading communists—including former first secretary Edward Gierek—for their role in creating the nation's socioeconomic crisis. By 2:00 A.M. the ZOMOs had surrounded the Metropol Hotel in Gdansk where many members of the National Coordinating Commission were staying. Moving quickly from room to room, they hustled union activists into waiting trucks while antiterrorist troops looked on from atop the hotel. An hour later, Gdansk Party chief Tadeusz Fiszbach appeared at Walesa's apartment with the provincial governor and six policemen. The police carried crowbars and were prepared to break down the door if Walesa resisted. Walesa went quietly and soon boarded a plane for Warsaw. There he would spend the next few weeks under house arrest in a government villa.[134]

At 6:00 A.M. on 13 December, General Jaruzelski appeared on Polish television and radio to announce formally the "introduction, by a decision of the Council of State, of a state of war throughout the country."[135] He explained that a new Military Council of National Salvation, made up of twenty-one military officers, would run the country until further notice.[136] Its influence would extend to all sectors of society, both national and local. In the words of General Jaruzelski, the council had "appointed its representatives, the military commissars, at all levels of state administration as well as certain economic institutions. The commissars have been given authority to supervise the activities of [all] units of state administration. . . . Let no one count on weakness or vacillation."[137] Jaruzelski defended his decision to introduce martial law on the grounds that Poland was sliding toward chaos, poverty, and famine. Extremists, he argued, threatened to effect a "complete partition of the socialist Polish state."[138] In the interest of political and economic stability, therefore, the military was stepping in to impose order. A long list of new laws would, it was hoped, help the authorities restore "normalcy" and communist control in Poland.[139]

Resistance to the crackdown was weak and uncoordinated. The arrests virtually decapitated Solidarity of its entire leadership. Moreover, no plans existed for a general strike under such conditions. The National Coordinating Commission simply had not considered martial law a likely enough event for which to prepare. Consequently, each individual enterprise was on its own in deciding how to respond.[140] Some did go on strike. When security forces moved in to crush worker resistance, some even met violence with violence, using whatever implements were at hand. In one Silesian coal mine, the resulting melee ended in nine deaths. Within a week, however, Jaruzelski was able to extinguish the last traces of open opposition in Poland.

At Sunday Mass on 13 December, Archbishop Glemp indicated that the Church, too, had been forced to accept the new state of affairs in Poland. "In our country," he conceded, "the new reality is martial law. As we understand it, martial law is a new state, and a state of severe laws which suspend many civic achievements. . . . Opposition to the decisions of the authorities under martial law could cause violent reprisals, including bloodshed, because the authorities have the armed forces at their disposal. We can be indignant, shout about the injustice of such a state of affairs. . . . But this may not yield the expected results."[141] In other words, the preservation of life was more important than political change, and thus Poles ought to acclimate themselves to the new situation as best they could. Glemp concluded, emotionally: "I shall plead, even if I have to plead on my knees: Do not start a fight of Pole against Pole." The state could not have been more delighted with Glemp's appeal and distributed copies of it throughout Poland. While many resented its concession to communist rule, the homily did play a significant role in tempering society's immediate resistance to martial law.[142]

As Jaruzelski consolidated his control in Poland, the Kremlin looked on with a tremendous sense of relief. Without the involvement of a single Soviet tank or platoon, Moscow had successfully engineered a favorable "normalization" in Eastern Europe. As it contacted its ambassadors throughout the communist world, the sense of victory was unmistakable. "A good impression has been created by W. Jaruzelski's address to the people," the Soviet dispatch read, "in which, in our view, all the basic questions were given appropriate emphasis. In particular, what is especially important is that the address reaffirmed the leading role of the PPR to the socialist obligations stipulated by the Warsaw Pact."[143]

The Poles had finally taken decisive steps against Solidarity, and all indications were that the operation was going smoothly. "In our preliminary evaluation," the Kremlin told its allies, "the measures taken by the Polish friends are an active step to repulse counter-revolution, and in this sense they correspond with the general line of all the fraternal countries."[144] Moscow promised to provide continuing moral, political, and economic assistance to the Poles as needs arose. The tacit message was clear—there would be no Soviet military involvement in the crackdown. The matter would be left to the Poles themselves. For the first time in the history of postwar Europe, Moscow had fully entrusted the fate of East European communism to the East European communists themselves. With the apparent success of this policy in Poland, the era of Soviet military guarantees had come to an end.

Conclusion

In terms of the evolution of Soviet bloc policy, the events of late 1981 might initially appear rather anticlimactic. Following the high drama that had taken place in June, Moscow's efforts to cope with the ramifications of noninterventionism seem almost preordained. Hemmed in by their own decision to avoid military involvement at all costs, Soviet leaders continued through much of this period to rattle sabers, condemn Party revisionism, and hope for the best. Nevertheless, the perceptions that characterized Soviet discussions until the proverbial eleventh hour are of unparalleled importance in considering the fate of the Brezhnev Doctrine. Between the spring of 1968 and the spring of 1981, Soviet leaders had moved from an integrationist bloc policy, based on socialist internationalism, to a recognition of fundamental contradictions among the interests of the socialist nations. As the Polish example illustrates, by 1981 this recognition had prompted an abandonment of Soviet guarantees to the beleaguered communist regime in Poland. Yet while the June resolution clearly reflected this new recognition, it did so at a time when the future of communist rule in Poland was unpredictable. The question therefore remained: Would the Soviets maintain their sangfroid if and when communism appeared likely to fall before an opposition offensive?

The discussions of late 1981 offer convincing evidence that Moscow was prepared to allow Polish communism to collapse rather than introduce its own troops into the crisis. On the very eve of Jaruzelski's emergency declaration in December 1981, the future of communist rule in Poland looked far more bleak than it had in June. The repeated rescheduling of the declaration, notwithstanding a resolution by the PZPR Central Committee to begin the crackdown, left Soviet leaders wondering if Jaruzelski ever intended to take "decisive action." The general seemed to be doing all that he could to shift the burden of Poland's woes onto the Kremlin. His requests for financial and trade assistance struck the Soviet leaders as just short of outright extortion, gambling the future of Soviet-Polish relations on the interest of domestic stabilization. Hence, when Jaruzelski inquired about Soviet military assistance, Moscow perceived yet another attempt to place the burden of "normalization" on Soviet shoulders. In the context of Kania's earlier reluctance to use force, it appeared entirely possible that Jaruzelski would also continue to retreat rather than act to crush the national opposition. Moreover, as that opposition prepared a general strike and popular demonstrations against the government, the final confrontation certainly did not appear to be far off.

Yet the Soviet leadership did not reconsider its June resolution against military intervention. On the contrary, it grew more convinced of the need to defend vital Soviet interests such as access to Western markets and products and preservation of Soviet prestige within the international community. Foreshadowing Gorbachev's turn to the "common European home," the Soviet leadership placed a higher priority on its ties with Western Europe than on its responsibility to allied socialist governments. Despite the dire prognosis for communist rule in Poland, early December 1981 found such men as Andropov, Gromyko, and Ustinov, key figures in the decision to invade Afghanistan, dead set against going into Poland. As Andropov pointed out in plain language, Western sanctions on the Soviet Union would be a serious burden on the country, both economically and politically. The USSR had to look out for itself above all. Indeed, he argued, that was the "main line" of Soviet policy. Andropov was not at all ambiguous about the consequences of this policy. Should Poland fall under the control of Solidarity, he concluded simply, then that's the way it would have to be.

Of course, that is not what ultimately transpired in late 1981, as the Polish Interior Ministry and General Staff successfully used their own forces to drive Solidarity underground. In terms of later Soviet policy, this achievement meant that Moscow's June decision would remain secret for more than ten more years. On the strength of its reputation, the obsolete Brezhnev Doctrine would continue to check the evolution of political change in Eastern Europe until 1989. Indeed, there are many who still argue that the doctrine survived as a policy option until then, ever present as a viable last alternative in the minds of the Soviet leadership. As this study has endeavored to demonstrate, that perception simply does not correlate with the Politburo resolutions of 1981. As General Gribkov, the former chief of staff of the Soviet armed forces, confirms, "Nineteen eighty-nine? No, it died early. It died in 1980–81. The fact that we didn't send troops into Poland shows that the Brezhnev Doctrine—that is, the resolving of problems by force—was dead."[145]

Conclusion

THE CONCLUSION OF THE POLISH SOLIDARITY CRISIS in late 1981 left the Brezhnev Doctrine of Limited Sovereignty very like the man after whom it had been named: Both had become mannequins propped up by a fading imperial power desperate to preserve its role in world affairs. Following the heady successes at bloc integration in the early 1970s, mounting domestic problems in the USSR itself had prompted Moscow to reevaluate its East European commitments consistent with a narrower, less internationalist perception of Soviet interests. By the end of that decade, the sudden collapse of relations with the United States, economic stagnation, declining international prestige, and a military stalemate in the mountains of Afghanistan had combined to weaken the Kremlin's hand in world affairs. In the process, the crisis-prone region of Eastern Europe had become as much a liability as an asset. Economic mismanagement, dissident activism, and emergent nationalism compounded in the 1970s to create a considerable burden on Soviet resources. In the face of perennial legitimacy crises, its local regimes had become too reliant on the trump card of Soviet military might to preserve communist rule. This was particularly true of Poland, the country that Moscow had long regarded as the keystone of the socialist edifice in Eastern Europe.

Consequently, at the outset of the 1980s, the prospect of bold military strikes into the region no longer appeared to be consistent with Soviet national interests, even if it meant the loss of this most important European client-state. Years before Mikhail Gorbachev would initiate his historic "new thinking" in Soviet foreign policy, Moscow was already cognizant of the need to base the future of European socialism on regime legitimacy rather than on Soviet bayonets. The Kremlin accordingly relinquished its earlier insistence on enforced orthodoxy and gradually began to search for a new paradigm of limited diversity in bloc relations. Increasingly permissive Soviet leaders provided greater political autonomy to their client-states, eager to encourage resolution of internal problems without resort to Soviet assistance. In the wake of the Polish crisis of 1980–81, a policy of greater forbearance in the bloc commanded support at every level of the Soviet Party bureaucracy. Though still unaware of their accomplishment, the Polish people had forced the Soviet colossus into an imperial retreat from which it would never recover.

This process of imperial decline had unfolded over a period of many years, synchronized with the evolution of Soviet ideological perceptions. Beginning with the invasion of Czechoslovakia in 1968, a renewed concern for political unity had taken hold in bloc relations, relinquishing as misconceived Khrushchev's policy of "separate paths to socialism." During the Prague Spring, Soviet leaders convinced themselves that counterrevolution was possible—indeed even probable—in conditions of peaceful socialist reform. One need not wait, they reasoned, for the violent insurrections witnessed twelve years earlier in Hungary before taking decisive action against anticipated revolts. Deviation from established Soviet norms afforded sufficient cause for military intervention into the domestic affairs of an allied communist state. In this manner, ideological orthodoxy came to define Soviet national and security interests to a degree unparalleled since the death of Stalin in 1953.

For much of the decade that followed, "normalization" remained the watchword of Soviet policy in Eastern Europe. In the Kremlin's peculiar doublespeak, this meant the preservation of Soviet political and economic norms through tight integration, policy coordination, and, if necessary, military intervention. Indeed, the Central Committee's own top secret analysis indicates the degree to which violation of Czechoslovak state sovereignty formed the very foundation of Soviet normalization efforts in 1968–69. Though at a loss to explain the nearly unanimous support in Czechoslovakia for Party reformers, Moscow operated on the conviction that they constituted a minority cabal in league with the West and bent on the overthrow of socialism. As such, it missed the essential accomplishment of the Prague Spring—namely, that a ruling communist party in Eastern Europe had at last managed to engender a measure of genuine popular support among its own people. This might have provided considerable insight into the perennial problem of communist legitimacy and its reliance on the Soviet military. But Moscow's ideological outlook precluded any such sympathetic assessment of the Prague Spring.

One need not grapple here with the elusive hypothetical question of whether Soviet bloc communism was "reformable" or not. Doubtless, if Moscow had not intervened to crush the Prague Spring in 1968, Dubcek would have overseen the creation of a system considerably different from that which persisted in the Soviet Union. Nonetheless, the alternative to greater permissiveness was a state of political dependence on Soviet military force. As Zdenek Mlynar astutely observed in 1990, "Any genuine reform program in the European countries of the Soviet bloc would be bound, sooner or later, to change their internal regimes. Economic and political reforms would move them away from the Soviet model, in line with their own historical traditions and special conditions. However, if the USSR sees such developments as threatening to its interests or security, and if it fails to allow the necessary degree of autonomy and tries to suppress independent developments by force, it will be unable to agree to any real guarantees for the smaller members of the bloc to go their own way."[1] In short, reluctance to permit greater autonomy in Eastern Europe would ensure its perpetual reliance on Moscow. While this was certainly an attractive proposition in the early history of the bloc, by the 1980s it carried responsibilities that the Soviet Union simply could no longer assume.

The principal challenge facing the region's communist parties in the 1980s was their obvious lack of popular legitimacy. True, it was systemic weakness that brought the bloc to the verge of socioeconomic ruin. Yet local communists managed to stay in power under these adverse conditions for more than a decade as long as Moscow appeared to guarantee their political fortunes. Although communist mismanagement and popular resentment had brought the bloc to its knees, it would take the withdrawal of Soviet guarantees to decapitate it. In the absence of any alternative source of legitimacy, the region's communist governments would then fall like so many dominoes.

During the Prague Spring, Alexander Dubcek generated genuine advocacy for his regime while maintaining the Party's grip on power. His removal in 1969 shattered the prospect of widespread popular support for communism in Eastern Europe. Instead, Moscow's normalization galvanized communist reliance on Soviet military guarantees. The intrinsic weakness of this new Brezhnev Doctrine, however, was its reliance on force and stealth to solve political problems. When military intervention eventually proved untenable, communist control in Eastern Europe promised invariably to collapse, as it did in 1989. Consequently, by modeling its bloc policy on the perceived successes of the Czechoslovakia invasion, Moscow committed itself to an all-or-nothing approach of forcing regional orthodoxy. This left Moscow very little room to maneuver by the 1980s, when domestic priorities forced a reassessment of its military commitments in Eastern Europe.

An additional obstacle facing the Soviets in the early 1980s was the degree to which they had publicly embraced "socialist internationalism" a decade earlier. As the ideological engine of bloc integration after 1968, this set of principles rested on the notion that socialist interstate relations were free of intrinsic contradictions. Its evolution as a central tenet of Soviet foreign policy mirrored the consolidation of Soviet control in the Warsaw Pact and the Council for Mutual Economic Assistance. Still, the decision in the mid-1970s to introduce dramatic price increases for deliveries of Soviet energy products to CMEA nations suggested an incongruity of national interests in Soviet perceptions.

By the end of that decade, Moscow regarded issues of international prestige virtually on an equal footing with socialist internationalism, as Kremlin deliberations over the fate of Afghan "communism" reveal. While Soviet leaders did ultimately elect to send troops into Afghanistan, their early inclination had been to show restraint in the interest of preserving Soviet military resources and international reputation. Only when Kabul seemed poised to shift its allegiance toward the West did Moscow abandon this position in favor of militant action. The result was a sharp decline in Soviet prestige around the world, an escalation of East-West tensions, and an exceedingly costly war from which Moscow would struggle to escape for ten years. In the name of socialist internationalism, the Soviet Union now faced international isolation, economic sanctions, mounting casualties, social disaffection, and dramatic hikes in military spending. It needed little more to drive home the point that the promotion of international communism might occasionally be at variance with Soviet national interests.

The dramatic events that followed in Poland brought into sharp relief the burden that Eastern Europe had become for the Kremlin leadership. A full decade after they had set out to normalize communist rule in Eastern Europe, Brezhnev and his associates once again faced an allied nation at the point of popular revolt. Mismanaged growth policies, a ballooning national debt, and rising consumer expectations had long since prompted Poles to regard their communist leaders as foreign intruders. As a result, a semilegal civil society had emerged in the late 1970s, fueled by a growth in anti-Soviet nationalism, religious solidarity, and popular discontent. Recognizing the revolutionary potential of Polish developments, Soviet leaders worked to limit the spread of a broader regional crisis. While encouraging Polish communists to deal decisively with "antisocialist elements," the Soviets focused on their own domestic interests by countering the spread of religious nationalism along the Polish-Soviet border. The Ostpolitik of Pope John Paul II clearly posed a threat to communist legitimacy everywhere in the bloc. But rather than confront the Vatican on behalf of the entire socialist alliance, Moscow attempted simply to contain the Catholic renaissance within Eastern Europe so as not to imperil the Soviet Union itself.

At this stage the shift was subtle but significant. The onetime tight identification of East European stability with vital Soviet interests had begun to erode. Since the seventeenth century, Poland had been considered the key to Russian security, both military and ideological.[2] Consequently, Moscow's decision to engage Catholic nationalism primarily at its own frontiers rather than in Poland itself was remarkably short-sighted. The challenge that Pope John Paul posed to Polish communism greatly exceeded its potential impact in the Soviet Union. And yet, despite Poland's traditional significance in Soviet strategic planning, Moscow showed very little creativity in its collaboration with Warsaw on this issue. Even if further research should prove conclusively that the KGB coordinated the attempted assassination of the Polish pope, this subordination of Polish stability in 1979 and 1980 will remain one of the great miscalculations of the twentieth century. After all, it was in the crucible of Poland's national and religious renaissance that its people tempered the bonds of their civil society, thereby creating the viable alternative that would eventually eclipse communist rule in 1989.

If in the late 1970s the Soviet leadership failed to foresee that events were heading toward a collapse of communist power, they were in good company. Notwithstanding the early stirrings of civil opposition in Poland, few specialists, either Eastern or Western, predicted that existing instabilities might someday bring down the entire system. As Martin Malia correctly notes, "To be sure, a number of observers, particularly dissidents living under the system, did perceive that it was too fatally flawed to be reformed, but they were usually dismissed by social-science Sovietology. Thus almost everyone, on both the Left and the Right, took Soviet prowess with too grim a seriousness, whether as an ideal or as an adversary."[3] It is for this reason that the Polish Solidarity crisis became the conclusive test of the post-Prague normalization policy in Eastern Europe. Unlike the Prague Spring or the pope's new Ostpolitik, the Solidarity crisis elicited an immediate presentiment of counterrevolution from the Kremlin leadership. Therefore it provides an ideal test case for exploring the degree to which Moscow's ideological commitment to socialist internationalism withstood the evolution of Soviet national interests.

At the outset, Moscow's response to the strikes in Poland bore a striking resemblance to its position on earlier regional crises. By manipulating local communist authorities, it sought a rapid normalization of affairs by every means possible. However, as already discussed, the notion that communist authorities might somehow "win back" any degree of popular legitimacy had died with the Prague Spring. The militant promises of socialist internationalism had underscored this political reality for more than a decade, and the time had come for Moscow to face the consequences. In practice this meant that very early in the crisis Soviet leaders were forced to entertain the real possibility of launching an armed intervention. Moreover, the crisis also presented Moscow with the colossal economic requirements of a nation driven to the point of collapse by years of graft and mismanagement. Poland had indeed become a tremendous liability to the Soviet Union. Tighter integration along the pattern of previous years offered little more than the opportunity for the Kremlin to deplete Soviet resources in a desperate attempt to prop up Poland's disintegrating economy. Furthermore, there was no guarantee that such assistance could halt the Polish free fall without permitting unorthodox departures from Soviet political and economic norms.

Early signs suggest that few members of the Soviet leadership ever strongly supported anything more than a limited use of allied troops in Poland. But as communist rule there appeared increasingly jeopardized, the pressure to consider a full-scale Warsaw Pact intervention became difficult to ignore. When the question first arose in the fall of 1980, the Solidarity movement was still in its early stages; it did not yet constitute an unmanageable threat to the Warsaw regime. Nevertheless, in accordance with Moscow's post-1968 definition of "counterrevolution," the mere ideological challenges that Solidarity was raising compromised the existing Polish system.

What differentiated this situation from the Prague Spring was not merely the fact so often cited that "Poles are not Czechs" but also that the government in Warsaw remained committed, in word if not always in deed, to the restoration of "normalcy" along Soviet lines. Although the Kremlin regularly lamented Kania's failure to act "decisively," Soviet leaders had not concluded by December 1980 that the counterrevolution had effectively seduced his leadership into heresy. Therefore, it remained simply to coax, cajole, or coerce the Poles into adopting a traditional normalization strategy on their own. This effort climaxed at the dramatic Warsaw Pact Summit of 5 December 1980, when Moscow and its allies deliberately misled Polish leaders with the specter of a joint intervention poised to strike Poland. While this feint was briefly successful, the Polish nation soon returned to a tense political standoff as Warsaw proved unwilling to crush Solidarity with military force.

In Moscow, Soviet leaders regarded Warsaw's restraint as political retreat. By mid-1981, following the uproar in Poland over the Bydgoszcz incident, this retreat began to look like a rout. Solidarity, it appeared, was fast becoming a party unto itself with far more popular support than had the ruling PZPR. Indeed, its communist supporters were poised to assert the union's influence over the PZPR itself at the Ninth Party Congress in July. Nevertheless, despite indications of a possible coup in the making, all attempts to motivate a Polish declaration of martial law had proved ineffective. Communism in Poland was clearly imperiled.

And yet, when Defense Minister Ustinov consulted the Soviet General Staff on the question of military intervention in June, his officers were nearly unanimous in their rejection of violent measures. The experience of Afghanistan suggested lessons that they felt were relevant to the Polish crisis. Soviet international prestige had suffered when the vast majority of the UN General Assembly had voted to condemn Moscow's invasion of Afghanistan. This had struck a solid blow to the Soviet objective of swaying the ideological "correlation of forces" throughout the world in favor of communism. Subsequent American sanctions hurt the Soviet economy while emphasizing the importance of Moscow's residual trade with

Western Europe. The ensuing rise of East-West tensions after 1979 placed these remaining European links on unstable footing as well. Certainly Soviet access to badly needed technological imports would not have withstood an invasion of Poland. Nor would negotiations toward securing a removal of American medium-range ballistic missiles from Europe. In short, the risks connected with socialist internationalism had become totally incompatible with the Kremlin's narrower perception of Soviet national interests. If forced to make a choice between East European communism and détente, the General Staff advised in favor of the latter. This outlook resonated clearly in the Kremlin as well. "If a new leadership comes to power," Suslov had concluded about Poland, "we will cooperate with it. We cannot subject our country to international condemnation yet again."

Granted, the conclusions reached in June constituted a theoretical policy position. Polish communism was not at the point of collapse just yet, and so there was still the possibility of a reversal. For the time being, however, this decision did reveal that the priorities and relative concerns of the Soviet leadership lay far from the preservation of communist unity in Eastern Europe. In a moment of tremendous historical import, Moscow had faced up to the bankruptcy of its erstwhile bloc policy honestly and with candor. No longer would Moscow equate blocwide orthodoxy with the vital national interests of the USSR. Quietly, almost imperceptibly, the Brezhnev Doctrine was slipping into history. What remained was an empty shell reliant on surviving fears to maintain stability in bloc affairs.

The decisive test of Moscow's new position on Poland came in December 1981 when Jaruzelski's government seemed to have approached the edge of disaster. Solidarity's preparations for a general strike, complete with antigovernment demonstrations scheduled for mid-December, suggested to the Soviets the start of a popular uprising. Should Jaruzelski fail to act, he would very likely be forced to concede defeat to the Polish counterrevolution. The final battle was nigh, Soviet leaders felt, and yet Jaruzelski continued to equivocate on the declaration of martial law, reversing his earlier objections to outside intervention in an apparent bid to abdicate full responsibility for the coming crackdown. If the Kremlin was going to reverse its earlier decision, the eleventh hour had come.

Yet not one member of the Politburo proposed doing so. To the contrary, at their December 10 meeting the Soviet leaders offered a litany of arguments for holding true to their June renunciation of armed intervention. For all the reasons enumerated six months earlier—particularly fear of Western sanctions—the Soviet Union could not even consider sending troops into Eastern Europe. Tested in the heat of an apparently decisive moment, the June resolution now assumed its place as the bottom line in Soviet bloc policy. Polish civil society, with the support of a vigilant West, had driven the Soviet colossus into retreat. The rollback of communist authoritarianism in Europe that would climax in the rout of 1989 had already begun.

Thanks to Jaruzelski's successful imposition of martial law in Poland, this fatal blow to socialist internationalism remained a closely guarded secret known only to Moscow's top political and military leaders. Nevertheless, its impact on bloc relations did become increasingly evident in the drift that characterized the Kremlin's East European policies during the period 1982–85. Historians have hitherto attributed this development to the fact that Brezhnev's death in 1982 forced Soviet leaders to focus on affairs back home.[4] Indeed, as this study has sought to demonstrate, the shift of focus toward Soviet home fires had been under way for a number of years before Brezhnev's death. Moreover, the foregoing analysis suggests as well that an essential cause of the drift after 1982 was Moscow's new effort to transform its relations with Eastern Europe in the wake of the Polish crisis. From an earlier insistence on bloc unity the Kremlin was groping its way toward what Hélène Carrère D'Encausse has termed "enlightened tolerance."[5] Aware that another explosion of social unrest might well expose the promises of socialist internationalism for the sham that they had become, Soviet leaders began to explore a return to limited "national communism."

That this policy evolution took on the appearance of drift was due to the reality that the shift had been essentially forced on the Politburo as a function of Soviet weakness. Consequently, there was little enthusiasm at first behind the search for new principles to replace military threats as the guarantee of socialist rule in Eastern Europe. This is not to suggest that the Kremlin leadership had begun to doubt the priority it had assigned to Soviet domestic interests during the Polish crisis. According to Nikolai Kolikov, a longtime consultant working for the Central Committee's Liaison Department, "The most important interests from our perspective were the development of the economy and the development of the Soviet Union itself."[6] What remained to be seen was whether the old guard of the Kremlin elite, fashioned in the ideological furnace of the Stalin era and committed to Soviet hegemony in Eastern Europe, could translate this conviction into policy initiatives.

For many, the election of Yuri Andropov to succeed Leonid Brezhnev on 22 November 1982 carried the promise of greater Soviet latitude vis-à-vis Eastern Europe. Before assuming control of the KGB, Andropov had been Soviet ambassador to Hungary (1954–57) and later worked as head of the Central Committee's Department for Liaison with Communist and Workers Parties of Socialist States (1957–62). Andropov was therefore far better acquainted than any of his colleagues with the situation in Eastern Europe, its strengths and its weakness. In January 1983, Andropov publicly asserted that relations with the socialist nations took precedence in Soviet foreign policy. It is difficult to judge how seriously to regard this claim. On the one hand, the ongoing sellout of socialist internationalism in exchange for maintaining a grip on East-West détente renders Andropov's assertion little more than a platitude in retrospect. As Kolikov notes, "The rejection of the Brezhnev Doctrine was a rejection of this priority, because ultimately relations with the United States were also a priority. . . . We understood perfectly well that without normal relations between the Soviet Union and the United States of America there could be no serious reconstruction [perestroika]."[7]

On the other hand, the case of Hungary's return to the New Economic Mechanism suggests that Andropov was open to the reassertion of greater diversity in the bloc. Even before the declaration of martial law in December 1981, the Soviet leadership had received secret reports from Bogomolov Institute scholars warning that a crisis similar to that in Poland was brewing in Hungary. One report, forwarded to the CMEA in late August 1981, predicted that "the possibility of a complication in the social sphere and disruption of internal political stability in the country worries the Hungarian leadership very seriously, especially in connection to the turn which events have taken in Poland."[8] Hoping to head off a wholesale economic collapse, Kadar had begun reintroducing elements of NEM in Hungary beginning in 1979 while Moscow was focused on the tensions in Poland and Afghanistan.[9] In the opinion of many Hungarian specialists, his efforts paid off. It was, they argued, the unique characteristics of the Hungarian system that had enabled Hungary to avoid Poland's fate.[10] When forced to answer for this divergence from uniform bloc policy in 1982, Kadar reasserted old arguments that NEM should be viewed in purely practical, nonideological terms. "It is a question of objective conditions rather than of ideology," he claimed in October 1982.[11] As Charles Gati observes, "The Kadar regime began to advocate a new formulation about the legitimacy of upholding the 'national interest' in a socialist country's foreign policy."[12]

Andropov's reluctance to insist on full conformity with Soviet economic norms suggests that Kadar's argument found a sympathetic audience in Moscow less than a year after concern for similar "objective conditions" in the USSR had overcome ideological commitments to Poland. Doubtless Andropov was also considering the fact that the economic decline that had given birth to Solidarity still continued to plague East European regimes, including the one in Budapest. Moreover, these conditions were only liable to worsen in the near term. Poland and Romania were at the point of defaulting on their international debts, and Hungary and the GDR seemed certain to join them soon. In October 1982, Kadar reportedly cautioned the Soviets through his subordinates that "a financial crash in Hungary in this regard would carry an extremely negative propaganda significance; it would sharpen still more the problem of cooperation between East and West; it would create diplomatic difficulties for the entire [socialist] camp, particularly for the GDR whose situation may still worsen in relation to Kohl's rise to power."[13] Considering Moscow's abiding concern for preserving relations with the West, this argument must also have struck a nerve in the Kremlin. However, Hungarian foreboding did not stop here. A fundamental restructuring of socialist bloc relations was essential, argued Jozsef Marjai, vice president of Hungary's Council of Ministers. In what would come to be remarkably predictive words, Marjai admonished the Soviets, "We are talking about the fate of the socialist system. It is easy to lead anything to collapse, for this one simply has to do nothing; but to correct it will already be much more difficult, if not impossible."[14]

It was on the strength of such arguments as these that the Hungarians were permitted to continue with their economic reforms, provided they did not translate into political liberalism. Andropov even dispatched the Soviet Politburo's agricultural specialist, Mikhail Gorbachev, to study Hungary's farming policies in 1983. That year, at both the June and August Central Committee plena, Andropov criticized earlier Soviet economic reforms as ineffective and halfhearted.[15] Hungary, on the other hand, once condemned for its innovations, was now regarded as a model of agricultural progress. Due to his untimely death in 1984, Andropov's efforts to learn from Eastern Europe saw few concrete results. But his openness to change and diversity in socialist economic policy marked a significant departure from the integrationist policies of the Brezhnev era. While still carefully circumscribed, national communism had crept back into socialist Europe, altering the form, if not yet the content, of selected internal developments. Its impact in Hungary was exemplary in this respect. As Rudolf Tokes observes, "The overwhelming influence of the regional hegemon [the USSR] imposed limits on the extent of systemic change in Hungary. Some of the 'limits' were spelled out in official statements; others were simply understood as the modus operandi of a Soviet-led alliance system. In any event, the unequal relationship was flexible enough to permit cosmetic changes within the existing system, including modest experimentation from the early 1980s on, with Hungary's financial and trading links with the West."[16]

Meanwhile, the winds of change had begun to blow through Moscow's corridors of power at all levels of the Party bureaucracy. Rumors and confidential discussions fed speculation regarding the question of new initiatives in Eastern Europe. Many argued for a much lighter degree of Soviet control in the region, one that did not involve Moscow in every little detail of East European life. Moreover, they continued, if nations facing economic difficulties such as Hungary and Poland were permitted to reach domestic solutions, then Moscow might be spared having to provide them with debilitating levels of assistance. They pointed to Hungary, noting that greater Soviet permissiveness toward Hungarian reforms had yet to result in a turn from Moscow's influence.[17] While the top leadership had only recently begun to process this persuasive reasoning, many members of the Central Committee apparat had believed it since the 1970s. Nikolai Kolikov recalls, "There was always among the apparat, at least at the level where I worked as a consultant, a notion that of course policy toward the East European countries had to change. . . . It had to change in order to afford them more freedom to act, to give them more space and more independence. Only then could we keep them in our orbit. . . . If not by force, then give them the ability to formulate their own policies."[18]

It was at this stage, in 1983–84, that Andropov's heir apparent, Mikhail Gorbachev, began receiving reports from the Bogomolov Institute appraising him of the need for reforms in bloc policy. The Soviet Union, these reports argued, had a standard of living which was far below that enjoyed throughout most of Eastern Europe.[19] Since 1976, Eastern Europe had maintained a trade surplus in its relations with Moscow which had run into the billions of rubles. In 1981–82 alone this surplus amounted to 8.5 billion rubles, or roughly 14 percent of Soviet–East European trade.[20] The reports painted a picture of Soviet–East European relations that cried out for reform precisely because existing mechanisms were no longer consistent with Soviet national interests. By familiarizing himself with this material on the eve of his rise to power, Gorbachev was beginning what would become a long practice of mastering the issues and problems of the region himself. His leading adviser on East European affairs, Georgii Shakhnazarov, later wrote that Gorbachev "had to study a tremendous amount of material which touched on the historical basis and contemporary conditions of the links with each neighboring country. He mastered this material surprisingly fast—in large degree because while a member of the Politburo and a secretary of the Central Committee he had absorbed all of the information pertaining to these questions which made its way up to the top leadership."[21]

By the time Gorbachev came to power in 1985, the cause of more progressive reforms was gaining momentum in the Soviet Union. Aleksandr Tsipko, a former consultant to the Central Committee's International Department and Bogomolov Institute scholar, recalls that "French journalists who wrote at the start of perestroika that the breeding ground of counterrevolution in the USSR was the headquarters of communism, the CPSU Central Committee, were right. Working at that time as a consultant to the International Department of the CPSU Central Committee, I discovered, to my surprise, that the mood among the highest hierarchy of that organization did not differ at all from the mood in the Academy of Sciences or in the humanities institutes. . . . It was clear that only the complete hypocrite could believe in the supremacy of socialism over capitalism. It was also clear that the socialist experiment had suffered defeat."[22] Reflecting back on the point when Gorbachev assumed power, Aleksandr Yakovlev, the "architect of perestroika," suggests that Brezhnev-era conformity was already becoming a memory. He claims that by 1985 "the parties in, let's say, Hungary or Poland were not actually communist parties. They were already becoming in many instances social democratic parties. Even here [in the USSR] the lesson of social democracy had also occurred to us. . . . In 1985 a shift occurred to social democracy, that is, from revolution to reform. . . . We of course denied it. We wouldn't tell anyone that we were shifting over to social democracy. I rejected this and played this kind of game. But, in fact, in 1985 we said, right folks, we are moving to reforms. Let's forget about revolutions. That was the fundamental question that made the communist Central Committee into social democrats."[23]

Radio Free Europe analyst Elizabeth Teague points to an address that Gorbachev gave in Warsaw in late June 1986 as evidence that he had begun to reassess the meaning of the Polish crisis. She notes that his remarks indicated that "socialist governments must adapt in response to changing circumstances. Otherwise . . . stagnation could set in and economic and social problems grow to 'dangerous proportions.' " The experience, Teague offers, prompted a wholesale reevaluation of Brezhnev-era policies. The Polish lesson, in Gorbachev's opinion, "applied to the Soviet Union as much as to the other socialist states. The USSR . . . was 'learning from the errors and miscalculations of the past.' But the shock of Poland's worker unrest did open the eyes of a new generation of Soviet leaders to the dangers of continuing the policies of the Brezhnev leadership, and alerted them to the need for a change of course in Soviet social policy. The Polish events served, in short, to shape the contours of the Soviet reform debate."[24]

Gorbachev himself confirmed that this reassessment extended to Soviet foreign policy while participating in a remarkably candid exchange with American scholars at the Kennan Institute in Washington, D.C., on 7 December 1999. Describing the scene in Moscow during the 1985 funeral of Konstantin Chernenko, his immediate predecessor, he noted that all the East European Communist Party leaders were present for the occasion and that he had taken that opportunity to discuss his foreign policy objectives with them. "I would like to tell you that we will respect your sovereignty," he told them, "your independence." At the same time, he noted that Moscow's laissez-faire policy would entail greater disengagement from the problems facing the region. Ultimately, he told the allies, "all of the responsibility for the policies that you carry out in your countries lies with you. We will be friends. We will be partners. But our relationship will be built on this basis."[25]

While this early assertion of Gorbachev's "new thinking" might come as a surprise to many historians, he admits that it was not much of a discovery for the East European leaders. "Even Brezhnev, Andropov, and Chernenko had said the same thing before me to them," he continued. Once the decision had been taken to abandon further intervention in Eastern Europe, Gorbachev asserted, "we never retreated from that rule. I never retreated from the rule of respecting sovereignty, independence, and not interfering in internal affairs. There were moments when they actually appealed to us—some of them appealed to us to intervene. But our ambassadors told them what needed to be told. So that the Brezhnev Doctrine, or the doctrine of limited sovereignty, was ended even before Chernenko was buried. We buried it even before Chernenko was buried."[26] In fact, the doctrine had suffered a quiet death four years earlier in Poland, a casualty of the divergent national interests that, even then, had already begun to tear the Soviet empire apart.

While the persistent fear of Soviet intervention continued to temper reformism in Eastern Europe, Gorbachev knew from the experience of 1980–81 that, when push came to shove, Moscow could no longer play its trump card of intervention. The future of socialism in the region depended on the East European regimes themselves and their ability to manage problems in accordance with local strengths and traditions. For the time being, though, belief in the bogeyman of Soviet intervention bought Gorbachev time to change socialist bloc relations in a gradual fashion. As Nikolai Kolikov again points out, "This doesn't mean that [Gorbachev] should have come out immediately saying that we are rejecting this doctrine and that we will be acting in an absolutely different way. Why? Because he recognized perfectly well that every rejection of that kind against the collective defense of socialism in the East European countries could definitely harm these countries from the perspective of the stability of the system there. And therefore, it was rather later that this became formalized."[27] Once it did, the response that Moscow had been fearing since 1981 finally came to pass, as communist regimes gave way before a tidal wave of pent-up popular resentment.

Moscow's gradual loosening of controls after the Polish crisis of 1980–81 was thus the beginning of this attempt to restore national diversity in socialist bloc relations. It was a reluctant admission that national customs could divide the once monolithic socialist camp—that divergent national interests were indeed possible among communist states. Consequently, the start of Gorbachev's reform program in Eastern Europe must be seen in the context of a policy shift that had already begun in the final years of the Brezhnev era. Similarly, the stunning events of 1989 ought to be seen as the final act of an enduring drama that stretches back to 1968 and the collapse of any popular belief in "socialism with a human face." This legacy ensured that Gorbachev's best efforts to rally public support for socialism in Eastern Europe only served to open a Pandora's box of cynical opposition throughout the region. The one thing that had suppressed this wave of popular opposition for years had been the threat of Soviet tanks. Though the Soviets sought to find a means of redressing this situation after 1981, the biblical caveat against "living by the sword" had long since taken on a new meaning for Moscow. Years of relying on force alone to guarantee communist rule in Eastern Europe had left the Soviets with no viable alternatives. The unheralded demise of the Brezhnev Doctrine in 1981 had virtually guaranteed the complete imperial collapse in Europe that Moscow suffered in 1989. Powerless to stop it, the Soviets simply did their best to ensure that they were not drawn into the political disaster. As ever, Soviet national interests continued to dictate the policy of the moment.

On Christmas Day 1989, with the execution of Romania's Nicolae Ceausescu and his wife, the last communist monopoly in the Soviet bloc collapsed, bereft of the guarantee Moscow had once so assertively championed. That night in Berlin, as they brought Beethoven's "Ode to Joy" to its stunning conclusion, Bernstein's combined orchestra and chorus uniting East and West celebrated the end of the Cold War with a slight modification of Schiller's hopeful poetry:

> *Freedom*, bright spark of divinity
> Daughter of Elysium,
> Fire-inspired we tread
> Thy sanctuary.
> Thy magic power reunites
> All that custom has divided.
> All men become brothers
> Under the sway of thy gentle wings.

Notes

Abbreviations

APRF: Arkhiv Presidenta Rossiskoi Federatsii (Archives of the President of the Russian Federation, known as the Presidential Archive, Moscow)

d.: delo (file or dossier)

f.: fond (fund, the most comprehensive organizational grouping within an archival collection)

MEIMO: *Mirovaia Ekonomika i Mezhdunarodnye Otnoshenii* (World Economy and International Relations)

o.: opis' (inventory)

pac.: paczka (packet)

PAP: Polska Agencja Prasowa (Polish Press Agency)

per.: perechen' (list)

SAMPO: Siftung Archiv der Massenorganisationen und Parteien der ehemaligen DDR im Bundesarchiv (Foundation "Archive of the Mass Organizations and Parties of the Former GDR" in the German Federal Archive, Potsdam)

tom: volume

TsKhSD: Tsentr Khraneniia Sovremennoi Dokumentatsii (Center for the Preservation of Contemporary Documentation, the former CPSU Party Archives, Moscow)

Introduction

1. The single, yet unforgettable, exception was Romania, where a brutal civil war raged for days before security forces loyal to Nicolae Ceausescu were finally defeated.

2. See especially Mark Kramer, "Beyond the Brezhnev Doctrine," *International Security* 14, no. 3 (Winter 1989–90); Charles Gati, *The Bloc That Failed: Soviet-East European Relations in Transition* (London: I. B. Touris, 1990); Karen Dawisha, *Eastern Europe, Gorbachev, and Reform: The Great Challenge*, 2d ed. (Cambridge: Cambridge University Press, 1990); William G. Hyland, *The Cold War Is Over* (New York: Times Books, 1990); Jerry F. Hough, "Gorbachev's Politics," *Foreign Affairs* 68, no. 5 (Winter 1989–90); Sidney Blumenthal, *Pledging Alliance: The Last Campaign of the Cold War* (New York: HarperCollins, 1990); Ralf Dahrendorf, *Reflections on the Revolution in Europe* (New York: Times Books/Random House, 1990); Jeane J. Kirkpatrick, *The Withering Away of the Totalitarian States . . . and Other Surprises* (Washington, D.C.: American Enterprise Institute, 1990); Michael Howard, "The Springtime of Nations," *Foreign Affairs* 69, no. 1 (Winter 1990); William H. MacNeill, "Winds of Change," *Foreign Affairs* 69, no. 4 (Fall 1990); Robert G. Kaiser, "Gorbachev: Triumph and Failure," *Foreign Affairs* 70, no. 2 (Spring 1991); Richard Perle, "Military Power and the Passing Cold War," in *After the Cold War: Questioning the Morality of Nuclear Deterrence*, ed. Charles W. Kegley Jr. and Kenneth L. Scwab (Boulder: Westview, 1991); and Richard Pipes, "Gorbachev's Russia: Breakdown or Crackdown," *Commentary* 89, no. 3 (March 1990).

3. See Daniel Deudney and G. John Ikenberry, "The International Sources of Soviet Change," *International Security* 16, no. 3 (Winter 1991), and Gati, *The Bloc That Failed*.

4. See Hough, "Gorbachev's Politics"; Valerie Bunce, "The Empire Strikes Back: The Evolution of the Eastern Bloc from a Soviet Asset to a Soviet Liability," *International Organization* 39, no. 1 (Winter 1985); Paul Marer, "Has Eastern Europe Become a Liability to the Soviet Union: (III) The Economic Aspect," in *The International Politics of Eastern Europe*, ed. Charles Gati (New York: Praeger, 1976); and Peter

Summerscale, "Is Eastern Europe a Liability to the Soviet Union," *International Affairs* 57, no. 4 (Autumn 1981).

5. The classic work outlining this approach is Jan Vanous and Michael Marese, *Soviet Subsidization of Trade with Eastern Europe: A Soviet Perspective* (Berkeley: Institute of International Studies, University of California, 1983). Their conclusions have been challenged, however, by some who argue that Soviet bloc subsidization was cyclical, with the Soviets occasionally playing the role of recipient. See, for example, Vlad Sobell, *The CMEA in Crisis: Toward a New European Order?* (New York: Praeger, 1990).

6. Robert A. Jones, *The Soviet Concept of "Limited Sovereignty" from Lenin to Gorbachev: The Brezhnev Doctrine* (New York: St. Martin's, 1990).

7. Bradley R. Gitz, *Armed Forces and Political Power in Eastern Europe: The Soviet/Communist Control System* (New York: Greenwood, 1992).

8. See Oleg Bogomolov, "Meniaiushchiisia oblik sotsializma" (The Changing Face of Socialism), *Kommunist*, no. 11 (1989); Mikhail Gorbachev, "Sotsialisticheskaia ideia i revoliutsionnaia perestroika" (The Socialist Idea and Revolutionary Transformation), *Kommunist*, no. 18 (1989); El'giz Pozdnyakov and Irina Shadrina, "O gumanizatsii i demokratizatsii mezhdunarodnykh otnoshenii" (Concerning the Humanizing and Democratizing of International Relations), *Mirovaia Ekonomika i Mezhdunarodnye Otnoshenii* (World Economy and International Relations), no. 4 (1989); Georgii Shakhnazarov, "Vostok-Zapad: K voprosu o deideologizatsii mezhgosudarstvenykh otnoshenii" (East-West: Toward the Question of Deideologization of Intergovernmental Relations), *Kommunist*, no. 3 (1989); "Peremeny v Tsentral'noi i Vostochnoi Evrope: S zasedaniia Komissii TsK KPSS po voprosam mezhdunarodnoi politiki, 15 iiunia 1990g." (Changes in Central and Eastern Europe: From a Meeting of the CPSU CC Commission on the Questions of International Politics), *Izvestiia TsK KPSS*, no. 10 (1990); "Vostochnaia Evropa na puti k obshcheevropeiskomu sotrudnichestvu" (Eastern Europe on the Path to Common European Cooperation), *Novaia i Noveishaia Istoriia* (New and Contemporary History), no. 1 (1990); and T. F. Yakovleva, *Politicheskie protsessy v Vostochnoi Evrope (80-e gg.)* (Political Processes in Eastern Europe [1980s]) (Moscow: Academy of Social Sciences of the CC CPSU, 1991).

9. See, for example, Christopher Andrew and Oleg Gordievsky, *KGB: The Inside Story* (New York: Harper Perennial, 1990); A. I. Gribkov, "Doktrina Brezhneva i pol'skii krizis nachala 80-kh godov" (The Brezhnev Doctrine and the Polish Crisis of the Early 1980s), *Voenno-Istoricheskii Zhurnal* (Military History Journal), no. 9 (1992); Georgii Shakhnazarov, *Tsena svobody: Reformatsiia Gorbacheva glazami ego pomoshchnika* (The Price of Freedom: The Gorbachev Reforms through the Eyes of His Assistant) (Moscow: Rossika Zevs, 1993); Mikhail Gorbachev, *Memoirs*, trans. Georges Peronansky and Tatjana Varsavsky (New York: Doubleday, 1995); Anatoly Dobrynin, *In Confidence: Moscow's Ambassador to America's Six Cold War Presidents (1962–1986)* (New York: Times Books, 1995); Valery L. Musatov, *Predvestniki buri: Politicheskie krizisy v Vostochnoi Evrope* (Ominous Clouds: Political Crises in Eastern Europe) (Moscow: Nauchnaia kniga, 1996); O. T. Bogomolov and S. P. Glinkina, "Pervye uroki ekonomicheskoi transformatsii v stranakh tsentral'noi i vostochnoi Evropy 90-x godov" (The First Lessons of Economic Transformation in the Countries of Central and Eastern Europe), *Novaia i Noveishaia Istoriia*, no. 3 (1997); and A. I. Gribkov, *Sud'ba Varshavskogo dogovora: Vospominaniia, dokumenty, fakty* (The Fate of the Warsaw Pact: Reminiscences, Documents, and Facts) (Moscow: Russkaia Kniga, 1998).

10. *Pravda*, 3 October 1988.

Chapter One

1. Throughout this study I refer to the nations of the Soviet bloc as both "socialist" and "communist." This choice is based above all on the fact that the Soviet and East European parties themselves used both terms to refer to themselves. Moreover, in doing so, they understood their system to be quite distinct from the type of social democracy practiced in the West. My use of the terms is not meant to imply any normative outlook on the nature of socialism but simply to be consistent with the terminology that arose in bloc discussions.

2. Mikhail Heller and Aleksandr M. Nekrich, *Utopia in Power: The History of the Soviet Union from 1917 to the Present* (New York: Summit Books, 1986), 527.

3. Alexander M. Kirov, "Hungary, 1956," in *Soviet Military Intervention in Hungary, 1956,* ed. Jeno Gyorkei and Miklos Horvath (Budapest: Central European University Press, 1999), 131.

4. Ibid., 132.

5. Joseph Rothschild, *Return to Diversity: A Political History of East Central Europe since World War II,* 2d ed. (Oxford: Oxford University Press, 1993), 156. Rothschild notes that Rákosi never returned to Hungary but rather died in the Soviet Union on 5 February 1971, "still professing the correctness of his positions."

6. For further discussion of the Polish "October," see Chapter 4.

7. Kirov, "Hungary, 1956," 132.

8. Ibid.

9. Ibid., 133–34.

10. Jeno Gyorkei and Miklos Horvath, "Additional Data on the History of the Soviet Military Occupation," in Gyorkei and Horvath, *Soviet Military Intervention in Hungary,* 11.

11. Ibid., 12.

12. Johanna Granville, "Imre Nagy, Hesitant Revolutionary," *Cold War International History Project Bulletin,* no. 5 (Spring 1995): 23.

13. Gyorkei and Horvath, "Additional Data," 22–23.

14. Csaba Bekes, "New Findings on the 1956 Hungarian Revolution," *Cold War International History Project Bulletin,* no. 2 (Fall 1992): 2.

15. Kirov, "Hungary, 1956," 141.

16. Ibid.

17. Ibid., 144. Mikoyan was vice president of the Soviet Council of Ministers (deputy prime minister), while Suslov was Moscow's leading ideologist. Both were members of the top Soviet party leadership.

18. Janos M. Rainer, "The Yeltsin Dossier: Soviet Documents on Hungary, 1956," *Cold War International History Project Bulletin,* no. 5 (Spring 1995): 25.

19. Kirov, "Hungary, 1956," 144–45.

20. Granville, "Imre Nagy," 27.

21. Rothschild, *Return to Diversity,* 159.

22. Kirov, "Hungary, 1956," 149.

23. Ibid., 152. Speaking to members of the crowd after his speech, he offered the opinion, "It is strange that the Soviet Union does not understand that troops must leave the country immediately" (ibid.).

24. Ibid., 154.

25. Ibid., 161.

26. Bekes, "New Findings on the 1956 Hungarian Revolution," 3.

27. Granville, "Imre Nagy," 27.

28. Ibid.

29. Bekes, "New Findings on the 1956 Hungarian Revolution," 3.

30. Ibid.

31. Ibid.

32. Although the group called for the creation of a clandestine army, its only weapon at the time of arrest was an old, rusty handgun. See Heller and Nekrich, *Utopia in Power,* 619–20.

33. Karen Dawisha, *The Kremlin and the Prague Spring* (Berkeley: University of California Press, 1984), 15.

34. APRF, "Rabochaia zapis' zasedanii Politbiuro, 1968g." (Working Notes of a Politburo Session, 1968), 93–95, cited in R. G. Pikhoia, "Chekhoslovakiia, 1968 god. Vzgliad iz Moskvy po dokumentam TsK KPSS" (Czechoslovakia, 1968: The View from Moscow according to the Documents of the CPSU CC), *Novaia i*

Noveishaia Istoriia, no. 6 (1994): 8; unless otherwise noted, all translations are my own. This is the first of two articles based almost entirely on the archival holdings of the APRF and the TsKhSD. Pikhoia worked with important documents that have since been reclassified. Therefore his analysis is an extremely valuable source of insight into the details of Soviet perceptions on the Czechoslovak crisis.

35. APRF, "Rabochaia zapis' zasedanii Politbiuro, 1968g.," 92, cited in Pikhoia, "Chekhoslovakiia, 1968 god," 8. See also Dawisha, *The Kremlin and the Prague Spring*, 25–26.

36. Harvey W. Nelsen, *Power and Insecurity: Beijing, Moscow, and Washington, 1949–1988* (Boulder: Lynne Rienner, 1989), 68.

37. Jiri Valenta, *Soviet Intervention in Czechoslovakia, 1968: Anatomy of a Decision*, rev. and expanded ed. (Baltimore: Johns Hopkins University Press, 1991), 26.

38. Dawisha, *The Kremlin and the Prague Spring*, 82–83.

39. The Slovak Communist Party was a part of the larger Czechoslovak Communist Party, created ostensibly to ensure the fair representation of the Slovak minority within the larger party. There was no similar Czech wing of the party, just as in the Soviet Union there was no Russian Communist Party alongside those of the other republics.

40. Rothschild, *Return to Diversity*, 168.

41. Ibid.

42. Valerii Musatov, "The Inside Story of the Invasion," *New Times International* 16 (April 1992): 37.

43. Dawisha, *The Kremlin and the Prague Spring*, 31.

44. Pikhoia, "Chekhoslovakiia, 1968 god," 9. Andropov was quite familiar with the details of the Hungarian crisis, as he had played a key role from Budapest at the time, engineering the eventual Soviet invasion. When he speaks of the "first and second echelons" he seems to suggest that, despite their apparent dedication to reforming communism, the reformers in Czechoslovakia will invariably begin to demand the introduction of Western-style democratization before long, just as occurred in Hungary twelve years earlier.

45. Zdenek Mlynar, *Nightfrost in Prague: The End of Humane Socialism*, trans. Paul Wilson (New York: Karz Publishers, 1980), 114–15.

46. Pikhoia, "Chekhoslovakiia, 1968 god," 10.

47. Ibid., 12.

48. Pavel Tigrid, "Czechoslovakia: A Post-Mortem II," *Survey*, Winter/Spring 1970, 114.

49. *Pravda Pobezhdaet* (Truth Prevails) (Moscow: Izdatel'stvo politicheskoi literatury, 1971), 136, quoted in Dawisha, *The Kremlin and the Prague Spring*, 44.

50. Eugen Steiner, *The Slovak Dilemma* (Cambridge: Cambridge University Press, 1973), 171.

51. Valenta, *Soviet Intervention in Czechoslovakia*, 31; Pikhoia, "Chekhoslovakiia, 1968 god," 13.

52. Dawisha, *The Kremlin and the Prague Spring*, 59–60.

53. APRF, "Rabochaia zapis' zasedanii Politbiuro, 1969g.," 200–220, cited in Pikhoia, "Chekhoslovakiia, 1968 god," 15.

54. Ibid.

55. *Zapis vystoupeni na setkani prvnich tajemniku UV KS BLR, MLR, NDR, PLR a SSSR v Moskve, 8 kvetna 1968 (13:00–20:00)* (Minutes about the Performance at the Meeting of the First Secretaries of the CC of CPs BPR, MPR, GDR, PPR, and USSR in Moscow, 8 May 1968 [13:00–20:00]), Czechoslovakia's government commission for analyzing the years 1967–70, Z/P2, quoted in Valenta, *Soviet Intervention in Czechoslovakia*, 167.

56. Pikhoia, "Chekhoslovakiia, 1968 god," 15–16.

57. Ibid., 17.

58. Bilak became first secretary of the Slovak Communist Party after Alexander Dubcek left the position to become head of the statewide CSCP.

59. See George Klein, "The Role of Ethnic Politics in the Czechoslovak Crisis of 1968 and the Yugoslav Crisis of 1971," *Studies in Comparative Communism* 8, no. 4 (Winter 1975): 368, and Steiner, *Slovak Dilemma*, 174–76.

60. Steiner, *Slovak Dilemma*, 181.

61. "Zapis' besedy v TsK KPSS s rukovoditelyami bratskikh partii Bolgarii, Vengrii, Germanii, Pol'shi, 8 maya 1968 goda" (Notes from a Meeting of the CPSU CC with the Leaders of the Fraternal Parties of Bulgaria, Hungary, Germany, and Poland, 8 May 1968) (TOP SECRET), in Archiv Komise vlady CSFR pro analyzu udalosti let 1967–1970, Z/S2, and "Vecny scenar invaze: Rozhovor o pozadi udalosti pred triadveceti lety" (Actual Scenario of the Invasion: A Discussion about the Background of the Events That Occurred Twenty-three Years Ago), *Lidove noviny*, 17 January 1991, 10, both cited in Mark Kramer, "The Prague Spring and the Soviet Invasion of Czechoslovakia: New Interpretations," in *Cold War International History Project Bulletin*, no. 3 (Fall 1993): 3. Kramer draws extensively on newly released archival materials from the Czech state archives in this article.

62. Pikhoia, "Chekhoslovakiia, 1968 god," 17–18.

63. APRF, "Rabochaia zapis' zasedanii Politbiuro, 1968g.," 357–98, cited in ibid., 20.

64. See Valenta, *Soviet Intervention in Czechoslovakia*, 170.

65. APRF, "Rabochaia zapis' zasedanii Politbiuro, 1968g.," 357–98, cited in Pikhoia, "Chekhoslovakiia, 1968 god," 20.

66. Dawisha, *The Kremlin and the Prague Spring*, 189.

67. Arkhiv Vneshnei Politiki Rossiskoi Federatsii, Moscow, f. 059, o. 58, per. 124, d. 571, ll. (pages) 145–49, "Top Secret Telegram from Ambassador Stepan Chervonenko to Moscow regarding the CPCz CC Presidium's Decision Not to Attend the Warsaw Meeting, July 9, 1968," in *The Prague Spring, 1968*, ed. Jaromír Navrátil et al., trans. Mark Kramer, Joy Moss, and Ruth Tosek (Prague: Central European University Press, 1998), 207.

68. Valenta, *Soviet Intervention in Czechoslovakia*, 170.

69. Erwin Weit, *At the Red Summit: Interpreter behind the Iron Curtain* (New York: Macmillan, 1973), 210. Weit was Gomulka's interpreter and was present at the Warsaw summit.

70. *Pravda*, 18 July 1968, cited in Navrátil et al., *Prague Spring*, 235.

71. Dawisha, *The Kremlin and the Prague Spring*, 210–11.

72. Alan Levy, *Rowboat to Prague* (New York: Grossman, 1972), 262–63.

73. Dawisha, *The Kremlin and the Prague Spring*, 218.

74. APRF, "Rabochaia zapis' zasedanii Politbiuro, 1968g.," 419, cited in Pikhoia, "Chekhoslovakiia, 1968 god. Vzgliad iz Moskvy po dokumentam TsK KPSS" (Czechoslovakia, 1968: The View from Moscow according to Documents of the CPSU CC), pt. 2, *Novaia i Noveishaia Istoriia*, no. 1 (1995): 34–35.

75. *New York Times*, 30 April 1968.

76. Valenta, *Soviet Intervention in Czechoslovakia*, 14.

77. *Pravda*, 19 July 1968, quoted in Dawisha, *The Kremlin and the Prague Spring*, 232–33. Former KGB resident Oleg Gordievsky later revealed that this story had been entirely fabricated by Department A of the KGB's First Chief Directorate. See Christopher Andrew and Oleg Gordievsky, *KGB: The Inside Story* (New York: Harper Perennial, 1990), 484.

78. *Pravda*, 22 July 1968.

79. Dawisha, *The Kremlin and the Prague Spring*, 312. Chervonenko faced considerable criticism following the invasion for relying for his information on members of the CSCP who were about to be purged and thus had a vested interest in exaggerating the dangers of the Prague Spring. See ibid.

80. Valenta, *Soviet Intervention in Czechoslovakia*, 175.

81. Christopher Andrew and Vasili Mitrokhin, *The Sword and the Shield: The Mitrokhin Archive and the Secret History of the KGB* (New York: Basic, 1999), 252–53.

82. Ibid., 255.

83. Andrew and Gordievsky, *KGB*, 483.

84. Oleg Kalugin, "KGB poka ne meniaet printsipov . . ." (The KGB Has Not Yet Changed Its Principles), *Komsomol'skaia Pravda*, 20 June 1990, 2.

85. Oleg Kalugin, "Otkrovennost' vozmozhno, lish' kogda za toboi zakroetsia dver': General KGB o KGB" (Openness Is Possible Only When You Close the Door behind You), *Moskovskie Novosti* 25 (24 June 1990): 11, quoted in Kramer, "Prague Spring and the Soviet Invasion of Czechoslovakia," 6.

86. One alternative source of information should have been the Institute of the Economics of the World Socialist System (IEMSS), the division of the Academy of Sciences whose job it was to keep the Central Committee appraised of developments in Eastern Europe. However, following the invasion of August 1968, the director of this institute, Gennadiy Sorokin, was replaced by a member of the Central Committee's Department for Liaison with Socialist States, Oleg Bogomolov. The cause was disappointment with the quality of the information IEMSS had provided during the crisis. See Jonathan Valdez, *Internationalism and the Ideology of Soviet Influence in Eastern Europe* (Cambridge: Cambridge University Press, 1993), 52–53.

87. Following Dubcek's agreement to continue bilateral talks with Moscow, the Soviets had finally begun to withdraw their troops. However, in mid-July Soviet troops were still in the country. Moreover, the units that had withdrawn remained encamped along the Czechoslovak border. See James H. Polk, "Reflections on the Czechoslovakian Invasion," *Strategic Review* 5 (Winter 1977): 30–37.

88. Dawisha, *The Kremlin and the Prague Spring*, 246–47.

89. APRF, "Rabochaia zapis' zasedanii Politbiuro, 1968," 425.

90. Ibid.

91. Jiri Pelikan, "The Struggle for Socialism in Czechoslovakia," *New Left Review*, no. 71 (January/February 1972): 25.

92. *Pameti Vasila Bil'aka: Unikatni svedectvi ze zakulisi KSC* (Memoirs of Vasi Bilak: Unique Insight behind the Scenes of the Czechoslovak Communist Party), 2 vols. (Prague: Agentura Cesty, 1991), 2:86–89, cited in Kramer, "Prague Spring and the Soviet Invasion of Czechoslovakia," 3.

93. "Dopis A. Kapeka," in Archiv Komise vlady CSFR pro analyzu udalosti let 1967–1970, Z/S21, cited in Kramer, "Prague Spring and the Soviet Invasion of Czechoslovakia," 3.

94. Dawisha, *The Kremlin and the Prague Spring*, 265.

95. Navrátil et al., *Prague Spring*, 296.

96. Pikhoia, "Chekhoslovakiia, 1968 god," pt. 2, 38–39.

97. Dawisha, *The Kremlin and the Prague Spring*, 263.

98. Mark Kramer, "A Letter to Brezhnev: The Czech Hardliners 'Request' for Soviet Intervention, August 1968," in *Cold War International History Project Bulletin*, no. 2 (Fall 1992): 35 (emphasis added). Kramer has translated the full text of the letter here.

99. Kramer, "Prague Spring and the Soviet Invasion of Czechoslovakia," 3.

100. Pikhoia, "Chekhoslovakiia, 1968 god," pt. 2, 39–41.

101. Kramer, "Prague Spring and the Soviet Invasion of Czechoslovakia," 3.

102. Valenta, *Soviet Intervention in Czechoslovakia*, 188.

103. Pikhoia, "Chekhoslovakiia, 1968 god," pt. 2, 42.

104. Ibid., 43.

105. *Stenograficky zaznam schuzky Varsavske petky v Moskve dne 18.8.1968 k rozhodnuti o intervenci a projednani planu* (Minutes of a Meeting of the Warsaw Five in Moscow, 18 August 1968, on the Decision about Intervention and Discussion of the Plan), CSCP Party Archives Z/S 22, 392–93, quoted in Kramer, "Prague Spring and the Soviet Invasion of Czechoslovakia," 3.

106. It is important to note that Romania refused to participate in the intervention on the grounds that it constituted a violation of Czechoslovak state sovereignty. Romanian Communist Party leader Nicolae Ceausescu worried that Romania's

own sovereignty would be violated next in response to his penchant for flaunting Soviet leadership in Eastern Europe.

107. Dawisha, *The Kremlin and the Prague Spring*, 279.

108. Kadar's meeting with Dubcek on 17 August was the Hungarian leader's last-ditch attempt to stave off in Czechoslovakia the fate that had befallen his country twelve years earlier. He is reported to have said to Dubcek at this meeting, "Do you *really* not know the kind of people you're dealing with?" See Mlynar, *Nightfrost in Prague*, 157. On Kadar's readiness to support the invasion, see APRF, "Vypiska iz protokola No. 95 Politbiuro TsK ot 17 avgusta 1968g." (An Extract from Protocol no. 95 of the CC Politburo from 17 August 1968), cited in Pikhoia, "Chekhoslovakiia, 1968 god," pt. 2, 44.

109. Pikhoia, "Chekhoslovakiia, 1968 god," pt. 2, 45.

110. Zdenek Mlynar, "August 1968," in *Communist Reformation*, ed. G. R. Urban (London: Maurice Temple Smith, 1979), 132.

111. "Telegram from the Embassy in the Soviet Union to the Department of State," in *Foreign Relations of the United States, 1964-1968*, vol. 17, *Eastern Europe*, ed. James E. Miller (Washington, D.C.: Government Printing Office, 1996), 211-12.

112. "Memorandum of Conversation," in *Foreign Relations of the United States, 1964-1968*, 212-14.

113. Ibid.

114. Ibid.

115. See APRF, f. 3, o. 91, d. 308, 25-26, cited in Pikhoia, "Chekhoslovakiia, 1968 god," pt. 2, 36 (emphasis added). For further discussion of this perception that the United States was reluctant to become involved in Czechoslovakia in 1968, see Mlynar, *Nightfrost in Prague*, 241; A. Paul Kubricht, "Confronting Liberalization and Military Invasion: America and the Johnson Administration Respond to the 1968 Prague Summer," in *Jahrbücher für Geschichte Osteuropas*, new ser., 40 (1992): 197-212; and Dawisha, *The Kremlin and the Prague Spring*, 252-53.

116. Pikhoia, "Chekhoslovakiia, 1968 god," pt. 2, 45.

117. Ibid. The Soviets had good reason to hope that Svoboda would see things their way. Twenty years earlier, in 1948, he had confined the army to barracks to keep it from opposing the Communist takeover in Czechoslovakia.

118. Valerii Leonidovich Musatov, "Krizisy v Evropeiskikh sotsstranakh (Vengriia—1956g., Chekhoslovakiia—1968g., Pol'sha—1980-81gg.) i politika Sovetskogo Soiuza" (Crises in the European Socialist Countries [Hungary—1956, Czechoslovakia—1968, Poland—1980-81] and the Politics of the Soviet Union) (Candidate of Historical Sciences diss., Diplomatic Academy of the Russian Foreign Affairs Ministry, 1995), 116.

119. APRF, "Vypiska iz protokola No. 95 Politbiuro TsK ot 17 avgusta 1968g.," cited in Pikhoia, "Chekhoslovakiia, 1968 god," pt. 2, 44.

120. Joseph L. Nogee and Robert H. Donaldson, *Soviet Foreign Policy since World War II* (New York: Pergamon, 1981), 94.

121. Hans J. Morgenthau, *Politics among Nations: The Struggle for Power and Peace*, 5th rev. ed. (New York: A. A. Knopf, 1973), 92.

122. Dawisha, *The Kremlin and the Prague Spring*, 311.

Chapter Two

1. Zdenek Mlynar, *Nightfrost in Prague: The End of Humane Socialism*, trans. Paul Wilson (New York: Karz Publishers, 1980), 146-47. See also Archive of the Federal Government Commission of Czechoslovakia, Russian file, Archive of the External Policy of the USSR, R43, cited in Kieran D. Williams, "Czechoslovakia, 1968," *Slavonic and East European Review* 74, no. 1 (January 1996): 86.

2. Mlynar, *Nightfrost in Prague*, 147.

3. Ibid.

4. Fred H. Eidlin, *The Logic of "Normalization": The Soviet Intervention in Czechoslovakia of 21 August 1968 and the Czechoslovak Response* (New York: Columbia University Press, 1980), 42, 65.

5. Mlynar, *Nightfrost in Prague*, 150–51.

6. Valerii L. Musatov, "Krizisy v Evropeiskikh sotsstranakh (Vengriia—1956g., Chekhoslovakiia—1968g., Pol'sha—1980-81gg.) i politika Sovetskogo Soiuza" (Crises in the European Socialist Countries [Hungary—1956, Czechoslovakia—1968, Poland—1980-81] and the Politics of the Soviet Union) (Candidate of Historical Sciences diss., Diplomatic Academy of the Russian Foreign Affairs Ministry, 1995), 117.

7. Mlynar, *Nightfrost in Prague*, 177–83. No such revolutionary tribunal had been formally established under Alois Indra. The arresting officer appears to have been acting in accordance with Soviet assumptions regarding the shape of the expected quisling government.

8. Gordon H. Skilling, *Czechoslovakia's Interrupted Revolution* (Princeton: Princeton University Press, 1976), 504.

9. *Tanky proti Szezdu*, Protocol dokumenty XIV sjezdu KSC (Tanks against the Congress, Protocol Documents of the Fourteenth Congress of the Czechoslovak Communist Party) (Vienna: Europ Verlag, 1970), 35–36, cited also in Eidlin, *Logic of "Normalization,"* 49.

10. Eidlin, *Logic of "Normalization,"* 50.

11. Viktor Suvorov, *Osvoboditel'* (Liberator) (St. Petersburg: Konets Veka, 1993), 191.

12. Mlynar, *Nightfrost in Prague*, 180.

13. Quoted from a flyer in the "Czechoslovakia 1968 Collection," cited in Eidlin, *Logic of "Normalization,"* 216.

14. Robert Littell, ed., *The Czech Black Book* (New York: Praeger, 1969), 74–75. This important source of firsthand accounts of the intervention was put together by the Institute of History, Czechoslovak Academy of Sciences, in September 1968.

15. Eidlin, *Logic of "Normalization,"* 225.

16. Mlynar, *Nightfrost in Prague*, 190.

17. Ibid., 191–94.

18. Ibid., 196.

19. S. M. Zolotov, "Shli na pomoshch druz'iam" (They Went to the Aid of Friends), *Voenno-Istoricheskii Zhurnal*, no. 4 (April 1994): 18.

20. Suvorov, *Osvoboditel'*, 175–76.

21. See, for example, Thomas T. Hammond, ed., *Witnesses to the Origins of the Cold War* (Seattle: University of Washington Press, 1982), for evidence of this behavior in the firsthand accounts of Western observers.

22. Littell, *Czech Black Book*, 92.

23. Eidlin, *Logic of "Normalization,"* 44.

24. Ibid., 246 n.

25. Mlynar, *Nightfrost in Prague*, 204.

26. "Vpad byl neodvratny: V srpnu 1968 melo byt zatceno na ctyricet' tisic cechu a slovaku" (Intervention Was Unavoidable: In August 1968 Forty Thousand Czechs and Slovaks Were to Be Imprisoned: *Mlada fronta*, 21 August 1990, 1, cited in Mark Kramer, "The Prague Spring and the Soviet Invasion of Czechoslovakia: New Interpretations," in *Cold War International History Project Bulletin*, no. 3 (Fall 1993): 3.

27. *Protocol ze setkani stranickych a vladnich delegaci Bulharska, NDR, Polska, Mad'arska a SSSR, Moskva, 24–26.8., 1968* (Minutes about a Meeting of the Party and Government Delegation of Bulgaria, GDR, Poland, Hungary, and USSR, Moscow, 24–26 August 1968), Czechoslovak government commission, Z/P4 (Czech translation). Cited in Jiri Valenta, *Soviet Intervention in Czechoslovakia, 1968: Anatomy of a Decision*, rev. and expanded ed. (Baltimore: Johns Hopkins University Press, 1991), 192.

28. TsKhSD, f. 89, per. 38, d. 57, 30, quoted in Musatov, "Krizisy v Evropeiskikh sotsstranakh," 119.

29. Institute for Contemporary History (Prague) (USD), Archive of the CPCz CC (AUV KSC), F. 07/15, "Minutes of Soviet-Czechoslovak Talks in the Kremlin, August 23

and 26, 1968 (Excerpts)," cited in *The Prague Spring, 1968*, ed. Jaromír Navrátil et al., trans. Mark Kramer, Joy Moss, and Ruth Tosek (Prague: Central European University Press, 1998), 471.

30. BBC translation of Smrkovsky's speech, quoted in Eidlin, *Logic of "Normalization,"* 247.

31. Mlynar, *Nightfrost in Prague*, 240.

32. Ibid., 242.

33. On 28 August the Vysocany Central Committee dissolved itself after issuing a statement of support for Dubcek. See *Rude Pravo*, 29 August 1968.

34. TsKhSD, f. 89, per. 61, no. 6, "Nekotorye zamechaniia po voprosu podgotovki voenno-politicheskoi aktsii 21 avgusta 1968g." (Some Observations on the Question of the Preparations for Military-Political Action on 21 August 1968), 16 November 1982, 1. Former Central Committee International Department analyst Valerii Musatov, a member of the Central Committee staff in 1968, told the author in an interview in 1995 that he believes this briefing was prepared for General Secretary Brezhnev himself. Brezhnev would then have presented it orally to the Politburo. Because the letterhead has been removed from the top of this report, it is unclear precisely who prepared it for presentation to the Politburo. The document is stamped "Strictly secret," "Only [existing] copy," and "For oral report." Based on the amount of sensitive information contained therein, it could only have been prepared by either the KGB or the Central Committee apparat. It seems likely that it was the latter, as the report contains a considerably rigorous critique of the Soviet "special services," presumably attacking the work of the KGB during the operation. One would not expect this in a document prepared by the KGB itself.

35. Ibid.

36. Ibid., 16.

37. Valenta, *Soviet Intervention in Czechoslovakia*, 193.

38. TsKhSD, "Nekotorye zamechaniia," 3-4.

39. Littell, *Czech Black Book*, 20.

40. Karen Dawisha, *The Kremlin and the Prague Spring* (Berkeley: University of California Press, 1984), 323.

41. TASS in English 12:25 GMT and Moscow home service 13:00 GMT (BBC 1, 21 August 1968), cited in Eidlin, *Logic of "Normalization,"* 41.

42. Ibid., 56 n.

43. TsKhSD, "Nekotorye zamechaniia," 3.

44. Ibid., 4-5.

45. Ibid., 5.

46. Ibid., 6-7.

47. Ibid.

48. Christopher Andrew and Vasili Mitrokhin, *The Sword and the Shield: The Mitrokhin Archive and the Secret History of the KGB* (New York: Basic, 1999), 259.

49. TsKhSD, "Nekotorye zamechaniia," 13-14.

50. Ibid., 7-8.

51. Ibid., 16.

52. Ibid., 9.

53. Littell, *Czech Black Book*, 133-34.

54. TsKhSD, "Nekotorye zamechaniia," 8.

55. Ibid., 9-10

56. Ibid.

57. Ibid., 13.

58. Andrew and Mitrokhin, *Sword and the Shield*, 259-61.

59. *Radio Free Europe Central Monitoring Desk*, 12:15, 24 August 1968, cited in Eidlin, *Logic of "Normalization,"* 214.

60. Husak was elected first secretary of the Slovak Communist Party at the Slovak Party congress, replacing Bilak in the position.

61. *Vyber*, special ed., March 1969, 27, cited in Eugen Steiner, *The Slovak Dilemma* (Cambridge: Cambridge University Press, 1973), 189.

62. Steiner, *Slovak Dilemma*, 189.

63. Ibid., 210–11.

64. Dubcek served briefly as ambassador to Turkey until, by June 1970, he had lost this post along with his duties in the Federal Assembly and Slovak National Council, as well as his Party membership.

65. Danielle Hunebelle, "Dubcek Talks," *Look*, 29 July 1969, 23.

66. Steiner, *Slovak Dilemma*, 212. "Left-wing opportunism" was generally understood to refer to ultraconservative, Chinese-style communism, whereas "revisionism" referred to more liberal reforms.

67. Opponents of the treaty in the U.S. Senate, in West Germany, and in Japan were able to use the invasion as an excuse to prolong the ratification process. See Valenta, *Soviet Intervention in Czechoslovakia*, 160.

68. Ibid.

69. "Telegram from the Embassy in the Soviet Union to the Department of State," in *Foreign Relations of the United States, 1964–1968*, vol. 17, *Eastern Europe*, ed. James E. Miller (Washington, D.C.: Government Printing Office, 1996), 230.

70. R. A. Medvedev, *On Socialist Democracy* (New York: A. A. Knopf, 1975), 28.

71. Andrei Sakharov, *Memoirs*, trans. Richard Lourie (New York: A. A. Knopf, 1990), 289–90.

72. David Remnick, *Lenin's Tomb: The Last Days of the Soviet Empire* (New York: Vintage, 1994), 18.

73. Ibid.

74. Valenta, *Soviet Intervention in Czechoslovakia*, 162.

75. Still firmly Stalinist, the Albanian leadership had been on difficult terms with Moscow since the start of Khrushchev's de-Stalinization campaign in the 1950s. It gradually exchanged its pro-Moscow orientation for tighter relations with Beijing.

76. Valenta, *Soviet Intervention in Czechoslovakia*, 162.

77. Santiago Carillo, *"Eurocommunism" y Estado* (Barcelona: Editorial Critica, 1977), 166–67, quoted in ibid.

78. Christian F. Ostermann, "New Evidence on the Sino-Soviet Border Dispute, 1969–71," *Cold War International History Project Bulletin*, nos. 6–7 (Winter 1995–96): 187.

79. Ibid.

80. Harvey W. Nelsen, *Power and Insecurity: Beijing, Moscow, and Washington, 1949–1988* (Boulder: Lynne Rienner, 1989), 73; see also Arkady Shevchenko, *Breaking with Moscow* (New York: Alfred Knopf, 1985), 164–66, and Ostermann, "New Evidence," 188.

81. SAMPO-BArch J IV 2/202/359, translated from Russian by Mark H. Doctoroff, cited in Ostermann, "New Evidence," 192.

82. Ibid.

83. Robert L. Hutchings, *Soviet–East European Relations: Consolidation and Conflict* (Madison: University of Wisconsin Press, 1983), 43.

84. Gorbachev's later failure to engineer reform in the Soviet bloc does not necessarily discredit the entire notion that socialism might have been subject to successful reforms. Even if the socialist system was ultimately doomed to fail by its internal contradictions, an effective reform policy might well have perpetuated its survival for many decades. However, Brezhnev's refusal to deal with the pressure for reform within the bloc ensured that future crises would arise sooner rather than later.

85. Zdenek Mlynar, *Cekoslovensky pokus o reformu* (The Czechoslovak Attempt at Reform) (Cologne/Rome: INDEX/LISTY, 1975), 260, cited in Hutchings, *Soviet–East European Relations*, 258.

Chapter Three

1. Sergei Kovalev, "O 'mirnoi' i nemirnoi kontrrevoliutsii" (Concerning "Peaceful" and Unpeaceful Counterrevolution), *Pravda*, 11 September 1968.

2. Sergei Kovalev, "Suverenitet: Internatsional'nye obiazannosti sotsialisticheskikh stran" (Sovereignty and the International Responsibilities of the Socialist Countries), *Pravda*, 26 September 1968.

3. Leonid Brezhnev, *Leninskim kursom: Rechi i stat'i* (By Lenin's Course: Speeches and Articles), vol. 2 (Moscow: Izdatel'stvo Politicheskoi Literatury, 1970), 329.

4. See Brezhnev's speech to the Congress of International Socialist Workers in June 1969 in ibid., 397–98.

5. Iu. Stepanov, "Proletarskii internatsionalizm—vazhneishii printsip marksizma-leninizma" (Proletarian Internationalism—the Most Important Principle of Marxism-Leninism), *MEIMO*, no. 11 (1976): 21.

6. I. I. Orlik, Valerii L. Musatov, and others tend to assert this viewpoint. See, for instance, Valerii L. Musatov, "Krizisy v Evropeiskikh sotsstranakh (Vengriia—1956g., Chekhoslovakiia—1968g., Pol'sha—1980–81gg.) i politika Sovetskogo Soiuza" (Crises in the European Socialist Countries [Hungary—1956, Czechoslovakia—1968, Poland—1980–81] and the Politics of the Soviet Union) (Candidate of Historical Sciences diss., Diplomatic Academy of the Russian Foreign Affairs Ministry, 1995).

7. See, for instance, Peter Summerscale, "The Continuing Validity of the Brezhnev Doctrine," in *Soviet–East European Dilemmas: Coercion, Competition, and Consent*, ed. Karen Dawisha and Philip Hanson (London: Heinemann Educational Books, 1981), 35.

8. J. F. Brown, *Eastern Europe and Communist Rule* (Durham: Duke University Press, 1988), 39.

9. Hungary remained on the fence, not willing to commit but not staunchly opposed either.

10. Hélène Carrère D'Encausse, *Big Brother: The Soviet Union and Soviet Europe*, trans. George Holoch (New York: Holmes and Meier, 1987), 227.

11. Ia. V. Iakimovich, "Voznikovenie mirovoi sotsialisticheskoi sistemy" (The Emergence of the World Socialist System), in *Sotsializm i mezhdunarodnye otnosheniia* (Socialism and International Relations), ed. A. P. Butenko (Moscow: Izdatel'stvo "Nauka," 1975), 115.

12. See Stepanov, "Proletarskii internatsionalizm," 21.

13. Ibid., 24.

14. See, for instance, Ia. Iakimovich, "Osnovanie printsipy vzaimootnoshenii sotsialisticheskikh stran" (The Foundation of the Principle of Mutual Relations among Socialist Nations), in Butenko, *Sotsializm i mezhdunarodnye otnosheniia*, 232–33.

15. Brezhnev speaking to the Berlin Conference in June 1976, cited in Stepanov, "Proletarskii internatsionalizm," 21–22.

16. Robert Hutchings points out that this arrangement "represented a new and somewhat paradoxical Soviet confidence in a multilateral approach to problems of alliance management and, derivatively, in the ability of their more loyal allies, chiefly the Bulgarians, Czechoslovaks, and East Germans, to help ensure that the desired consensus would prevail in multilateral negotiations." See his *Soviet–East European Relations: Consolidation and Conflict* (Madison: University of Wisconsin Press, 1983), 89.

17. *Pravda*, 18 June 1969.

18. Hutchings, *Soviet–East European Relations*, 89.

19. Georgii Shakhnazarov, *Tsena svobody: Reformatsiia Gorbacheva glazami ego pomoshchnika* (The Price of Freedom: The Gorbachev Reforms through the Eyes of His Assistant) (Moscow: Rossika Zevs, 1993), 121.

20. Richard F. Staar, *Yearbook on International Communist Affairs, 1972* (Stanford: Hoover Institution Press, 1972), 33.

21. *Scinteia*, 8 February 1969, cited in ibid.
22. Hutchings, *Soviet-East European Relations*, 157.
23. Staar, *Yearbook on International Communist Affairs, 1972*, 55.
24. Kadar interview, Budapest Radio, 17 March 1971, cited in ibid., 41.
25. Rudolf L. Tokes, *Hungary's Negotiated Revolution: Economic Reform, Social Change, and Political Succession, 1957-1990* (Cambridge: Cambridge University Press, 1996), 104.
26. Ibid., 105.
27. Charles Gati refers to the period 1972-79 as Hungary's "lost years." See his *Hungary and the Soviet Bloc* (Durham: Duke University Press, 1986), 166.
28. Hutchings, *Soviet-East European Relations*, 65.
29. A. S. Bakhov, *Organizatsiia Varshavskogo dogovora* (The Organization of the Warsaw Pact) (Moscow: Nauka, 1971), 90, and N. N. Rodinov et al., eds., *Organizatsiia Varshavskogo dogovora, 1955-1979: Dokumenty i materially* (The Organization of the Warsaw Pact, 1955-1979: Documents and Materials) (Moscow: Politizdat, 1975), 114.
30. Richard Pipes, "Documentation," *Orbis*, Winter 1988, 29.
31. See *24th Congress of the CPSU, 30 March-9 April 1971: Documents* (Moscow: Novosti Press Agency, 1971), 13.
32. Hutchings, *Soviet-East European Relations*, 74.
33. *Scientia*, 6 February 1970, cited in Robin Alison Remington, *The Warsaw Pact: Case Studies in Communist Conflict Resolution* (Cambridge: MIT Press, 1971), 132.
34. See *Sovremennye problemy razoruzheniia* (Contemporary Problems of Disarmament) (Moscow: Mysl Publishing House, 1970).
35. Pipes, "Documentation," 29.
36. The Soviet press was replete with references to this point in the days and weeks surrounding the exercises. See Remington, *Warsaw Pact*, 155.
37. Richard F. Staar, ed., *Yearbook on International Communist Affairs, 1971* (Stanford: Hoover Institution Press, 1971), 82.
38. Hutchings, *Soviet-East European Relations*, 155.
39. Ibid., 160.
40. Ibid., 25-26.
41. Brown, *Eastern Europe*, 147.
42. *Kozgazdasagi Szmele* (Budapest), no. 6 (6 June 1975), quoted also in ibid., 113.
43. Robert R. King and James F. Brown, *Eastern Europe's Uncertain Future: A Selection of Radio Free Europe Research Reports* (New York: Praeger, 1977), 114.
44. Ibid.
45. Ibid.
46. Ibid., 88.
47. See Iu. Shiriaev, "Sotsialisticheskaia integratsiia i mezhdunarodnoe razdelenie truda" (Socialist Integration and the International Division of Labor), *MEIMO*, no. 1 (1975): 19.
48. Hutchings, *Soviet-East European Relations*, 83.
49. Iu. Shiriaev, "Sotsialisticheskaia integratsiia i mezhdunarodnaia ekonomicheskoe sotrudnichestvo" (Socialist Integration and International Economic Cooperation), *MEIMO*, no. 6 (1976): 20-23.
50. George R. Feiwel, "Economic Development and Planning in Bulgaria in the 1970s," in *The East European Economies in the 1970s*, ed. Alec Nove, Hans-Hermann Höhmann, and Gertraud Seidenstecher (London: Butterworths, 1982), 227-29.
51. Hungary actually began the trend during its 1961-65 plan, though its growth had stagnated by 1970.
52. Although differences between them narrowed everywhere except in East Germany.

53. Trend and Nikolaev, "Consumer Communism," 157.

54. I. Dudinskii, "Mirovaia sotsialisticheskaia sistema—novaia mezhdunarodnaia istoricheskaia obshchnost" (The World Socialist System—a New International Historical Community), *MEIMO*, no. 10 (1975): 22.

55. See, for example, Hutchings, *Soviet-East European Relations*, 162.

56. Shiriaev, "Sotsialisticheskaia integratsiia i mezhdunarodnaia ekonomicheskoe sotrudnichestvo," 20.

57. Hutchings, *Soviet-East European Relations*, 162–63.

58. Ibid., 164–65.

59. Raymond L. Garthoff, *Détente and Confrontation: American-Soviet Relations from Nixon to Reagan*, rev. ed. (Washington, D.C.: Brookings Institution, 1994), 527.

60. These included "respect for sovereignty and sovereign equality, nonresort to the threat or use of force, inviolability of frontiers, territorial integrity, peaceful settlement of disputes, nonintervention in internal affairs, respect for human rights and fundamental freedoms, equal rights and self-determination of peoples, cooperation among states, and fulfillment of international obligations." See ibid.

61. Ibid., 527–28.

62. Kevin Devlin, "Communism in Europe: The Challenge of Eurocommunism," *Problems of Communism* 26, no. 1 (January–February 1977): 3.

63. Stepanov, "Proletarskii internatsionalizm," 24.

64. "Conference of the Communist Parties of Europe: A Declaration by M. Azcarate," *Mundo Obrero*, 25 November 1975, cited in Devlin, "Communism in Europe," 8.

65. J. F. Brown, Charles Andras, and Kevin Devlin, "The Major External Influences: The Soviet Union, East-West Cooperation, and Eurocommunism," in King and Brown, *Eastern Europe's Uncertain Future*, 26.

66. Ibid., 27.

67. *L'Humanité*, 1 July 1976, cited in Devlin, "Communism in Europe," 16; Yu. Stepanov, "Proletarskii internatsionalizm—vazhneishii printsip marksizma-leninizma" (Proletarian Internationalism—the Most Important Principle of Marxism-Leninsim), *MEIMO*, no. 11 (1976): 24.

68. Anatoly Dobrynin, *In Confidence: Moscow's Ambassador to America's Six Cold War Presidents (1962–1986)* (New York: Times Books, 1995), 345.

69. Ibid., 345–46.

70. Ibid., 346.

71. Ibid.

72. *La Stampa*, 8 December 1976, cited in Brown, Andras, and Devlin, "Major External Influences," 29.

73. Heneghan, "Civil Rights Dissent in Eastern Europe," 230.

74. Romania did not enjoy the same preferential treatment, no doubt thanks to Ceausescu's independent foreign policies. Moscow charged world market prices for deliveries of oil to the Romanians.

75. George W. Hoffman, "Energy Dependence and Policy Options in Eastern Europe," in Robert G. Jensen, Theodore Shabad, and Arthur W. Wright, *Soviet Natural Resources in the World Economy* (Chicago: University of Chicago Press, 1983), 661.

76. Brown, *Eastern Europe*, 125.

77. Martin J. Kohn, "Soviet-East European Economic Relations, 1975–78," in Joint Economic Committee, *Soviet Economy in a Time of Change*, vol. 1 (Washington, D.C.: Government Printing Office, 1979), 250–53.

78. Brown, *Eastern Europe*, 127.

79. Moscow eventually stepped in with low-cost, 2.5–3 percent loans to many East European governments in the early 1980s, particularly Poland, the GDR, and Bulgaria. See ibid., 138.

80. Speaking with Soviet foreign minister Eduard Shevardnadze in 1987, Afghan president Nadjibulla admitted that "in April 1978 what transpired in Afghanistan

was not at all a revolution and not even an uprising, but a coup." Quoted in G. M. Kornienko, *Kholodnaia voina: Svidetel'stvo ee uchastnika* (The Cold War: Testimony of Its Participant) (Moscow: Mezhdunarodnye Otnosheniia, 1995), 189.

81. Ibid.

82. Ibid.

83. Vladimir Bukovskii, *Moskovskii Protsess* (Moscow Process) (Moscow: Russkaia Mysl', 1996), 296–97. Bukovskii gained access to hundreds of archival records from the TsKhSD and the APRF, lengthy excerpts from which he provides in his book along with his own commentary.

84. Ibid.

85. Ibid., 299.

86. Ibid., 300.

87. Ibid., 301.

88. Numerous political observers have speculated that these two motives might have driven the Soviet decision to invade Afghanistan.

89. Bukovskii, *Moskovskii Protsess*, 305.

90. In separate discussions with Defense Minister Dmitrii Ustinov, Deputy Prime Minister Hafizullah Amin had offered the same warning. Ibid., 306.

91. Ibid., 307.

92. Ibid.

93. Ibid., 308.

94. Ibid. Brezhnev remained ill throughout this period and thus was not present for these discussions. See ibid., 296.

95. Kornienko, *Kholodnaia voina*, 192.

96. Ibid.

97. Bukovskii, *Moskovskii Protsess*, 315.

98. Ibid., 309. See also Kornienko, *Kholodnaia voina*, 191.

99. Bukovskii, *Moskovskii Protsess*, 316–17.

100. The former Soviet ambassador to the United States, Anatoly Dobrynin, recalls in his memoirs: "The KGB became more and more deeply involved. Our secret service did not trust Amin and considered him a CIA agent who might turn to the Americans for help (he had studied at Columbia University). That was the essence of the KGB reports to the Politburo." See *In Confidence*, 436.

101. Kornienko, *Kholodnaia voina*, 193.

102. Ibid., 195.

103. R. A. Medvedev, "Pod kontrolem naroda" (Under the Control of the People), *Voenno-Istoricheskii Zhurnal*, no. 2 (March–April 1999): 70.

104. Garthoff, *Détente and Confrontation*, 1032. Garthoff cites Major General Zia Yusif-zade, "Protecting the Country and the People," *Bakinskii rabochii*, 19 December 1980, along with Gaidar Aliev, *Bakinskii rabochii*, 25 December 1980.

105. The KGB had sent Lieutenant Colonel Mikhail Talebov to Kabul in the late fall with instructions to poison Amin, but his efforts had failed. See Christopher Andrew and Oleg Gordievsky, *KGB: The Inside Story* (New York: Harper Perennial, 1990), 574.

106. Medvedev, "Pod kontrolem naroda," 69.

107. Kornienko, *Kholodnaia voina*, 196. See Garthoff, *Détente and Confrontation*, 954, for a discussion of this move by NATO.

108. Bukovskii, *Moskovskii Protsess*, 320. Absent members Dinmukhamed Kunaev (first secretary of Kazakhstan), Grigori Romanov (first secretary of the Leningrad Oblast), and Vladimir Shcherbitskiy (first secretary of Ukraine) each had to sign the resolution prior to the start of hostilities. This assertion by Bukovskii, on the strength of archival evidence, calls into question earlier assertions by Eduard Shevardnadze that nonvoting candidate members of the Politburo were not consulted on the decision to invade. Indeed, he argues that he and Mikhail Gorbachev both heard about the invasion for the first time from the national

news reports after it had already begun. See *International Herald Tribune*, 24 October 1989. Kornienko writes that the Central Committee later approved the invasion decision at its regularly scheduled plenum in June 1980. "To my surprise," he notes, "after some brief information, not only did no one voice any doubts about the decision that had been taken, but no one even asked a single question about what was happening—everyone voted with one voice: 'approved.'" See Kornienko, *Kholodnaia voina*, 197.

109. Andrew and Gordievsky, *KGB*, 575.

110. Medvedev, "Pod kontrolem naroda," 68.

111. Garthoff, *Détente and Confrontation*, 1020.

112. Ibid., 1022.

113. Vladimir Kuzichkin, "Coups and Killing in Kabul," *Time*, 22 November 1982.

114. Garthoff, *Détente and Confrontation*, 1022.

115. Andrew and Gordievsky, *KGB*, 575.

116. Garthoff, *Détente and Confrontation*, 1021.

117. Kornienko, *Kholodnaia voina*, 197.

118. Garthoff, *Détente and Confrontation*, 1022.

119. In the words of Grigorii Kornienko, "The negative international consequences for the Soviet Union in the broad context of the 'Cold War' turned out to be clearly more serious and long-lasting than those who had taken the fatal decision to send Soviet troops into Afghanistan had anticipated." See *Kholodnaia voina*, 196–97.

120. Donald W. Treadgold, *Twentieth-Century Russia*, 7th ed. (Boulder: Westview, 1990), 489.

121. See Glenn R. Chafetz, *Gorbachev, Reform, and the Brezhnev Doctrine: Soviet Policy toward Eastern Europe, 1985–1990* (Westport: Praeger, 1993), 33.

122. Brown, *Eastern Europe*, 94.

123. Medvedev, "Pod kontrolem naroda," 73.

124. Kornienko, *Kholodnaia voina*, 199.

125. Ibid., 198.

126. Hutchings, *Soviet–East European Relations*, 94.

Chapter Four

1. See Norman Davies, *Heart of Europe: A Short History of Poland* (New York: Oxford University Press, 1983), 3.

2. See Zbigniew K. Brzezinski, *The Soviet Bloc: Unity and Conflict*, rev. and enl. ed. (London: Oxford University Press, 1967), 223.

3. At the time Soviet marshal Konstanty Rokossowski was a member of the Polish Politburo, deputy premier, and minister of national defense. Sent after World War II to Poland by Stalin, he was made a citizen of Poland in 1949. He joined the Politburo in 1950 and became deputy premier in 1952. He was expelled from the PZPR CC and Politburo in October 1956 and recalled to the USSR in November 1956. Back in Moscow he became deputy minister of national defense. See L. W. Gluchowski, "Poland, 1956: Khrushchev, Gomulka, and the 'Polish October,'" *Cold War International History Project Bulletin*, no. 5 (Spring 1995): 38 n.

4. Secret notes from the discussions of 11 and 12 January 1957 between the delegates of the Chinese People's Republic and Poland, Archiwum Akt Nowych, Warsaw, KC PZPR (PZPR CC), pac. 107, tom 5, str. (pages) 83, 85–88, 93–95, cited in ibid., 44.

5. Ibid.

6. Nikita Khrushchev, *Khrushchev Remembers: The Glasnost Tapes*, trans. and ed. Jerold L. Schecter, with Vyacheslav W. Luchkov (Boston: Little, Brown, 1990), 115.

7. See Jacek Kuron, *Wiara i wina: Do i od komunizmu* (Belief and Guilt: Before and after Communism) (Warsaw: BGW, 1990), 119, cited in Mark Kramer, "Hungary and Poland, 1956: Khrushchev's CPSU CC Presidium Meeting on East European Crises, 24 October 1956," *Cold War International History Project Bulletin*, no. 5 (Spring 1995): 51.

8. T. Rakowska-Harmstone, Christopher Jones, and Ivan Sylvian, *Warsaw Pact: The Question of Cohesion, Phase II*, vol. 2, *Poland, German Democratic Republic, and Romania* (Ottawa: ORAE Extra-Mural Paper no. 33, November 1984), 66. See also Andrew A. Michta, *Red Eagle: The Army in Polish Politics, 1944–1988* (Stanford: Hoover Institution Press, 1990), 51.

9. Michta, *Red Eagle*, 51.

10. From a report presented by Czechoslovak Party leader Antonín Novotný to the Czechoslovak Politburo titled "Zprava o jednani na UV KSSS 24. rijna 1956 k situaci v Polsku a Mad'arsku" (Report of the CPSU CC Session on 24 October 1956 concerning the Situation in Poland and Hungary) (Statni ustredni archiv [SUA] Fond 07/16, Svazek 3), cited in ibid., 54. Novotný was present at the Soviet Politburo meeting at which Khrushchev reported on the situation in Poland and Hungary in October 1956.

11. The first article of the 1956 Soviet-Polish Treaty on the Legal Status of Soviet Troops Temporarily Stationed in Poland reads, "The temporary stationing of Soviet troops in Poland will in no way infringe on the sovereignty of the Polish State and can not lead to their interference in the internal affairs of the Polish People's Republic." See "Dogovor mezhdu pravitel'stvom Soiuza Sovetskikh Sotsialisticheskikh Respublik i pravitel'stvom Pol'skoi Narodnoi Respubliki o pravovom statuse Sovetskikh voinsk, vremenno nakhodiashchikhsia v Pol'she" (Treaty between the Government of the Union of Soviet Socialist Republics and the Government of the Polish People's Republic on the Legal Status of Soviet Troops Temporarily Located in Poland), in Ministry of Foreign Affairs of the USSR, *Sbornik deistvuiushchikh dogovorov soglashenii i konventsii zakliuchennykh SSSR s inostrannymi gosudarstvami: Vypusk XIX destvuiushchie dogovory, soglasheniia, i konventsii, vstupivshie v silu mezhdu 1 ianvaria i 31 dekabria 1957 goda* (Collection of Active Treaties, Agreements, and Conventions Concluded by the USSR with Foreign Governments: Issue XIX Active Treaties, Agreements, and Conventions Coming into Force between 1 January and 31 December 1957) (Moscow: Gosudarstvennoe izdatel'stvo politicheskoi literatury, 1960), 101.

12. Ibid.

13. Nicholas G. Andrews, *Poland, 1980–81: Solidarity versus the Party* (Washington, D.C.: National Defense University Press, 1985), 15.

14. J. F. Brown, *Eastern Europe and Communist Rule* (Durham: Duke University Press, 1988), 167–68.

15. Ryszard J. Kuklinski, "Wojna z narodem widziana od srodka" (War with the People Seen from the Center), *Kultura*, April 1987, 14, cited in Michta, *Red Eagle*, 68.

16. Ibid.

17. Official estimates put the death toll at forty-five, with unofficial reports suggesting far more. See Brown, *Eastern Europe*, 167. Colonel Ryszard Kuklinski puts the number of dead at 44 and wounded at 1,164. See Kuklinski, "Wojna z narodem," 14, cited in Michta, *Red Eagle*, 69.

18. Andrews, *Poland, 1980–81*, 16.

19. Michta, *Red Eagle*, 69.

20. Andrews, *Poland, 1980–81*, 16.

21. Michta, *Red Eagle*, 70. Michta notes that he draws some of his perspective from A. Ross Johnson, "Soviet Military Policy in Eastern Europe," in *Soviet Policy in Eastern Europe*, ed. Sarah Meiklejohn Terry (New Haven: Yale University Press, 1984), 267. On Brezhnev's dislike of Gomulka, he cites Adam Bromke, "Poland under Gierek: A New Political Style," *Problems of Communism*, September–October 1972, 14.

22. See Brown, *Eastern Europe*, 168, for a discussion of this point.

23. Timothy Garton Ash, *The Polish Revolution: Solidarity, 1980–82* (London: Jonathan Cape, 1983), 12–13.

24. Brown, *Eastern Europe*, 171.

25. Ibid., 172–74.

26. Garton Ash, *Polish Revolution*, 16.

27. Sarah Meiklejohn Terry, "The Future of Poland: Perestroika or Perpetual Crisis," in *Central and Eastern Europe: The Opening Curtain?*, ed. William E. Griffith (Boulder: Westview, 1989), 183.

28. Garton Ash, *Polish Revolution*, 16–17.

29. Michta writes that "according to a story circulated in Poland after the confrontation, when asked for the military's help, stiff-lipped Jaruzelski allegedly informed Gierek that, 'Polish soldiers would never fire at Polish workers.' Whether this story is true or not, it is clear that the 1976 crisis did not escalate to the point where a direct intervention of the armed forces was needed to restore order." Cited from an interview between Dale Herspring and former Polish officers from 1978 in A. Ross Johnson, Robert W. Dean, and Alexander Alexiev, *East European Military Establishments: The Warsaw Pact Northern Tier* (New York: Crane Russak, 1980), 61; see Michta, *Red Eagle*, 72.

30. Michta, *Red Eagle*, 71–72.

31. Josef Paestka, *Pol'skii Krizis 1980–1981gg.: Chto k nemu prevelo i chemu on uchit* (The Polish Crisis, 1980–1981: What Led to It and What It Teaches), trans. from the Polish (Moscow: Progress, 1981), 38.

32. Andrews, *Poland, 1980–81*, 20.

33. Adam Michnik, *Letters from Prison and Other Essays* (Berkeley: University of California Press, 1985), 144.

34. Garton Ash, *Polish Revolution*, 18.

35. Adam Bromke, "Opposition in Poland," *Problems of Communism*, September–October 1978, 49.

36. Marek Turbacz, "Mozliwościdzilania opozycji w Polsce" (Possibilities for Opposition Activities in Poland), *Aneks*, nos. 16–17 (1977): 22–23.

37. Peter Raina, *Independent Social Movements in Poland* (London: L.S.E./Orbis, 1981), 373.

38. Ibid., 374.

39. Garton Ash, *Polish Revolution*, 23–24.

40. Ibid.

41. Raina, *Independent Social Movements in Poland*, 379.

42. *Le Figaro*, 9 October 1979.

43. See Terry, "Future of Poland," 188–89.

44. *Le Figaro*, 10 June 1980.

45. Translated in Jack Bielasiak, ed., *Poland Today: The State of the Republic* (Armonk, N.Y.: M. E. Sharpe, 1981), 77–78.

46. Garton Ash, *Polish Revolution*, 31.

47. Paestka, *Pol'skii Krizis*, 22.

48. Figures cited in Wlodzimerz Brus, "Aims, Methods, and Political Determinants of the Economic Policy of Poland, 1970–80," in *The East European Economies in the 1970s*, ed. Alec Nove, Hans-Hermann Höhmann, and Gertraud Seidenstecher (London: Butterworths, 1982), 95.

49. Ibid.

50. *Politika*, no. 15 (9 April 1977): 4, cited in ibid., 101.

51. Brus, "Aims, Methods, and Political Determinants," 106. Figures are given in terms of current prices.

52. Figures cited in Wlodzimerz Brus, "Economics and Politics: The Fatal Link," in *Poland: Genesis of a Revolution*, ed. Abraham Brumberg (New York: Random House, 1983), 38–39.

53. Jozef Kusmirek, "O czym wiedzialem" (Things I Have Known), published originally in the KOR journal *Krytyka*, no. 3 (Winter 1978/1979); translated and reproduced in Brumberg, *Poland*, 145.

54. Paestka, *Pol'skii Krizis*, 21.

55. Vladimir Wozniuk, *From Crisis to Crisis: Soviet-Polish Relations in the 1970s* (Ames: Iowa State University Press, 1987), 82.

56. Garton Ash, *Polish Revolution*, 16. In terms of indebtedness per capita, in 1979 Poland actually ranked third ($527 per capita) behind Hungary ($660 per capita) and East Germany ($547 per capita). See Brus, "Economics and Politics," 27.

57. Brus, "Aims, Methods, and Political Determinants," 130–31.

58. *New York Times*, 29 September 1979, 26.

59. Brus, "Aims, Methods, and Political Determinants," 129, 131–32.

60. Robert L. Hutchings, *Soviet–East European Relations: Consolidation and Conflict* (Madison: University of Wisconsin Press, 1983), 200.

61. Paestka, *Pol'skii Krizis*, 31.

62. Ibid., 39–40.

63. General A. I. Gribkov, interview by author, Moscow, 29 August 1995. I am indebted to General Gribkov, the former chief of staff of the Soviet Armed Forces, for providing me with his own annotated copy of Paestka's book.

64. See the commentary of Yurii Stepanovich Novopashin in Jonathan Valdez, *Internationalism and the Ideology of Soviet Influence in Eastern Europe* (Cambridge: Cambridge University Press, 1993), 52–53. Notwithstanding this complaint, Novopashin points out that it was important to Bogomolov that the institute's warnings be on record. The reports submitted in the late 1970s, though largely ignored by the Politburo, protected Bogomolov and his scholars from another shake-up following the events of 1980–81.

65. R. A. Medvedev, "Pod kontrolem naroda" (Under the Control of the People), *Voenno-Istoricheskii Zhurnal*, no. 2 (March–April 1999): 69–70.

66. Carl Bernstein and Marco Politi, *His Holiness: John Paul II and the Hidden History of Our Time* (New York: Doubleday, 1996), 9. While the central assertion of this work, that Pope John Paul II actively collaborated with the Reagan administration to bring down communism around the world, remains highly controversial, it does contain a number of very useful interviews conducted by the authors with former Soviet and East European policymakers.

67. Christopher Andrew and Vasili Mitrokhin, *The Sword and the Shield: The Mitrokhin Archive and the Secret History of the KGB* (New York: Basic, 1999), 269.

68. St. Stanislaw was a bishop in the city of Kraków in the eleventh century. After he excommunicated King Boleslaus, the king had him killed. As a result, Pope Gregory VII put Poland under interdict, prompting King Boleslaus to fall from power. St. Stanislaw later became the patron saint of Poland.

69. Bogdan Szajkowski, *Next to God . . . Poland: Politics and Religion in Contemporary Poland* (New York: St. Martin's, 1983), 63.

70. John Paul II, *The Redeemer of Man*, encyclical letter of His Holiness Pope John Paul II (Boston: St. Paul Editions, 1979), 37–38.

71. Tad Szultc, *Pope John Paul II: The Biography* (New York: Scribner, 1995), 299.

72. See George Weigel, *The Final Revolution: The Resistance Church and the Collapse of Communism* (New York: Oxford University Press, 1992), 130.

73. Cited in ibid., 132.

74. John Paul II, *Pilgrim to Poland, John Paul II* (Boston: St. Paul Editions, 1979), 208–9.

75. Ibid.

76. Szajkowski, *Next to God*, 72.

77. Janusz Onyszkiewicz, interview by George Weigel, Warsaw, 10 June 1991, quoted in Weigel, *Final Revolution*, 134.

78. Garton Ash, *Polish Revolution*, 30.

79. Andrew and Mitrokhin, *Sword and the Shield*, 513.

80. TsKhSD, f. 89, per. 32, no. 13, "O merakh po protivodeistviiu politike Vatikana v otnoshenii sotsialisticheskikh stran" (Concerning the Measures for Opposing Vatican Policy regarding the Socialist Countries), 13 November 1979, 21–26. This file contains Soviet KGB, Politburo, and Central Committee documents pertaining to Vatican policy dating from September 1979 to September 1980.

81. Ibid., 25–26.

82. Ibid., 4.

83. Ibid.

84. *Litaunus*, no. 4 (1972): 55–69, cited in Alexis Ulysses Floridi, S.J., *Moscow and the Vatican* (Ann Arbor: Ardis Publishers, 1986), 164.

85. Andrew and Mitrokhin, *Sword and the Shield*, 500.

86. Ibid., 503, 513.

87. Ibid., 513–14.

88. TsKhSD, "O merakh po protivodeistviiu politike Vatikana," 5.

89. Ibid., 5–6.

90. Ibid.

91. Ibid., 2–3, 16. The "eyes-only" sections were sent only to Yurii Andropov, Andrei Gromyko, Boris Ponomarev, Mikhail Zimianin, Konstantin Rusakov, Vladimir Kuroedov, Leonid Zamiatin, and E. Tiazhel'nikov.

92. Christel Lane, *Christian Religion in the Soviet Union: A Sociological Study* (London: George Allen and Unwin, 1978), 209.

93. TsKhSD, "O merakh po protivodeistviiu politike Vatikana," 2–3, 16.

94. Ibid., 1. It should be noted that the "eyes-only" sections were not sent to these parties.

95. Ibid., 30–31.

96. Ibid., 32.

97. Ibid., 33.

98. Ibid., 35.

99. I. Grigulevich, "Prisposablivaias' k deistvitel'nosti" (Accommodating to Reality: Religion in Today's World), *Sovetskaia Latviia*, 14 May 1980; *Pravda Ukrainy*, 20 May 1980; *Kommunist*, 14 June 1980; *Kommunist Tadzhikistana*, 6 July 1980; and *Sovetskaia Litva*, 24 September 1980.

100. Grigulevich, "Prisposablivaias' k deistvitel'nosti"; translated in "Assessing Catholicism under John Paul II," *Current Digest of the Soviet Press* 32, no. 22 (2 July 1980): 8.

101. Ibid., 9.

102. TsKhSD, "O merakh po protivodeistviiu politike Vatikana," 28. The secretaries involved were, respectively, E. Tiazhel'nikov, L. Zamiatin, and A. Cherniaev.

103. Ibid., 38.

104. Claire Sterling, "The Plot to Murder the Pope," *Reader's Digest*, September 1982, 82–83.

105. Claire Sterling, "Bulgaria Hired Agca to Kill Pope, Report of Italian Prosecutor Says," *New York Times*, 10 June 1984, and Bernstein and Politi, *His Holiness*, 299.

106. Nicholas Gage, "The Attack on the Pope: New Link to Bulgarians," *New York Times*, 23 March 1983.

107. Bernstein and Politi, *His Holiness*, 306–7.

108. Sterling, "Bulgaria Hired Agca to Kill Pope."

109. Nicholas Gage, "Bulgarian Agents Described as Ready to Do Moscow's Bidding," *New York Times*, 23 March 1983.

110. This resulted after a high-ranking KGB officer defected to the West, prompting the expulsion of 105 Soviets from Great Britain. See ibid.

111. Christopher Andrew and Oleg Gordievsky, *KGB: The Inside Story* (New York: Harper Perennial, 1990), 639–40.

112. Andrew and Mitrokhin, *Sword and the Shield*, 522.

113. Bernstein and Politi, *His Holiness*, 298.

114. Andrzej Paczkowski, "Poland, the 'Enemy Nation,'" in Stephane Courtois et al., *The Black Book of Communism: Crimes, Terror, Repression*, trans. Jonathan Murphy and Mark Kramer (Cambridge: Harvard University Press, 1999), 272; Vladimir Abarinov, *The Murderers of Katyn* (New York: Hippocrene Books, 1993), 371–72; and

Keith Sword, *Deportation and Exile: Poles in the Soviet Union, 1939–48* (New York: St. Martin's, 1995), 25–27.

115. See Natal'ia Lebedeva, *Katyn': Prestuplenie protiv chelovechestva* (Katyn: Crime against Humanity) (Moscow: Progress Kultura, 1994), 318.

116. *New York Times*, 9 February 1941.

117. Sword, *Deportation and Exile*, 22–23.

118. The assertion belongs to Iwo Cyprian Pogonowski, writing in Abarinov, *Murderers of Katyn*, 372.

119. Lebedeva, *Katyn'*, 312. Lebedeva asserts that the arrests were by no means a simple coincidence of the invasion. The lists of those to be arrested had been prepared prior to the Soviet invasion of September 1939.

120. TsKhSD, f. 89, per. 14, nos. 1–20, 10. (This collection includes a number of documents with separate titles, all of which pertain to the Katyn issue.) Note that the exact numbers included 14,736 in prisoner of war (POW) camps, 97 percent of whom were Polish, and 18,632 in special NKVD camps, 10,632 of whom were Polish. This meant the Beria had over 25,000 prisoners in mind when drafting his dispatch to Stalin. Although all were sentenced to execution, a later report, drafted almost exactly nineteen years later on 3 March 1959, states that the number of those executed was 21,857. It is believed that some of the prisoners were separated from the rest before the executions and allowed to live. These were targeted for communist indoctrination (largely unsuccessful) and later became the core of the Polish communist army and government. However, the number of those spared is placed at only a few hundred. (See Salomon W. Slowes, *The Road to Katyn: A Soldier's Story*, ed. Wladyslaw T. Bartoszewski, trans. Naftali Greenwood [Oxford: Blackwell, 1992], xvi.) Therefore, it is not clear why such a large discrepancy exists between the 1939 and 1959 KGB statistics.

121. TsKhSD, f. 89, per. 14, nos. 1–20, 5.

122. There is no indication of where the remaining three full members of the Politburo—Andreyev, Khrushchev, and Zhdanov—stood on the issue. Their names do not appear anywhere on the document.

123. Abarinov, *Murderers of Katyn*, 373.

124. Nicholas Bethell, "Officers Were Shot One by One—at a Rate of 250 a Night," *Observer*, 6 October 1991.

125. According to Andrzej Paczkowski, the number of Polish military personnel liquidated in these executions numbered 14,587. Of the roughly 11,000 remaining prisoners from a variety of professions, he estimates that 7,305 were shot. The resulting figure of 21,892 roughly approximates the official Soviet indications from 1959 of 21,857 killed. See Paczkowski, "Poland, the 'Enemy Nation,' " 370.

126. Abarinov, *Murderers of Katyn*, 375.

127. Mikhail Heller and Aleksandr M. Nekrich, *Utopia in Power: The History of the Soviet Union from 1917 to the Present* (New York: Summit Books, 1986), 403.

128. At this point attention focused on the missing military officers. It was only after the release of Soviet archival documents that historians discovered the fate of the many thousands of other victims who died alongside the soldiers.

129. J. K. Zawodny, *Death in the Forest: The Story of the Katyn Forest Massacre* (South Bend: University of Notre Dame Press, 1962), 10.

130. *Izvestiia*, 16 April 1943.

131. Louis FitzGibbon, *Katyn: A Crime without Parallel* (London: Tom Stacey, 1971), 128–29, and Heller and Nekrich, *Utopia in Power*, 404.

132. Louis FitzGibbon, *Unpitied and Unknown* (London: Bachman and Turner, 1975), 56, cited in Slowes, *Road to Katyn*, xix.

133. Winston Churchill, *The Second World War* (Boston: Houghton Mifflin, 1948–53), 4:761.

134. Interim Report of the U.S. Congressional Select Committee, 2 July 1952; reproduced in FitzGibbon, *Katyn*, 201.

135. Slowes, *Road to Katyn*, xxvii.

136. TsKhSD, f. 89, per. 14, nos. 1–20, 12–13.

137. Ibid., 13–14. The destruction order from the Politburo was handwritten as well. Marked "project top secret," it bears no date or signature, only the attestation "Decree of the Presidium of the CC CPSU."

138. TsKhSD, f. 89, per. 14, nos. 1–20, Démarche for the Soviet Ambassador in London, with Copy Sent to the Soviet Ambassador in Warsaw, 15–16.

139. Ibid., 18–23.

140. Ibid., 24.

141. Ibid.

142. Ibid., 27.

143. Perhaps worried about the potentially explosive nature of the rally, the local bishop refused to permit a Mass to be held at the demonstration in memory of those slain in the Katyn affair. Poles ought to pray for all their compatriots who perished in the war, the episcopate argued, and not only for the victims of Katyn. Ibid.

144. TsKhSD, f. 89, per. 67, no. 4, "Spravka Genkonsul'stva SSSR 'Ob antisovetskoi aktsii antisotsialisticheskikh grupp v Shchetsine v aprele 1980 goda'" (Concerning the Anti-Soviet Actions of Antisocialist Groups in Szczecin in April 1980). Note that the foregoing description of the meeting is drawn from Timofeev's report.

145. Ibid., 2.

146. TsKhSD, f. 89, per. 67, no. 3, "Informatsiia Genkonsul'stva SSSR v Gdan'ske 'Ob Antisovetskom Sborishche v Gdanske 3 maia 1980 goda'" (Information of the General Consul of the USSR concerning an Anti-Soviet Mob in Gdansk on 3 May 1980), 1.

147. Ibid., 2.

148. *L'Humanité*, 3–4 August 1980, 4.

Chapter Five

1. Soviet discussions lump Solidarity together with KOR and Poland's other dissident movements into a single "opposition" camp. Consequently, I will refer to Solidarity and the Polish opposition interchangeably. While differences certainly existed among the respective groups that came together under the Solidarity umbrella, their collective opposition to many elements of the existing system did merit this generalization.

2. Nicholas G. Andrews, *Poland, 1980–81: Solidarity versus the Party* (Washington, D.C.: National Defense University Press, 1985), 25.

3. Vladimir Wozniuk, *From Crisis to Crisis: Soviet-Polish Relations in the 1970s* (Ames: Iowa State University Press, 1987), 13.

4. Daniel Singer, *The Road to Gdansk* (New York: Monthly Review Press, 1981), 213–17. It should be noted that at the time of the strikes the Polish workweek, as elsewhere in the communist world, was six days long, running from Monday through Saturday.

5. "Minutes no. 13 of the Meeting of the [PZPR] Political Bureau, July 18, 1980," in *Poland, 1980–1982: Internal Crisis, International Dimensions*, Compendium of Declassified Documents and Chronology of Events Prepared for an International Conference in Jachranka, Poland, by the Institute for Political Studies of the Polish Academy of Sciences, the National Security Archive at George Washington University, and the Cold War International History Project at the Woodrow Wilson Center, November 1997.

6. Timothy Garton Ash, *The Polish Revolution: Solidarity, 1980–82* (London: Jonathan Cape, 1983), 34.

7. *Foreign Broadcast Information Service [FBIS] Daily Report, Eastern Europe*, 24 July 1980, D3; *FBIS Daily Report, Soviet Union*, 22 July 1980, F1.

8. TsKhSD, f. 89, per. 66, no. 2, "Postanovlenie Politbiuro TsK—o tezisakh dlia besedy

s predstavitelem pol'skogo rukovodstva" (Resolution of the CC Politburo— concerning the Theses for a Meeting with a Representative of the Polish Government), 3 September 1980, in "Dokumenty 'Komissii Suslova'. Sobytiia v Pol'she v 1981 g.," *Novaia i Noveishaia Istoriia*, no. 1 (1994): 89.

9. *Der Spiegel*, 4 August 1980, cited in *FBIS Daily Report, Eastern Europe*, 6 August 1980, G3–G5.

10. Andrews, *Poland, 1980–81*, 27–28.

11. Peter Raina, *Independent Social Movements in Poland* (London: L.S.E./Orbis, 1981), 486–88.

12. Garton Ash, *Polish Revolution*, 44.

13. *Pravda*, 15 August 1980.

14. It was rumored that a Party faction led by Kania took over effective control of the government from Gierek as early as 16 August, leaving the latter as first secretary in name alone. See *Nowe Drogi*, nos. 10–11 (October–November 1980): 46.

15. Garton Ash, *Polish Revolution*, 48.

16. Wojciech Gielzynski and Lech Stefanski, *Gdansk. Sierpien '80* (Warsaw: KiW, 1981), 66–67.

17. Garton Ash, *Polish Revolution*, 48.

18. "Protokol Nr. 28 z posiedzenia Biura Politycznego KC PZPR 29 sierpnia 1980 r." (Protocol no. 28 from a Meeting of the PZPR CC Politburo 29 August 1980), 29 August 1980 (Secret), in *Tajne Dokumenty Biura Politycznego: PZPR a "Solidarnosc" 1980–1981* (Secret Documents of the Polituburo: PZPR vs. Solidarity, 1980–1981), ed. Zbigniew Wlodek (London: Aneks, 1992), 84–90.

19. "Minutes no. 26 of the Meeting of the Politburo of the Central Committee of the Polish United Workers' Party, August 27, 1980," 6, in *Poland, 1980–1982*.

20. "Posiedzenie Sztabu MSW, 29.VIII.1980 r." (Staff Meeting of the Interior Ministry, 29 August 1980), 29 August 1980 (Top Secret), in Archiwum Urzedu Ochrony Panstva (AUOP), Sygnatura 2309/IV, tom 2, stonica 1, cited in Mark Kramer, "'In Case Military Assistance Is Provided to Poland': Soviet Preparations for Military Contingencies, August 1980," *Cold War International History Project Bulletin*, no. 11 (Winter 1998): 103.

21. See Bruce Porter, "Phases in the USSR's Response to the Labor Unrest in Poland," *Radio Liberty* 71/81, 17 February 1981.

22. Cited in *FBIS Daily Report, Eastern Europe*, 26 August 1980, D5–D6.

23. Stanislaw Kania, *Zatrzymac konfrontacje* (To Stop Confrontation) (Warsaw: Polska Oficyna Wydawnicza "BGW," 1991), 33–34.

24. TsKhSD, f. 89, per. 66, no. 1, "Postanovlenie Politbiuro TsK k voprosu o polozhenii v PNR" (Resolution of the CC Politburo on the Question of the Situation in the PPR), 25 August 1980, 1.

25. Kramer, "'In Case Military Assistance Is Provided to Poland,' 108.

26. *Kommunist*, no. 8 (1980).

27. Garton Ash, *Polish Revolution*, 58–59.

28. *Solidarnosc*, no. 8, the newsletter of the new independent labor movement, cited in *Labor Focus on Eastern Europe* 4, nos. 1–3 (Spring–Autumn 1980): 22.

29. *Radio Free Europe Polish Situation Report 16*, 1980.

30. Garton Ash, *Polish Revolution*, 66.

31. *Labor Focus*, 47.

32. *Pravda*, 1 September 1980.

33. *FBIS Daily Report, Eastern Europe*, 3 September 1980, E1.

34. Ibid., 9 September 1980, D1.

35. *Izvestiia*, 6 September 1980, cited in Wozniuk, *From Crisis to Crisis*, 105.

36. TsKhSD, "Postanovlenie Politbiuro TsK," 87.

37. Ibid.

38. Kramer, "'In Case Military Assistance Is Provided to Poland,'" 104.

39. TsKhSD, "Postanovlenie Politbiuro TsK," 88.

40. Ibid.

41. Ibid. It is interesting to compare this assertion with those of Paestka and the DiP discussed in the previous chapter. There is, quite clearly, a strong contrast between them.

42. Ibid., 89.

43. Reuters, 12 September 1980.

44. PAP, 13 September 1980, cited in *FBIS Daily Report, Eastern Europe*, 15 September 1980, G1.

45. TASS, 12 September 1980.

46. TsKhSD, f. 89, per. 67, no. 5, "Politzapiska Genkonsul'stva SSSR v Gdan'ske 'O sobytiiakh na Gdan'skom Poberezhe i v drugikh voevodstvakh Konsul'skogo Okruga v avguste 1980 goda' " (Political Assessment of the Consul General of the USSR in Gdansk concerning the Events on the Gdansk Waterfront and in Other Voivodships of the Consular District in August 1980), 15 September 1980.

47. Ibid., 2.

48. Ibid., 5.

49. Ibid., 13.

50. Ibid., 10. Vakhrameev's choice of words here was significant. The most memorable use of the term "dual power" in Soviet history is connected with the situation in Petrograd just prior to the October 1917 Bolshevik Revolution.

51. Ibid.

52. Ibid., 11.

53. Ibid., 16.

54. Ibid. As an addendum to the dispatch, Vakhrameev included the twenty-one demands of the Gdansk strike committee translated into Russian. See ibid., 17–18.

55. Garton Ash, *Polish Revolution*, 77.

56. *Pravda*, 20 September 1980. It is widely believed that the author A. Petrov was actually *Pravda* lead editor Viktor Afanasyev.

57. "Telegram from U.S. Ambassador to Moscow Thomas Watson to the Department of State, 'Polish Diplomat on Polish International Situation and Potential Soviet Response,' September 19, 1980," 2, in *Poland, 1980–1982*.

58. Ibid., 2–3.

59. TsKhSD, f. 89, per. 46, no. 59, "O nekotorykh dopolnitel'nykh merakh po organizatsii propagandy i kontrpropagandy v sviazi s sobytiiami v Pol'she" (Concerning a Number of Additional Measures for the Organization of Propaganda and Counterpropaganda in Connection with the Events in Poland), 4 October 1980, 6.

60. Ibid., 6–8.

61. Testimony of Colonel Ryszard Kuklinski in Richard Pipes, "Documentation," *Orbis*, Winter 1988, 15. This interview with Kuklinski originally appeared in 1986 in the Parisian Polish-language journal *Kultura*.

62. Garton Ash, *Polish Revolution*, 80.

63. "KKP ['Solidarity' National Coordination Commission] Statement, October 24, 1980," in *Poland, 1980–1982*.

64. Geremek, interview by Timothy Garton Ash, 4 November 1980, cited in Garton Ash, *Polish Revolution*, 81.

65. *Ljubljana Delo*, 25 October 1980, cited in *FBIS Daily Report, Eastern Europe*, 31 October 1980, D2.

66. Zbigniew Brzezinski, *Power and Principle: Memoirs of the National Security Advisor, 1977–1981* (New York: Farrar, Straus, Giroux, 1983), 464–65.

67. Jan B. de Weydenthal, Bruce D. Porter, and Kevin Devlin, *The Polish Drama, 1980–1982* (Lexington: Lexington Books, 1983), 110.

68. *Zolnierz Wolnosci*, 27 October 1980, cited in *FBIS Daily Report, Eastern Europe*, 13 November 1980, G2.

69. Figures cited in *Radio Free Europe Polish Situation Report 19*, 20 October 1980.

70. TsKhSD, f. 89, per. 42, no. 34, "Materialy k druzhestvennomu rabochemu vizitu v SSSR pol'skikh rukovoditelei" (Materials for the Friendly Working Visit of the Polish Leadership in the USSR), 29 October 1980, 1.

71. Ibid., 2.

72. Ibid.

73. Ibid., 2–3.

74. Kramer, " 'In Case Military Assistance Is Provided to Poland,' " 106.

75. The CIA at the time estimated that the Soviets would have to use as many as thirty divisions to invade a resistant Poland. See Robert M. Gates, *From the Shadows: The Ultimate Insider's Story of Five Presidents and How They Won the Cold War* (New York: Simon and Schuster, 1996), 163–64.

76. Apparently the preparations that had begun only days before in Warsaw had yet to be reported to Moscow.

77. TsKhSD, "Materialy k druzhestvennomu rabochemu vizitu," 3.

78. Soviet and East European studies of socialism in practice during this period did, and often still do, refer to it as "real socialism."

79. "Minutes no. 13 of the Meeting of the Secretariat of the Central Committee of the Polish United Workers' Party, October 25, 1980," in *Poland, 1980–1982*.

80. TsKhSD, "Materialy k druzhestvennomu rabochemu vizitu," 4.

81. Ibid., 5.

82. Ibid., 6.

83. Ibid. See also Wojciech Jaruzelski, with Marek Jaworski and Wlodzimierz Loznski, *Stan Wojenny Dlaczego . . .* (Why Martial Law) (Warsaw: Polska Oficyna Wydawnicza "BGW," 1992), 34.

84. A cut in deliveries to the other East European countries controverted the promise Premier Aleksei Kosygin had made to them in 1979 that Moscow would guarantee to maintain existing delivery levels in the years to come. See ibid.

85. *Pravda*, 31 October 1980.

86. TsKhSD, f. 89, per. 42, no. 35, "K itogam vizita v SSSR pervogo sekretaria Pol'skoi ob'edinennoi rabochei partii t. S. Kania i predsedatelia Soveta Ministrov PNR, t. Iu. Pinkovskogo" (Summing Up the Visit to the USSR of the First Secretary of the Polish United Workers Party Comrade S. Kania and the President of the PPR Soviet of Ministers Comrade Y. Pinkovski), 31 October 1980, 2.

87. Ibid.

88. Ibid.

89. Ibid., 3.

90. Ibid., 4.

91. Ibid., 3.

92. Ibid., 4.

93. TsKhSD, f. 89, per. 46, no. 81, "O nekotorykh dopolnitel'nykh merakh po kontroliu za rasprostraneniem pol'skoi pechati v SSSR" (Concerning Some Additional Measures for Controlling the Distribution of the Polish Press in the USSR), 4 October 1980, 105.

94. There were 150 such institutions in Moscow and an additional 80 outside Moscow. See ibid., 106.

95. Ibid.

96. Ibid., 106–8.

97. Ibid., 103.

98. Ibid., 102.

99. Garton Ash, *Polish Revolution*, 82.

100. Though Soviet troops were on a war footing near the Polish border, the footage used is believed to have come from earlier joint exercises, as was evident from the leaves on the trees in the footage—a rarity in November. Nevertheless, these films

have convinced some observers that the exercises were, in fact, going on at the time they were broadcast.

101. Garton Ash, *Polish Revolution*, 83.
102. Ibid., 84.
103. Ibid., 87.
104. Pipes, "Documentation," 15.
105. This "first-use" doctrine dated back to the 1950s at the time of the first deployments of U.S. tactical nuclear weapons in Europe.
106. Jaruzelski, *Stan Wojenny Dlaczego*, 35.
107. Garton Ash, *Polish Revolution*, 90.
108. TsKhSD, f. 89, per. 67, no. 6, "Spravka Genkonsul'stva SSSR v Gdanske 'O deiatel'nosti oppozitsionnykh elementov na Gdan'skom Poberezh"e v usloviiakh novoi obshchestvenno-politicheskoi situatsii' " (Information from the Consul General of the USSR in Gdansk concerning the Activities of Opposition Elements on the Gdansk Waterfront under the Conditions of the New Sociopolitical Situation), 25 November 1980, 5.
109. Ibid., 1.
110. Ibid., 2.
111. Warsaw Domestic Service Radio, 24 November 1980, cited in *FBIS Daily Report, Eastern Europe*, 26 November 1980, G1.
112. *Pravda*, 27 November 1980.
113. Garton Ash, *Polish Revolution*, 92–93.
114. Pipes, "Documentation," 16.
115. Ibid., 9, 12.
116. Ibid., 16.
117. Ibid.
118. Ibid., 17.
119. Ibid.
120. Kramer, " 'In Case Military Assistance Is Provided to Poland,' " 109 n.
121. A. I. Gribkov, "Doktrina Brezhneva i pol'skii krizis nachala 80-kh godov" (The Brezhnev Doctrine and the Polish Crisis of the Early 1980s), *Voenno-Istoricheskii Zhurnal* (Military History Journal), no. 9 (1992). See also *New York Times*, 11 November 1997, for Marshal Kulikov's assertions.
122. Gribkov, "Doktrina Brezhneva," 54. Note that members of the Soviet armed forces were often used as additional labor to bring in the autumn harvest.
123. Ibid., 53.
124. Ibid., 54.
125. Kania, *Zatrzymac konfrontacje*, 82.
126. "Transcript of the Meeting of the Politburo of the Central Committee of the Bulgarian Communist Party, October 21, 1980 [excerpts]," 3, in *Poland, 1980–1982*.
127. "Transcript of the Meeting of the Politburo of the Central Committee of the Bulgarian Communist Party, October 25, 1980 [excerpts]," 3, in *Poland, 1980–1982*.
128. TsKhSD, "Materialy k druzhestvennomu rabochemu vizitu," 5.
129. Deutsche Presse Agentur (Hamburg), 10 November 1980, cited in *FBIS Daily Report, Eastern Europe*, 10 November 1980, E2.
130. Kania, *Zatrzymac konfrontacje*, 82.
131. *Bratislava Pravda*, 1 November 1980, cited in *FBIS Daily Report, Eastern Europe*, 4 November 1980, D1.
132. *Rude Pravo*, 6 November 1980, cited in *FBIS Daily Report, Eastern Europe*, 10 November 1980, F2.
133. Kania, *Zatrzymac konfrontacje*, 83.
134. Ibid.
135. Garton Ash, *Polish Revolution*, 95.

136. Jaruzelski, *Stan Wojenny Dlaczego*, 36.

137. Ibid.

138. Gribkov, "Doktrina Brezhneva," 54.

139. Ibid.

140. It is not clear precisely how the Poles were advised of the new starting date for the exercises. Jaruzelski writes that Marshal Kulikov phoned Kania with the news on 3 December (see *Stan Wojenny Dlaczego*, 36). Kania's account, while confirming this date, states that it was General Jaruzelski who brought him the news after being informed by Kulikov (see *Zatrzymac konfrontacje*, 84).

141. Jaruzelski, *Stan Wojenny Dlaczego*, 37; Kania, *Zatrzymac konfrontacje*, 84.

142. Gribkov, "Doktrina Brezhneva," 54–55.

143. Kania, *Zatrzymac konfrontacje*, 84.

144. Pipes, "Documentation," 18.

145. Kania, *Zatrzymac konfrontacje*, 84.

146. Garton Ash, *Polish Revolution*, 95.

147. Kania, *Zatrzymac konfrontacje*, 85.

148. Ibid.

149. Research in the former East German state archives now confirms that Erich Honecker strongly advocated an invasion in the fall of 1980, convinced as he was that Solidarity represented a greater danger to socialism than had the Prague Spring. See "Stasi Documents Revealed: German Guns Were Ready," *Warsaw Voice*, 7 November 1993, 6. Interestingly, though, East Germany later rejected the notion that the Warsaw Pact had seriously considered invading Poland. The summit, it would come to admit, had been convened as "a substitute for intervention, a means of exerting maximum psychological pressure on Poland short of physical invasion." Garton Ash, *Polish Revolution*, 99.

150. U.S. ambassador to Yugoslavia, Lawrence Eagleburger, reported to Washington on 21 November 1980 that "Romania is adamantly opposed under any circumstances to outside intervention in Poland." He cited highly placed local sources to the effect that "Ceausescu's public comments in Romania which seemed to suggest possible Romanian support for intervention if the Polish party could not maintain control were designed exclusively for internal Romanian consumption." See "Telegram from U.S. Ambassador to Belgrade Lawrence Eagleburger to the Department of State, 'Ceausescu's Views on Outside Intervention in Poland,' " 3, in *Poland, 1980–1982*.

151. Jaruzelski, *Stan Wojenny Dlaczego*, 44–45. Jaruzelski writes: "After several years I discovered that before speaking with us, still on the evening of 4 December, all of the other delegations met. Then the decision was taken, but still not to invade. From unofficial information I know that the strongest opponents of intervention [were] we two sharply different figures, Kadar and Ceausescu, though the latter regarded the situation in Poland as especially grave. Honecker and Bilak took the most radical stance. What took place later in our presence was therefore above all a demonstration, pressure, a serious warning, but in our case, this was our first warning." Ibid.

152. Gribkov, "Doktrina Brezhneva," 55.

153. General A. I. Gribkov, interview by author, Moscow, 29 August 1995.

154. Ibid.

155. Szlachcic apparently failed to relay this information to Kania at the time. See Kania, *Zatrzymac konfrontacje*, 96.

156. *Cetka* in English, 3 December 1980, cited in Weydenthal, Porter, and Devlin, *Polish Drama*, 113.

157. Michael Dobbs, *Down with Big Brother: The Fall of the Soviet Empire* (New York: Alfred A. Knopf, 1997), 61.

158. Jaruzelski, *Stan Wojenny Dlaczego*, 37.

159. Brezhnev certainly had in mind a very specific understanding of "democracy," which revolved around the democratic centralism of Soviet-style Marxism-Leninism.

160. Kania, *Zatrzymac konfrontacje*, 89.

161. Jaruzelski, *Stan Wojenny Dlaczego*, 37.

162. "Stenographic Minutes of the Meeting of Leading Representatives of the Warsaw Pact Countries in Moscow, December 5, 1980," 3, in *Poland, 1980–1982*.

163. Ibid., 4.

164. Ibid., 4–5.

165. Jaruzelski, *Stan Wojenny Dlaczego*, 39. This statement does not appear in the stenographic minutes of the meeting. However, the translated minutes contain a number of ellipses suggesting missing material.

166. "Stenographic Minutes of the Meeting of Leading Representatives," 9.

167. Ibid., 12.

168. Ibid., 13.

169. Ibid., 14–15.

170. Ibid., 16–18.

171. Kania, *Zatrzymac konfrontacje*, 90.

172. Ibid., 91.

173. Jaruzelski, *Stan Wojenny Dlaczego*, 42.

174. Ibid.

175. Zbigniew Brzezinski, "White House Diary, 1980," *Orbis*, Winter 1998, 41, 43.

176. TASS International Service in Russian, 0815 GMT, 8 December 1980, cited in *FBIS Daily Report, Soviet Union*, 8 December 1980.

177. Sydney I. Ploss, *Moscow and the Polish Crisis: An Interpretation of Soviet Policies and Intentions* (Boulder: Westview, 1986), 48.

178. *Pravda*, 11 December 1980.

179. Weydenthal, Porter, and Devlin, *Polish Drama*, 114.

180. Radio Moscow and *Pravda*, 12 December 1980, cited in ibid., 115.

181. *Der Spiegel*, 15 December 1980.

182. *La Republica*, 11 December 1980, cited in *FBIS Daily Report, Eastern Europe*, 15 December 1980. The PCI had warned Moscow on 6 December not to invade Poland, implying that it would consider severing relations with the CPSU if this occurred. See *L'Unita*, 6 December 1980, cited in *FBIS Daily Report, Western Europe*, 10 December 1980.

183. Gribkov, "Doktrina Brezhneva," 55.

184. Garton Ash, *Polish Revolution*, 101. Significantly, it was on 14 December that the Rural Solidarity movement held its founding congress in Warsaw. Denied a farmers union in the court decision of 22 October that had ignited the "registration crisis," the movement met while awaiting a ruling on its appeal of this decision.

185. Radio Warsaw, 18 December 1980, cited in *Radio Free Europe: Polish Situation Report 23*, 20 December 1980.

186. *Frankfurter Allgemeine Zeitung*, 6 February 1980.

187. At this early point, in 1980, it is not clear whether détente with Europe would have collapsed as completely. On 29 October 1980, American NSC adviser Zbigniew Brzezinski wrote in his diary that "the Germans have told us at the Quad meeting [four-power conference with Britain, France, West Germany, and the United States] that détente should not be victim of such intervention; in other words the Germans are saying that in the event of a Soviet intervention the Germans would be prepared to continue with their East-West relationship. This was the best proof yet of the increasing Finlandization of the Germans." Later, however, on 4 December, Brzezinski received assurances from the German ambassador to the United States that Bonn "would probably move forward with economic sanctions in the event Poland was invaded." Though the government might not want to, he said, popular opinion would compel such a forceful response. See Brzezinski, "White House Diary, 1980," 34, 37.

188. Ibid., 48.

189. David Binder, "U.S. Cautioning on Intervention in Polish Crisis," *New York Times*, 3 December 1980.

190. Brzezinski, *Power and Principle*, 465.

191. See Kuklinski quoted in Pipes, "Documentation," 18.

192. The fact that in November Brezhnev had scheduled a three-day trip to India for early December offers additional evidence that this assessment is accurate. If Moscow had intended to send troops into Poland on 8 December, it is hard to imagine the general secretary making plans to leave the country on 7 December. See Weydenthal, Porter, and Devlin, *Polish Drama*, 114.

Chapter Six

1. A. I. Gribkov, "Doktrina Brezhneva i pol'skii krizis nachala 80-kh godov" (The Brezhnev Doctrine and the Polish Crisis of the Early 1980s), *Voenno-Istoricheskii Zhurnal* (Military History Journal), no. 9 (1992): 55.

2. General A. I. Gribkov, interview by author, Moscow, 29 August 1995.

3. This campaign had begun earlier in the fall, but on 22 October 1980 the Polish Supreme Court had ruled against it. By December the movement had begun to seek an appeal of that decision.

4. Timothy Garton Ash, *The Polish Revolution: Solidarity, 1980–82* (London: Jonathan Cape, 1983), 110–12.

5. Radio Moscow, 18 January 1981, cited in Lawrence Sherwin, "More Accusations about 'Solidarity' in Soviet Media," *Radio Liberty* 32/81, 20 January 1981.

6. Richard D. Anderson Jr., "Soviet Decision-Making and Poland," *Problems of Communism*, March–April 1982, 24.

7. Gribkov, "Doktrina Brezhneva," 55.

8. Tsipko had spent two years working at the Institute of Philosophy and Sociology of the Polish Academy of Sciences in Warsaw. His report is contained in the recently declassified collection of secret reports from the former Institute of Economy of the World Socialist System labeled "Fond 1933s, Delo No17s-633, 05 ianvaria 1981g.–17 iiunia 1981g." The report itself, with its accompanying letter from institute director O. T. Bogomolov to Yuri Andropov, is titled "Zapis' besed v Pol'she starshego sotrudnika IEMSS AN SSSR A. S. Tsipko" (Notes from Meetings in Poland of A. S. Tsipko, Senior Research Fellow of the IEMSS USSR Academy of Sciences), dated 20 January 1981.

9. Ibid., 7.

10. Ibid., 8–9.

11. Ibid., 11.

12. Ibid., 12–13.

13. Ibid., 13–14.

14. Ibid., 17, 25.

15. Ibid., 32.

16. TsKhSD, f. 89, per. 42, no. 36, "O poezdke delegatsii partiinykh rabotnikov KPSS vo glave s t. Zamiatinym, L. M. v Pol'shu" (Concerning the Travel to Poland of a Delegation of CPSU Party Workers under Comrade L. M. Zamiatin), 22 January 1981, 2.

17. Ibid.

18. Ibid.

19. "Report: From the Visit to Katowice of a Soviet Group with Comrade L. M. Zamyatin on January 16, 1981," 2, in *Poland, 1980–1982: Internal Crisis, International Dimensions*, Compendium of Declassified Documents and Chronology of Events Prepared for an International Conference in Jachranka, Poland, by the Institute for Political Studies of the Polish Academy of Sciences, the National Security Archive at George Washington University, and the Cold War International History Project at the Woodrow Wilson Center, November 1997.

20. TsKhSD, "O poezdke delegatsii," 4.

21. Ibid., 5.

22. Ibid.

23. Ibid., 5–6.

24. *Krasnaia Zvezda*, 23 January 1981.

25. Radio Moscow, 31 January 1981, cited in Lawrence Sherwin, "Rural Solidarity Provides Soviet Media with a New Target," *Radio Liberty* 59/81, 2 February 1981.

26. "CIA National Intelligence Estimate (NIE 12.6-81), 'Poland's Prospects over the Next Six Months,' January 27, 1981," 2, in *Poland, 1980–1982*.

27. Yakov Samoilov, "Soviet Economic Aid for Poland," *Radio Liberty* 49/81, 2 February 1981. By contrast, the Soviets estimated that they would spend approximately 4 billion rubles subsidizing Poland's normalization in 1982. See TsKhSD, f. 89, per. 66, no. 7, "Rabochaia zapis' zasedaniia Politburo Ts.K.—K voprosu o polozhenii v Pol'she" (Working Notes of a Meeting of the CC Politburo—on the Question of the Situation in Poland), cited in Mark Kramer, "Poland, 1980–81: Soviet Policy during the Polish Crisis," *Cold War International History Project Bulletin*, no. 5 (Spring 1995): 135.

28. TsKhSD, "O poezdke delegatsii," 5–6.

29. Ibid., 6.

30. Garton Ash, *Polish Revolution*, 116.

31. Ibid., 118.

32. *Radio Free Europe: Polish Situation Report*, 19 February 1981, 3.

33. The government refused to register Rural Solidarity as an official union and so used the term "alliance" instead in the Rzeszow Agreement of 18 February 1981, which guaranteed "the inviolability of peasants' private property, especially land, and the right to inherit it as well as the recognition of private farming as a lasting and equal element in [Poland's] national economy." See Garton Ash, *Polish Revolution*, 132–33.

34. Andrew A. Michta, *Red Eagle: The Army in Polish Politics, 1944–1988* (Stanford: Hoover Institution Press, 1990), 68.

35. *Materialy z Dziejow Polski* (Between October 1956 and December 1970: Sources on Polish History) (Warsaw: Wydawnictwo Spoleczne KOS, 1985), no. 2, 137, cited in ibid., 69.

36. A. Ross Johnson, Robert W. Dean, and Alexander Alexiev, *East European Military Establishments: The Warsaw Pact Northern Tier* (New York: Crane Russak, 1980), 61.

37. Michta, *Red Eagle*, 72.

38. Garton Ash, *Polish Revolution*, 144.

39. Ibid., 145.

40. "'Meeting with L. Zamyatin,' February 18, 1981," 2, in *Poland, 1980–1982*.

41. Jan B. de Weydenthal, Bruce D. Porter, and Kevin Devlin, *The Polish Drama, 1980–1982* (Lexington: Lexington Books, 1983), 117.

42. Bruce Porter, "The Twenty-sixth Party Congress: Brezhnev on Soviet Foreign Policy," *Radio Liberty* 80/81, 23 February 1981.

43. *Pravda*, 5 March 1981, cited in Bruce Porter, "Soviet and Polish Leaders Meet in Moscow," *Radio Liberty* 102/81, 5 March 1981.

44. Kevin Ruane, *The Polish Challenge* (London: BBC Publications, 1982), 127–28.

45. General Anatolii Gribkov and other Soviet officers reportedly participated in the preparation of this exercise. Gribkov points out that only the military aspects of martial law were examined at this time. Political questions were left to government officials, notwithstanding Jaruzelski's presence in both circles. See Gribkov, "Doktrina Brezhneva," 48–49.

46. Richard Pipes, "Documentation," *Orbis*, Winter 1988, 20. Jaruzelski offered this assurance to the Soviets on 3 March after the conclusion of the congress.

47. Ibid.

48. Ibid.

49. For more than two months, Marshal Kulikov and General Gribkov had struggled to explain to impatient allied officers why they had to remain in the field for so

long. Each time they had reminded Moscow of the military pointlessness of the continuing maneuvers, Ustinov had become more annoyed with them. Gribkov, therefore, had resigned himself to following orders and used the time in Poland to tour Polish military facilities and defense industries. See Gribkov, "Doktrina Brezhneva," 55.

50. Garton Ash, *Polish Revolution*, 147–48.

51. Ibid., 148–50.

52. Ibid., 150.

53. TsKhSD, f. 89, per. 42, no. 37, "O besede tov. Brezhneva, L. I. s tov. E. Khonnekerom" (Concerning the Meeting of Comrade L. I. Brezhnev with Comrade E. Honecker), 12 March 1981, 3.

54. Ibid.

55. Garton Ash, *Polish Revolution*, 152.

56. These were the Soiuz-81 training maneuvers that Defense Minister Ustinov had spoken of in January. The first announcement of the planned Soiuz-81 exercises appeared in a TASS bulletin of 10 March 1981. Inasmuch as the coverage of the training was limited almost exclusively to maneuvers in Poland, it is assumed that Soiuz-81 was intended purely as political pressure on the Polish opposition consistent with Ustinov's recommendation of 22 January. See also Lawrence Sherwin, "Initial Soviet Media Response to Events in Bydgoszcz," *Radio Liberty* 128/81, 24 March 1981, and Bruce Porter, "Warsaw Pact Maneuvers and Poland: The Political Implications," *Radio Liberty* 118/81, 17 March 1981.

57. Although a majority of the PZPR Politburo is reported to have favored martial law at this time, Jaruzelski allegedly threatened to resign if the resolution passed. See Garton Ash, *Polish Revolution*, 152. On 26 March the *Financial Times* (London) reported that the question of martial law had arisen at the PZPR Politburo meeting of 23 March. Later, Poland's ambassador to Japan, Zdzislaw Rurarz, testified that he received a telegram on 27 March warning that emergency law might be declared soon. Thus, while Jaruzelski's threat to resign had blocked the move toward martial law, it would appear that some in the government remained convinced that the delay would be only temporary. See *Radio Free Europe: Polish Situation Report*, 21, 18 December 1981.

58. Garton Ash, *Polish Revolution*, 153.

59. Ibid., 154.

60. Ibid., 154–55.

61. TsKhSD, f. 89, per. 42, no. 38, "O resul'tatakh peregovorov s delegatsiei Pol'skoi Narodnoi Respubliki" (Concerning the Results of Negotiations with the Delegation from the Polish People's Republic), 26 March 1981, 2.

62. Ibid.

63. Ibid., 3.

64. Ibid.

65. Ibid.

66. Pipes, "Documentation," 22.

67. Radio Moscow, 26 March 1981, cited in Lawrence Sherwin, "Soviet Media Accuse 'Solidarity' of Causing Chaos and Anarchy," *Radio Liberty* 136/81, 30 March 1981.

68. *Voennyi Vestnik*, 26 March 1981.

69. Radio Moscow, 27 March 1981, cited in Sherwin, "Soviet Media Accuse 'Solidarity.'"

70. Garton Ash, *Polish Revolution*, 156.

71. The accusations were entirely fabricated. Radio Moscow would admit as much later in the day, though without identifying TASS as their author. Ibid., 158. See also Weydenthal, Porter, and Devlin, *Polish Drama*, 119–20.

72. "U.S. Defense Intelligence Agency, Information Report, 'Weekend of 28–29 March Ominous for Poland,' March 27, 1981," 2, in *Poland, 1980–1982*.

73. American secretary of defense Caspar Weinburger issued the warnings on 27 and 28 March 1981. See Weydenthal, Porter, and Devlin, *Polish Drama*, 120.

74. Garton Ash, *Polish Revolution*, 160.

75. Ibid.

76. Ibid., 163.

77. *Solidarity Weekly*, no. 2, 1, cited in ibid., 164.

78. "Report regarding a Confidential Discussion with the Supreme Commander of the Combined Military Forces of the Warsaw Pact . . . following . . . 'SOIUZ-81,' GDR Ministry of Defense, 7 April 1981," 2, in *Poland, 1980–1982*.

79. *Pravda*, 2 April 1981. See also Radio Moscow and TASS, 2 April 1981, cited in Weydenthal, Porter, and Devlin, *Polish Drama*, 123.

80. TsKhSD, f. 89, per. 42, no. 39, "K voprosu o polozhenii v Pol'she" (On the Question of the Situation in Poland), 2 April 1981, 2.

81. Ibid., 3.

82. Ibid.

83. Ibid., 4. Note here the absence of any serious discussion of Soviet intervention. On 4 April 1981 an article appeared in the *Los Angeles Times* which suggested that in late March the Soviet leadership had taken a vote on the question of intervention. Supposedly the vote had been six members in favor to six opposed, with Brezhnev casting the deciding vote against invasion. Documents from the Soviet Party Archives show no evidence that the Politburo seriously entertained an invasion at this time. Certainly, by early April the notion appears to have drawn no support at all in Politburo discussions.

84. Ibid.

85. Ibid., 5.

86. Ibid., 6.

87. Ibid., 6–7.

88. Ibid., 7.

89. Ibid.

90. Ibid., 8.

91. Gribkov, "Doktrina Brezhneva," 50.

92. Carl Bernstein and Marco Politi, *His Holiness: John Paul II and the Hidden History of Our Time* (New York: Doubleday, 1996), 280.

93. Gribkov, interview. Gribkov claims that the main reason he chose to publish his article "Doktrina Brezhneva" was to correct the mistaken belief in some quarters that he had arrested Kania and Jaruzelski on the night of 3 April 1981.

94. Gribkov, "Doktrina Brezhneva," 50.

95. Jaruzelski interview in Bernstein and Politi, *His Holiness*, 281.

96. Ibid. Note that Colonel Kuklinski would later report that "on April 3 in the evening, under the shelter of darkness, a Soviet aircraft brought Kania and Jaruzelski to face Brezhnev himself" (Pipes, "Documentation," 22). Kuklinski is clearly mistaken here. As the Politburo working notes indicate, the Poles met not with Brezhnev but with Andropov and Ustinov.

97. TsKhSD, f. 89, per. 42, no. 40, "Ob itogakh vstrechi t.t. Andropova, Iu. V. i Ustinova, D.S. s pol'skimi druz'iami" (Summarizing the Meeting of Comrades Y. V. Andropov and D. S. Ustinov with the Polish Friends), 9 April 1981, 2.

98. Ibid., 2–3.

99. Wojciech Jaruzelski and Stanislaw Kania interviewed in Bernstein and Politi, *His Holiness*, 282.

100. TsKhSD, "Ob itogakh vstrechi," 3.

101. Ibid.

102. It is interesting to note Jaruzelski's reversal on this point, as the plans he had presented to Moscow only a month earlier on 3 March had stipulated that the Sejm would *not* be consulted before declaring martial law.

103. TsKhSD, "Ob itogakh vstrechi," 3–4.

104. Bernstein and Politi, *His Holiness*, 283.

105. Ibid., 284.
106. TsKhSD, "Ob itogakh vstrechi," 6.
107. Ibid., 4.
108. Ibid., 8.
109. Ibid., 6.
110. Gribkov, "Doktrina Brezhneva," 50.
111. TsKhSD, "Ob itogakh vstrechi," 6–7.
112. Ibid., 7.
113. Ibid.
114. Pipes, "Documentation," 23.
115. Garton Ash, *Polish Revolution*, 172.
116. *Financial Times* (London), 16 April 1981.
117. TsKhSD, f. 89, per. 42, no. 41, "O besede tov. Brezhneva, L. I. s Pervym sekretarem TsK PORP tov. Kanei" (Concerning the Meeting of Comrade L. I. Brezhnev with the First Secretary of the PZPR CC Comrade Kania), 16 April 1981, 2.
118. Ibid., 3.
119. The authors of these reports included Chernenko, Andropov, Gromyko, Ustinov, Rusakov, Arkhipov, and Zamiatin. See TsKhSD, f. 89, per. 66, no. 3, "Postanovlenie Politbiuro TsK o razvitii obstanovki v Pol'she i nekotorykh shagakh s nashei storony" (Resolution of the CC Politburo concerning the Evolving Situation in Poland and Some Steps from Our Side), 23 April 1981. An English translation may be found in Kramer, "Poland, 1980–81," 130–31.
120. See ibid., 2.
121. Kramer, "Poland, 1980–81," 130.
122. See ibid.
123. Ibid.
124. Ibid., 131.
125. Ibid., 130.
126. Ibid., 131.
127. Ibid., 131–32.
128. TsKhSD, f. 89, per. 42, no. 42, "Ob itogakh peregovorov delegatsii KPSS s rukovodstvom PORP" (Summarizing the Negotiations of the CPSU Delegation with the PZPR Leadership), 30 April 1981, 3.
129. Ibid., 4.
130. Ibid., 2.
131. *Pravda*, 8 May 1981.
132. Polish television, 18 May 1981, cited in Sidney I. Ploss, *Moscow and the Polish Crisis: An Interpretation of Soviet Policies and Intentions* (Boulder: Westview, 1986), 93.
133. *Sztandur Mlodych*, 28 May 1981.
134. PAP Maritime Service, 31 May 1981, cited in Ploss, *Moscow and the Polish Crisis*, 94.
135. *Pravda*, 2 June 1981.
136. *Washington Post*, 8 June 1981. Gribkov suggests that this letter was timed to arrive just before the PZPR Central Committee plenum of 9–10 June. See Gribkov, "Doktrina Brezhneva," 50.
137. *Times* (London), 11 June 1981, cited in Garton Ash, *Polish Revolution*, 176.
138. *Nowe Drogi*, July 1981, 6, cited in Weydenthal, Porter, and Devlin, *Polish Drama*, 127.
139. Poland's Ambassador Ruarz, who later defected to the West, would testify as much before the U.S. Congress in December 1981. See "Statement to the U.S. Commission on Security and Cooperation," Zdzislaw Ruarz, 28 December 1981, cited in Weydenthal, Porter, and Devlin, *Polish Drama*, 128–29.
140. Ruane, *Polish Challenge*, 211. Predictably, thanks to Soviet pressures, Fiszbach was not reelected to the Central Committee at the Ninth PZPR Party Congress.

141. Gribkov, "Doktrina Brezhneva," 49.

142. General Gribkov described the results of both meetings in discussion with the author; however, he is unable to pinpoint their precise date any more specifically than "mid-June." Indeed, his "Doktrina Brezhneva" is even more vague, indicating that the meetings took place "in the second half of 1981." Gribkov, interview, and Gribkov, "Doktrina Brezhneva," 56.

143. Gribkov, "Doktrina Brezhneva," 56.

144. Gribkov, interview; Gribkov, "Doktrina Brezhneva," 56.

145. Gribkov, interview.

146. Gribkov, "Doktrina Brezhneva," 56.

147. Ibid.

148. Gribkov, interview. Gribkov was likely engaging in hyperbole here. The Third World members of the UN General Assembly certainly had more concern for the fate of one of their own in Afghanistan than they would have for Poland. Witness the fact that the African National Congress had supported the 1968 invasion of Czechoslovakia. Doubtless the central concern behind Gribkov's assertions was that the nations which were liable to become most enraged by a Soviet invasion would be those nations of Western Europe with which the Soviets were desperately trying to maintain some of the political and economic benefits of détente following the collapse of relations with Washington.

149. Gribkov, "Doktrina Brezhneva," 56.

150. Gribkov, interview.

151. Gribkov, "Doktrina Brezhneva," 56.

152. Gribkov, interview.

153. When asked what became of Brezhnev's promise not to abandon Poland in time of distress, General Gribkov replied simply that it became null and void with the abandonment of the Brezhnev Doctrine. Ibid.

154. Ibid. It is difficult to tell how seriously Kulikov intended this comment. Did he plan to act on his own initiative in Poland, against the wishes of Defense Minister Ustinov and the entire Politburo? It is hard to imagine that he genuinely thought that he could have managed to do so successfully, particularly without the cooperation of the other Warsaw Pact allies. Therefore, it is far more likely that these were the words of a bitterly disappointed man who had yet to come to terms with his defeat.

Chapter Seven

1. A. I. Gribkov, "Doktrina Brezhneva i pol'skii krizis nachala 80-kh godov" (The Brezhnev Doctrine and the Polish Crisis of the Early 1980s), *Voenno-Istoricheskii Zhurnal* (Military History Journal), no. 9 (1992): 57.

2. TsKhSD, f. 89, per. 42, no. 44, "Ob informatsii tov. Brezhneva, L. I. o besede s t. Kanei" (Information of Comrade L. I. Brezhnev concerning the Meeting with Comrade Kania), 18 June 1981, 2.

3. Ibid., 3.

4. In keeping with this promise, a moderate, Leslaw Tokarski, replaced the more liberal Jozef Klasa as head of the PZPR Department of Information Services, a development that greatly upset Solidarity. See *Solidarnosc*, special supplement, 11 September 1981.

5. TsKhSD, "Ob informatsii tov. Brezhneva," 3.

6. Ibid., 4.

7. Ibid., 4–5.

8. Soviet television, 20 June 1981, cited in Sidney I. Ploss, *Moscow and the Polish Crisis: An Interpretation of Soviet Policies and Intentions* (Boulder: Westview, 1986), 101.

9. *Chronology: Soviet and Soviet-Proxy Involvement in Poland, July 1980–December 1981*, Special Report no. 94 (Washington, D.C.: Department of State, Bureau of Public Affairs, 1982), 3.

10. "Information on the Talks between the Member of the Politburo of the CC of the

CPSU and the Minister of Foreign Affairs of the USSR, Com[rade] A. A. Gromyko, with the Leadership of the PZPR in Warsaw on July 3–5, 1981," in *Poland, 1980–1982: Internal Crisis, International Dimensions*, Compendium of Declassified Documents and Chronology of Events Prepared for an International Conference in Jachranka, Poland, by the Institute for Political Studies of the Polish Academy of Sciences, the National Security Archive at George Washington University, and the Cold War International History Project at the Woodrow Wilson Center, November 1997.

11. Warsaw Radio, 14 July 1981; *Pravda*, 15 July 1981.

12. *Izvestiia*, 17 July 1981.

13. *Pravda*, 15 July 1981.

14. Radio Warsaw, 19 July 1981, cited in Ploss, *Moscow and the Polish Crisis*, 109.

15. Bruce Porter, "Soviet Coverage of the Elections at the Polish Party Congress," *Radio Liberty* 288/81, 21 July 1981.

16. Traditionally this part of the election had been limited to the Central Committee alone.

17. Porter, "Soviet Coverage of the Elections at the Polish Party Congress."

18. "Report to the HSWP CC Politburo Containing Verbatim Transcript of July 21, 1981, Telephone Conversation between Stanislaw Kania and Leonid Brezhnev, July 22, 1981," in *Poland, 1980–1982*.

19. Timothy Garton Ash, *The Polish Revolution: Solidarity, 1980–82* (London: Jonathan Cape, 1983), 186.

20. Ibid., 191.

21. Ibid.

22. Ibid., 193.

23. "Excerpted Notes of Meetings of Solidarity's National Coordinating Commission in Gdansk, July 24–26, 1981," in *Poland, 1980–1982*.

24. *Pravda*, 5 August 1981.

25. *Washington Post*, 10 August 1981. The offers of assistance apparently arrived in Warsaw on 7 August. Note that they did not include a proffering of military intervention.

26. Ploss, *Moscow and the Polish Crisis*, 116.

27. *Pravda*, 16 August 1981.

28. Garton Ash, *Polish Revolution*, 202–3.

29. Ibid., 205.

30. "Forecast of the Anticipated Public Feelings and Conflicts with NSZZ 'Solidarnosc' and Other Politically Malevolent Groups in the Course of the Next Few Months, Prepared with Reference to the Situation on 17 August 1981: Conclusions and Proposals for Counteraction, PZPR CC, August 17, 1981," in *Poland, 1980–1982*.

31. Ploss, *Moscow and the Polish Crisis*, 120.

32. Ibid. (emphasis added).

33. Garton Ash, *Polish Revolution*, 212.

34. Ibid., 224–25.

35. *Solidarity Agency Bulletin*, no. 40, 301ff., cited in ibid., 225–26.

36. Garton Ash, *Polish Revolution*, 225.

37. Ibid., 213.

38. He received this response despite the fact that his proposal was consistent with the union's position during the "registration crisis" of October 1980.

39. Garton Ash, *Polish Revolution*, 223.

40. *Radio Free Europe: RAD Background Report*, no. 298, October 1981.

41. TsKhSD, f. 89, per. 42, no. 46, "Obmen mneniiami po pol'skomu voprosu" (Exchange of Opinions about the Polish Question), 10 September 1981, 2.

42. Ibid., 2–3.

43. Ibid., 2.

44. "Meeting of the General Secretary of the CC of the SED and the Chairman of the State Council of the GDR, Comrade Erich Honecker, on the Occasion of His Stay in Cuba with the First Secretary of the CC of the CP of Cuba and President of the State Council and Council of Ministers of the Republic of Cuba, Fidel Castro, on September 13, 1981, in Havana," 1–2, in *Poland, 1980–1982*.

45. TsKhSD, "Obmen mneniiami po pol'skomu voprosu," 3.

46. PAP, 18 September 1981, cited in Jan B. de Weydenthal, Bruce D. Porter, and Kevin Devlin, *The Polish Drama, 1980–1982* (Lexington: Lexington Books, 1983), 126.

47. *Le Monde*, 18 September 1981.

48. TsKhSD, f. 89, per. 42, no. 47, "Telegramma sovposla iz Berlina (spets. no. 598)" (Telegram from the Soviet Ambassador in Berlin [special no. 598]), 17 September 1981, 2.

49. " 'Report to the Politburo' from Hungarian Ambassador Jozsef Garamvolgyi, September 18, 1981," 2, in *Poland, 1980–1982*.

50. TsKhSD, "Telegramma sovposla iz Berlina," 2.

51. " 'In the Face of Statements by the PZPR CC, the Government of the PPR, and the CPSU CC,' Summaries of Responses by 'Solidarity' Cells, September 1981," 5–6, in *Poland, 1980–1982*.

52. Ibid., 6.

53. "Telegram from Ryszard Kuklinski ('Jack Strong'), September 15, 1981," in *Poland, 1980–1982*.

54. Richard Pipes, "Documentation," *Orbis*, Winter 1988, 25.

55. See Maxine Pollack and Janusz Bugajski, "Report on Poland: Solidarity's Tug of War," *Encounter* 58, no. 1 (January 1982).

56. Radio Warsaw, 24 September 1981, cited in Garton Ash, *Polish Revolution*, 123.

57. *Pravda*, 6–11 October 1981.

58. *Pravda*, 14 October 1981.

59. General A. I. Gribkov, interview by author, Moscow, 29 August 1995.

60. *Pravda*, 19 October 1981.

61. TsKhSD, f. 89, per. 66, no. 4, "Zapis' telefonnogo razgovora L. Brezhneva s V. Iaruzl'skim" (Notes of a Telephone Conversation between L. Brezhnev and W. Jaruzelski), 19 October 1981, cited in Mark Kramer, "Poland, 1980–81: Soviet Policy during the Polish Crisis," *Cold War International History Project Bulletin*, no. 5 (Spring 1995): 132.

62. Ibid.

63. Ibid., 133.

64. With the gears in motion for a declaration of martial law, Jaruzelski was not about to bring a fresh crop of pro-Solidarity conscripts into the armed forces. Note that this decision was consistent with Soviet recommendations voiced months earlier. See Garton Ash, *Polish Revolution*, 237.

65. Ibid., 239.

66. Radio Moscow, 30 October 1981, cited in Weydenthal, Porter, and Devlin, *Polish Drama*, 134.

67. Siwicki remained in Warsaw to "mind the store" while the rest of the general staff was on maneuvers.

68. Gribkov, interview.

69. Gribkov, "Doktrina Brezhneva," 57.

70. Ibid.

71. Significantly, Rusakov visited each of the member-nations of the Warsaw Pact alliance *except* Romania. Romania did not receive subsidized deliveries of Soviet energy products and so would not suffer from Moscow's decision to divert oil and gas to Poland. See TsKhSD, f. 89, per. 42, no. 48, "Ob itogakh poezdki t. Rusakova, K. V. v GDR, ChSSR, VNR, i NRB," 29 October 1981, 2.

72. Ibid., 2–3.

73. Ibid.

74. Ibid., 6.

75. Ibid., 3.

76. Mikhail Gorbachev, *Memoirs*, trans. Georges Peronansky and Tatjana Varsavsky (New York: Doubleday, 1995), 216.

77. TsKhSD, "Ob itogakh poezdki t. Rusakova," 6.

78. IEMSS, f. 1933s, d. no. 17s-633, 25 June 1981–21 October 1981, "Kontseptsiia dolgosrochnogo ekonomicheskogo sotrudnichestva SSSR i PNR" (Conception for Long-Term Economic Cooperation between the USSR and PPR), 31 October 1981. The report was written by L. S. Semenov, classified as "SECRET," and forwarded to S. I. Borodavhenko at the CMEA Intergovernmental Commission on Bilateral Economic and Scientific-Technical Cooperation: USSR-Poland.

79. TsKhSD, "Ob itogakh poezdki t. Rusakova," 6–7.

80. Ibid., 4.

81. G. M. Kornienko, *Kholodnaia voina: Svidetel'stvo ee uchastnika* (The Cold War: Testimony of Its Participant) (Moscow: Mezhdunarodnye Otnosheniia, 1995), 197–98.

82. TsKhSD, "Ob itogakh poezdki t. Rusakova," 4.

83. *Krasnaia Zvezda*, 30 October 1981.

84. *Pravda*, 7 November 1981.

85. *Pravda*, 11 November 1981.

86. "Pol'skii krizis i liniia KPSS," translated as "Secret Report on 'The Polish Crisis and the Line of the CPSU' presented by Mikhail Suslov to the CPSU Central Committee Plenum 16 November 1981," 5. Soviet archival document presented by Mark Kramer in a talk at the Woodrow Wilson Center on 13 December 2001 on the twentieth anniversary of the imposition of martial law in Poland. The document is a transcript of Suslov's remarks to the plenum.

87. Ibid., 18–19 (emphasis in the original).

88. Brezhnev invited Jaruzelski for consultations in Moscow to be held 14–15 December. At this point, Jaruzelski had not yet scheduled the imposition of martial law to begin on 13 December.

89. TsKhSD, f. 89, per. 66, no. 5, "Postanovlenie Politbiuro TsK—o prieme v SSSR partino-gosudarstvennoi delegatsii PNR i ustnoi poslanii L. Brezhneva V. Iaruzel'skomu" (Resolution of the CC Politburo—concerning the Reception in the USSR of a Party-State Delegation from the PPR and the Statement of L. Brezhnev to W. Jaruzelski), 21 November 1981, cited in Kramer, "Poland, 1980–81," 133.

90. Ibid., 133–34.

91. Ibid., 134.

92. Ibid.

93. Garton Ash, *Polish Revolution*, 257–58.

94. Wojciech Jaruzelski, with Marek Jaworski and Wlodzimierz Loznski, *Stan Wojenny Dlaczego . . .* (Why Martial Law) (Warsaw: Polska Oficyna Wydawnicza "BGW," 1992), 391.

95. See the report of Yuri Andropov in TsKhSD, f. 89, per. 66, no. 6, "Rabochaia zapis' zasedaniia Politbiuro TsK—k voprosu o polozhenii v Pol'she" (Working Notes from a Meeting of the CC Politburo—on the Question of the Situation in Poland), 10 December 1981, cited in Kramer, "Poland, 1980–81," 135–36.

96. See the observations of Bernard Guetta in *Le Monde*, 1 December 1981.

97. *L'Unita*, 27 January 1982, cited in Weydenthal, Porter, and Devlin, *Polish Drama*, 137.

98. This according to Ambassador Zdzislaw Rurarz. See Weydenthal, Porter, and Devlin, *Polish Drama*, 135.

99. A conference of socialist foreign ministers met 1–2 December in Bucharest. At the same time, Warsaw Pact defense ministers met in Moscow 1–4 December, while a news agency summit met in Prague 1–3 December. An article in *Le Monde*,

published on 18 December of that year, claimed that the Poles informed their allies of their intention to move against Solidarity at one or all of these meetings.

100. Kevin Ruane, *The Polish Challenge* (London: BBC Publications, 1982), 270–72.

101. Nicholas G. Andrews, *Poland, 1980–81: Solidarity versus the Party* (Washington, D.C.: National Defense University Press, 1985), 249. See also Jaruzelski, *Stan Wojenny Dlaczego*, 387.

102. Richard Spielman, "Crisis in Poland," *Foreign Policy*, no. 49 (Winter 1982–83), 30–31.

103. Jaruzelski, *Stan Wojenny Dlaczego*, 387–90.

104. In preparation for this eventuality, Polish ship captains were being instructed to remain in neutral waters to avoid seizure by Western creditors. See TsKhSD, "Rabochaia zapis' zasedaniia Politbiuro TsK," 134–35.

105. Ibid., 136.

106. Ibid., 137.

107. Ibid., 135–36. Dmitrii Ustinov reinforced Rusakov's version of the story, arguing that "with regard to what Comrade Kulikov allegedly said about the introduction of troops into Poland, I can say in full responsibility that Kulikov never said this. He simply repeated what was said by us and by Leonid Ilyich that we would not leave Poland in the lurch. And he perfectly well knows that the Poles themselves requested us not to introduce troops." See ibid., 137.

108. Ibid., 135.

109. Ibid., 136.

110. Ibid.

111. Ibid. (emphasis added). Andropov's perception of Western intent was quite accurate. Great Britain was already in the process of coordinating a strong European response to the prospect of Soviet invasion in late 1980. Former British prime minister Margaret Thatcher writes in her memoirs: "From about the same time [late 1980] we began to draw up measures to punish the Soviet Union in such an eventuality. Peter Carrington and I agreed that we should respond in a measured, graduated way depending on the situation we faced. We foresaw four possibilities: a situation in which the use of force by the Polish Government against Polish workers was imminent, or had already taken place, or one in which Soviet intervention was imminent, or had already taken place. We agreed that ineffective sanctions would be worse than useless, but sanctions would have to hit the Soviets harder than they hit us." See Margaret Thatcher, *The Downing Street Years* (London: Harper Collins, 1993), 252.

112. TsKhSD, "Rabochaia zapis' zasedaniia Politbiuro TsK," 137.

113. Ibid. (emphasis added).

114. Ibid.

115. Mark Kramer, "The Anoshkin Notebook on the Polish Crisis, December 1981," *Cold War International History Project Bulletin*, no. 11 (March 1999): 17–31.

116. Ibid., 19.

117. Ibid., 22 (emphasis added).

118. Ibid., 24.

119. Ibid. It is indeed ironic, in light of his position taken in June for intervention, that Kulikov would have been the one to dash Jaruzelski's hopes for outside military assistance. Significantly, however, Anoshkin's comment here suggests that Kulikov retained his desire to intervene as late as December 1981.

120. *Pravda*, 10 December 1981.

121. *Slowo Powszechne*, 12 December 1981, cited in Garton Ash, *Polish Revolution*, 260.

122. *Labor Focus* 5, nos. 1–2, 25ff., cited in Garton Ash, *Polish Revolution*, 260.

123. Garton Ash, *Polish Revolution*, 234–35.

124. Jaruzelski, interview in *Gazeta Wyborcza*, 20 February 1993.

125. Ibid., 14 December 1992.

126. Jaruzelski, *Stan Wojenny Dlaczego*, 402.

127. Jaruzelski's testimony in Sejm Commission, 9–10 March 1993, *Sad Nad Autorami Stanu Wojennego* (The Trial of the Authors of Martial Law) (Warsaw: BGW, 1993), 235, cited in Michael Dobbs, *Down with Big Brother: The Fall of the Soviet Empire* (New York: Alfred A. Knopf, 1997), 76.

128. Garton Ash, *Polish Revolution*, 260. Polish forces had been trained in large part by the Soviet KGB on the most minute details of the crackdown months earlier. They had models built of each town and city, which were then used to show Polish forces precisely where they would be standing and maneuvering in the days to come. The models were reportedly detailed to the point that soldiers could be shown exactly what doorways to occupy at the start of martial law. Following the smooth introduction of emergency law, Vladimir Kriuchkov, head of the KGB's First Main Directorate (dealing with foreign intelligence activities), received a decoration for his central role in preparing this training for the Polish forces. Sergei Grigoriev, interview by author, Newport, Rhode Island, 16 August 1994.

129. Dobbs, *Down with Big Brother*, 78–79.

130. *Le Monde*, 16 December 1982.

131. *Washington Post*, 16 November 1982.

132. Dobbs, *Down with Big Brother*, 79.

133. Garton Ash, *Polish Revolution*, 261.

134. Dobbs, *Down with Big Brother*, 79.

135. *Trybuna Robotnicza*, 14 December 1981.

136. This was not the first the nation had heard of this Council of National Salvation. As early as mid-October of that year, the Solidarity news agency had reported its existence. At the time, however, it was said to consist of only six members, led by Generals Jaruzelski and Kiszczak. See Garton Ash, *Polish Revolution*, 234.

137. Weydenthal, Porter, and Devlin, *Polish Drama*, 238.

138. Andrews, *Poland, 1980–81*, 256.

139. These new regulations included severance of communications with the outside world, as well as within Poland itself; establishment of a national curfew; a ban on travel between cities and outside one's place of residency; a ban on meetings, societies, and organizations; suspension of trade unions and other organizations; closure of schools and universities; a ban on publication of most newspapers and magazines; military control of radio and television, as well as of certain industries; and the seizure and closure of Solidarity offices throughout the country.

140. Andrews, *Poland, 1980–81*, 257.

141. Carl Bernstein and Marco Politi, *His Holiness: John Paul II and the Hidden History of Our Time* (New York: Doubleday, 1996), 337–38.

142. Garton Ash, *Polish Revolution*, 269.

143. TsKhSD, f. 89, per. 66, no. 7, "Postanovlenie Politbiuro TsK—Ob informatsii rukovodstva bratskikh stran po po'skomu voprosu" (Resolution of the CC Politbiuro—concerning Information about the Polish Question for the Leadership of the Fraternal Parties), 12 December 1981, cited in Kramer, "Poland, 1980–81," 138.

144. Ibid.

145. Gribkov, interview.

Conclusion

1. Zdenek Mlynar, *Can Gorbachev Change the Soviet Union? The International Dimensions of Political Reform*, trans. Marian Sling and Ruth Tosek (Boulder: Westview, 1990), 137.

2. As Zbigniew Brzezinski points out, "There appears to be little doubt that Poland, due to its geographical position, was the primary objective of Soviet policy in East Central Europe. A non-Communist Poland would have resulted in the exclusion of the USSR from Central Europe." Zbigniew Brzezinski, *The Soviet Bloc: Unity and Conflict*, rev. and exp. ed. (Cambridge: Harvard University Press, 1967), 9.

3. Martin Malia, *The Soviet Tragedy: A History of Socialism in Russia, 1917–1991* (New York: Free Press, 1994), 5–6.

4. Charles Gati argues, for instance, that "the Polish era of 'socialist renewal' in 1980–81 should be understood against the background of Brezhnev's illness in the late 1970s and the brief tenures of Yuri Andropov and Konstantin Chernenko in the early 1980s—a long period of immobilism in the Kremlin which in turn contributed to weakness and confusion at the top in Poland as well." He goes on to note, "While in some cases such immobilism in the Kremlin culminated in a crackdown, in several other cases the East European reaction was to take advantage of the Soviet leaders' preoccupation with the struggle for succession—and make such changes as an attentive and vigorous Kremlin might have opposed. When the cat's away the mice will play." See Gati, *The Bloc That Failed: Soviet–East European Relations in Transition* (Bloomington: Indiana University Press, 1990), 60.

5. Hélène Carrère D'Encausse, *Big Brother: The Soviet Union and Soviet Europe*, trans. George Holoch (New York: Holmes and Meier, 1987), 217.

6. Nikolai P. Kolikov, interview by author, Moscow, 13 April 1995.

7. Ibid. It should be noted that Kolikov was not familiar with the documentary evidence that illustrated the move of Moscow's top leadership away from the Brezhnev Doctrine in the early 1980s. The shift he had in mind was the emergence of Gorbachev and his move away from the doctrine. Clearly, however, these two processes were all of a piece, a logical continuation that began with the events of the late 1970s and early 1980s.

8. IEMSS, f. 1933s, d. no. 17s-633, 25 June–21 October, "O valiutnom polozhenii VNR" (Concerning the Currency Situation in the Hungarian People's Republic), 31 October 1981, by N. S. Osipov. The report was labeled "SECRET" and forwarded to Deputy Chairman Inozemtsev at Gosplan, as well as to the Department for Liaison with Communist and Workers Parties of Socialist States and the Soviet representatives at CMEA.

9. Paul Marer writes, "Recognizing that significant competition between producers is indispensable for an efficiently functioning market mechanism, a series of steps were taken: several trusts and enterprises were broken up into smaller units; setting up new small- and medium-sized business ventures in the socialized sector was facilitated; the scope of legalized private sector activities was expanded and restrictions on them eased; some competition in the foreign trade field was introduced; the size of the central bureaucracy was cut to provide fewer opportunities to meddle into enterprise decisions; new methods of appointing enterprise managers were introduced; and new financial institutions were created." See Marer, "Economic Reform in Hungary: From Central Planning to Regulated Market," in *East European Economies: Slow Growth in the 1980s*, vol. 3, *Country Studies on Eastern Europe and Yugoslavia* (Washington, D.C.: Government Printing Office, 1986), 248–49.

10. In October 1982, the vice president of the Hungarian Council of Ministers, Jozsef Marjai, told visiting Bogomolov Institute scholar M. A. Usievich that despite the many difficulties facing Budapest, "in general, thanks to our system, we have all the same not had to introduce martial law in our country." See IEMSS, f. 1933s, d. no. 17s-633, 20 May 1982–29 November 1982, "Zapis' besedy s zamestitelem Predsedatelia Soveta Ministrov VNR t. I. Mar'iai" (Notes of a Meeting with Deputy Chairman of the HPR Soviet of Ministers, Comrade I. Marjai), 3 November 1982, by M. A. Usievich. This report was labeled "SECRET" and forwarded to Brezhnev's apparent successor, Yuri Andropov. (Note: Usievich was the head of the IEMSS Hungarian sector.)

11. He offered this assertion to M. A. Usievich during her visit to Budapest that October. See IEMSS, f. 1933s, d. no. 17s-633, 20 May 1982–29 November 1982, "Zapis' besedy s pervym sekretarem TsK VSRP tovarishchem Ianoshem Kadarom" (Notes of a Meeting with the HSWP CC First Secretary, Comrade Janos Kadar), 3 November 1982, by M. A. Usievich. This report was marked "SECRET" and forwarded to Yuri Andropov.

12. Importantly, Kadar was not seeking to employ nationalism to enhance his

legitimacy, inasmuch as doing so would create problems for the Warsaw Pact alliance. There were simply too many ethnic Hungarians living in neighboring states to open the question of nationalism for discussion. Rather, by asserting the importance of national interest, Kadar hoped to make a case for tighter relations with the West. Accordingly he claimed that small and medium-size countries had a responsibility to maintain cordial relations "at a time of 'superpower' discord." See Charles Gati, *Hungary and the Soviet Bloc* (Durham: Duke University Press, 1986), 175.

13. Ferenc Havasi, Central Committee secretary for economic policy in Budapest, interview by M. A. Usievich, Budapest, October 1982. Havasi claimed in the interview to be quoting Kadar directly. See IEMSS, f. 1933s, d. 17s-633, "Osnovnye voprosy iz besedy s sekretarem TsK VSRP po ekonomike tov. F. Khavashi" (Fundamental Questions from a Meeting with the HSWP CC Economic Secretary, Comrade F. Xavasi), 3 November 1982, by M. A. Usievich. This report was labeled "SECRET" and forwarded to Yuri Andropov.

14. In the course of December 1982–January 1983, Marjai held a number of discussions with IEMSS scholars on the problems of cooperation in the CMEA. He met with Oleg Bogomolov, M. A. Usievich, and the institute's secretary for international relations, V. M. Zegal'. See IEMSS, f. 1933s, d. 17s-633, 12 January 1983–23 September 1983, "Zapis' besed s zamestitelem Predsedatelia Soveta Ministrov Vengerskoi Narodnoi Respubliki tov iosefom Mar'iai" (Notes of a Meeting with Deputy Chairman of the Soviet of Ministers of the Hungarian People's Republic, Comrade Josef Marjai), 26 January 1983, by Oleg Bogomolov. This report was marked "SECRET" and forwarded to General Secretary Yuri Andropov.

15. *Pravda*, 16 June 1983 and 16 August 1983. See also Oleg Bogomolov, "Obshchee dostoianie: Obmen opytom sotsialisticheskogo stroitel'stva" (Common Property: Exchanging the Experience of Socialist Construction), *Pravda*, 14 March 1983.

16. Rudolf L. Tokes, *Hungary's Negotiated Revolution: Economic Reform, Social Change, and Political Succession, 1957–1990* (Cambridge: Cambridge University Press, 1996), 33.

17. Sergei Grigoriev, who worked as executive secretary of the Soviet-Chinese Friendship Association from 1979 to 1984—an organization run by the Central Committee Liaison Department—offered these reflections on the outlook in Moscow in the early 1980s during an interview with the author in Newport, Rhode Island, 16 August 1994.

18. Kolikov, interview.

19. See IEMSS, f. 1933s, d. 17s-633, 12 January 1983–23 September 1983, "Osnovnye pokazateli zhiznennogo urovnia naseleniia v SSSR i evropeiskikh stranakh SEV v 70-e i pervoi polovine 80-kh godov" (Fundamental Indicators of the Standard of Living for the Populations in the USSR and European Countries of the CMEA in the 1970s and First Half of the 1980s), 27 January 1983, by L. S. Lichkina. This report was labeled "SECRET" and forwarded to M. S. Gorbachev at the Central Committee and to the Soviet representative at CMEA.

20. See IEMSS, f. 1933s, d. 17s-633, 12 January 1983–23 September 1983, "Ob ekonomicheskoi effektivnosti sotrudnichestva SSSR so stranami SEV" (Concerning the Economic Effectiveness of the Cooperation between the USSR and the CMEA Countries), 17 February 1983, by N. A. Ushakova. This report was labeled "SECRET" and forwarded to M. S. Gorbachev at the Central Committee and to the Soviet representative at CMEA.

21. Georgii Shakhnazarov, *Tsena svobody: Reformatsiia Gorbacheva glazami ego pomoshchnika* (The Price of Freedom: The Gorbachev Reforms through the Eyes of His Assistant) (Moscow: Rossika Zevs, 1993), 100.

22. Aleksandr Tsipko in the preface to Aleksandr Yakovlev, *Predislovie Obval Posleslovie* (Moscow: Novosti, 1992), 4.

23. Aleksandr Yakovlev, interview by author, Moscow, 30 August 1995.

24. Elizabeth Teague, *Solidarity and the Soviet Worker: The Impact of Polish Events of 1980*

on Soviet Internal Politics (London: Croom Helm, 1988), 316. Teague is quoting Gorbachev from a TASS bulletin of 30 June 1986.

25. Mikhail Gorbachev speaking to the Director's Forum at the Woodrow Wilson Center for Scholars, Washington, D.C., on 7 December 1999.

26. Ibid.

27. Kolikov, interview.

Index

Spring as "peaceful," 66; in Afghanistan, 89, 93; Soviets refuse to recognize Polish riots of 1970 as, 104; in USSR, 253

Crimea, 133

Cuba: receives CMEA investment money, 78

Czechoslovakia: 1968 invasion of, 4, 6, 35, 37, 49, 69, 83, 89, 99, 105, 107, 131, 137, 139, 154, 191, 213, 229, 234, 244, 245; revisionism in, 17, 18; and Prague Spring, 17–63, 131; and Action Program, 20, 22, 56; "second center" in, 22, 48; and "Warsaw Letter," 24, 28, 48; "normalization" of, 24, 39–63; prospects for Western sabotage in, 25–26, 50, 70; armed forces of, 27; Fourteenth CSCP Congress in, 28; Revolutionary Government in, 28, 32, 44; official postinvasion declaration in, 34, 50; quislings in, 39, 40, 41, 42, 44, 55, 193, 195; resistance flyers in, 43, 50; possible division into East and West Czechoslovakia, 45; and Moscow talks of August 1968, 46; and Moscow Protocol, 48, 55; Ministry of Internal Affairs, 53–54; and purge of CSCP under Husak, 56, 57; role in preserving directed consensus in bloc discussions, 72; and socialist division of labor, 77; Soviet-Czechoslovak treaty of 1970, 82, 83; and crisis in Poland, 156, 164; Jaruzelski's role in, 177; as model of passive resistance for Poland, 185

Czechoslovak News Agency, 50

Czubinski, Lucjan, 152

Daniel, Yuri, 16

Dawisha, Karen, 37

Democratic centralism, 72

Department for Liaison with Communist and Workers Parties of Socialist States, 250

Der Spiegel (West Germany), 133, 167

D'Estaing, Giscard, 168

Détente, 37, 58, 69, 70, 76, 84, 92, 164; collapse of with United States, 96, 97, 168, 248; and Soviet reliance on Western Europe for stability, 98, 168, 248–49, 251; and religious affairs, 117

DiP (Experience and Future), 109

Directed consensus, 72, 75

Disinformation, 54; campaign in Czechoslovakia, 52

Dobrynin, Anatoly (Soviet ambassador to United States), 33, 34, 86, 87

Dolgikh, Nadimir, 233

Dual power, 141

Dubcek, Alexander, 17–32 passim, 37, 40, 42, 43, 44, 46, 47, 48, 52, 54, 56, 57, 61, 146, 163, 189, 193, 195, 244, 245

Dudinskii, I., 70

Duzhavna Sigurnost (DS), 120–21

Dzur, Martin (Czechoslovak minister of defense), 40

Eastern Rite Catholic Church, 19

East Germany. *See* German Democratic Republic

Economic levers (USSR), 25, 191, 203, 232–33, 234, 236, 253

Economic sanctions, Western, 5, 228, 232, 234, 236, 242, 248–49

Eidlin, Fred, 45

Epishev, A. A.: and decision not to invade Poland, 199–202

Eurocommunism, 59, 66, 85, 86, 87; rifts in by 1980, 97; as model of socialism, 194, 203

European Community (EC), 86

European Economic Community (EEC), 77, 168

Experience and Future (DiP), 109

Falin, Valentin, 167

Federal Republic of Germany (FRG), 68

Filipov, Grisha (member of Bulgarian Politburo), 156

Firiubin, N. P. (Soviet ambassador to Yugoslavia in 1956), 15

Fiszbach, Tadeusz, 134, 135, 199, 239

FROG missiles, 59

Front of National Accord (Poland), 228

Garamvolgyi, Jozsef, 219

Garthoff, Raymond L., 94, 95

Garton Ash, Timothy, 106, 152; on influence of Pope John Paul II in Poland, 115; on threat of general strike in Poland, 186; and Poland's "self-limiting revolution," 211

Gati, Charles, 251

Gdansk, 142

Gdansk Accords (1980), 119, 141, 144, 151, 220, 237

Georgia (Soviet republic), 189

Geremek, Bronislaw, 145, 182, 211

German Democratic Republic (GDR), 24, 25; and invasion of Czechoslovakia, 35; relations with FRG, 68; crisis of 1953 in, 69; military commitment to, 76; and socialist division of labor, 77; implements socialist economic integration, 78; liquidity crisis in, 88; indebtedness and, 111; armed forces in, 146, 186; sharp tone of with Poland, 156–57; Stasi secret police in, 161; threatens to curtail deliveries of uranium to USSR, 224; importance of Poland to, 234

Gero, Erno, 11, 12

Gierek, Edward, 80, 99, 135, 162; assumes power in riots of 1970, 105, 107; fires Jaroszewicz, 109; loyal communist opposition to policies of, 109; and Polish indebtedness, 110, 111; and failure of import-led growth, 112, 144, 174; on visit of Pope John Paul II to Poland in 1979, 114; and price rises of 1980, 132, 133; inquires about possibility of Soviet intervention, 136; replaced by Kania, 140; and riots of 1976, 178; internment of under martial law, 239

Gierek, Leopold (organizer of Poland's first unofficial free-union cell), 108

Glavlit, 150, 151

Glemp, Joseph Cardinal, 227, 240

Godunov, Boris, 130

Gomulka, Wladyslaw, 11, 22, 32, 47, 50; replaced by Edward Gierek, 80; replaces Ochab, 101; copes with Polish "October," 101–2; collapse of government of in riots of 1970, 105

Gorbachev, Mikhail, 2, 3, 4, 5, 7, 9, 254; new thinking in foreign policy, 4, 5, 243, 254; and Solidarity crisis, 147, 216; on decline of Soviet economy, 225; turn to "common European home," 242; studies East European reform issues, 252, 253

Gordievsky, Oleg, 27, 121

Goskomizdat USSR, 117

Gosplan, 148, 184, 203, 233

Gostelradio, 143

Gostelradio USSR, 117

Gottwald, Klement, 17

Grabski, Tadeusz, 192, 195, 210

Grechko, Andrei (Soviet defense minister), 17, 23, 45, 59

Gribkov, Anatolii, 155, 156, 161, 167, 172, 173, 199, 207, 208, 221, 223, 226; and Brest meeting, 189, 190, 192; and decision not to invade Poland, 199–202, 235; on death of Brezhnev Doctrine, 242

Grigulevich, I., 119, 122

Grishin, Viktor, 209, 210

Gromyko, Andrei, 136, 137, 187–88, 209; and Prague Spring, 20, 23, 27, 28, 34, 87; and Afghanistan, 89, 91, 92, 94; on election of Polish pope, 113; condemns Gdansk Accords, 139; on Jaruzelski, 146; on risk of counterrevolution in Poland, 147; misgivings about Kania's government, 175, 183, 188, 217; and coordination with East European Communists on Poland, 193; counsels restraint in dealing with Poland, 217; on Soviet refusal to intervene militarily in Poland, 235

Healthy forces: in Czechoslovakia, 21, 28, 31, 32, 39; in Poland, 139, 194, 229

Hegedus, Andras (prime minister of Hungary in 1956), 12

Helsinki Final Act (1975), 66, 85, 86; and "third basket" on human rights, 86, 87

Hitler, Adolf, 125

Honecker, Erich, 72, 161, 163, 217, 218

Hungary, 24, 234, 244; Revolution of 1956 in, 9, 11, 12, 16, 36, 37, 49, 62, 69, 137; Revolution of 1848 in, 11; battle for Budapest, 13; Communist Party in, 14; National Smallholders and Social Democratic (Petofi) Parties in, 14; Soviet withdrawal from Budapest, 14; stationing of Soviet troops in, 14; arrest and trial of Nagy in, 15–16; invasion of, 19; and invasion of Czechoslovakia, 35; and socialist division of labor, 77; as stimulus to CMEA, 77; and trade in CMEA, 79; consumerism in, 81; liquidity crisis in, 88; and New Economic Mechanism (NEM), 106, 251–52; indebtedness and, 111; and Polish crisis, 164, 191; and Ambassador Jozsef Garamvolgyi, 219. See also Kadar, Janos

Hupalowski, Tadeusz, 155

Husak, Gustav, 55, 56; replaces Dubcek, 56; and Polish crisis, 161, 164, 218, 224

Hutchings, Robert, 60, 74, 76, 98

Ideology, 36

Indebtedness: East European, 82, 98; Polish, 110, 111, 112, 129, 232, 246, 251

Independent Students' Union (NZS), 142

India, 166

Indra, Alois, 32, 34, 42, 44, 46, 47

Institute of the Economics of the World Socialist System (IEMSS or "Bogomolov Institute"), 113, 225, 251, 253. See also Bogomolov, Oleg T.

Intelligentsia: in USSR, 58; in Poland, 103, 107, 123, 141, 181, 209

International Labor Organization (ILO), 134

International law: violations of, 53, 62

International Monetary Fund (IMF): Polish membership in, 111

International peace movement: and KGB, 116

International Red Cross, 125

Iran, 90, 91, 93; Ayatollah Khomeini comes to power in, 113–14

Iron Curtain, 1, 57, 84, 126

Izvestiia, 139, 143, 218

Jagielski, Mieczyslaw, 140, 183

Janczyszyn, Ludwik (commander in chief of Polish navy), 135

Janiszewski, Michal, 189

Jarosezewicz, Piotr, 106, 109

Jaruzelski, Wojciech: and riots of 1970, 104; refusal to fire on fellow Poles in 1976, 106, 128; on arming Citizens' Militia, 135; and Kuklinski, 154, 155; on WTO summit in December 1980, 158, 159, 165, 167–68, 169; becomes prime minister, 171, 177–80; deals with Soviets, 181, 188–93, 197, 213; and Bydgoszcz incident, 182; and question

99, 100, 122–29; establishment of communist rule in Poland in, 100; annexations to Western Soviet Republics in, 116

Yakovlev, Aleksandr, 254
Yugoslavia: and Prague Spring, 23, 58; and Helsinki process, 85; refusal to attend Paris Conference in 1980, 97; and Polish crisis, 157; introduction of martial law in Kosovo, 190; model of socialism in, 194, 196

Zabinski, Andrzej, 181, 195, 210
Zagladin, Vadim, 167

Zahir-Shah, King, 89
Zamiatin, L. M., 136, 174–75, 176, 177, 178, 203, 208, 216
Zelenov, V. (Soviet consul in Gdansk), 153
Zhivkov, Todor, 47, 157, 161, 162, 192, 218, 224
Zhukov, Georgii (Soviet defense minister in 1956), 12, 13
Zimianin, Mikhail, 23, 136
Zionism, 27, 103, 174
Zolnierz Wolnosci, 166
ZOMOs (Mechanized Units of the Citizens Militia), 230, 231, 239
Zpravy, 51

The New Cold War History

MATTHEW J. OUIMET,
The Rise and Fall of the Brezhnev Doctrine in Soviet Foreign Policy
(2003)

PIERRE ASSELIN,
A Bitter Peace: Washington, Hanoi, and the Making of the Paris Agreement
(2002)

JEFFREY GLEN GIAUQUE,
Grand Designs and Visions of Unity:
The Atlantic Powers and the Reorganization of Western Europe, 1955–1963
(2002)

CHEN JIAN,
Mao's China and the Cold War
(2001)

M. E. SAROTTE,
Dealing with the Devil:
East Germany, Détente, and Ostpolitik, 1969–1973
(2001)

MARK PHILIP BRADLEY,
Imagining Vietnam and America:
The Making of Postcolonial Vietnam, 1919–1950
(2000)

MICHAEL E. LATHAM,
Modernization as Ideology:
American Social Science and "Nation Building" in the Kennedy Era
(2000)

QIANG ZHAI,
China and the Vietnam Wars, 1950–1975
(2000)

WILLIAM I. HITCHCOCK,
France Restored:
Cold War Diplomacy and the Quest for Leadership in Europe, 1944–1954
(1998)